Complete Encyclopedia of the SALTWATER AQUARIUM

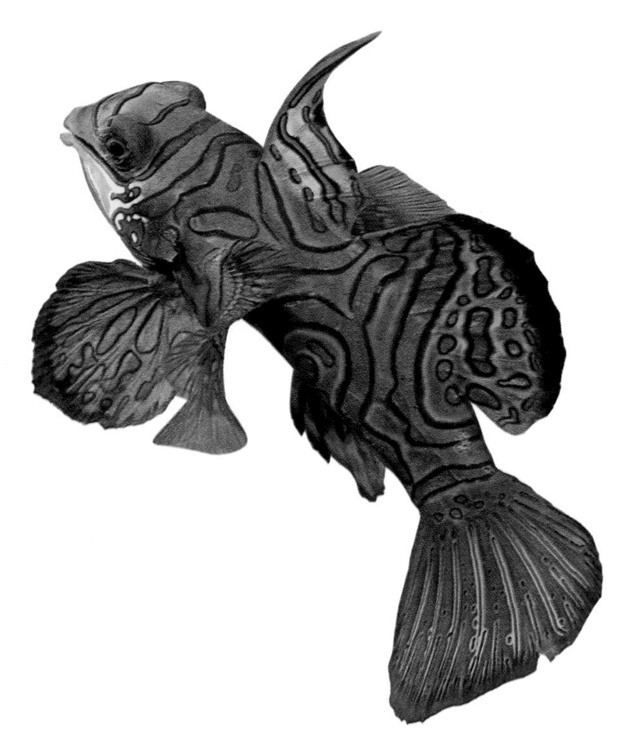

Complete Encyclopedia of the SALTWATER AQUARIUM

NICK DAKIN
FOREWORD BY JULIAN SPRUNG

FIREFLY BOOKS

A FIREFLY BOOK

Published by Firefly Books Ltd. 2003

First printing

Publisher in Cataloguing-in-Publication Data (U.S.)
(Library of Congress Standards)

Dakin, Nick.
Complete encyclopedia of the saltwater aquarium/
Nick Dakin. — 1st ed.
[400] p. : col. ill. , photos. ; cm.
Includes index.
Summary: An encyclopedic reference for setting up, stocking, and maintaining a saltwater aquarium.
ISBN 1-55927-817-6
1. Marine aquariums — Handbooks, manuals, etc.
2. Marine aquarium fishes — Handbooks, manuals.
I. Title.
639.34/2 21 SF457.1.D135 2003

National Library of Canada Cataloguing in Publication Data

Dakin, Nick
Complete encyclopedia of the saltwater aquarium/
Nick Dakin ; foreword by Julian Sprung.
Includes index.
ISBN 1-55297-817-6
1. Marine aquariums. I. Title.
SF457.1.D35 2003 639.34'2 C2003-901084-8

CREDITS
Managing Editor: Anne McDowall
Editor/Consultant: John Dawes
Editorial: Ideas into Print
Design: John Heritage/Stuart Watkinson
Picture Editor: Tony Moore
Index: Stuart Craik
Colour reproductions: Regent Publishing Services
Filmset: SX Composing Ltd.
Computer graphics: Phil Holmes and Stuart Watkinson
Production management: Consortium
Print production: Sino Publishing House Ltd.

Published in Canada in 2003 by
Firefly Books Ltd.
3680 Victoria Park Avenue
Toronto, Ontario, M2H 3K1

Published in the United States in 2003 by
Firefly Books (U.S.) Inc.
P.O. Box 1338, Ellicott Station
Buffalo, New York 14205

Printed in China

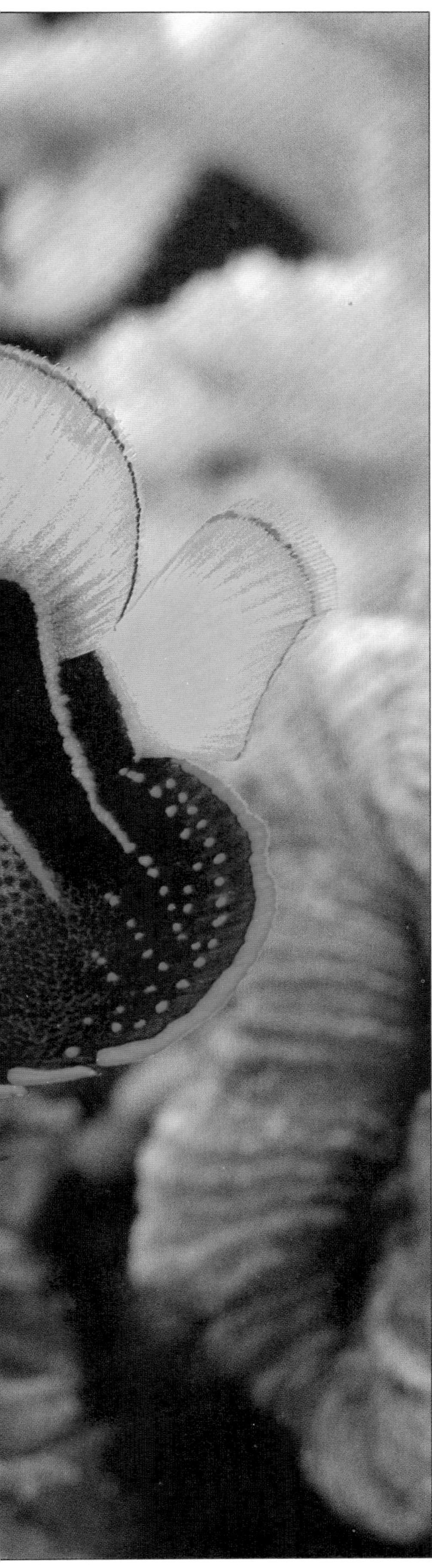

This book has been prepared by a team of experts in the fields of fishkeeping, marine biology, diving, environmental studies, fisheries, conservation and health care. The authors are listed here in alphabetical order with details of their contributions.

THE AUTHORS

Adrian Exell
Part One: What is a Marine Fish?

Colin Grist
Part Two: Setting up the Aquarium
Part Three: Marine Fish and Invertebrate Care

Martyn Haywood
Part Five: Tropical Marine Invertebrates

Les Holliday
Part One: The Coral World of Fishes

Stan Kemp
Part One: Collection and Conservation

Dick Mills
Part Four: Tropical Marine Fishes
Part Six: The Coldwater Aquarium

Sue Wells
Part One: What is an Invertebrate?

THE CONSULTANTS

John Dawes
Dr Keith Banister

SPECIALIST ADVISERS

Neil Marks
Part Two: Setting up the Aquarium
Part Three: Marine Fish and Invertebrate Care

Andrew Caine
Part Two: Setting up the Aquarium

Julian Sprung
Julian is a marine biologist, diver and consultant, with many years of experience of keeping marine fish and invertebrates. He regularly lectures on aquatic subjects and is contributing editor of the US magazine *Freshwater and Marine Aquarium*.

Half-title page: The Mandarinfish (Synchiropus splendidus).
Title page: A Pistol Shrimp (Synalpheus sp.) at rest on a Tridacna clam.
Left: The Blue-girdled, or Majestic, Angelfish (Euxiphipops navarchus).
Page 9: A spectacular and colourful tropical marine invertebrate aquarium.

Contents

FOREWORD

A marine aquarium is a living work of art, an attraction for the eyes and the imagination. Seeing the fabulously coloured marine creatures within an aquarium, we are astonished that these little gems are actually alive. The brilliance of their colours is matched equally by improbable shape, texture and pattern, while the way these creatures move is fascinating. The delicate undulations of the Mandarinfish's pectoral fins, the fireworks display of pulsing *Xenia*, a soft coral, or the effect of the motion of water over the flowing fins of say, a *Pinatus* Batfish, or a field of coral polyps, is hypnotic.

The marine aquarium affords a window to the sea far away from its pounding shores, and a window to the unknown. It is precisely this element of mystery that holds the most enduring attraction for hobbyists, who learn about animal behaviour, biology, chemistry, and ecology from exposure to an aquarium. When it is a marine aquarium, there is a particular satisfaction in the knowledge that you are taming a little piece of the sea.

Sometimes the aquarium will not be tamed, however, and every hobbyist suffers moments of frustration because aquarium keeping is not, and never will be, an exact science. Living systems do not respond like machinery. Only experience and patience will allow you to achieve reproducible success.

Our hobby has undergone periods of enthusiasm and periods of waning interest. Every time a new product or filter is introduced, one hears claims that *the* solution has been found to the successful, maintenance-free marine aquarium, and this attracts new hobbyists and re-attracts the old salts who gave up. Patience, knowledge, and experience will always succeed where the exaggerated claims fall short. Still, there is a purpose to such claims. They dispel a myth and widely accepted view that has long been an obstacle to the growth of the hobby: the perception that marine aquariums are impossible to keep. I can't recall how many times after I mentioned that I was a marine aquarist, a new acquaintance would blankly utter, "Oh, I've heard that marine aquariums are impossible . . ." My reply is that a marine aquarium is as difficult or easy as you make it.

With that in mind, you can use this book as a guide to help you decide just what kind of marine environment to create, and how to do it. You can start with a small, simple system, a painless dip of a toe to test the water, but, eventually, you might just dive right in. Don't drown! You have many options, but you must be patient and avoid taking on too much responsibility too quickly.

The 'fish only' tank, or one that primarily emphasizes fish, has long been the mainstay of the marine aquarium hobby. Showy angelfishes, butterflyfishes, tangs and wrasses cruising among the skeletons of dead or fake coral is the stuff of most public displays. This type of display also typifies the first marine aquarium for most hobbyists. Whole displays may also be made with the fascinating partnership of anemones and clownfishes. And few hobbyists escape the attraction of the seahorse. Those fond of danger choose lionfishes and moray eels.

A more recent trend in marine aquarium keeping is the fascinating creation of whole ecosystems. This aspect of the marine hobby focuses primarily on the duplication of tropical coral reefs and lagoon settings, but also includes temperate or 'coldwater' reef environments. Both are covered in this book. 'Reef tanks' are especially fascinating because the decor is dynamic – ever changing as it grows. Each time you view the aquarium there may be a new discovery, a new pet, or growth. While older systems achieve success through a sort of clinical maintenance, the modern trend toward duplicating a natural environment achieves stability through the cultivation of rich populations of animals, plants, and micro-organisms, so that little external filtration may be required at all.

Now, as there are more technical gadgets and sophisticated forms of filtration available to hobbyists than ever before in the history of aquarium keeping, an appreciation of the simplest forms of creating a successful aquarium is returning. While the idea of using live rock to create a naturally balanced aquarium is not new, only now is it popular and widely accepted. One of the most fascinating things about the hobby of marine aquarium keeping is that, as we learn more about the environments we create and the creatures we keep, the techniques and technology continue to evolve.

The future of our hobby is bright. Advances in the care, propagation and aquaculture of marine species have brought an exciting new aspect of marine aquarium keeping within our reach. The trend towards environmental awareness and concern about depleting the natural resources makes captive propagation of marine life a positive alternative. Much progress is being made in this endeavour through the work of expert aquarists and active aquarium societies.

These organizations of aquarists now have a multiple duty: conservation, regulation, education and captive propagation are presently on club agendas. If we are to continue to enjoy and learn from our hobby, we must actively ensure that the methods of capture and care of the creatures we keep are responsible, for while our impact on the marine environment is minuscule compared with the destruction from industrial development and pollution, to proceed wrecklessly in our endeavour is counter-productive. Most people who enjoy the rewards of marine aquarium keeping are also sensitive to environmental issues. As marine aquarists, we know the value of increasing public awareness of the marine environment by exposing people to the beauty and wonder of a healthy marine aquarium.

PART ONE

THE MARINE ENVIRONMENT

The stunning beauty and the staggering diversity of animals to be found in and around the world's oceans often defies the imagination. Rich tapestries of life are delicately interwoven, providing a balanced ecosystem virtually unrivalled in the natural kingdom. In this opening section we shall be trying to gain an overview of life on the coral reef, looking at such widely ranging topics as the use of camouflage, cleaning symbiosis and reef activity by night and day. This vital background information can be of invaluable assistance when you are trying to recreate a successful mini-environment.

We also examine the biological make-up of marine fishes and invertebrates; understanding how each creature has developed and adapted to survive a life in seawater can teach us important lessons in the care of marine livestock. We consider fish senses and patterns of reproduction, as well as finding out how and why they differ from their freshwater cousins, and take a look at the amazing diversity of invertebrates – the most adaptable of creatures, filling every conceivable niche in the marine environment.

The final chapter in this section – Collection and Conservation – seeks to demonstrate that the aquarist can play an important part in the conservation of the world's seas by demanding that this important resource is managed respectfully. It is encouraging to note that the marine hobby has made positive and practical contributions to various Third World economies by providing much-needed jobs in the collection of fish and invertebrates and in the production of artificial corals. With proper organization, the reefs of the world can be regarded as a renewable resource – it is up to the hobbyist to use it wisely.

Left: *Who could fail to be impressed by this inviting underwater scene captured photographically off the island of St Lucia. Squirrelfishes shelter beneath coral ledges as sea fans sway gently in the warm sea current; all is harmony.*

The Coral World of Fishes

The first and overwhelming impression of any coral reef is the sheer brilliance, abundance and diversity of the reef fishes. Brightly coloured, gaudily patterned fish of every conceivable body shape dart among the corals or hang in huge shoals in midwater. It is not unusual to find 20 or more species living closely together on just one small coral outcrop, and large reef areas, such as the Great Barrier Reef of Australia, can be home to a remarkable 2000 species.

In such a crowded environment, the competition for food and space is ever present. In order to survive and to get the most from their surroundings, reef fishes have adapted in shape and behaviour to live in various parts of the reef and become dependent on different food sources. Feeders on coral polyps and the tiny worms and crustaceans that live in cracks and holes in the reef have needlelike snouts and highly compressed body shapes to allow them easy access to deep crevices that other fishes cannot reach. Teeth may be fused together to form a parrotlike beak for scraping off algae covering the coral or combined with powerful jaws to feed on the coral itself. The main food source for the majority of reef fishes, however, is other fish, and 'eat or be eaten' is the general rule for survival.

Offence and defence on the reef

To overcome the immense difficulties of surviving in such a competitive situation, reef fishes have developed an armoury of weapons and defence strategies and these are used by predator and prey alike. Here, we look briefly at a number of these strategies for survival on the reef.

Cryptic camouflage

Camouflage is a universal strategy on the coral reef. Predators use it to conceal themselves as they lie in wait to surprise any unsuspecting prey coming within their reach and many less aggressive species hide behind the cloak of camouflage as a means of evading predation. A good

Below: *Animals that use camouflage as a defence often have the amazing ability to rapidly change colour and markings to match their surroundings. The Yellow-spotted Stingray is one of these creatures and is almost undetectable at times.*

example of the former is the Indo-Pacific Giant Moray Eel (*Gymnothorax javanicus*), which reaches over 2m (6.6ft) in length and hides within crevices and holes in the reef, perfectly camouflaged to mimic the surrounding coral. This formidable fish feeds on a wide variety of reef fishes and its gargantuan proportions indicate just how successful its hunting technique can be. A good example of defensive camouflage is seen in the Yellow-spotted Stingray (*Urolophus jamaicensis*). This small, placid ray from shallow sandy Caribbean waters hunts by excavating depressions in the sand to expose the small shellfish and various other invertebrates on which it feeds. To elude its predators, the body of the ray is covered in yellow spots that blend with the seabed and it has a chameleonlike ability to change colour, shade and pattern to match its surroundings. If all else fails, a further weapon is provided by a sharp venomous spine at the base of the tail, which is known to deter the ray's most ardent predators, including large Lemon and Hammerhead Sharks.

Behavioural camouflage

Behavioural camouflage is seen in the tropical Atlantic Trumpetfish (*Aulostomus maculatus*), a common reef fish that often hovers vertically, nose down, among gorgonians and sea whips, cleverly hiding in wait for passing small fishes and shrimps. Closely related to seahorses and pipefishes, this bizarre creature has an elongated body with a head extended into a long, trumpet-shaped snout. It can often be observed adopting a further subterfuge, using other, non-aggressive fishes, such as herbivorous surgeonfishes, as cover

Right: *The Atlantic Trumpetfish is a clever hunter. Blending in with the surrounding sea whips, it adopts a nose-down position and hovers realistically, moving gently to and fro with the current, ready to engulf any small fish or shrimp that ventures too close.*

to sneak up on its prey. Almost invisible within a shoal of slow-moving surgeonfishes, the Trumpetfish will suddenly dart out and pounce on a small fish or shrimp, sucking the unsuspecting prey into its tube-shaped mouth.

The power of advertising

Camouflage coloration is one method to deceive a predator or gain a meal, but by far the largest number of coral reef fishes are gaudy and colourful. Bright colours and patterns can serve purposes other than simply to adorn. It often pays to advertise, and if you are a fish that evades predation by having poisonous or distasteful flesh it is important that predators know this before deciding to sample you for themselves. Bright yellow, especially combined with black spots or bars, is a universally recognized indication of a poisonous species, and is used by terrestrial as well as aquatic animals. The juvenile phase of the Indo-Pacific Cube Boxfish (*Ostracion cubicus*) is an excellent example, using this type of livery to advertise the poisonous mucus covering its body.

Above: *When combined with black spots, the bright yellow body of the Cube Boxfish provides an effective way of warning would-be predators of the poisonous mucus covering its flesh.*

The art of deception

Butterflyfishes (family Chaetodontidae) are among the most attractive reef fishes and have a 'state of the art' ability to use colour and pattern to aid their survival. They have a disclike, highly compressed body and often display bold patterns that disguise the fish by breaking up its body outline or masking conspicuous features such as the eyes. Such disruptive coloration serves as an effective means of evading capture, and many eye-masked species take the illusion one stage further by employing conspicuous false eyes on the base of the tail or on the dorsal fin. This confuses predators into attacking the 'wrong end', while the fish dashes off in the opposite direction.

Drastic measures

Not all reef fishes employ disguise or deception to survive; many have evolved other strategies to protect themselves. This is shown to perfection by members of the porcupinefish family (Diodontidae). Porcupinefishes are easily recognized by the prominent spines that cover the head and body. These erect spines are a major deterrent and are made even more emphatic by the fishes' extraordinary ability to inflate themselves with water into spiky balls at least double their original size, effectively preventing attacking predators from swallowing them whole. In addition to this impressive defence mechanism, the horny skin and poisonous flesh act as a further discouragement, and the parrotlike beak is capable of delivering a nasty bite.

Unfortunately, porcupinefishes have not evolved a defence mechanism effective against their worst enemy – man! The very ability that protects porcupinefishes in the wild has resulted in their downfall. Inflated specimens are popular as souvenirs and many are collected for the curio trade, dried, varnished and offered for sale as mantleshelf ornaments or lampshades. The Bridal Burrfish (*Chilomycterus antennatus*), one of four

Above: *The Bridal Burrfish has an impressive armoury of weapons. Its sharp spines, horny skin and beaklike mouth deter most predators.*

Above right: *More ardent predators would soon discover the Burrfish's second line of defence, an ability to inflate to double its size or more.*

Below: *Fully inflated, the once tiny Burrfish becomes a spiky ball; its size, and its now erect spines preventing predators from swallowing it whole.*

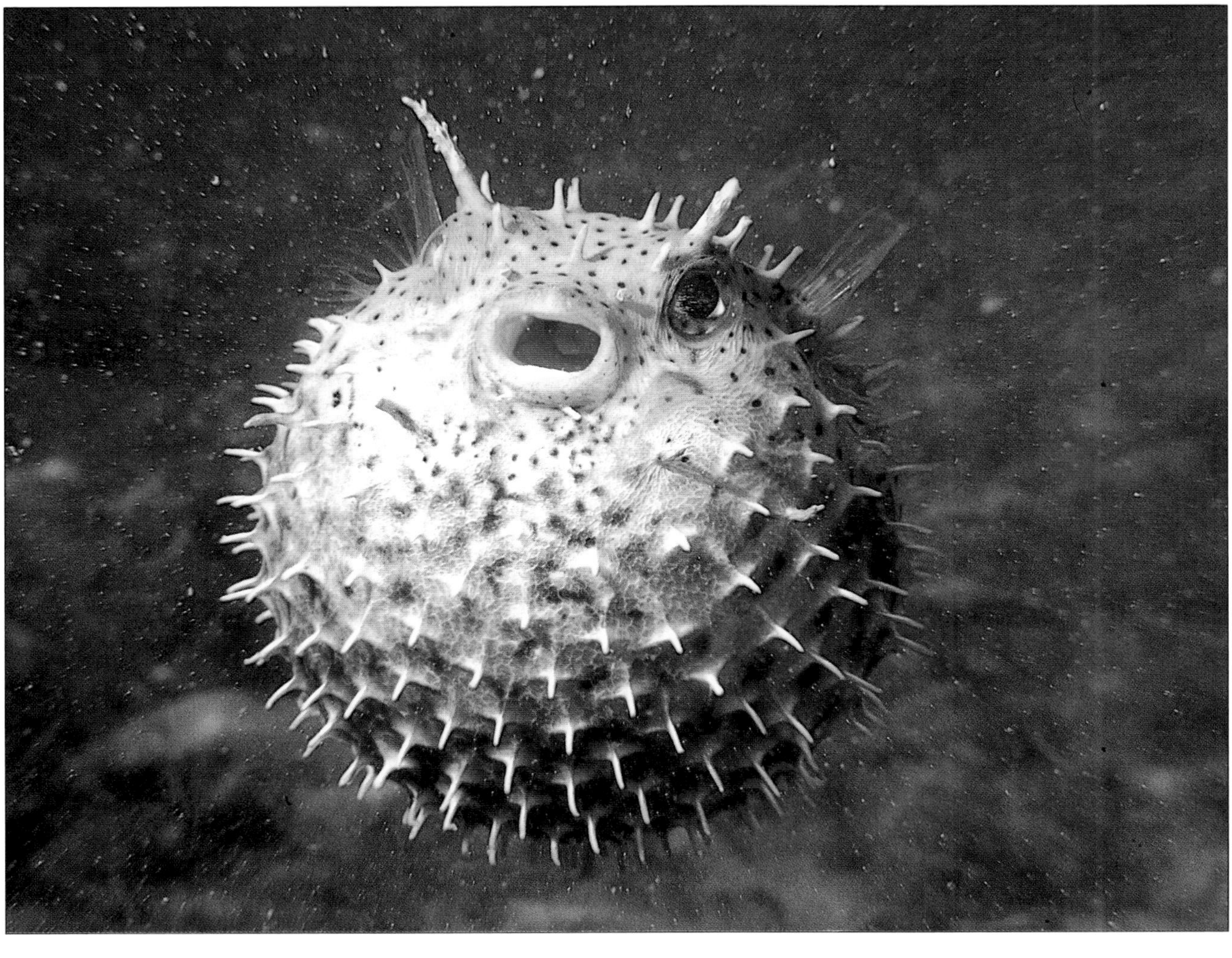

porcupinefish species represented in the Caribbean, is rapidly becoming threatened due to the large numbers taken for sale, and there is an urgent need to protect this particular species.

Living in harmony

Not all living interactions on the reef are based on aggressive predator/ prey relationships. Within the teeming diversity of plants and animals that live together on a coral reef, there are many examples of widely differing life forms involved in intricate and interdependent liaisons. After all, the very existence of a coral reef depends upon a symbiotic relationship between the stony coral polyps and the microscopic zooxanthellae algae that live within their tissues.

One of the most interesting of the mutually beneficial associations is that between clownfishes and their host anemones. These brightly coloured fish are found singly or, more often, as a pair or small group hovering above their host anemone and seek a safe haven within its venomous tentacles at the first hint of danger. The immunity enjoyed by clownfishes has only recently become properly understood. The clownfish acquires its immunity from the otherwise deadly stinging cells of the anemone by the dual strategy of manufacturing a sugar-based mucus to disguise its natural protein body composition and by slowly covering itself with a layer of mucus from the anemone. (In fact, young 'unprotected' clownfishes have been observed 'dashing' through the tentacles of an anemone to pick up some of the mucus.) The main trigger mechanism that activates the anemone's nematocysts, or stinging cells, is the protein-based mucus covering most fishes. As the anemone is naturally equipped to avoid stinging itself by recognizing its own mucus, it is deceived by the clownfish's 'cloak of disguise' into assuming that the fish is part of itself.

The clownfish obviously benefits from the safe protection offered by the anemone's tentacles but any advantage to the anemone is less clear. One theory is that the bright coloration of the clownfishes acts as a warning to would-be predators of the deadly consequences of approaching too closely to the tentacles. Of course, this also keeps potential prey fish at bay, but it seems that anemones only feed on fish 'by chance', with juvenile 'inexperienced' fish being the most common victims. The bulk of the anemone's food source is composed of other invertebrates and zooplankton.

Above: *The association between the clownfish and its host anemone is well known. The dependence the clown attaches to its host is such that the numbers of anemones available on a reef can directly effect the size of the clown population.*

A life of service

Cleaning symbiosis is a further type of mutually beneficial arrangement, which is common on land as well as underwater. Coral reefs have many examples of this fascinating practice; over 50 coral reef species of fish and quite a number of invertebrates have given up the conventional means of hunting for food and live by cleaning parasites, small pieces of dead tissue and fungus from the fish living on or visiting the reef.

Cleaner species often set up business at particular locations on the reef, known as 'cleaning stations'. The large numbers of fish they attract often form into orderly queues as they patiently wait their turn to be groomed. The cleaners provide an essential service in relieving their 'clients' of parasites and minor infections, while earning themselves a meal at the same time. The tactile experience resulting from the cleaning process often seems to be enjoyed, some clients living in close association with, and becoming very protective towards, their cleaners. The relationship between client and cleaner usually works to a defined set of rules. The cleaner is allowed to perform its duties all over the body, even inside the mouth and in the gill cavities, and in turn can trust its host not to make a meal of its defenceless companion in the process.

Cleaning symbiosis has evolved to become a very specialized

Above: *Several Cleaner Wrasse* (Labroides dimidiatus) *perform cleaning duties on a large Queen Angelfish, which has visited their station.*

arrangement. There are full-time cleaners, those that mix normal feeding patterns with part-time cleaning, and the juveniles of certain species which act as cleaners only when young. The list of juvenile cleaners includes many species, of which young angelfishes and butterflyfishes are perhaps the most familiar examples. It is not uncommon to find the juveniles of a number of different species working in combination to service a cleaning station or joining forces with a full-time cleaner.

Cleaning gobies (*Gobiosoma* spp.) and cleaner wrasses (*Labroides* spp.) are the two main groups of full-time cleaner fishes, the gobies performing the service in the tropical West Atlantic and the labrids filling the same niche in the Indo-Pacific. There are six species of the cleaner goby, of which the Neon Goby (*Gobiosoma oceanops*), which employs a dazzling, electric blue lateral stripe to advertise its cleaning service, is perhaps the best known. The Cleaner Wrasse (*Labroides dimidiatus*) sports a similar blue lateral stripe, a trademark of many full-time cleaners, and is one of a number of cleaner wrasse species distributed over the Indo-Pacific.

Cleaner shrimps head the list of invertebrate cleaners and are represented by the Caribbean Red-backed, or Painted Lady, Shrimp (*Lysmata grabhami*), the Indo-Pacific *L. amboinensis* and the circumtropical Coral-banded Shrimp (*Stenopus hispidus*). The cleaning methods used by cleaner shrimps are very similar to those adopted by cleaner fish. They also establish cleaning stations and attract clients by sporting conspicuous patterns and coloration and by waving their white, threadlike antennae.

Below: *This Cube Boxfish does not object in the least to being cleaned by a specialist shrimp, the brightly coloured* Lysmata amboinensis.

Daytime on the reef

During the daytime, the coral reef is often a crowded place. From the early grey of morning to the bright, sunlit hours of midday, there is a progressive increase in the numbers of fish and other animals venturing into activity until, finally, the water and the surface of the reef are filled with movement. Hundreds of colourful fishes hang in shoals or busily forage for food. Small damselfishes hover just above outcrops of staghorn corals, never straying far away and always ready to dash to safety at the first sign of danger. Suddenly, a large predator in the form of a grouper or Barracuda moves in for the kill, the distressed victim relaying a warning message across the reef and causing momentary panic as fish dive for cover in all directions.

These daytime predators arrive at dawn to feed, and are succeeded by huge populations of fish that graze and browse. These grazers fully exploit the many food sources provided by the reef. The herbivores feed on the algal turf growing in the niches between the living coral or use their chisel-like teeth to scrape off the thin film of algae adhering to coral surfaces. Parrotfishes are the most common of these algal grazers and can form large shoals, systematically grazing large areas of submerged reef flat. Surgeonfishes also form aggregations and are the true farmers of the reef, reserving large areas of reef flat for the shoal and protecting their fields of algae from other herbivores. The tiny herbivorous damselfish *Stegastes nigricans*, found in the Red Sea and Indo-Pacific, follows a similar practice, tending and cleaning its square metre or so of algal turf and, despite its diminutive size, pugnaciously defending its adopted territory from other much larger herbivores that try to take over.

The coral polyp grazers are represented by members of the butterflyfish family, with their long, forcep-shaped snouts perfectly designed for reaching into crevices in the coral and their laterally compressed bodies allowing access through the narrowest of gaps. Well named, these colourful marine 'butterflies' flit among the coral heads like their airborne counterparts fluttering from flower to flower. The angelfishes, closely related to the butterflyfishes, form a further group of grazers that devote the daylight hours to browsing on sponges and algae. In the Caribbean and tropical West Atlantic, where sponges feature as one of the largest constituents of the reefs, angelfishes are often prolific, flourishing on the rich pastures available to them.

The major remaining group of animals of the daytime can also be distinguished by their feeding patterns. These are the midwater feeders searching for food in the currents laden with zooplankton that often sweep along the reef edge. Indo-Pacific communities of these fishes would include various damselfishes and the Golden Jewelfish (*Anthias squamipinnis*), which hang in clouds close to the reef. The Pennant Butterflyfish (*Heniochus diphreutes*), a species quite unusual for members of the butterflyfish family, also patrols along the reef in aggregations of many hundreds to feed in this manner. The Caribbean counterparts of this group would include the Creole Wrasse (*Clepticus pharrai*) and the Sergeant Major Damselfish (*Abudefduf saxatilis*).

Carnivorous corals, with tentacles withdrawn, rest and await the richer pickings of the night, when the zooplankton will rise from the depths to feed and in turn provide a meal for the millions of hungry coral polyps. Bathed in sunlight, the corals by day are transformed into tiny greenhouses, their symbiotic microscopic algae harnessing the energy of the sun to benefit their coral hosts. Many other reef animals have entered into a similar partnership with these tiny zooxanthellae, including anemones, sponges and clams. The huge Giant Clam (*Tridacna gigas*) of the Indo-Pacific is an excellent example, which can reach more than 1m (3.3ft) across and weigh 254kg (560lb). Living in shallow, brightly lit water, the clam exposes its colourful fleshy mantle that houses large numbers of zooxanthellae. By

Below: *Coral reefs are busy places during the day. A variety of different fish species may share a good feeding position in the current.*

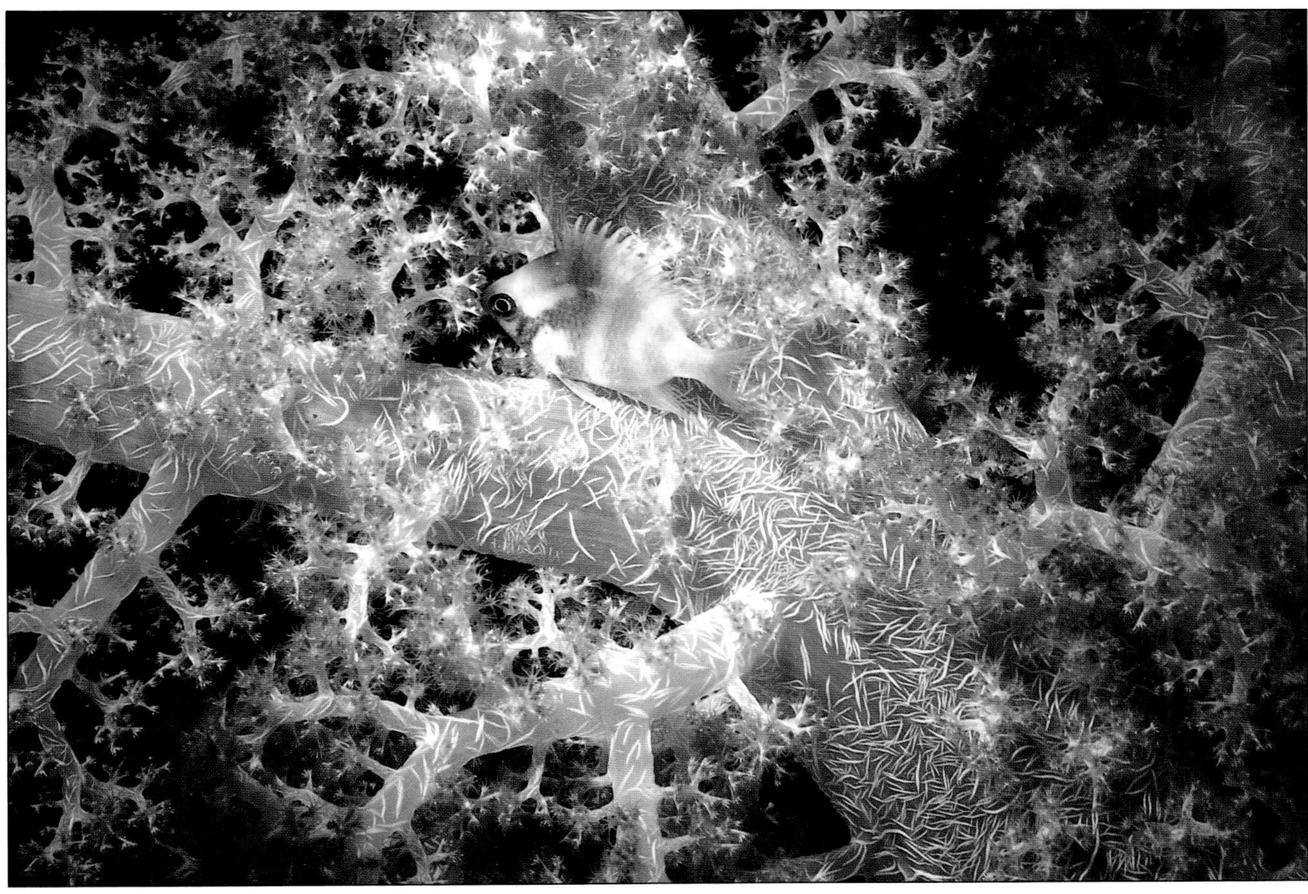

maintaining just the right levels of algae in its tissues, the clam is often able to rely upon them for nutrition. The clam will control the algae population by consuming only sufficient of their numbers to maintain optimum levels.

By mid-afternoon, the search for food has subsided and the reef becomes a more relaxed place. The major predators have returned to deeper water and, as the light wanes, the animals of the daytime prepare for darkness, scurrying to safety in the recesses of the reef.

The reef at night

The pressures on food sources and space are such that activity continues throughout the 24-hour period, and the reef at night is a lively place. Before the night's proceedings can take place, however, the members of the daytime community must withdraw to safe retreats.

The midwater feeders are the first to leave, realizing how vulnerable they are to attack from dusk predators, such as large mackerel or jacks, in the fading light. They are followed quickly by the herbivores. Disc-shaped surgeonfishes disperse from their shoals and wriggle into incredibly small clefts in the reef flat. Large solitary parrotfish become very defensive at this time and may either nervously take flight if approached or hold their ground, making mock aggressive displays. Presently, some species of parrotfish will select a hole in the reef and settle inside it for the night, enveloping themselves in a cocoon

Above: *A dainty damselfish* (Amblyglyphidodon *sp.) is well concealed among the branches of a soft coral during a long Red Sea night.*

Below: *This parrotfish is enveloped in a mucous shroud. This is thought to discourage predators by masking the fish's shape and scent.*

of mucus. This mucus shroud deceives predators, both by disguising the fish's outline and also by masking its taste to confuse those that hunt by using this sense. (A highly developed sense of taste can assist underwater predators in much the same way as a keen sense of smell serves terrestrial predators.)

Many reef fish change colour at night, predators as well as their potential victims. They may take on more muted shades or, surprisingly, use bright red coloration as effective camouflage in the nightly battle for survival. Soldierfishes and squirrelfishes have large eyes and a pink or red coloration – a good indication that these fishes are nocturnal predators. Their squirrel-like eyes are an adaptation to their nocturnal mode of life and the gaudy pink or red livery really does act as low-light-level camouflage. This is because water quickly filters out red wavelengths of light, making pink and red appear grey or black in the gloomy depths.

One nocturnal reef fish, the aptly named Flashlight Fish (*Photoblepharon palpebratus*), confounds all recognized theories of night-time coloration. This tiny, sombre grey fish, common in the Red Sea and Indo-Pacific, sports a pair of elliptical 'flashlights', one beneath each eye. These luminescent organs are filled with bacteria that can generate light by a series of biochemical reactions. The light produced not only helps the fish to hunt but also actively attracts the zooplankton on which it feeds. It is easy to assume that these points of light act as beacons to attract would-be predators, but in reality the reverse is true. Flashlight Fishes hunt in shoals, using their glowing lights as an important means of communication, and this tends to confuse predators rather than entice them. These extraordinary fishes can turn their 'flashlights' on and off at will by manipulating muscles beneath the eye.

As darkness falls, fish are not the only predators in action. The reef itself springs into life, as corals spread their delicate tentacles to trap passing zooplankton with batteries of lethal stinging cells. Crinoids, feathery armed relatives of the starfishes, make for the highest points on the reef and spread their arms to take the plankton soup.

Herbivorous feeders are generally associated with the daytime reef community, but *Diadema* sea urchins, slow-moving, open-reef animals that defend themselves with long, needle-sharp spines, are an exception. Each night, they migrate from the reef slope up onto the reef flat pastures, now vacated by their daytime occupants, and feed undisturbed on the algae. Brightly coloured sea slugs appear from beneath the coral rubble at the base of the reef edge and join the sea

Below: *A shoal of fish, mainly squirrelfish, occupy a cave at night, where it matters little whether they swim the right way up or upside down!*

urchins, some species grazing on algae while the carnivorous ones – the nudibranchs – feed on sponges and coral polyps, seemingly immune to the stinging nematocysts.

The nightly saga of the reef unfolds and continues until dawn, while daytime feeders rest, to live and feed another day.

The coral web of life

The coral reef and adjacent areas of mangrove swamp and lagoon seem able to support an endless diversity of life. Living organisms claim two essential requirements from their environment: a habitat and a food supply, both available in abundance on the reef and in nearby waters. The fundamental interaction between the members of the huge complex community of animals, plants and bacteria that make up the reef ecosystem is based on the food chain. In fact, this chain is so complex that it is more appropriate to think of it as a food web. The two main ingredients that fuel this system are the energy of the sun and the supply of nutrients in the form of decomposing organic matter. Since these nutrients are a product of the organisms living within the ecosystem, they form the bond that makes the food chain a never-ending process.

The first level of feeders are the plants, the so-called primary producers that use the energy of the sun to convert the nutrients into living matter by the process of photosynthesis. (Just to complicate matters, there are some fishes and invertebrates, called benthic feeders, that feed directly on detritus before it is broken down into nutrients and processed by the plants.) The many herbivorous fishes and other reef animals occupy the next level since they take advantage of the food source represented by the plants. Such herbivores include browsers and grazers that feed on algae and on plant material growing on the reef itself.

The connection between plant life and the next group of feeders is by way of the zooplankton, simple, tiny animal life forms that float in the water and feed on microscopic plants known as the phytoplankton. The zooplankton thus form the basis of a wide range of different feeding strategies. For example, animals such as corals feed directly on the zooplankton (but also rely heavily on their symbiotic relationship with the zooxanthellae in their tissues). Other carnivorous creatures feed on small fishes and invertebrates that have in turn fed upon the zooplankton. At the top of the 'feeding tree' are the large carnivores that feed on a wide range of animals in the other levels of the coral web of life.

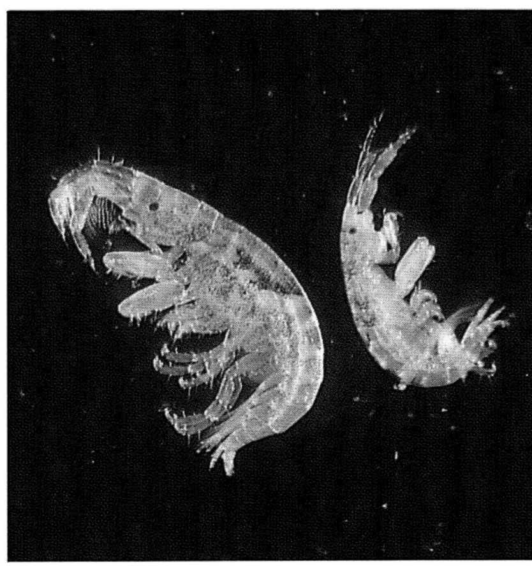

Above: *Microscopic zooplankton – simple animal life forms – are the staple diet of a multitude of fish and invertebrate species.*

Above: *Moray eels are voracious predators, and will quickly capture any fish that is foolish enough to pass too close to their lair.*

This very simple classification does not reflect the true complexity of the reef feeding pattern. There are omnivorous fishes and other animals, for example, that feed on both animal and plant material. Also, feeding patterns and food preferences often change during the life cycle of some members of the reef community; zooplankton-feeding juveniles may become herbivores or carnivores as adults and some species may move from shallow waters to feed in deeper waters at a later stage in their lives.

Reef fishes can be classified into five groups by their adult feeding pattern:

Feeders on algae, such as parrotfishes, surgeonfishes, some damselfishes, and blennies.

Feeders on zooplankton, such as cardinalfishes, fusiliers, some damselfishes, jewelfishes, manta rays and whale sharks.

Feeders on sessile invertebrates, which include the coral and sponge feeders and are represented by butterflyfishes and angelfishes.

Feeders on large invertebrates (e.g. molluscs, crustaceans and echinoderms), such as snappers, stingrays, puffers, boxfishes, triggers, some wrasses and emperors.

Feeders primarily on fish, such as many sharks, barracudas, groupers, moray eels, cornetfishes, needlefishes and scorpionfishes.

A number of fish families, such as the triggerfishes, damselfishes, wrasses, puffers and boxfishes, are omnivorous and where these are included above, the category shows their main feeding preference.

What is a Marine Fish?

Seawater covers 71 percent of the earth's surface. However, huge tracts of the ocean are fathomless deeps, largely devoid of life. These are the aquatic desert lands, lacking in essential nutrients and thus unable to support a food chain without an input from the overlying 'layers'.

The thousands of species of marine fish mostly inhabit the narrow bands of the shallow, nutrient-rich waters – the continental shelves, which teem with life. These species of fish have evolved over millions of years to fill every conceivable niche, each species supremely suited in form and function to its own particular aquatic existence.

There are two main groups of fish: elasmobranchs, with their cartilaginous skeletons include sharks, dogfish and rays, but these do not, on the whole make suitable home aquarium subjects. Of more interest to the fishkeeper are the larger, more highly developed group of teleosts, or bony fish.

What is a marine teleost?

It is actually very difficult to give a completely watertight definition of a teleost. However, the following features are shared by most species: they spend all their life in water and would die out of it; they have a bony skeleton, including a skull; they have fins with spines and rays (see *Locomotion*); they possess a swimbladder used in buoyancy control; they have outwardly orientated gills, sited in a cavity (buccal cavity), which is covered by a bone flap (operculum, see *Respiration*); their bodies are typically covered with protective scales; they have a unique sense organ called a lateral line (see *Senses*); they are cold-blooded, i.e. poikilothermic, (which means their body temperature matches that of the water surrounding them).

Building on that basic definition, this section of the book will look briefly at how fish are adapted to live in the demanding aquatic environment. A basic knowledge of marine fish anatomy and physiology will improve your understanding of the creatures in your care.

Body shape

Marine fish come in all shapes and sizes. Their external body form is a function of the environment in which they have evolved and of the way they live. Some of the factors dictating a fish's evolved shape are: how active it is; how it feeds; whether it is a predator or potential prey (this is a relative term in the sense that a predator may, in turn, be preyed upon); and its defence and attack systems necessary for survival. This is best illustrated with a couple of examples. The Leopard Moray Eel (*Gymnothorax tesselatus*) has a long, serpent-like body, the only finnage being a dorsal fin extending the length of the body.

Below: *The Moray Eel has a snake-like body, which is well adapted to slipping into rock crevices, where the creature lurks ready to ambush passing prey.*

They swim laboriously with a sinuous undulation of the body. They have traded locomotory efficiency for a powerful form, which hides easily in crevices and cracks in the coral. Here a moray will lie in wait, ready to ambush unsuspecting fish swimming past, which it grabs in its massive tooth-filled jaws. Compare this with the bizarre appearance of the Lionfish (*Pterois volitans*). This has a body form much more typical of our concept of a fish, but has developed elaborate finnage with long flowing fins tipped with venomous spines. This gives the illusion of a much larger fish to predators, which are further dissuaded by the venomous spines. The fish also uses its outspread fins to manoeuvre small prey fish into a corner with no hope of escape from its large, well developed jaws.

Locomotion

Seawater is over 800 times denser than air. Moving through it is fraught with problems, such as drag, negative buoyancy and the sheer effort required to force a body through such a dense medium. Locomotory adaptation, like body form, is closely linked to a fish's lifestyle and its need for locomotion. We have seen above two examples of the moray eel and lionfish, where predatory feeding tactics dictate the species' body form at the expense of locomotory efficiency. The moray eel's body has hardly any locomotory adaptations, although the powerful muscles are ideal for the final uncoiling lunge that completes the ambush. The lionfish's flowing fins create drag which limits swimming speed. However, lionfish have a well-developed swimbladder, which is an adjustable air sac that allows them to hang motionless at any level in the water. The careful manoeuvring of a lionfish is accomplished by subtle fin movements, which prove an effective steering mechanism. Most fish dwelling on the reef, like the lionfish, have two types of muscle; a small portion is brown muscle, which is used for continuous activity because it is very well supplied with oxygen-rich blood, while the larger proportion of body mass is made up of white muscle, which can be used only for short bursts of emergency, high-speed swimming because of the poorer oxygen supply.

Continuously swimming midwater fish, which cruise over or on the edge of the reef, such as Barracuda (*Sphyraena barracuda*) have a body form supremely suited to a high-speed locomotion in water. Their bodies are optimally streamlined to minimize energy for reducing drag and aiding displacement. Swimbladders are either absent or much reduced, cutting down cross sectional area, and, therefore, drag. Muscle is primarily brown for constant speed swimming. Fins are minimal size and only used for turning. They are usually retracted during swimming.

Above: *Although slow swimmers, Lionfish possess well-developed swimbladders, enabling them to hang almost motionless in the water.*

Below: *Barracuda* (Sphyraena barracuda) *are adapted for speed. The body is streamlined and muscle developed for prolonged speed swimming.*

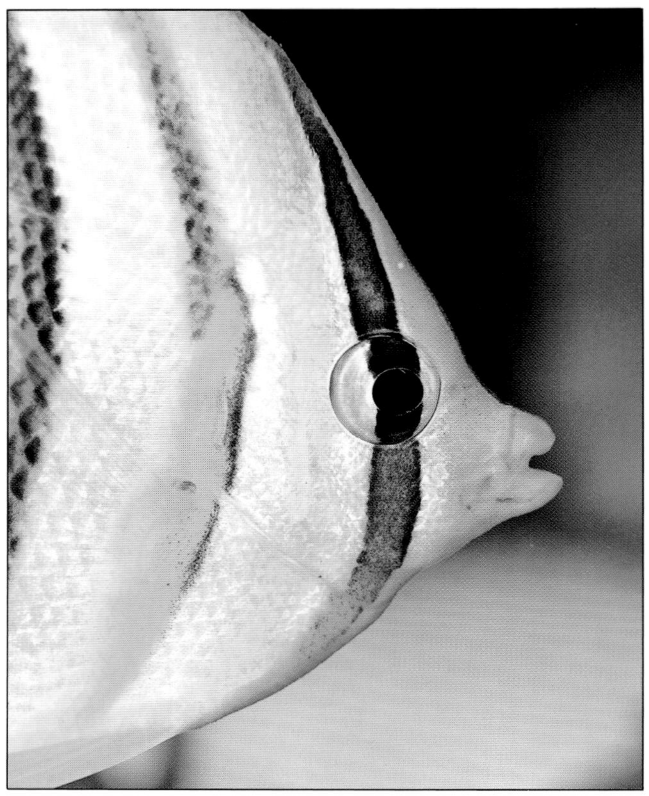

Senses
Marine fish need to be aware of what is happening around them. Sensory equipment is needed for communication, navigation, attack, defence and food location.

Sight In the crystal-clear waters of a tropical reef, sight is a key sense. Fishes' eyes are somewhat similar in structure to those of most other vertebrate animals, but usually possess a spherical lens. Fish can focus selectively on both near and far-away objects, their field of view

Above left: *The butterflyfish's eyes are set well to the side of the head, giving good all-round vision and early warning of possible dangers.*

Above right: *Coral Trout are predators and need forward-set eyes to concentrate all their attention on their potential prey.*

being determined by the position of the eyes on the head. Butterflyfish (*Chaetodon* spp.) with eyes on the side of the head have a wide field of view on both flanks, which is good for defence. Predators such as Coral Trout (*Cephalopholis miniatus*), on the other hand, have forward-facing eyes, which enable better detailed focussing on the prey ahead. Examination of eye structure and behaviour suggests fish have better colour vision than we do. The glorious colours of most reef fish are used in territorial and reproductive behaviour to communicate with each other.

Sound Water is a denser medium than air and sound travels further and faster as pressure waves through the aquatic world. Fish use two systems to sense these pressure waves. Firstly, they have a sensitive lateral line system. This consists of a series of canals and pits set just below the skin surface, the main lateral line running along the mid

Eye position and field of view

Predatory fishes

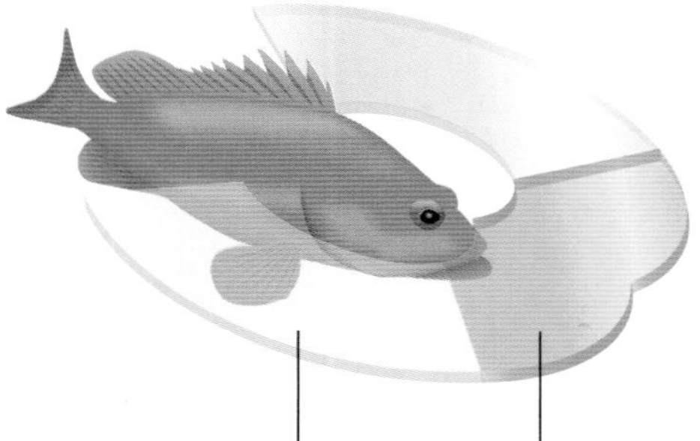

Non-predatory fishes

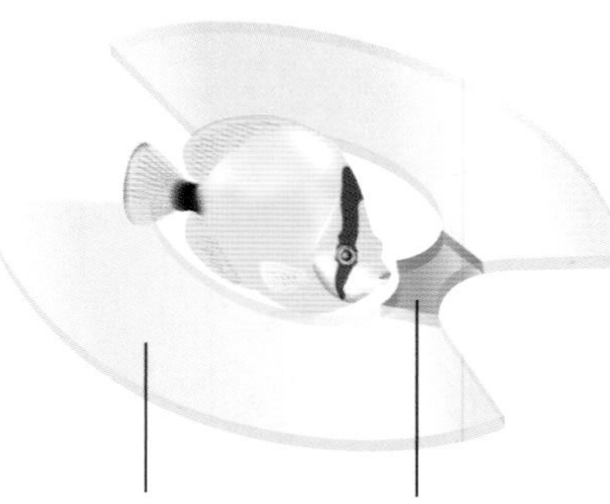

Left: *The eyes of a predator are set well to the front of the head, thus concentrating most vision in a forward direction and on to the prey ahead. A grazing fish has a wide all-round field of vision due to eyes set to the side of the head – an essential development as a defence against predators.*

line of each flank in most species. Background noise is tuned out and only low-frequency sounds 1/10 to 200 Hertz are picked up by the lateral line. This mechanism can be used for pressure wave echo sounding, which allows the fish (like a bat with its echo sonar) to navigate in the dark around obstacles. Fish also have an inner ear, which picks up higher frequency sound up to 8000 Hz. Sound is used in communication by fish and ultrasonic equipment used on a reef will reveal a cacophony of grunts, squeaks and clicks as fish attract, threaten and 'talk' to each other.

Orientation Sense receptors in the inner ears and closely related structures enable the fish to orientate themselves in a three-dimensional aquatic environment.

Smell and taste Most chemicals dissolve into water and readily diffuse through it. The difference between taste and smell is blurred in the aquatic environment so they are both encompassed in the term 'chemoreception'. Fish have special chemoreceptor sites concentrated in their nasal openings, scattered in the mouth around the head and, in some species, in other parts of the body. Fishes' sense of smell is over one million times more acute than our own. The olfactory sense is vital to fish both for discovering food and for communicating. To communicate with smell, fish release chemical messages, 'smells' called pheromones.

Co-ordination and control The co-ordination and control of body processes in response to external and internal stimuli is achieved by the brain in co-operation with highly developed nerve and endocrine (gland/hormone) systems. The brain receives and assimilates information from the sensory organs and then co-ordinates and stimulates the correct response from the appropriate organs in the body. The brain also integrates reflex actions, such as breathing, and is the site of learning and memory.

Nutrition
Fish have evolved the ability to exploit many different food sources. There are species that are solely carnivorous, such as fish-eating groupers (*Cephalopholis* spp.), and vegetarian species, such as many tangs (*Acanthurus* spp.) which graze macro- and micro-algae. Many species are omnivores, eating a combined diet of vegetable and meat matter. Individual species have

Below: *Tangs spend much of the day grazing on macro- and micro-algae, especially in highly oxygenated surge areas, where growth is most prolific.*

evolved specialized mouth structures that allow them to cope with specific food sources, and digestive systems tuned to deal effectively with their diet. For instance, fish eaters have a short gut with a stomach, which prolongs contact with special enzymes in an acid environment to encourage protein breakdown.

Osmoregulation

Fish are literally parcels of fluids within a fluid environment. In both marine and freshwater fish there is a difference between the salt concentration of the environment and their body fluids. Since the two are separated in places by very thin membranes, notably the gills, it is not surprising that there is a constant tendency for salt and water to flow in or out of the fish's body. The processes at work here are called diffusion and osmosis. If two solutions of different concentration are separated by a permeable membrane, such as those that form the biological boundaries of a fish, the ions of the salt will move by diffusion through the membrane from the more concentrated to the weaker solution, while the water molecules will move in the opposite direction by osmosis to dilute the stronger solution. As in many natural processes, there is a tendency towards equilibrium.

For a fish's body to work efficiently, it is essential that it maintains its internal salt/water balance at a constant level, in spite of the salt concentration of the water in which it lives. Fish counteract the natural forces of diffusion and osmosis by means of a process called osmoregulation. Here we see how the 'priorities' differ in marine and freshwater fish.

In freshwater fish, the body fluid has a higher concentration of salt than the surrounding environment. The tendency is therefore for water to flow in and for salts to be lost from the tissues. To counteract the first process, freshwater fish have very efficient kidneys, which excrete water very rapidly. Salt loss is minimized by efficient reabsorption of salt from urine before it is excreted, and active uptake of salt through special cells in the gills and from the food ingested by the fish.

Since seawater has a higher concentration of salt than the body fluids in marine fish, there is a constant tendency for water to be lost from the tissues and salt to flow in. Marine fish solve the dehydration problem by drinking large amounts of water and excreting little urine. The influx of salt is counteracted by selectively absorbing only a few salts from the sea water they drink and using energy to eliminate salts through special cells in the gills.

Respiration

Fish require oxygen for life. The vital processes by which they remove it from their aquatic environment and transfer it to the cells is called respiration. Freshwater contains only five percent of the oxygen present in air and saltwater contains 20 percent less oxygen than freshwater. Therefore, a marine fish's respiration system needs to be very efficient. It is essential to move large volumes of relatively oxygen-deficient water over the absorption surfaces to allow sufficient oxygen to be taken up. This transport mechanism also has to be energy-efficient because, as we have seen, water is 800 times denser than air.

To generate the necessary water flow, fish use the structure of their mouth and buccal cavity, plus the gill covers and their openings, the opercula, to produce a very effective low-power pump. This produces a constant flow of water over the gas-absorption surfaces of specialized respiration structures called gills. To absorb oxygen efficiently, the gill structures need to present a large surface area and a thin wall between the oxygen-carrying water and the blood. These parameters are limited by the fact that the more ideal gills become for gaseous exchange, the more likely they are to promote osmoregulatory problems, since

Osmoregulation in marine and freshwater fish

Marine fish

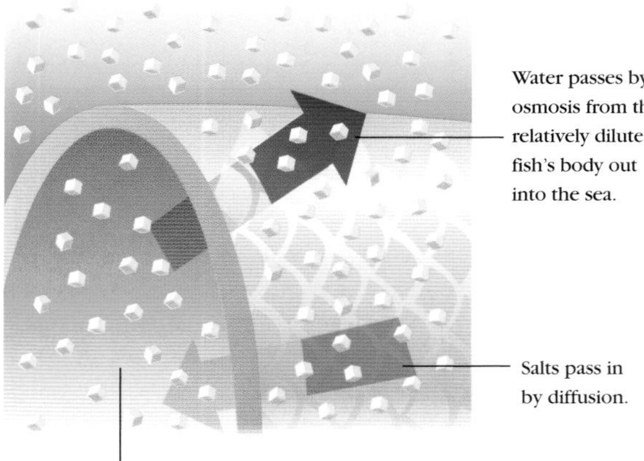

Water passes by osmosis from the relatively dilute fish's body out into the sea.

Salts pass in by diffusion.

The body fluids have a lower salt concentration than the surrounding water.

Freshwater fish

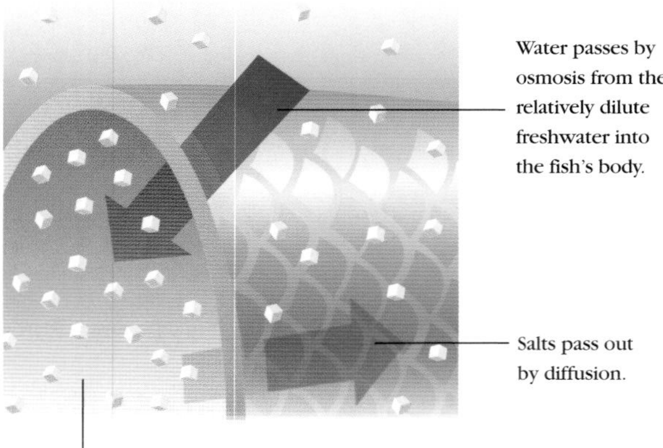

Water passes by osmosis from the relatively dilute freshwater into the fish's body.

Salts pass out by diffusion.

The body fluids have a higher salt concentration than the surrounding water.

Pumping cycle in fish respiration

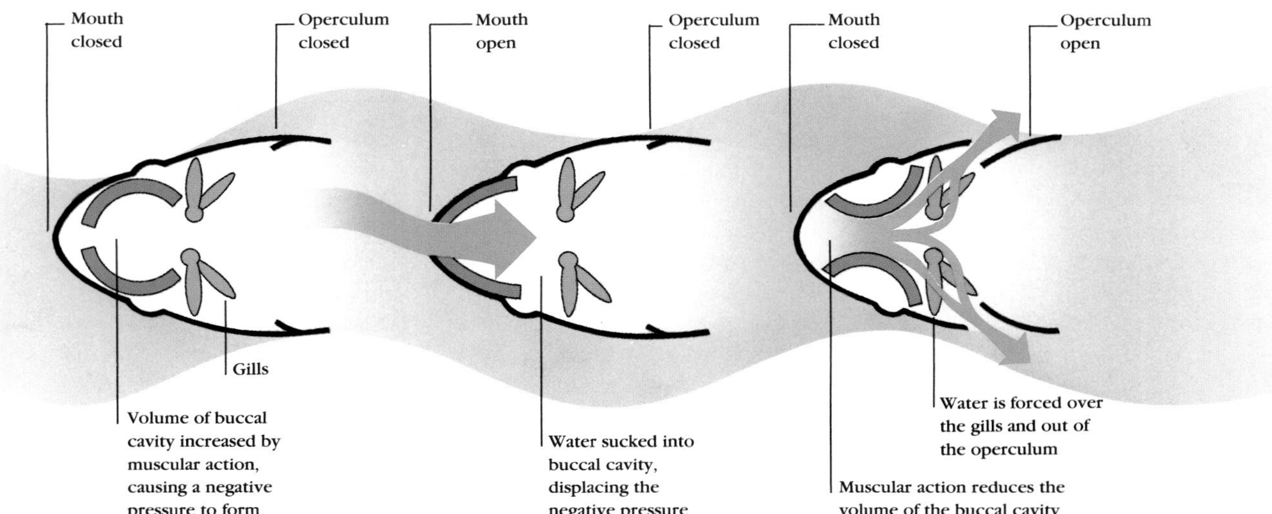

they provide an ideal site for water influx or loss. Gill structures, therefore, represent a compromise between the requirements for respiration and osmoregulation.

Oxygen is absorbed into the blood by simple diffusion. The blood flowing into the gills has a lower oxygen concentration than the surrounding water, so oxygen moves into the blood to redress the balance. This process is further improved by the fact that blood is pumped in the opposite direction to the water moving over the gills. This counter-current system ensures that the blood oxygen level remains below that of the water right across the gills and allows many fish to remove up to 80 percent of the water's oxygen content. The oxygen is actively picked up by haemoglobin in the red blood cells and transported to the body tissues, where a relatively high carbon dioxide level, allied to relatively lower oxygen concentrations in the fish's tissues, causes the oxygen to be given up for use in the cells' essential functions.

Carbon dioxide is a waste product of metabolism but, since this is soluble in the blood, it poses no problems in removal, diffusing out easily through the gill walls.

Reproduction

Survival of fish species clearly depends on their ability to reproduce themselves. Therefore, with around 27,000 living species in our seas and fresh waters, it is hardly surprising to find that they have developed a wide variety of successful strategies. All reproductive strategies are different means of applying the energy allocated to producing offspring in the most efficient way; that is, balancing the number and size of eggs or young produced with the amount of effort applied in parental care. For instance, damselfish and clownfish pair up and lay relatively small clutches of fairly large demersal eggs, which are guarded and tended by the parents.

Contrast this with Yellow Tangs (*Zebrasoma flavescens*), which come together in large shoals and breed above the reef at the full moon when currents run strong. They broadcast millions of small eggs – and even larger numbers of sperm. Later, the juveniles hatch out and become part of the vulnerable plankton where they are left to their own devices.

Sex on the reef is a fascinating subject. Many species, such as clownfish, even have the ability to change sex. All members of a group are male, except for the dominant specimen which becomes a female. When she dies the next most dominant male changes sex and takes on her role.

Above: *A pair of Fire Clownfish* (Amphiprion frenatus) *tend their eggs.*

What is an Invertebrate?

The term 'invertebrate' is a convenient catch-all title, loosely covering all those animals that do not have a backbone (or vertebral column) and an internal skeleton. Invertebrates range in size from microscopic planktonic animals to giant squid, fierce predators that roam the deep, colder waters of the world. There are so many species of invertebrate animals that it is difficult to estimate the total number involved. Of the two million species of animals in the world, about 97 percent are invertebrates. Land-living insects, spiders and worms make up a large proportion of these, but there are probably just as many invertebrate species in the seas as on the land.

The range of marine invertebrates is so vast that there is no sea habitat in which they do not occur. The species found in aquarium shops come primarily from the shallower, warm waters of the tropics, but the cold waters of the Poles contain massive populations of shrimps, anemones, sponges and the like.

So adaptable are invertebrates that they have even overturned one of the major, and previously unassailable, scientific precepts, namely that in the first instance all life on earth is primarily dependent upon the sun's energy. (For example, a cabbage captures light energy through photosynthesis and is then eaten by a rabbit that in turn becomes food for a fox.) Now, however, scientists have discovered a small but flourishing ecosystem of bacteria, sponges, molluscs, crabs and filter-feeding worms that exist at depths impenetrable by the sun's rays. The primary energy source for these creatures is submarine volcanic activity in the form of heat and emitted chemicals.

Naturally, these creatures are beyond the scope of the home aquarist, but even so, the invertebrate keeper is faced with selecting and housing creatures with widely different lifestyles and requirements. In this chapter we take a closer look at each phylum (major group) of animals of interest to the aquarist. As well as illustrating and describing the structure and behaviour of species suitable for the aquarium, this overview features some of the other fascinating animals that make up the diverse world of invertebrates. Clearly, keeping marine invertebrates is not a challenge to be taken up lightly, but the reward is a window onto an absorbing and often unseen world.

Phylum PORIFERA

In evolutionary terms, sponges are the most primitive animals likely to be of interest to the marine hobbyist. When alive, they look very different from the familiar dried sponges used in the bath. Unfortunately, many are difficult to transport – exposed to the air they soon die – and only a few are regularly available. However, many species can be found in well-established 'living reef' tanks, where they usually arrive as accidental introductions with living rock (see page 106), and some of the encrusting tropical species are very attractive. Deep-water sponges are generally white, pale yellow or green, but there are a number of brightly coloured species – green, yellow, orange, red and purple – particularly from shallow tropical waters. The purpose of these colours, caused by pigments, is unknown but it has been suggested that they could have a warning function or could protect the sponge from the sun's rays.

At a conservative estimate, there are at least 5,000 sponge species, but 10,000 may be nearer the number. Most are marine, with one freshwater family of about 150 species.

Habitat

Sponges are found in all seas wherever there is a suitable substrate for their attachment, such as rocks, shells, corals, plants, boats, pilings, oil rigs and all the other objects that man provides. They are particularly abundant in shallow waters of the continental shelf. In some areas, sponges are so plentiful that they make up 80 percent of all living matter. Commercial bath sponges may occur in large beds, which make them easy to collect. Sponges have been described as living hotels, their chambers providing temporary or permanent accommodation for a vast number of other organisms, ranging from algae to fish. For example when the 'residents' of some Caribbean loggerhead sponges were counted, there were several thousand shrimps in each sponge. And the sponge threadworm can occur in tens of thousands in a single sponge, making up a significant proportion of its weight.

Left: *Sponges take on many shapes, colours and forms, enabling them to colonize most situations.*

Although some sponges are eaten by sea slugs, turtles and some fish, many are toxic, particularly if their preferred habitat is in an exposed site. The toxins deter predators, help to keep the sponge free of larvae, etc. and protect the sponge from colonization by corals and other sponges.

Shapes and sizes

Most sponges are irregular in shape; the shapes often depend on the water current, the space available and the substrate to which the sponges are attached. In strong water currents they often grow as rounded or flattened clumps, but in calm water they may take on a branching appearance. A number of species form encrustations over any solid object, taking its shape. Confusingly, sponges of the same species may look very different under different conditions, making identification difficult.

Sponges vary greatly in size, ranging from less than 1cm (0.4in) to approximately 2m (6.6ft) in height and diameter. Deepwater species tend to be particularly enormous, with the largest species being found in the Caribbean and Antarctic. Some may not grow once they are mature, and some Antarctic sponges are known not to have grown for ten years. Given a good food supply in the tank, many small sponges grow quite rapidly.

Structure

Sponges are unlike any other group of marine invertebrates in that they are simply aggregations of cells and have no true tissues or organs. They are also incapable of movement. Not surprisingly, early naturalists assumed they were plants and it was not until the 1800s, when a sponge pumping water was observed through a microscope, that it was finally realized that they are animals.

Above: *These dramatic sponge 'chimneys'* (Verongia *sp.) expel water and waste material through the exhalent opening at the top of each stack.*

The name Porifera means 'pore-bearer'. This reflects the fact that cells making up a sponge enclose a system of canals and chambers that open to the surface through many small openings, or pores. The simplest sponges are vase-shaped, with a central cavity surrounded by a wall containing the pores. Special cells, known as collar cells, line the inner wall and draw a current of water in through the pores by means of their whiplike hairs, or flagella. The water current supplies the sponge with oxygen and food particles before passing out through the large opening at the top – the osculum – taking waste material with it. Sponges are very efficient filter feeders, the collar cells straining and ingesting bacteria and minute organic particles from the water. Because these particles are too small for many other species to use, sponges are well adapted to living in the nutrient-impoverished waters of the tropical seas.

Larger sponges need a more efficient filtering system to supply all their needs, so the body wall becomes increasingly convoluted. In the more complex species, the central body cavity disappears completely and is replaced with small chambers housing the collar cells. A number of large volcano-shaped processes may develop, each bearing an osculum out of which the current passes. Sometimes, the water current can be detected as much as 1m (3.3ft) above large sponges. The volume of water pumped through a sponge can be remarkable; for example, in one species it has been calculated that a sponge 10cm (4in) high and 1cm (0.4in) in diameter can pump 22.5 litres (5 gallons) of water a day.

Sponge cells often lie in a gelatinous medium, supported on a 'skeleton' of spicules or fibrous material called spongin, which is why sponges feel firm to the touch. Sponge spicules, usually invisible to the eye, look like slivers of glass and their different shapes are an important aid in identifying species. if you rub a sponge between finger and thumb, you can feel the spicules, but take care; in some sponges the spicules penetrate the surface and can irritate the skin.

A simple sponge

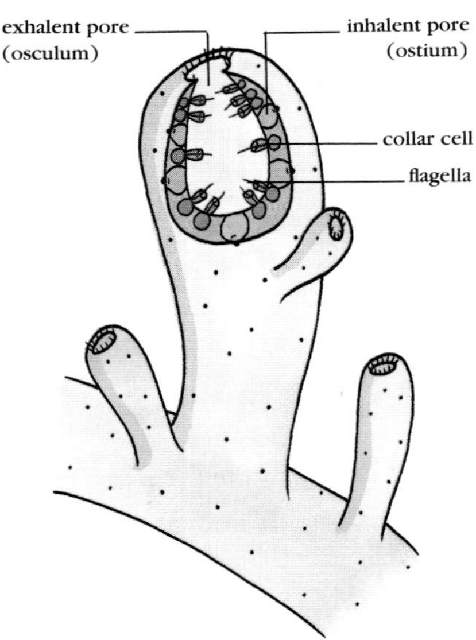

A complex sponge

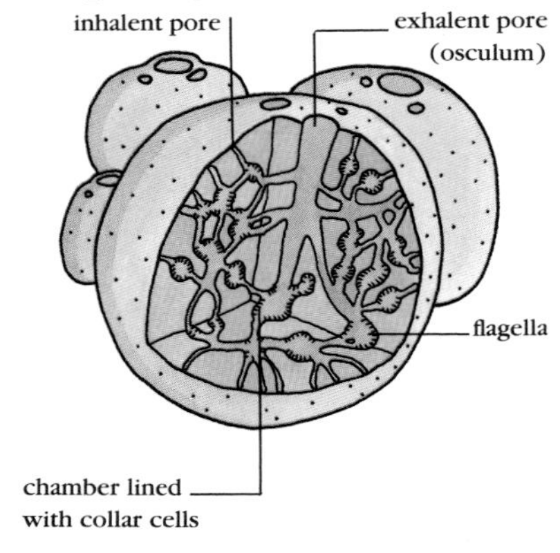

Sponge classification

Sponges are divided into four main groups according to their type of skeleton. The Calcarea, the simplest sponges, have calcareous spicules. The Hexactinellida have six-rayed siliceous spicules and include the beautiful deep-water glass sponges, such as the Venus Flower Basket, *Euplectella aspergillum*. The Sclerospongiae have massive limy skeletons composed of calcium carbonate, siliceous spicules and organic fibres and can easily be mistaken for corals.

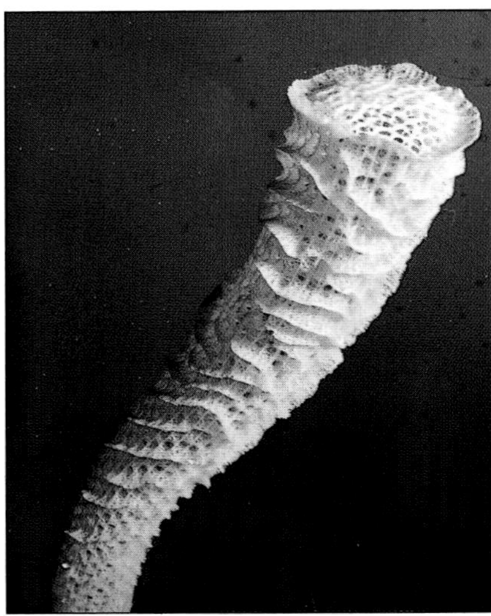

Above: *The skeleton of the Venus Flower Basket* (Euplectella aspergillum) *is often prized as a decorative ornament.*

The Demospongiae is the largest group, encompassing species with variously shaped siliceous spicules, a spongin skeleton or a mixture of both. This group includes the sponges of interest to the marine hobbyist, as well as the bath sponges and the boring sponges. The bath sponges have been harvested in the Mediterranean for centuries (the Romans used them for padding their helmets, as well as for bathing) and, more recently, in Florida waters. They are allowed to dry in the sun until the soft tissues rot, leaving the spongin skeleton. Boring sponges are in fact quite interesting; their name arises from the fact that they bore through rocks, stony corals and bivalve shells, probably by secreting an acid to dissolve the calcium carbonate. They eventually cause the death of their host and can be quite a pest in commercial oyster beds.

Sponge spicules

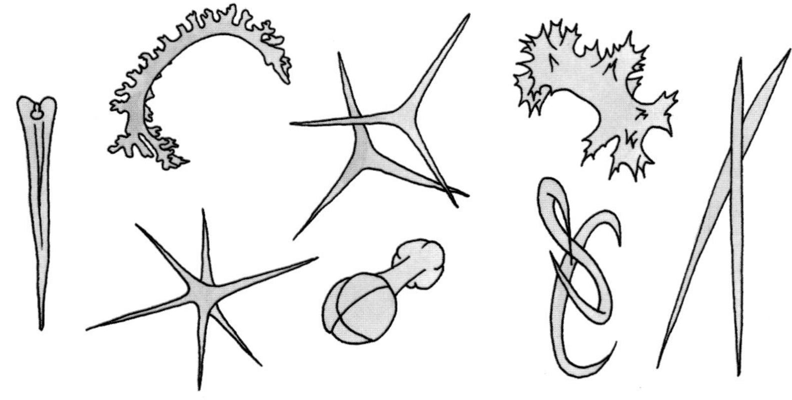

Reproduction

Like the majority of marine invertebrates, sponges reproduce by releasing eggs and sperm which, after fertilization, form larvae that float in the plankton before settling in a suitable place and developing into a new sponge. Sponges also have remarkable powers of regeneration; complete new animals will grow from small detached or broken pieces.

Phylum CNIDARIA

The phylum Cnidaria consists of a vast group of animals, the majority of which are marine. They include jellyfish, sea anemones, sea fans and corals, and are found throughout the world, from the coldest depths to the sun-baked shallows of tropical lagoons. Cnidarians play an immensely important role in marine communities and, like sponges, often provide a habitat as well as food for other invertebrates and fish. Many cnidarians are of interest to the aquarium hobbyist especially in 'living-reef' aquariums, i.e. those aiming to recreate a section of coral reef. However, it is only fairly recently that many aquarists have succeeded with any but a very limited number of species. In the last ten years, a higher quality of salt mixes, a recognition of the importance of trace elements and stable specific gravities, and improved lighting, filtration and nitrate reduction techniques have all contributed to simplifying the maintenance of corals and anemones in the aquarium. But given that these animals populate such widely different habitats, it is impossible to accommodate them all within one set of environmental conditions.

Structure

Cnidarians seem very variable in appearance, ranging in size from tiny *Hydra* to coral heads (colonies of polyps) several metres across. However, they are all characterized by a radially symmetrical body plan. This means that if you slice horizontally through a cnidarian you will find the body organs arranged in an even circle around a central axis. The body is basically a simple sack, or stomach, with a single opening used both as a mouth and as the exit through which waste is ejected. This is usually surrounded by tentacles armed with tiny stinging cells called nematocysts, used for catching food. Each nematocyst ejects a hollow thread, like a harpoon, into the body of the prey and injects a paralyzing poison. Sessile (non-moving) cnidarians also use nematocysts to protect the living space around them from other animals, including encroaching individuals of the same species.

Above: *Cnidarians such as this anemone play an important role in marine communities, providing a protective habitat for other animals.*

Polyps and medusae

All cnidarians exist in one of two alternative forms: the polyp, usually attached to rocks or other objects, or the free-swimming medusa. Some groups occur only as polyps and some only as medusae, but some pass through both phases, starting as polyps before budding off medusae as part of their life cycle. A sea anemone is a typical polyp, cylindrical in shape, attached to the substrate at the base end, and with mouth and tentacles at the free end. Polyps often have an external or

Stinging cells (nematocysts)

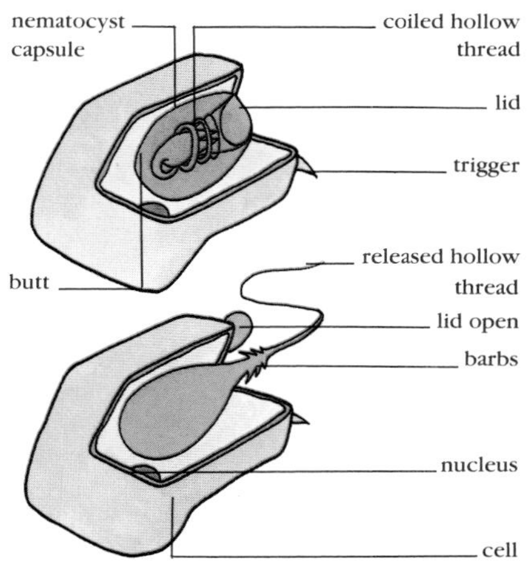

A jellyfish

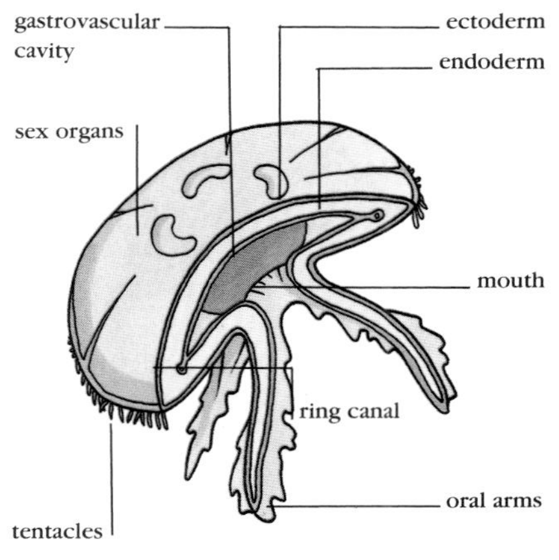

internal skeleton, as in the corals, and many form colonies by budding off new polyps from the parent polyp. Jellyfish are typical free-swimming medusae, the bell-shaped body having a convex upper surface, below which hang the mouth and tentacles. Medusae are rarely colonial. They swim by alternate contractions of two sets of muscle, which cause them to pulsate. The arms and tentacles often develop into complex shapes to deal with a variety of prey.

Classification
There are approximately 10,000 species of cnidarian, divided into three main groups: the Hydrozoa, the Scyphozoa and the Anthozoa.

The Hydrozoa are mainly marine, but a few species occur in fresh water. The group contains the tiny sea firs (hydroids) and also the complex floating colonies that make up the Portuguese men-of-war. The fire corals that are found on coral reefs and that produce painful rashes if touched, also feature in this group. Hydrozoans characteristically have both polyp and medusa phases.

The Scyphozoa include all the jellyfish, and the medusa phase if predominant. Jellyfish are well named – even the firmest ones contain 94 percent water. They are highly mobile, and very graceful in the water, swimming by contracting their umbrella-shaped bodies, but they are largely at the mercy of the sea currents. Most species are carnivorous and catch animals with their tentacles, which are armed with nematocysts. They are still virtually unknown in aquariums, perhaps because so many of them are venomous. Tropical species can be extremely dangerous and one jellyfish has tentacles up to 20m (66ft) long. A few species feed by wafting currents through their mouths and trapping food in strands of mucus. Jellyfish reproduce by releasing fertilized eggs into the sea. These develop into small larvae that float among the plankton in the ocean currents.

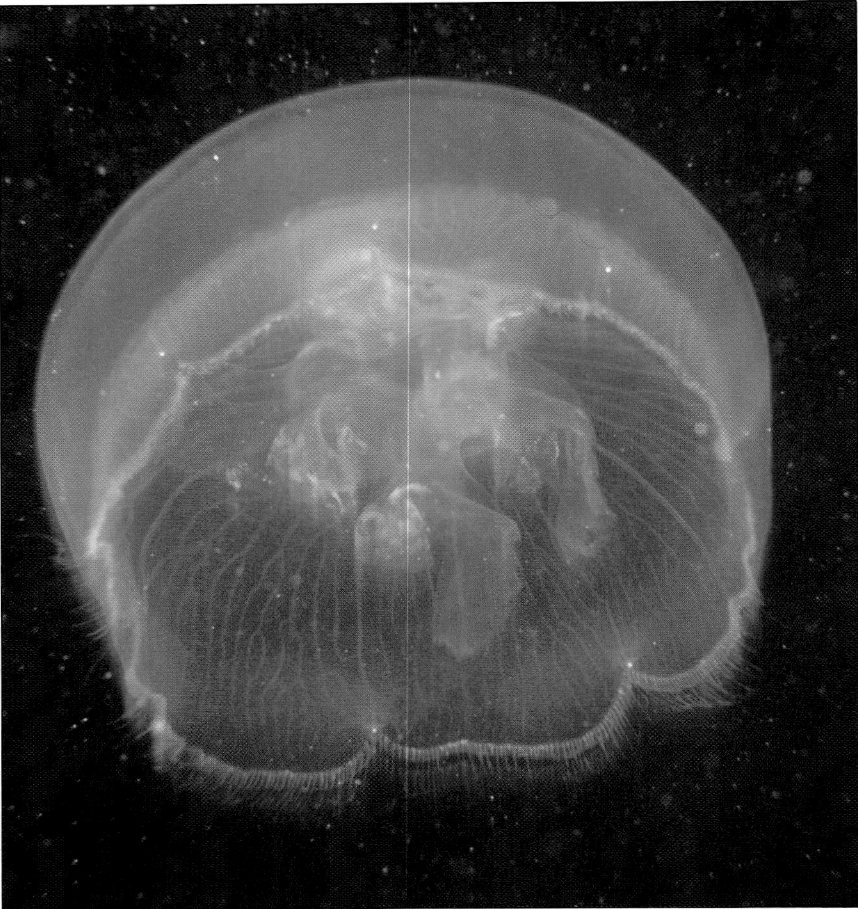

Above: *The graceful beauty of the jellyfish belies the fact that it is often highly carnivorous in nature, catching animals with its tentacles.*

The Anthozoa are the largest group of cnidarians. They have no medusa phase and include some 6,000 species. These are of greatest interest to the aquarist, as they include the sea anemones and corals, once known as 'flower animals'. Many corals and anemones are filter feeders or rely on zooxanthellae, but a large number benefit by being fed directly with small pieces of fish or shrimp, sprinkled over the animal or lightly pushed among the tentacles once or twice a week.

The body structure of sea anemones is based on a simple polyp, with multiples of six tentacles around the mouth. In some species, the base is modified for burrowing, but more usually anemones are attached to hard objects by means of a suckerlike disc. Although most seem to remain rooted to the spot, some can move by creeping over rocks. Species of *Stomphia* even leave their rock and swim away when touched by a starfish or predatory sea slug. Tropical anemones are generally larger than their temperate relations and can reach up to 1m (39in) in diameter. Sea anemones are often brightly coloured and a single species may have several different colour forms. Some anemones have zooxanthellae but most catch living prey, including fish, using the nematocysts (see page 31) on their tentacles.

Others trap organic particles in the water in mucus streams propelled towards the mouth by the tentacles. Several of the large anemones are host to clownfishes, *Amphiprion* sp., that live in their tentacles. The fish are protected by the anemone, and themselves provide protection for their host by deterring predatory fish. They also provide a cleaner service for the anemone. Anemones can reproduce

What are zooxanthellae?

Like several other groups of marine invertebrates, many cnidarians have small single-celled plants or algae, called zooxanthellae that live in the body tissues. Both animal and plant appear to benefit from this symbiotic association, which is particularly common in corals. The cnidarian probably uses the carbohydrates and oxygen produced by the zooxanthellae and the latter use the animal's waste products and assist in the assimilation of vital trace elements from the surrounding water. In the United States and West Germany there is much intensive study into the functions of these algae and the more that is discovered, the more vital they appear to be. Although it has been said that up to 90 percent of their food energy is obtained from these zooxanthellae, hard corals, for example, still need to capture planktonic organisms to survive. The *Tridacna* clams also play host to algae within their tissues but, unlike the corals, these clams will ingest the algae if they are hungry. With the advent of suitable lighting, it is now possible to satisfy the needs of the zooxanthellae in the domestic aquarium. Generally speaking, cnidarians with beige, brown, green or blue colouring have zooxanthellae and thus require strong lighting of the correct spectrum if these algae are to function correctly; like all plants they produce food through the process of photosynthesis, for which light is essential. In contrast, cnidarians within the colour range of purple, through red to orange and yellow usually lack zooxanthellae. They are often deep-living and generally do not require, or appreciate, intense lighting.

by budding off from the polyp, but they also reproduce sexually by releasing sperm and eggs.

Also of interest to aquarists is a small group of anthozoans that are effectively halfway between anemones and corals. These are the zoanthids, such as the green polyps (see page 316). They resemble small anemones but are colonial. There is no skeleton or basal disc, but the polyps have one or two rings of smooth slender tentacles. Zoanthids encrust rocks and even other animals, such as sponges and corals. The false corals, which include the mushroom polyps (see page 316) are also in a halfway position. Their polyps resemble those of true corals, but have no hard external skeleton. The tentacles often have clubbed tips and are arranged in rings around the mouth.

Anthozoans with eight tentacles

Corals that do not build reefs are classified in another group of the Anthozoa and have an eight-tentacle body plan, unlike the six-tentacle plan of sea anemones and hard corals. This group includes soft corals, sea pens, sea feathers, sea whips, sea fans and also the precious red and pink corals. They are generally colonial, with an internal calcareous or horny skeleton and tentacles that are often branched or featherlike. The precious corals are deep-water or cave-dwelling species and are not suitable for the aquarium, but their beautiful coloured calcareous skeletons are used for jewellery.

Below: *The delicate and intricate tracery of the sea whip's tentacles are appreciated to best effect when seen in close-up, as here.*

A sea anemone

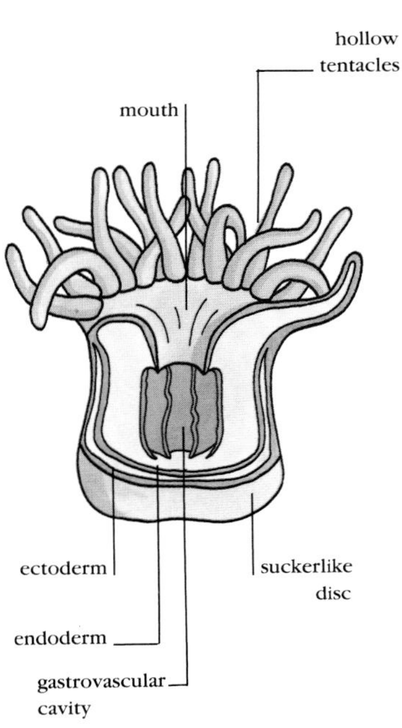

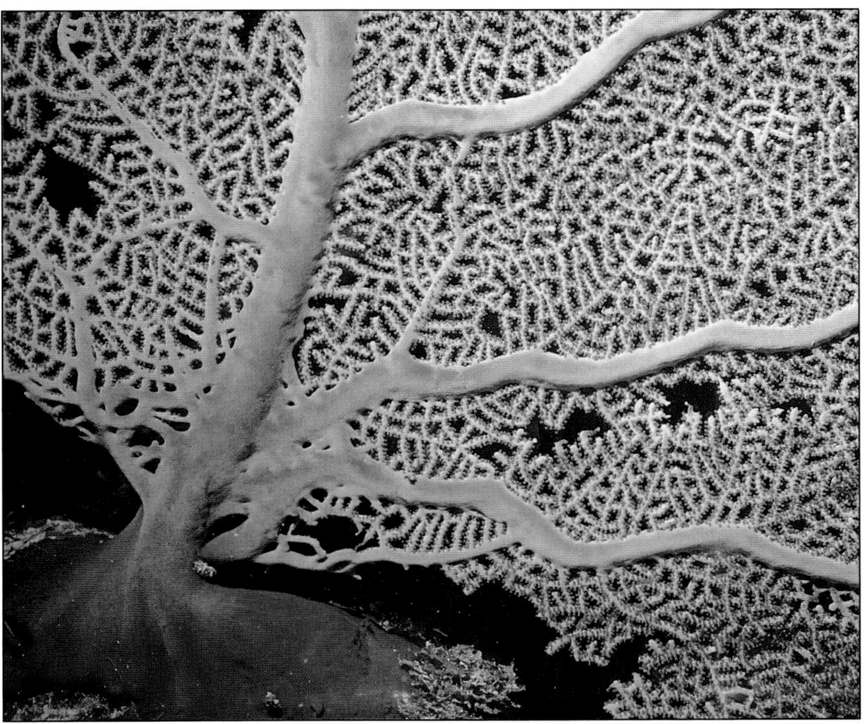

Soft corals include the leather corals, pulse corals and cauliflower corals (see pages 324-325). They are not as demanding to keep in the aquarium as the hard corals, but still need good water quality and husbandry. The polyps protrude from a fleshy mass, which is sometimes lobed, and is strengthened by calcareous spicules. Deep-water species tend to have more spicules and so are more rigid than shallow-water forms, which are subjected to a greater wave force. The polyps can be completely withdrawn into the body.

Sea pens and sea feathers (see page 323) are fleshy colonies, with short polyps arising from the sides of a central polyp. The lower end of this main polyp forms a stalk that is buried in soft sediments and several species can retract into the mud if disturbed. The skeleton is made of calcareous spicules and may reach 1m (39in) in height. Some sea pens emit waves of glowing phosphorescence when disturbed. They are usually found on the sandy and muddy bottoms of sheltered bays and harbours.

Horny corals (see page 314), a group of species that look rather like plants, includes sea whips and sea fans. The main stem is firmly attached to a hard surface by a plate or tuft of creeping branches. The stem has a central strengthening rod that is generally made out of a horny material called gorgonin (these species are often referred to as 'gorgonians'), although some species have a calcareous skeleton. The short polyps are found all over the branches of the colony but are absent from the main stem. Colonies are often brightly coloured and may reach a height of 3m (10ft). They often provide a home for sponges and hydroids, bryozoans and brittle stars, which stick to their branches.

Hard or stony corals Many corals have calcareous external skeletons and the biggest group of these – the stony corals – are responsible for building coral reefs. They are most often shades of beige and green, although some are blue or pink. The stony corals are in the same group as sea anemones and have a six-tentacle body plan. The coral animal is basically a tiny sea anemone sitting in a chalky cup, but colonies of these animals can build structures as enormous as the Australian Great Barrier Reef, some 2000km (1260 miles) long and consisting of over 2500 separate reefs. In colonial stony corals, individual polyps may be as small as 5mm (0.2in) in diameter, but in some solitary forms, such as *Heliofungia*, the polyp may be as much as 50cm (20in) in diameter. Brain corals (see page 306) are so-named because the polyps are arranged in continuous rows, so that the skeleton has longitudinal fissures in a brainlike mass. The polyps in colonial forms are connected laterally and lie over the limestone skeleton that they secrete. Coral reefs are built up over thousands of years; as old ones die, new colonies form on top.

A coral reef provides a habitat for sea anemones and other corals, as well as for a wide variety of other marine invertebrates, fish and plants. Reef-building corals need warm, clear water – the temperature should rarely drop below 21°C (70°F) – and are easily suffocated by sediment. Coral reefs are often described as oases in an oceanic desert, because the tropical waters in which they occur are very poor in nutrients compared with temperate waters. As a result, if too much food is introduced into a tank, many stony corals will retract their tentacles. Clear water is also needed by the zooxanthellae, on which stony corals heavily depend. To build their skeletons, stony corals need a high pH level and a good reserve of calcium in the water. Without this, they do not flourish and appear to come 'unstuck' from their bases. They can, however, survive in the sea in colder, darker waters, but in such situations their capacity to secrete limestone is reduced and reefs are not formed.

Reef corals grow in many different shapes, depending on their preferred position and water depth. Deeper corals and those in sheltered, still waters tend to form branches, while corals in exposed positions are usually compact. New coral colonies can grow from broken fragments of larger colonies if the conditions are right; this is one way in which coral reefs recover from damage inflicted by storms and hurricanes. Stony corals also reproduce sexually by releasing sperm and eggs. Recently, it has been discovered that corals on the Great Barrier Reef all spawn on the same night, once a year. The reef becomes covered with a mass of swirling eggs and sperm; the reason for this extraordinary event is not yet clearly established, but it could be that it confuses predators.

Above: *The feathery tips of these polyps 'pulse' in a rhythmical action, capturing tiny food particles and absorbing oxygen.*

Phylum PLATYHELMINTHES

The large group of wormlike creatures known as flatworms includes the various parasitic flukes and tapeworms well known to aquarists and studiously avoided by them! However, most fishkeepers would be delighted to come across some of the large and colourful flatworm species found on coral reefs. Unfortunately, these are rarely imported, even though they are fairly common in the wild.

Above: *This species,* Pseudoceros bajae, *is a typically colourful and interesting flatworm, which is much sought after by marine aquarists.*

Below: *In common with many species in the animal kingdom, the black and yellow warning colours of this flatworm indicate that it may be poisonous.*

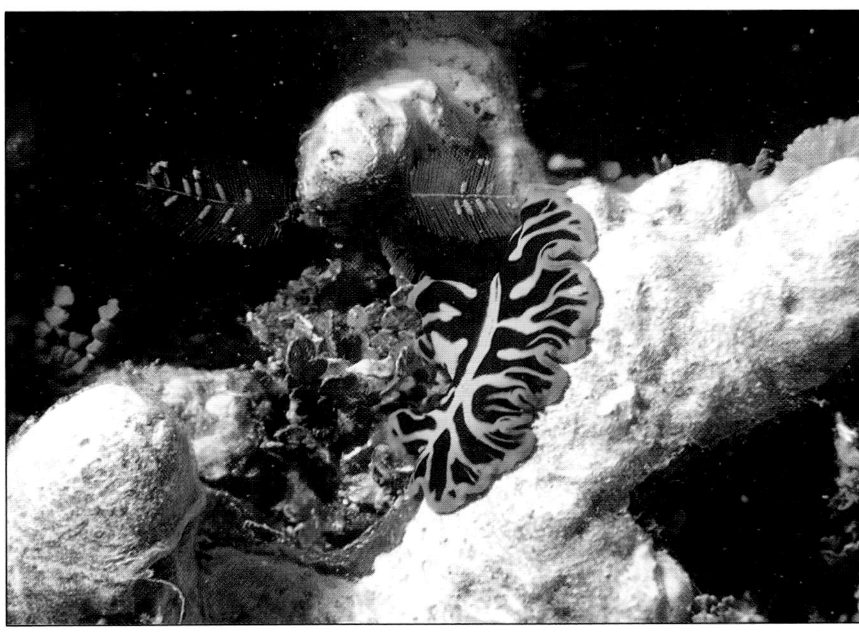

Structure

Flatworms are the most primitive worms and their ancestors occupied a key position on the evolutionary tree leading to the higher animals. The flatworm gut is still a simple, blind-ended tube, and respiration occurs throughout the body surface, but there is an excretory system, muscles along the lines of those found in higher animals and a centralized nervous system, with a tiny brain.

Flatworms are generally small and sombre in colour, and a few are green due to the presence of zooxanthellae. However, the most attractive species – and those of interest to the aquarist – are extremely brightly patterned, often with some form of banding or striping. These species reach about 5cm (2in) in length and are in the family Pseudocerotidae from the Indo-Pacific. This family is in a group characterized by their branching guts. Like most flatworms, the body is flattened, but in this group it is wafer thin and has a leaflike shape, being almost as broad as it is long. They have a recognizable head, usually with numerous pairs of eyes and often a pair of sensory tentacles.

Function and behaviour

The unpleasant flukes and tapeworms belong to the class Trematoda and Cestoda, whereas the free-living flatworms are in the class Turbellaria, of which there are about 4,000 species. Free-living flatworms differ from the parasitic forms in that their body is covered with cilia, which, with the muscles, produce the characteristic gliding movement and create the 'turbulence' that has given rise to the group's name. Most of the free-living flatworms are marine and live on the bottom of shallow waters in the intertidal zone, although a few swim freely in the water. They are generally more active at night. The majority are carnivorous. The mouth opens on the underside of the body and sometimes has a muscular tube or funnel-like pharynx that can be extruded through the mouth to grasp or pierce food. The animal digests its prey by releasing enzymes over it and sucking the softened food into the mouth.

Reproduction

Free-living flatworms are hermaphrodite, i.e. they have both male and female organs, but they do not normally fertilize themselves. After copulation between two individuals, a large egg mass is laid from which hatch small larvae. Many flatworms also reproduce asexually by dividing, and freshwater flatworms can regenerate complete animals from small pieces. It is not known whether this also applies to the tropical marine flatworms.

Phylum ANNELIDA

This large group of invertebrates contains the segmented worms, many of which are marine. They have long, soft bodies and are oval in cross-section. The rings on the body, from which the name Annelida derives (in Latin, 'anulus' means a ring), are not merely external, but involve many of the internal organs. These animals have no solid skeleton, but gain rigidity from hydraulic pressure in the fluid-filled body cavity. Alternate contraction of two sets of muscle – one circular and the other longitudinal – allows the animal to move. Most species, apart from the leeches, have bristles or chaetae, protruding from each segment. These also help them to move and may be adapted for other purposes as well. Annelids have a more or less straight gut, with a mouth at one end and an anus at the other. Other characteristics indicate their much higher level of evolution in comparison to the invertebrates discussed so far, namely a good circulatory system and the presence in each segment of excretory organs and a compact mass of nerve cells called a ganglion. There are three main groups of annelids.

Oligochaetes

The class Oligochaeta consists mainly of the familiar terrestrial earthworms, but also includes some important marine species, although none of these is of interest to the aquarist. The diversity and abundance of marine oligochaetes in estuaries and sheltered coasts is only just being realized. Many are able to tolerate high levels of dissolved organic matter and occur in polluted habitats.

Leeches

Hirudinea – or leeches – are mostly bloodsucking external parasites. There are only a few marine species; most of them are in a single family and feed on fish body fluids.

Polychaetes

The segmented worms of interest to the aquarist are all in the class Polychaeta, the bristleworms. This is the largest and most primitive group of annelids, and the majority are marine. They are often strikingly beautiful and very colourful and, unlike the other two groups of annelids, they show enormous variation in form and lifestyle. Apart from the head and terminal segments, all the segments are identical, each with a pair of flattened, fleshy lobelike paddles called parapodia, which are used for swimming, burrowing and creating a feeding current. The bristles, or chaetae, on the parapodia are immensely variable between species. In the sea mice, for example, they form a protective mat

Below: *The Sea Mouse* (Aphrodita *sp.) does not much resemble a worm, owing to its extended bristles, which form a protective covering over the animal.*

over the back of the worm and give the animal a furry appearance. The bristles of fireworms, on the other hand, are long and poisonous for defence, and are shed readily if a worm is attacked. Fireworms are voracious predators that usually feed on corals, but are known to attack animals, such as anemones, ten times their size. The species *Hermodice carunculata* is sometimes accidentally introduced into the home aquarium; take great care when handling it.

Polychaetes can be split into two groups on the basis of their behaviour. The mobile polychaetes are free-living forms with well-developed parapodia used for swimming and, often, for burrowing in the sand and mud. Many of them live under boulders and coral heads, and are common on coral reefs. This group also includes tube dwellers that leave their tubes to hunt for food. By contrast, the sedentary polychaetes are tube dwellers that rarely, if ever, leave their tubes, obtaining food with their tentacles.

In tube dwellers, the tentacles usually form a crown that catches food particles in the water. These are carried to the mouth by cilia on the tentacles. Mobile polychaetes often have an eversible pharynx, ending in fierce jaws that seize other animals or suck their body fluids, or grasp large pieces of plant material. The body surface provides sufficient area for respiration in small polychaetes, but larger ones need gills. In tube dwellers, these are usually situated near the tentacles and water is drawn past them by special movements of the body.

Ragworms, which live in the intertidal zone in muddy habitats, are mobile polychaetes, and well known to fishermen who often use them as bait. They live in U-shaped burrows, emerging only to feed on plant and animal debris on the surface. Lugworms, also familiar as bait, spend their entire lives in burrows, filtering sediment through the gut and leaving worm casts on the surface. Both worms respire by directing a current of water through their burrows by regular body contractions.

The tubeworms are the only polychaetes of real interest to the aquarist. Both the fan or featherduster worms in the family Sabellidae and the 'Christmas tree' worms in the family Serpulidae make excellent aquarium inhabitants and are recommended for beginners. They are sedentary, spending all their lives in their tubes, and are the most attractive of all the polychaetes.

Above: *The main body of the Christmas Tree Worm remains deep in the coral, but the two branches of stiff tentacles extend above the surface.*

A fanworm

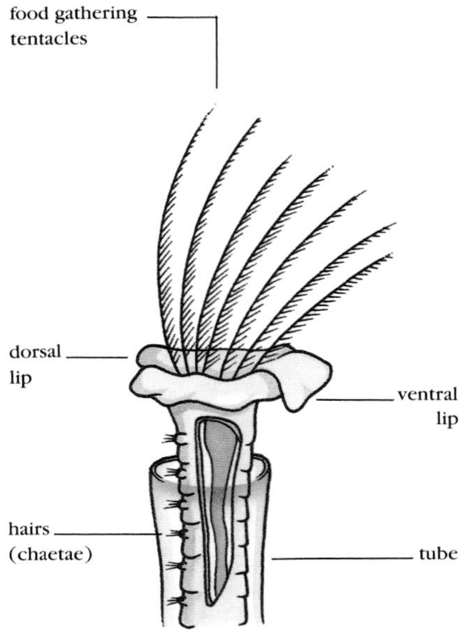

In tubeworms, the parapodia are degenerate, there are no jaws and the heads are reduced. Instead, feathered, rather stiff tentacles radiate from the head to form an almost complete crown, which is used both as a gill and for feeding. Particles of food are trapped on the branches of each tentacle and channelled to the central rib, from where they flow in a stream of mucus to the mouth. Fanworms have colourful orange, green or purple tentacles forming the crown. Serpulids often have more brightly coloured blue and red tentacles, which may act as a warning device. Fanworms can contract their crown with startling rapidity, thanks to giant nerve fibres, which run from one end of the body to the other within the main nerve cord. The tentacles are extremely sensitive and will respond even to the shadow of a hand passing over the tank.

The cylindrical lower part of the

body is protected by a tight tube, secreted by the animal and made of a parchmentlike mucus. Serpulid worms are smaller and produce a tube of a stony calcareous material. As extra protection, a calcareous 'plug' may be present to block the entrance of the tube after the tentacles have been withdrawn. The serpulid group of worms also includes the tiny *Spirorbis* worms, which are often found on rocks and the bottom of boats as calcareous tubes arranged in a flat spiral about 3.3mm (0.12in) in diameter.

Annelid reproduction

Most annelids have sex cells in each segment; some species are hermaphrodite, but in others there are animals of both sexes. At certain times of year, the sex cells are shed into the sea, where fertilization takes place and a ciliated larva is formed. In some cases, the worms die after shedding the sex cells.

Reproduction in polychaetes often involves swarming, which helps to ensure that sperm and eggs are released at the same time, rather like the corals on the Great Barrier Reef. There is often a special sexual phase that looks quite unlike the normal burrowing individual, with enlarged eyes and parapodia for swimming.

Above: *Red-banded Fanworms* (Potamilla fonticula) *may be found both in small colonies, as seen here, or as isolated individuals.*

Below: *The parts of a fan worm are clearly seen here – feathery tentacles, outer tube and (at the bottom of the picture) the normally unseen worm.*

The palolo worm from the South Pacific, though not an aquarium species, is worth mentioning because it is so strange. These worms have sex cells in the rear segments only. These segments change shape and colour and, when ready, this rear section breaks off and rises to the surface, where the eggs and sperm are shed. All the palolo worms do this on one night, near dawn, at full moon in November. When all the segments have risen to the surface, the sea takes on the appearance of vermicelli, turning milky white when the eggs and sperm are released. Meanwhile, the front part of the worm remains in the coral and rocks and regenerates the missing parts. But perhaps strangest of all is the behaviour of the people who live on the islands in this part of the world; the palolo worm is considered a great delicacy and on the appointed day people venture out in boats at dawn and collect buckets of the worm segments as they rise to the surface!

Another interesting polychaete is the fireworm from Bermuda. When the worms come to the surface, the females start to emit a greenish phosphorescent glow. This attracts the males, which dart towards the females, emitting flashing lights at the same time. As the different sexes approach each other, the sex cells are shed.

Phylum CHELICERATA

King, or horseshoe, crabs, sea spiders and a few mites are the only marine species in this large group that is dominated by the spiders, mites and ticks. The chelicerata are related to crustaceans and insects, all animals with an external skeleton, or cuticle, made of a material called chitin. The body of a chelicerate has just two sections: the cephalothorax at the front, which includes the head and legs, and the abdomen at the back, which may have some appendages. The name chelicerata arises from the fact that instead of the antennae found in insects and crustaceans, these animals have a pair of pincerlike mouthparts called chelicerae.

The horseshoe crabs are the only species in this group of interest to aquarists. They are extremely primitive animals; over 300 million years, ago, horseshoe crab ancestors looked much like their modern descendants. They were once widespread and included many species. Today, however, there are only four species, which are considered as 'living fossils'.

Structure

Horseshoe crabs are light greenish grey to dark brown in colour and can reach a length of 60cm (24in). Males are generally smaller than females. They have a heavily armoured body, and look as if they should be taking part in a science fiction film! The front section (cephalothorax) is covered by a horseshoe-shaped carapace, hinged to the abdomen; the domed shape of the carapace helps the animal to burrow through the mud. Horseshoe crabs have been described as 'walking museums', as the carapace is often covered with large numbers of other organisms, including algae, coelenterates, flatworms, bryozoans and molluscs. The crab has a long mobile tail spine, a telson, which helps it to move and to right itself if it is accidentally overturned. Immature crabs have spines along the top of the telson, but these do not grow and so appear proportionately smaller as the crab gets older; they may help the young crab to burrow, and act as a deterrent to predators.

There are five pairs of walking legs on the front section. The first four pairs have pincer tips and heavy bases that are used for moving food into the mouth. The fifth pair has an even heavier base that is used to crush thin-shelled molluscs, and a whorl of spines to sweep away silt as the animal burrows. The back section of the crab has several pairs of appendages, five of which form gill books – an adaptation unique to horseshoe crabs. These look like the leaves of a book and act as gills for respiration. The gill books are also used for movement by young horseshoe crabs, which swim along upside down.

Behaviour

Horseshoe crabs live on the bottom of sandy and muddy bays and estuaries, and only return to the beach to breed. They generally move along the bottom with a stiff-legged gait, but are capable of swimming in quieter water. They feed on a wide variety of other invertebrates, including worms and molluscs, digging in the mud and passing the food to their mouths with their pincer-tipped front legs. The American horseshoe crab, *Limulus polyphemus*, can consume at least 100 young soft-shelled surf clams a day and seems able to detect this prey up to 90cm (36in) away.

A horseshoe crab

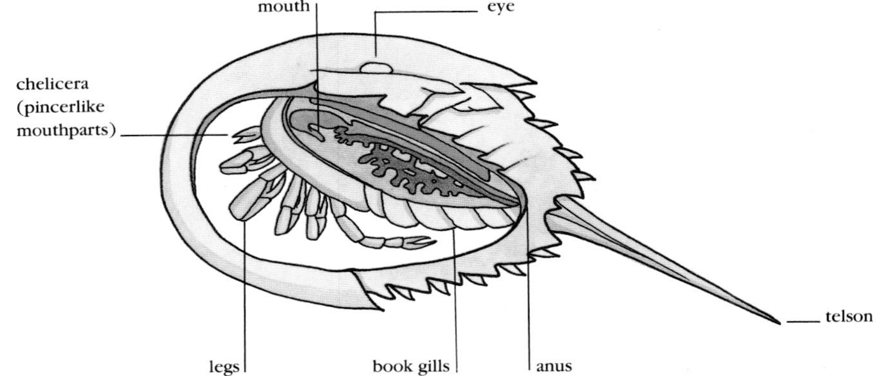

Reproduction

The breeding period is characterized by the migration of huge numbers of crabs into shallow waters along the shores of bays and estuaries. This is best known in North America, where the massive emergence of horseshoe crabs on the beaches of the Atlantic and Gulf of Mexico is one of the most spectacular phenomena of the coast. The crab makes a useful food for poultry and pigs, a good fertilizer, a bait for other fisheries, and has recently become very important in biomedical research. As a result, large harvests are taken during the breeding period. Thousands of crabs may be taken in each session and, at the peak of the fishery in the 1920s and 1930s, four to five million crabs were being collected annually.

The crabs migrate to the beaches, usually either at full or new moon and within two hours of high tide. The males move sideways to the shore and intercept females heading directly for the beach. The couples then proceed to the beach. The males fertilize the eggs as they are released, and the female lays them in an excavation in the sand, from several hundred to several thousand at a time. The adult crabs leave the beach as the tide ebbs and the eggs hatch in about five weeks. The young crab larvae emerge only at an appropriate high tide. Juveniles moult several times a year, burying themselves in the sand to protect themselves from predators; adults may moult once a year or even less.

Phylum CRUSTACEA

Crustaceans have aptly been called 'the insects of the sea'. Although there are some freshwater and terrestrial species, the majority are marine. They have invaded every possible habitat in the sea, from deep cold abysses to warm shallows, and have exploited every way of life in the same way as insects have on land. There are nearly 40,000 species, ranging in size from microscopic parasitic and planktonic animals to giant spider crabs from Japan with a leg span approaching 3m (10ft) and lobsters weighing up to 20kg (44lb). Many species are commercially important, such as the edible prawns, lobsters and crabs. Others are a major food source for higher animals. Crustaceans themselves are often active and efficient predators on invertebrates and fishes.

Structure

Crustaceans have a distinct head, thorax and abdomen, although in some species the two front sections fuse together. Most have a telson, or tail piece, and some have a rostrum, or spine, which projects between the eyes. The number of body segments, limbs and other appendages varies between species, but there are always two pairs of antennae on the head, often a pair of stalked, compound eyes, and at least three pairs of mouthparts. Whereas smaller crustaceans respire through the body surface, the larger crustaceans have gills, which are more complex in the more active species and often associated with the leg appendages. The appendages of crustaceans show a marked division of labour, different pairs being adapted for walking, feeding, respiration or reproduction. The tailfan found in many species – and used for swimming backwards – is also developed from appendages.

'Suits of armour'

Like insects and the horseshoe crabs, crustaceans have a cuticle of chitin that serves both as a suit of armour and a skeleton, and it is this 'crust' that has given rise to the name of the group. In most large crustaceans, it is strengthened with carbonate and other calcium salts to keep it rigid. In some species, this carapace, as it is known, can be thick enough to make the animal almost invulnerable to all but the most determined predators. The disadvantage of an exoskeleton is that it must be shed at intervals as the animal grows. At moulting time, the cuticle splits at the thorax and the animal squeezes itself backwards, leaving behind a perfect hollow replica of itself, which is sometimes eaten by its owner to reduce energy losses. The animal swells rapidly in size with fluid, so that the new cuticle is larger when it hardens than the old one. The body is then deflated, leaving space for growth. After moulting, the animal is soft-skinned and vulnerable; in a tank, be sure to provide plenty of hiding places for it to retreat into during this phase. Check that the pH level of the water is not too low,

Below: *A small colony of Gooseneck Barnacles* (Lepas ansifera) *is a common sight in the tropics. Note the stalks by which the barnacles are attached.*

otherwise the new shell may not harden properly and the animal will become deformed. Any leg or claw lost before moulting will be regenerated at the next moult, but make sure that the animal is not at a disadvantage in the tank and isolate it if necessary.

Minor crustacean groups

There are eight groups of crustaceans, but not all are considered here. One of the more primitive groups, the Branchiopoda, is largely freshwater, but may be familiar to aquarists because it includes the water flea, *Daphnia*, often used as food for small fish. The brineshrimp, *Artemia*, found in salt pans and ponds, also belongs to this group. The Copepoda include the tiny, usually transparent, herbivores with no carapace that make up most of the sea's plankton and are an important food source for many fish.

Barnacles

It is often not appreciated that barnacles – both the common conical ones and the stalked or gooseneck barnacles, such as *Lepas* (see page 330) – are crustaceans. All barnacles are marine and pass their adult lives attached to rocks or other suitable substrates. These include manmade objects – barnacles are major fouling organisms – and also living animals, such as crabs, turtles and whales. Although they could not look more different from shrimps, crabs and lobsters, dissection shows them to be closely related.

A barnacle has been described as 'an animal standing on its head within a limestone house and kicking food into its mouth with its feet'. It is attached to the substrate by a secretion from its antennae and is enclosed in a shell, developed from the cuticle, consisting of a number of plates. It feeds by circulating water through this and filtering out minute particles with the long, finely branched feet that now act as a filter-feeding mechanism. Goose barnacles are attached by stalks, and are so named because in medieval times it was believed that geese hatched from the egg-shaped shells. This confusion also gave rise to the common name of the barnacle goose! Barnacles have the strange habit of accumulating heavy metals, particularly zinc. Studies in the River Thames in the UK show that up to 15 percent of the dry weight of barnacles may be zinc. Since such high concentrations are easy to measure, barnacles are very useful for environmental monitoring.

Malacostracans

The largest group of Crustacea is the Malacostraca. It contains almost three quarters of all known crustaceans and many of the most interesting, popular and colourful of the marine hobbyist's invertebrates. It also includes many groups that are not kept in the aquarium, but which are important for other reasons. The isopods are usually flattened and include the familiar terrestrial woodlice, as well as many marine worms, which are usually bottom dwelling and rather dull in colour for camouflage purposes. The amphipods are laterally compressed and curved, with no carapace. The male is often larger than the female and rides on her back before mating. This group includes the sandhoppers that are found almost anywhere in the world on beaches when the tide is out. The tropical mantis shrimps (*Odontodactylus* sp.) have front legs adapted for seizing prey, similar to the terrestrial praying mantises; they lie in wait in front of their burrows for unsuspecting prey – usually fish – before striking. Another important group includes the shrimplike crustaceans of the open sea known as krill, which form the food of the great whales, seals, birds and squid in the southern oceans.

Decapods

The largest and most familiar crustaceans in the Malacostraca – the crabs, lobsters, crayfish, shrimps and prawns – are all in the Decapoda – literally 'ten feet'. They have five pairs of leglike appendages on the thorax and several rows of gills at the base of the legs, covered by the carapace. Most species are easy to

A typical decapod crustacean

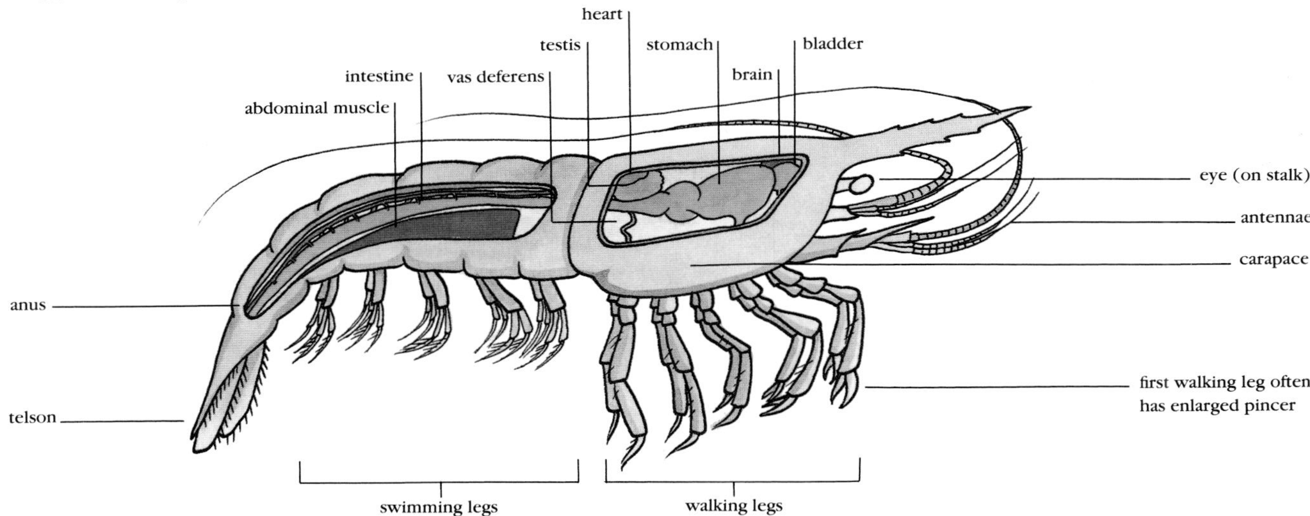

maintain in a domestic aquarium, where they tolerate less than perfect water conditions and accept almost anything remotely edible. They are a particularly interesting group of invertebrates as many are very active. Furthermore, they often display commensal behaviour, which literally means 'sharing food at the same table'. In the crustacean world, it means that they live in close association with other animals for mutual benefit. For example, shrimps and crabs, such as *Neopetrolisthes ohshimai* (see page 332) and *Periclimenes brevicarpalis* (see pages 338-9), are often found in the tentacles of sea anemones, between the spines of sea urchins or within the shells of molluscs. They benefit by 'stealing' scraps of their neighbour's food but many also help in keeping the neighbour and the surroundings clean. The Boxing Crab, *Lybia tessellata*, goes one step further and holds anemones in its claws for defence.

Shrimps and prawns

The shrimps and prawns are often laterally compressed, usually with light external skeletons, and include swimming and bottom-dwelling animals. By flexing the abdomen they can move fast enough to escape danger. People often think that shrimps and prawns are different species, but the names have no scientific meaning, although larger species are often called prawns. Some 350 species of this group are used by man for food. They also include the cleaner shrimps, some of which make good aquarium species, such as *Lysmata amboinensis*. Their characteristic coloration may help their 'clients' to locate them. Many other shrimps are suitable for the aquarium.

Lobsters and crabs

The lobsters and crabs are all bottom-dwelling walking animals. They move on only eight legs, the front pair being modified as huge claws. These are used for seizing and shredding prey, for protecting themselves and to proclaim their territories, as in fiddler crabs.

Above: *The Cleaner Shrimp* (Lysmata aboinensis) *makes a colourful and useful addition to the reef aquarium.*

The spiny lobsters, such as *Panulirus versicolor* (see page 335), have rather less well-developed but spiny claws. Spiny lobsters often migrate in enormous numbers. Observations have shown, for example, that *Panulirus argus* in the Caribbean may travel as much as 50km (31 miles) in the autumn, covering a distance of 15km (9 miles) each day. Up to 100,000 animals make the journey travelling in groups, one behind the other, and keeping together by touching and perhaps by using the row of spots clearly visible on the abdomen of the animal in front.

Lobsters with heavy claws are extremely long-lived and some may survive 100 years. They live in holes

Below: Panulirus versicolor, *the Purple Spiny Lobster, is a nocturnal feeder, rarely observed during daylight hours.*

on rocky bottoms and are mainly scavengers, but will eat live food. Some have an unpleasant tendency to cannibalize their weaker relatives. The larger lobsters have asymmetrical claws; a large one with rounded teeth that is used for crushing, and a smaller one with sharper teeth used for seizing and tearing their prey. The edible parts of the lobster are the well-developed muscles, particularly the ones in the abdomen that are used for swimming. Lobsters are most active at night and their eyes are comparatively poorly developed. Instead, they have sensory bristles all over the body and legs; some of these are sensitive to touch and others are sensitive to chemicals.

Hermit and porcelain crabs

The hermit crabs, porcelain crabs and squat lobsters are all intermediate in shape between lobsters and true crabs and are scavengers. Squat lobsters have large symmetrical abdomens usually flexed below their bodies rather like crabs, and porcelain crabs, such as *Neopetrolisthes ohshimai*, look very like their crab relatives. Hermit crabs, such as *Dardanus megistos* and *Pagurus prideauxi* (see pages 331 and 333), live in empty mollusc shells in order to protect their soft abdomens. They carefully choose a shell of exactly the right size, and change the shell as they grow. They usually choose right-handed shells, although sometimes they will use the rare left-handed shells. The shell is gripped by their specially adapted legs and its opening blocked by one or more claws.

'True' crabs

The 'true' crabs are usually carnivorous walkers on the seabed, although in some species the limbs are adapted for swimming. They have a very reduced abdomen, held permanently flexed below the front segments, which are fused. The carapace is large for the animal's size and extended at the sides. Crabs often have long eyestalks and can move sideways. All these adaptations make the crab a very efficient mover. They are found at all levels, from the deep ocean trenches – where a blind crab preys on the strange animals recently discovered 2.5km (1.6 miles) below sea level around hot vents – to the intertidal zone, beaches and even far inland on large islands. Crabs have a rapid escape reaction and can burrow backwards into mud or sand. Several species of crab, such as *Calappa flammea* (see page 330), cover their carapaces with living organisms, such as algae, sponges and other encrusting animals to provide camouflage or even a source of food.

Above: *The tiny Porcelain Crab* (Neopetrolisthes ohshimai) *lives among anemones' tentacles for protection. It has a complicated filter-feeding apparatus at the front of its head.*

Reproduction

Most crustaceans have separate sexes, although some are hermaphrodites. Terrestrial crabs and hermit crabs return to the sea to breed; their mating is usually seasonal, sometimes involving an elaborate courtship ritual. Many crabs mate while the female is still soft from moulting, the fertilized eggs being retained by the female until they hatch, either in a brood pouch or attached to the appendages. The eggs usually hatch into free-swimming larvae that metamorphose through various stages into the adult form. Several stages of larvae look very different from the adult; in fact, one stage – the zoea – looks so different that early naturalists classified it as a completely different animal!

Phylum MOLLUSCA

The Mollusca is one of the largest phyla in the animal kingdom, with more than 100,000 species. This group has long been important to man, both as a source of food and for its beautiful shells, used for a variety of decorative purposes. Molluscs are found in almost every habitat, and about half are marine. From the aquarist's point of view, many of the most attractive and interesting invertebrates are found within this group. All require good water conditions and, although some should be left strictly to experienced hobbyists, many species are well within the scope of the novice.

Structure

The body of a mollusc consists of a head (although this has been virtually lost in the bivalve group), a muscular foot and a 'visceral mass', which contains the digestive and other organs. The foot is used for gliding over the sea bottom, over rocks or vegetation. In some sea slugs, lobes of the foot are developed for swimming and in a great many species it is used for burrowing. Marine molluscs have gills, which in several groups – particularly the bivalves – are adapted for feeding. Many molluscs have a 'radula', a kind of tongue covered in hundreds of teeth, used for rasping at food. This is made of chitin and is secreted continuously, old rows of teeth at the front dropping off as they become worn.

The name Mollusca means soft-bodied but, like crustaceans, most molluscs (but not squids or octopods) have an external skeleton to protect and support the body. This is the shell, which is made of a material called conchiolin impregnated with calcium carbonate. Shells come in a wide variety of colours, patterns, shapes and textures that usually reflect the lifestyle of the animal. They may have regular lines or marks indicating interruptions of growth, which can occur in cold weather. Thus, some species can be aged in much the same way that trees can be aged from their growth rings. The inner layer of shell is often made of tiny blocks of crystalline calcium carbonate and is called nacre or, when the layer is thick, mother-of-pearl. A few species, such as the chambered nautilus and the pearl oysters, consist almost entirely of nacre. Some molluscs have very reduced shells, often internal, or have lost them altogether.

Shells have a variety of functions in addition to acting as a skeleton. Some species, such as the abalones and limpets, have shells that can be clamped tightly to windswept rocks to avoid dessication when the tide is out, or to avoid being removed by predators. Others have streamlined shells for burrowing. The razor shells are a good example; when alarmed, these can plunge into the sand by as much as 1m (39in). Perhaps the strangest shells of all are the carrier shells, *Xenophora*. Not content with the natural form of their own shells, they attach stones, bits of coral and other empty shells to the surface, perhaps to camouflage it.

All molluscs have a mantle – a fold of skin enclosing the gills, anus and various other glands and organs. Sometimes it is brightly coloured, perhaps as a warning; at other times it may be coloured to provide a camouflage. The mantle of a cowrie is extended back over the shell when the animal is active and its mottled colour provides good camouflage; it also means that the shell remains shiny and lustrous, unlike many other species whose shells become worn and covered with encrustations over time.

The mantle also secretes the shell and forms what is probably the most famous product of the mollusc – the pearl. Pearls are formed naturally when layers of mother-of-pearl are laid down around particles of grit lodged in the mantle cavity. Some molluscs can be persuaded to form 'cultured' pearls by inserting a tiny hard object, such as a minute piece of shell, into the animal. Commercial pearls come mainly from the pearl oysters, but many people are surprised to discover that other molluscs can form them. The queen conch can produce a delicate pink pearl, although this is

Below: *The Sea Hare* (Aplysia *sp.), a large Opisthobranch, releases a purplish poisonous dye from a gland in its mantle when it is attacked.*

not very valuable, and the largest pearl in the world – the pearl of Allah – came from a giant clam and weighs 6.4kg (14lb). The mantle may also secrete poisons for defence, in the form of acids, as in some cowries, or inks as in some sea slugs and the cephalopods.

A predatory univalve

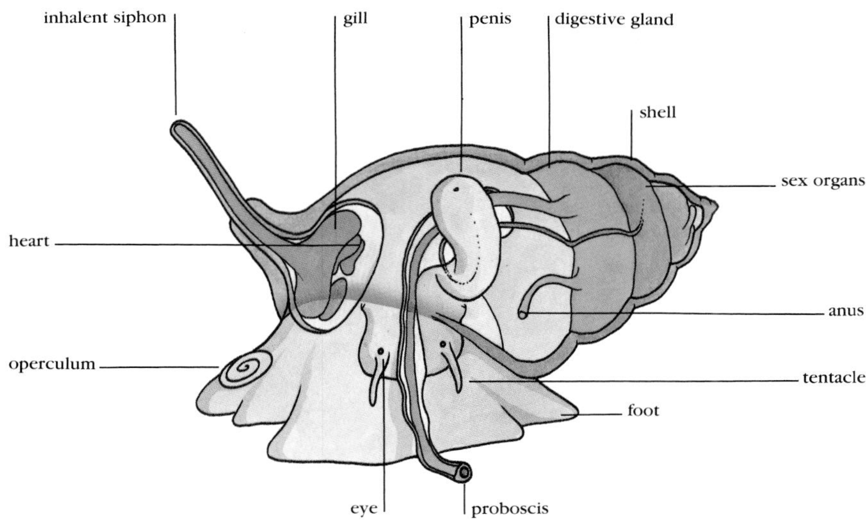

Reproduction

Marine molluscs either have separate sexes or are hermaphrodites. Apart from the cephalopods and a few other species, such as the Caribbean Queen Conch, which copulate, most shed their eggs and sperm into the sea at the same time and fertilization takes place in the water. In some cases, the eggs are laid on the bottom or on vegetation in clutches surrounded by a jellylike material. This can be spectacularly colourful, as in some sea slugs. As in many other marine invertebrate larvae, planktonic larvae called veligers develop and float in the ocean currents, often over huge distances. Oysters are known to have been dispersed in this way over 1300km (780 miles). Some species, such as the giant clams, have shorter planktonic lives and their ranges are therefore smaller. A few species have no planktonic stage and produce young that look identical to their parents; these species may have very narrow distributions.

Below: *The spotted shell of the Tiger Cowrie (seen here with egg capsules) is kept lustrous by the mantle, which expands when the cowrie is active.*

Classification

Molluscs are an extremely varied group, ranging from small parasitic clams that burrow into the arms of starfishes, to the giant squid that roam the deep waters of the oceans. Of the various groups of mollusc, the three largest are of interest to the aquarist.

Gastropods

The largest group, with 60,000-75,000 species, is the Gastropoda, or univalves. It includes the terrestrial slugs and snails, as well as vast numbers of marine and freshwater species. Gastropods have single shells, often strongly coiled, which usually open on the right-hand side. In species where the adults appear to have differently shaped shells, the juveniles practically always have coiled shells. The shape of the cowrie, for example, is obtained by the final large whorl of the shell enclosing the earlier smaller parts of the spiral within it, as can be clearly seen if an old shell is cut open. Some species have an operculum that operates as a trapdoor to close the shell. This is usually made of a horny material, but in some molluscs it is calcareous. The beautiful green operculum of the turban shell is used in jewellery and is known as a cat's eye.

Marine gastropods include herbivores, detritus feeders, carnivores and a few ciliary feeders, in which the radula is reduced or absent. The radula is usually closely adapted to the food that a species eats. The simplest gastropods are the limpets and abalones, both herbivores that use their hard radulas to rasp at seaweeds on rocks. Other herbivores are the cowries, spider shells and conchs. The Caribbean Queen Conch lives in sea-grass beds and propels itself over the bed using a modified operculum, resembling an outsize fingernail, that it jams into the sand, while the muscular foot heaves the animal forward.

Carnivorous gastropods have fewer, larger, more pointed teeth on a narrower radula than herbivores, and a proboscis that carries the mouth and radula. Whelks feed on dead organic matter, but will also prise open live bivalves by wedging the valves open with the edge of their shells to obtain the flesh inside. Dog whelks bore holes through the shells of other molluscs and barnacles using special teeth and then suck the tissues out. Cone shells have a long proboscis and harpoonlike teeth on the radula. They impale their prey, which includes small fishes, worms and other molluscs, on the radula, paralyze them with a nerve poison and swallow them whole. The poison can be fatal to man.

Many marine gastropods are burrowers and have siphons or tubes that extend from the mantle and sometimes the shell. These act as snorkels, enabling the animal to continue to draw a water current containing oxygen and food into their bodies. The siphons are also used to detect prey from a distance. Many marine gastropods have tentacles on the head, with eyes at the base.

Opisthobranchs are one group of gastropods of particular interest to the aquarist. They include the bubble snails, which have a very thin, almost translucent shell; the sea hares with a very reduced shell; and the sea slugs, with no shell at all, which can be considered the marine equivalents of land slugs.

Above: *The bright colours of sea slugs, such as this* Nembrotha *sp., are used to camouflage them among corals, or to warn predators that they are poisonous.*

Some opisthobranchs creep slowly along the sea bottom or over seaweed and corals, but many are agile and beautiful swimmers, such as the Spanish Dancer (see page 347), which swims in the surface of the oceans. The opisthobranchs are all hermaphrodites.

Sea hares (see page 346), with their prominent tentacles, are among the largest opisthobranchs and have internal gills and a simple internal shell plate.

Below: *A pair of colourful* Chromodoris lubocki *are responsible for laying a string of eggs, a fairly common occurrence in the marine aquarium.*

Sea slugs are often flamboyantly coloured, either as a warning if they are poisonous, or to camouflage them on the corals and seaweeds on which many species are found. The gills are often in the form of feathery plumes on their backs, and give rise to their other name – nudibranchs, or naked gills. The dorid group of nudibranchs, such as *Chromodoris* (see page 346), have gills in a small cluster at the rear, while the gills of the aeolid group are irregularly placed along the back. Aeolids can withdraw their gills into the body for defensive purposes, while those of dorids are permanently exposed. To counter this weakness, many of the dorids, which feed on anemones and stinging hydroids, 'pirate' the stinging cells (nematocysts) of their cnidarian food and re-use them in their gill tufts as protection against predators. Nudibranchs with smooth or warty backs have no visible gill mechanism and, in some cases, respiration may take place directly through the skin. Although these species tend to be less attractive than many of the dorids, they often prove hardier than the latter and more adaptable to aquarium life.

A bivalve

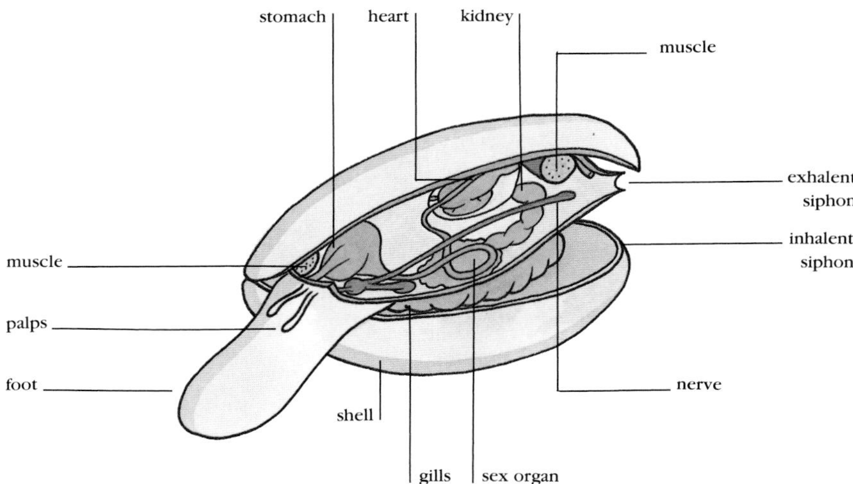

Many also have fleshy extensions of the digestive system on their backs.

A few sea slugs are herbivores, but many are 'grazing carnivores', which may seem a contradiction in terms until one realizes that they graze on sedentary animals such as corals, sponges and other invertebrates. Many have distinct dietary preferences and regularly occur in association with certain species. For example, *Chromodoris quadricolor* is found with the sponge *Latrunculia*. Unless the exact food preference is known, keeping these species in an aquarium is very difficult. As a general rule, it is a good idea to house all sea slugs in a well-stocked 'living reef' aquarium in the hope that they will find a suitable food source. Unfortunately, although sea slugs tend to be very attractive, they cannot, with a few exceptions, be recommended to beginners.

Bivalves

The bivalves are the second largest group of molluscs after the gastropods, with 15,000-20,000 species. They include many commercially important species, such as mussels, clams, oysters, scallops and cockles. Their shells, or valves, are in two, usually symmetrical, hinged parts, held together tightly by a pair of powerful muscles. As in the gastropods, bivalve shells can be very variable in shape, colour and texture, the largest being those of the giant clams (see page 343). In bivalves, the head has been lost and there is a pair of large gills, generally used for feeding as well as respiration. These are shaped like leaves or curtains and are covered with cilia that beat continuously to draw in a current. Plankton is trapped by mucus on the gills and carried by the cilia to the mouth. Many bivalves require a high concentration of organic matter in the water and tend to be found in coastal areas. Few can survive long out of water; intertidal species, such as mussels must close their shells tightly at low tide to retain water.

Most bivalves live a sedentary life on or in the seabed. Some, such as mussels and some of the oysters are attached to rocks and other hard substrates by strong elastic fibres, known as byssus threads. Bivalves feed on filtered phytoplankton or take in detritus with siphons that reach to the surface in burrowing species. Burrowers have a large flattened foot that digs through the sand or mud by a combination of muscle action and blood pressure.

Some bivalves are surprisingly mobile, particularly the cockles, which are capable of leaping, and the scallops, such as the Flame Scallop (see page 342), which swim by opening and closing their shells and expelling water from the mantle cavity so forcefully that they move under a form of jet propulsion. They have a row of tiny eyes around the mantle edge to detect danger and can therefore make a rapid escape from a predator. The boring molluscs, like the boring sponges, are aptly named for their lifestyle; as soon as the larvae settle, they start excavating into rock or coral, either by using their shell valves, which often have serrated edges, or drills, or by secreting an acid. The shipworms have long cylindrical bodies and bore into timber, using the excavated sawdust as food.

Below: *The giant clams (this is* Tridacna gigas*) are the largest bivalves.*

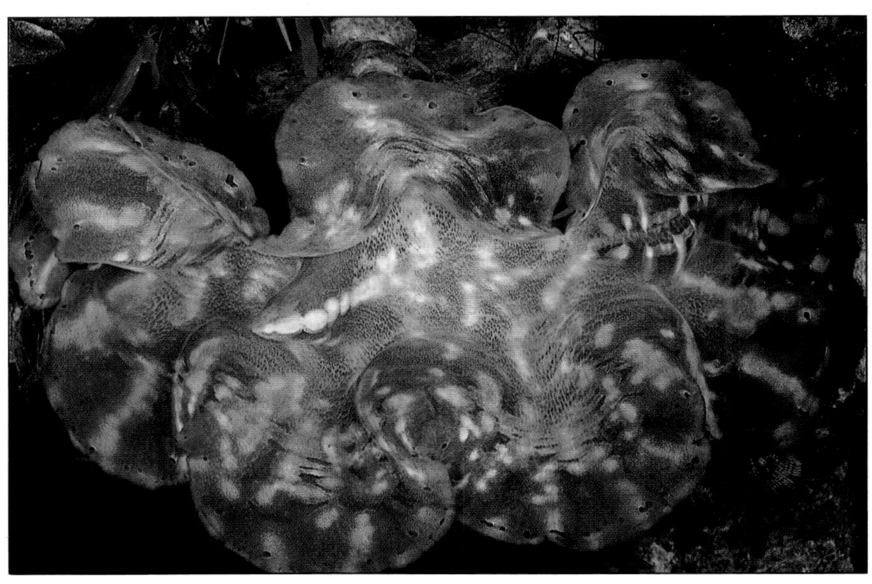

Cephalopods

With 650 species, the Cephalopoda is the third largest group, and includes squid, cuttlefish and octopi. They are the most highly developed molluscs and include some of the most intelligent and fascinating, if also rapacious, invertebrates in the world. The majority are quite large, and many species are totally unsuited to the home aquarium. These include the famous giant squid, which reaches a length of 20m (66ft)! Furthermore, comparatively few species are regularly available.

The shell is very reduced or even absent, and a complete shell is found only in the chambered nautilus. However, unlike gastropods, the nautilus only lives in part of its shell, the rest being divided into chambers which are filled with gas and used as a buoyancy organ. Cuttlefish and squid are unusual molluscs in having an internal shell. The flattened cuttlefish 'bone', often found on the beach, is comparatively soft; the squid 'pen' is very thin and reduced.

The mouth of a cephalopod is surrounded by tentacles, derived from the foot found in other molluscs. Octopi have eight tentacles, squid and cuttlefish have ten, and the chambered nautilus has 38. The tentacles have well-developed senses of touch and taste: those of the octopus (see pages 344-345) are extremely sensitive and can discriminate texture and pattern. All cephalopods are active predators on fish and crustaceans and use their tentacles to locate and capture prey. The mouth has a strong beak for tearing pieces from the prey, which is then pushed into the mouth by the radula. Their voracious appetites are an important consideration when you come to choose suitable tankmates. They are safe with most sessile (non-moving) invertebrates, but will catch and kill any moving animal available. They put a heavy demand on filtration systems, producing a lot of waste products and, at the same time, demanding ideal water conditions. Despite this, they are justifiably popular and can become quite tame.

A cuttlefish

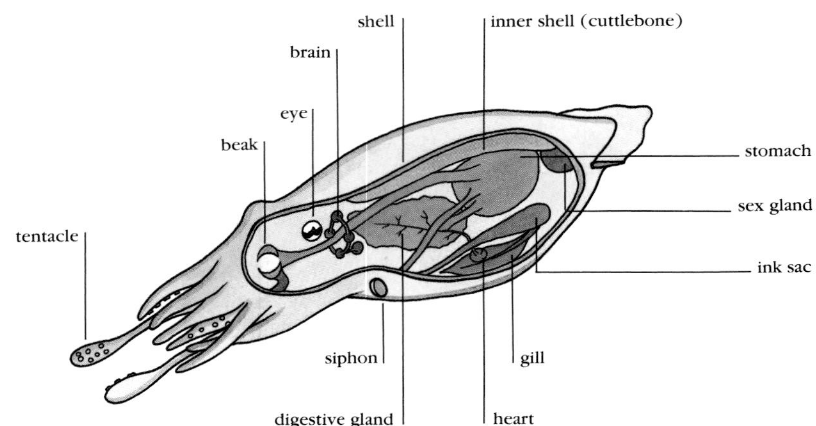

Unlike most molluscs, cephalopods are able to move very rapidly (they travel backwards, trailing their tentacles). The octopus usually crawls using the suckers on its arms, but it is capable of swimming. In the squid and cuttlefish, the mantle cavity has become a pump that squirts water through a funnel in a form of jet propulsion. The torpedo-shaped squid move around in shoals and reach the greatest swimming speeds of any marine invertebrates. There are even flying squid that can shoot out of the water and glide for some distance, sometimes travelling through the air at 25.5kph (16mph).

The cephalopods have well-developed eyes and the largest brains of all invertebrates. They are responsive to external stimuli – made possible by their giant nerve fibres, similar to those found in some worms – and can respond extremely rapidly to events signalling danger. Octopi even have a memory and can be trained. Many cephalopods are capable of rapid colour change and use this for camouflage, defence and copulation. Pigment cells, called chromatophores, in the skin expand or contract rapidly, sometimes producing stripes and patterns. By contracting completely they can make the squid almost invisible.

All cephalopods, except nautilus, have an ink sac containing the dark brown ink known as sepia. The cephalopod discharges the sac to produce a 'smoke screen' of ink that hangs like a cloud in the water, fooling the predator while the cephalopod escapes. However smoke screens are of little help to the squid, which form the main food of sperm whales; it has been estimated that the whales consume over 100 million tonnes in a year.

Reproduction

Unlike many other molluscs, cephalopods have separate sexes. Octopi go through an elaborate courtship ritual in which the male changes colour and arouses the female by stroking her. Then he transfers a sperm 'packet' on the tip of one of his arms into her mantle cavity, where it fertilizes the eggs. The eggs, as in other cephalopods, are large and yolky and are usually laid in the shelter of a crevice or shell. They are guarded by the female until they hatch as miniature versions of their parents. In some species, the female does not feed during this period of guardianship and dies after the eggs have been hatched. Squid generally lay their eggs in sticky clusters on rocks in open water. Cuttlefish eggs resemble bunches of grapes and may be washed up on the shore after a gale.

Phylum ECHINODERMATA

This group of entirely marine animals consists of about 6000 species and includes many that are of great interest to hobbyists, such as starfishes, sea urchins, sea lilies, feather stars and sea cucumbers, all of which show a huge variation in structure. However, they share certain constant features. One of the most striking common characteristics is the five-rayed radial symmetry, shown most clearly in the starfish. Like the lower invertebrates, they lack a distinct head, brain and complex sense organs. The nervous system consists mainly of nerve cords along the arms and simple receptor cells over the animal's surface, which respond to touch and chemicals in solution. However, many other aspects of their structure indicate that they are highly evolved invertebrates.

Structure

The skeleton is internal and consists of calcareous ossicles, or plates, that usually bear spines and ridges, from which the name Echinodermata – meaning spiny skinned – is derived. The skeleton is perforated by numerous tiny spaces, which makes it very light while remaining strong.

Echinoderms are also unique in possessing a water vascular system. This consists of five radiating canals containing sea water that connect by side branches to many hundreds of pairs of tube feet. Each tube foot, which in many species has a sucker at the end, can be moved by means of valves and muscles. There is a bladderlike reservoir at the base of the tube foot and when this contracts, water is forced into the foot and it extends. The tube feet are used in locomotion, respiration, feeding and sensory perception. On its own, a tube foot is a very weak structure, but by working with its neighbours in relays, sufficient pressure can be exerted to enable starfishes to pull apart the two shells of a mussel or cockle.

Starfish and sea urchins have extraordinary tiny protuberances over the body that look like minute tongs or forceps. These were once thought to be parasites on the animals, but are now known to be part of the body and are called pedicellariae. They may be on stalks or attached directly to the skeleton. They have two or more pincers, and their detailed structure is very variable. Their main function seems to be to remove sand and debris from the surface of the animal, but in some species they are used for defence, and may be capable of injecting poison.

Above: Pentagonaster duebeni, *the Biscuit Starfish, detects food by smell and can move towards it at a surprisingly fast pace.*

Behaviour

The echinoderms are mainly bottom-living marine animals. Some, such as starfishes, which feed on molluscs, are active predators. Others are filter-feeders, comparable with featherduster worms, that trap small particles of food on feathery appendages.

A starfish

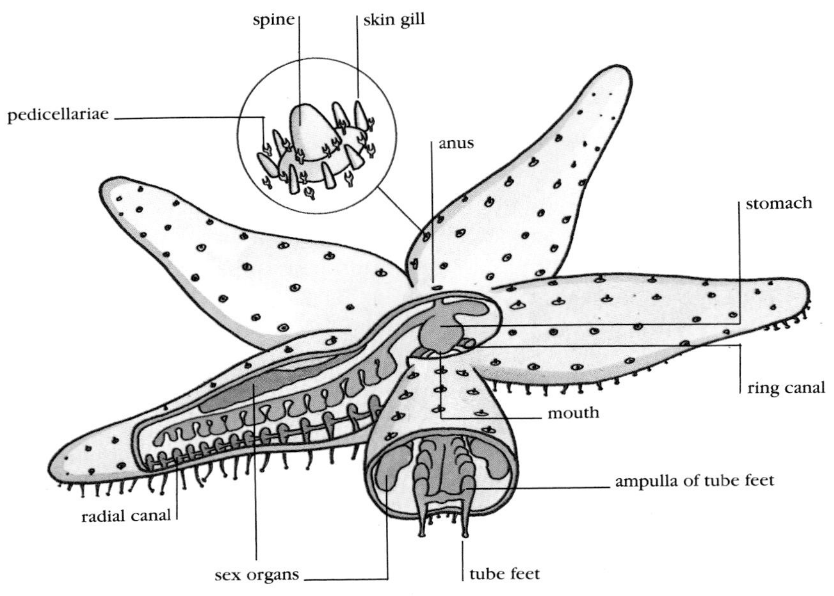

Others survive by sifting through the accumulated detritus on the seabed. A number of species are diurnal (active during the day), but many more confine their activities to the hours of darkness, when their, soft, unprotected bodies are less at risk from predators.

The very bright colouring of the tropical species, and the easy maintenance and often cosmopolitan diet of echinoderms, justifies their popularity among invertebrate keepers. Given good water conditions and a suitable diet, many species can be expected to live in the aquarium for several years. Like many invertebrates, echinoderms often live in close association with other animals. Small starfishes, shrimps and gobies live a well-camouflaged existence among the arms of crinoids, for example, or even inside the bodies of sea cucumbers, other starfishes and sea urchins, emerging only to feed. They are infrequent but welcome bonuses to the aquarium.

Echinoderms reproduce by shedding their eggs and sperm into the sea, where fertilization takes place. Surprisingly enough, the larvae are bilaterally, rather than radially, symmetrical and swim by means of ciliated bands on the body surface. They float in the currents before settling and metamorphosing into an adult.

Feather stars and sea lilies

The free-living feather stars that inhabit shallow seas are most abundant in the tropics. Both they and the stalked sea lilies of deeper waters are in the group known as crinoids. They are the most primitive echinoderms and their history is well documented from the large numbers of fossils, dating back about 500 million years, when crinoids were among the commonest animals in warm shallow seas. Thick beds of limestone in Derbyshire in the UK owe their existence to the accumulation of stalk segments from the ancestors of crinoid species found today. Only the few rare sea lilies now retain this stalk as adults, but the larvae of all crinoids are initially anchored to the substrate by a small stem before they break free and drift onto the reefs.

Crinoid arms are usually forked and branched and their tube feet lack suckers. The tube feet lie in a double row along the upper side of each arm and are used for respiration and feeding, small particles of matter sticking to the mucus on the feet. The sea lilies are fixed to the bottom and look rather like palm trees with upturned fronds. They feed on fine particles sieved from the water.

Feather stars, such as the Red Crinoid *Himerometra robustipinna*, have a central disc, or cup, from the underside of which grow the short, spiky 'cirri', or hooked appendages, that they use to grip rocks and corals. They can walk rather clumsily on their cirri or swim in a rather spectacular fashion, each arm beating up and down independently with undulations. The cup extends upwards and outwards into five arms that are usually repeatedly branched. These are edged with small extensions called pinnules, and the end result is an animal that looks not unlike a feathery shuttlecock. Their arms have a great degree of vertical flexibility but very little lateral movement, which makes them very brittle.

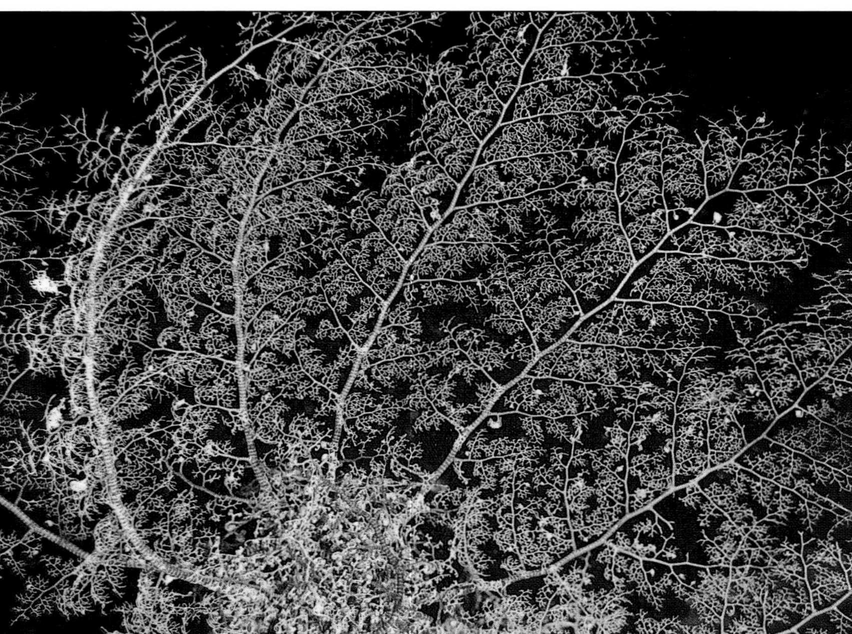

Above: *The delicate tracery of the arms of the basket stars is well illustrated in this Red Sea species. At rest, the arms are curled into a tight ball.*

Brittle stars and basket stars

Brittle stars, such as *Ophiomastix venosa* and basket stars, such as *Astrophyton muricatum* (see page 350), are in the group known as ophiuroids. Like the feather stars, these have a central disc and their tube feet lack suckers and are used for respiration and feeding only. The skeleton is made up of many ossicles, which fit tightly together. In brittle stars, the disc is flat and the long, thin and very mobile arms are clearly set off from it, unlike those of the starfish. In most brittle stars the arms are smooth, but a number of commonly imported species have short spiky extensions along the arms that may offer some protection from predators. The arms are capable of lateral movements and limited vertical movements, but cannot be coiled around objects. Brittle stars can move remarkably quickly, the arms propelling the animal with snakelike movements.

They feed either by collecting tiny edible particles on their arms as they wave them about, or by tearing off pieces of seaweed or dead fish. In the sea, they often live in huge beds and can form a seething carpet

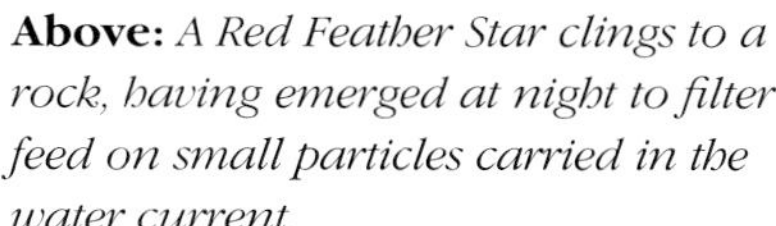

Above: *A Red Feather Star clings to a rock, having emerged at night to filter feed on small particles carried in the water current.*

Above: *Although the similarities are not obvious, the Long-spined Sea Urchin* (Diadema antillarum) *is a close relation of the starfishes.*

up to five animals deep. Like feather stars, brittle stars are very fragile, as the name implies, but they are able to regenerate lost arms very rapidly.

In basket stars, the five arms are divided and subdivided to form a greatly branched 'net' and they can be coiled around objects. During the day, they rest on sea fans or rock pinnacles, looking like loose balls of string, but at night, they spread their arms to produce a roughly circular trap, or 'basket', to catch whatever small food items the water currents bring their way.

Starfishes

The starfishes are the most familiar echinoderms and many are brightly coloured. They usually have five or more well-developed, stout arms radiating from the centre of the body. Like brittle and basket stars, these can regenerate relatively easily if damaged. The tube feet are on the underside of the arms and the mouth is in the centre of the underside. Many starfishes feed by everting the stomach through the mouth, encircling and digesting large food items, then retracting the stomach and moving on.

Although not as fast as brittle stars, they can detect food by smell, and crawl towards it at a surprisingly fast rate. Some feed on minute particles but most prey on live animals, forcing open shellfishes or chewing sponges. They can be serious pests of commercial oyster and mussel beds and the infamous Crown-of-thorns Starfish, *Acanthaster planci*, (see also page 58) can wreak havoc on a coral reef if large numbers congregate to feed on the coral polyps.

A sea urchin

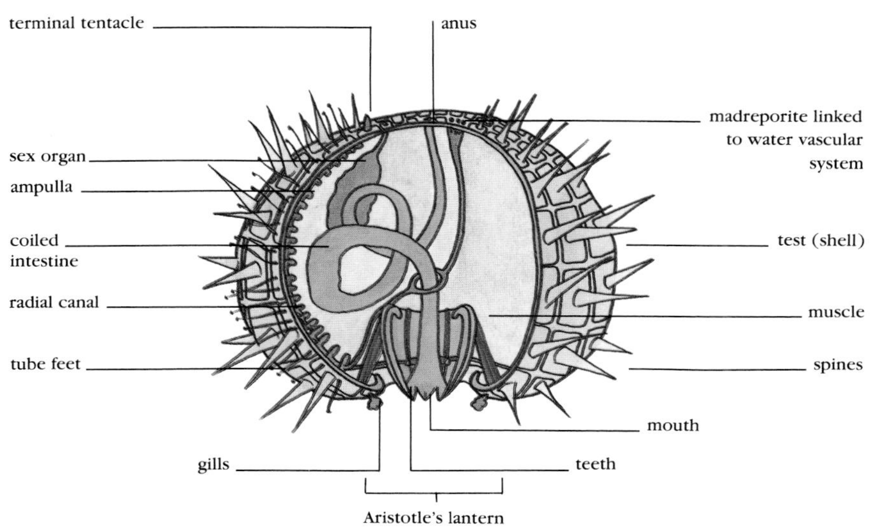

Sea urchins

The sea urchins and sand dollars in the group known as echinoids have globular or flat bodies with an internal shell, or 'test', of closely fitting plates. At first sight, they appear to bear little relation to the starfishes, but there are clear similarities. They can be thought of as starfish with their arms bent over their backs and their skeletal plates fused together. The tube feet vary in shape and function, and may be used for movement or creating currents in tunnels. Some urchins burrow in sand and mud, keeping a vertical shaft open to supply water for respiration. Others burrow into rock using the spines attached to the test to dig with. The shape of the spines is adapted to the species habitat; urchins that live on surf-beaten shores have short, stout spines, whereas those from calmer waters, such as *Diadema savignyi*, have longer spines. In addition to providing protection from predators, the spines may be used with the tube feet for climbing rocks.

Many urchins have a unique organ known as Aristotle's lantern, named after its discoverer. This consists of five hard calcareous teeth, suspended from a complex chewing apparatus, and ringing the mouth on the underside of the body. The teeth are used to scrape algal material from rocky surfaces. Sand dollars and heart urchins have no lantern. They burrow in the sand, collecting particles of detritus on their modified spines and tube feet.

Sea cucumbers

The sea cucumbers, or holothurians, are elongated, sausage-shaped echinoderms. The tube feet around the mouth have become sticky tentacles, which vary slightly from one species to another according to the size of the detritus particles on which they feed. Some sea cucumbers sweep the surface of the sand or mud with the tentacles, but others rely on water currents to bring food to them. Other tube feet over the body are used for locomotion. The skeleton is reduced to small crystals embedded in the skin and these produce a rough leathery feel.

When attacked, and possibly as a result of chemical changes in the habitat, sea cucumbers can discharge the stomach and its contents through the anus to help them escape. In the wild, the stomach and intestine are regenerated quickly, but avoid very deflated specimens when buying stock. An alternative defence adopted by the sea cucumber is to squirt out sticky threads. Amazingly enough, sea cucumbers are a gastronomic delicacy in the Far East, where they are known as *trepang*, or *bêche-de-mer*, the latter name coming from the Portuguese *'bicho-do-mar'* or 'worm-of-the-sea'.

A sea cucumber

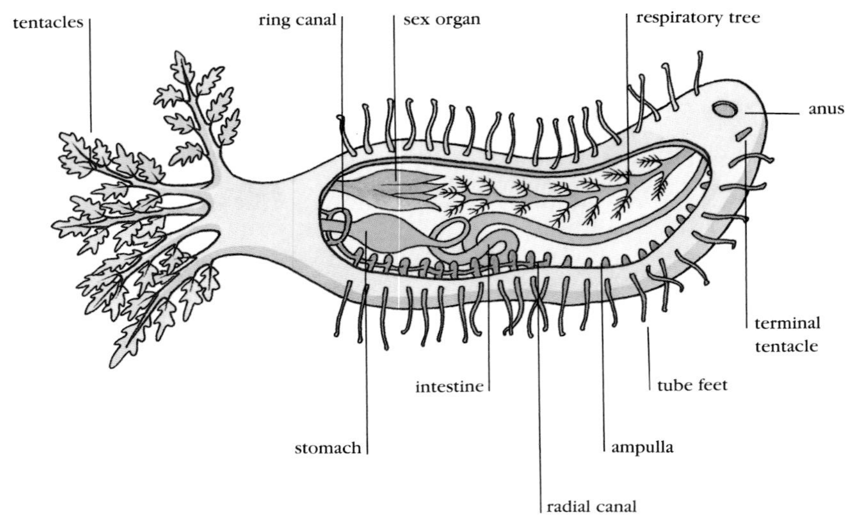

Right: Pseudocolochirus *sp. This vividly coloured sea cucumber is much in demand with marine aquarists, despite its invariably high price.*

Phylum CHORDATA

The majority of – and the most familiar – chordates are the vertebrates, or animals with backbones. However, there are some species within this phylum that represent the link between the vertebrates and the invertebrates and these are often known as the protochordates. They lack a true backbone, but have a stiff rod, or notochord, in their bodies in at least one stage in their life cycle, and a single hollow dorsal nerve cord. The sea squirts, or ascidians, are the only protochordates of interest to the hobbyist and even these usually arrive in the aquarium by accident.

There are over 1,000 species of sea squirts, many of which live on reefs. Some are solitary, and large individuals may be up to 50cm (20in) high. Others are colonial and form mats composed of many small individuals. They have a stiff, jellylike or leathery bag-shaped body called a tunic, with large inlet and outlet siphons, although colonial forms have a single communal outlet. Water is drawn in and passes through a strainer, where small particles of food are filtered out before the water is discharged. Their common name comes from their habit of squirting water if they are squeezed.

Sea squirt larvae are like tiny tadpoles and show the typical chordate characteristics. They have a notochord, sense organs and nervous system, all of which are lost when the larva settles and turns into the adult form. Salps are an interesting, free-swimming group of sea squirts that float in the open waters of the oceans. They are jellylike and reproduce by budding, the new individuals often remaining attached to the old ones, thus forming long strings. Many sea squirts are very colourful, such as *Distomus* spp., but they are inactive and have never become popular.

The other group of simple chordates contains less than 20 species. These have a notochord and are called lancelets, or amphioxus. They look like little transparent fish, and they burrow in coarse sand in shallow water, lying with their mouths exposed to sieve food from the water current. They sometimes aggregate in large numbers, and are fished and eaten in some parts of the world, particularly China.

A sea squirt

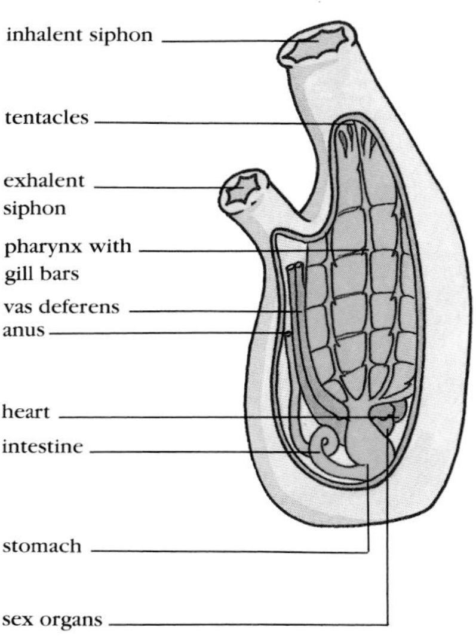

Below: *The inlet and outlet siphons of this small colony of sea squirts can be seen here. Note how some fuse together, while others remain as individuals.*

Collection and Conservation

In 1980, the International Union for the Conservation of Nature and Natural Resources published a seminal document on the relationship between just one species – humans – and all the others on this planet. It was written over several years, as a result of the slow appreciation of the increasing dominance of the one species over all the rest. This imbalance had to be redressed if possible or, to take the worst scenario, humankind had to be informed of the disastrous consequences if our current behaviour persisted. *The World Conservation Strategy* was not meant to be a document that advocated reversing time, eliminating sprawling cities and about half of the human population. Rather, it tried to establish the terms for as harmonious a balance as possible between dominant humans and the rest of the world's species, to the mutual benefit of both camps.

The document argued that the frequently misused and misunderstood concept 'conservation' simply means the management of human use of the world in such a way that it may yield the greatest sustainable benefit to the present generation and maintain this into future generations of both humans and other species (the majority). Humans are a part of the environment. It is not there for us. Therefore, we must live with it, not let it live and die for us, thereby effectively signing our own death warrants. (It is perhaps worth remembering here that a parasite can only be successful and survive if it does not kill its host.)

It may at first seem difficult to reconcile the keeping and selling of marine fishes and invertebrates with the conservation of the world's coral reefs for future generations, but these two aims are not mutually exclusive. It is possible for the marine conservationist and the aquarist to work hand in hand in examining different facets of conservation and collection. There can even be a two-way feedback in that the observations of one may be of benefit to the other. An observation of a detail of a fish's life by an aquarist may help the biologist understand one part of the jigsaw of reef life. Equally, the conservationist's or biologist's report that two particular species are, say, always found in close association at night can help the hobbyist improve the quality of life for the animals in his or her care.

The trade chains

In any type of retailing there must be cooperation at all levels of the chain, from before collecting on the coral reef to the final sale of a healthy fish to the hobbyist. There are, however, many limiting factors to consider, which start with the local fishermen and culminate in establishing concordance in all the worldwide trade chains.

There are two basic trade chains. Both start with the fisherman who collects the desired species. These are then sold on to a person variously described as a transporter, gatherer or middleman, who will visit a number of collectors and take the entire consignment to a holding facility. The holding facilities, which are often those of exporters, are usually close to international airports. Here, the fishes should be given time to recuperate from the stress of collection and transportation. Although the decision to provide a rest period for the fishes ought to be a deliberate one, it can also occur inadvertently while the exporter waits for enough consignments of the required species to build up to fulfil orders. The orders are then made up, the fishes packed appropriately, and flown out to a receiving wholesaler in Europe, America or Japan. A good wholesaler then quarantines the fishes and sells them on to a retailer, who sells directly to the public.

The other basic trade chain is one in which the retailers commission

Left: *The retail shop is the last link in a chain that starts with local fishermen, who collect the desired species and sell them to a transporter.*

or employ a consolidator. The consolidator is an agent who will work on behalf of several retail outlets to obtain the most competitive carriage rates from the airlines. This cuts out the need for the wholesaler so that the retail shop can offer the livestock for sale at a most competitive price. The disadvantage of the consolidator chain is that the range of species is generally more limited than that obtainable from wholesalers, and quarantine facilities have to be provided by the retailer.

As there are thousands of miles of collectable coral reefs, transport conditions and logistics are of fundamental importance. Coral fish are, by nature, delicate and do not respond well to poor treatment in catching, handling or transporting. The nature of transport from the point of collecting to the holding facility is a limiting factor in this stage of the chain. Most third world countries – where most fish are caught – do not have motorways or rail terminals near the coral reefs affording easy access to the holding facility. This may seem obvious, but it is a fact often overlooked by those examining the trade in corals and reef fishes. It has been calculated that over 99 percent of the world's coral reefs are logistically impossible, or at least financially unworthwhile, to collect from, as the transport overheads are so high.

Freight space, or more importantly the lack of it, will adversely affect the transport of coral reef fishes. As over 80 percent of the invertebrates and coral reef fishes sold in Europe originate in the Far East, space is at a premium. The 'mega-top' 747s that some airlines are using on a non-stop Far East or Europe service have a smaller volume of freight space available and, as the ageing fleet of 747 Jumbos is phased out, the situation may well get worse, the advantage of a non-stop flight being nullified by the smaller volume of freight capable of being transported. This man-made limitation could well be with us sooner than wished, and the law of supply and demand means that if goods cannot be shipped, and thus cannot reach the market in the volume demanded, there is no point in collecting them.

Twenty years ago, the holding facilities at many of the exporters were little more than concrete vats with primitive aeration systems (mostly, individual pumps with airstones to provide the oxygen and a weak water current). Biological filtration systems were unknown. Happily, this situation is now changing. There are several reasons for this. Firstly, the initial cost of the fish is higher; collectors are now encouraged to take more care in their collecting so that the fishes are in perfect condition. Secondly, some species of fish are less abundant, or live further from the collecting sites, than before. Thirdly, greater time is taken in obtaining and ensuring the fishes reach the exporter in good condition. More time is therefore expended by the collectors, who then demand a greater return from the exporter. The exporters' capital investment is therefore higher and if they do not take advantage of the latest technology to ensure the health of their stock they will lose more money than before.

Not all exporters in the Third World have become rich through their efforts. Many have to be helped financially to install sophisticated and beneficial holding systems. Often, this financial help comes from the importers in the northern hemisphere, who use the greater capital, to which they have more access, to provide better systems. The financial burden is spread, but

Below: *Large tanks, good filtration and effective monitoring are essential in a well-run holding station. Butterflyfish are sensitive and require extra care.*

Left: *Fish collectors carry a range of handnets and use each in the best way to herd a fish down to the main barrier net. They work quickly and carefully.*

the importers gain a benefit from the security of receiving high-quality, healthy fish. To this end, fish are now given temporary housing in all-glass aquariums, often individually, and provided with water-circulation plants with water being filtered through cartridge filters. There are also ultra-violet sterilizers and trickle filters, and ozone can be added via a protein skimmer, while a level of veterinary help is available if required.

Collecting methods

The three main methods of collecting fish are by net, trap or cyanide. Most fish are caught at depths of less than 10 metres by divers, using either a hooker pipe or a self-contained underwater breathing apparatus (SCUBA). A hooker is a low-pressure compressor at the surface in a boat or canoe moored above the diver. The airhose is fixed to the seabed and the divers take a lungful of air when necessary. The divers using the hooker system may work with ordinary goggles to aid their vision underwater. There are also those who use a full-face mask. In this case, the mask is filled with air from the hooker pipe which gives them a prolonged period of freedom. It is not uncommon for up to half a dozen divers to work off the same hooker pipe. Even when a face mask is used, the diver cannot go much deeper than the hooker hose can reach. SCUBA divers use a high-

Below: *A collector carefully disentangles a fish caught in the soft mesh of the barrier. This is done quickly and skilfully.*

pressure compressor to recharge their cylinders. This gives the divers greater freedom but is more expensive, both initially and in running costs.

On the seabed a fine-meshed nylon mono-filament net about 10 metres (33ft) long and 1 metre (40in) high is placed along a part of the sea floor. Weights keep the bottom of the net in place, while floats at the top keep it upright so that it resembles a curtain rising up from the bottom of the sea. The fish are chased into this barrier, become enmeshed, and are then carefully removed and placed in a 'goodie' bag. A variant of this technique is to bait the net with pieces of fish. The bait attracts some species, and others, discerning a feeding activity, come to investigate and are caught. The collectors then work along the net, picking out the fishes and putting them into the 'goodie' bag. The 'goodie' bag is usually of plastic about 60-75cm (24-30in) long and 45cm (18in) wide. The collected fish, of whatever species, are placed in the bag and the neck held closed by the diver. It is not normal for there to be interspecific aggression within the bag. The reason for this is unclear, but it may be that taking a fish away from its territory disorientates it and, having no familiar landmarks to defend, it just stays there with formerly antagonistic bedfellows.

Fish rarely try to bite their way out of the bag. Triggerfish will occasionally perforate the bag, but the holes are not big enough to allow the escape of the inmates and the triggerfish's dentition is not geared to producing anything more than nip-sized holes. What is interesting is that the surgeonfish do not seem to erect their caudal peduncle spines when they are in the 'goodie' bag. Netting bags are rarely used in the Philippines.

Drop nets are also used to collect fish. A drop net is a circular net with weights around the edge and a float at the centre. This is dropped over an area of reef and the fish chased into the raised central portion from which they are collected.

Fish traps vary in style in different parts of the world but, in essence, follow the same basic pattern. A trap is made of a net on a wooden frame measuring approximately one metre by two metres (40 × 80in). A cone, usually made of bamboo, leads into the net. Bait, of fish or meat, is fastened in the holding part of the net. Fish are attracted into the net by the bait and, once in, cannot get out. Quite why they cannot navigate out the way they came in is not understood, but there is deep fishy psychological reluctance to go downstream headfirst. It is possible that as water carrying the vital oxygen goes in through the mouth and out through the gill covers, facing the 'wrong way' may induce some feeling of breathlessness. However, whereas that logic seems to work for the common minnow trap, in which the netted neck is placed facing into the current and the fish enter by the knocked out punt, it does not seem to be valid for fish traps set around the coral reefs from Thailand to the Philippines. There appears to be no particular orientation. They are usually placed about 10-12 metres (approximately 30-40ft) down, well below low water mark and the surf zone (according to locality), on a

Below: *The final stage of transferring the catch of fish into a large plastic 'goodie' bag. Spare bags are tucked into the diver's waist belt.*

firm bottom and close to coral bosses. The position of the trap is rarely changed; it remains anchored to a rock or coral head. The trap is then visited once or twice a day and its contents collected.

Originally, these traps were used to catch food fish, but, of late, their efficacy in trapping aquarium fish in perfect condition has been realized. The bait and mesh size can be adjusted to obtain the desired species of the local fauna. All fishes caught at the deeper part of the diver's depth range, or in deep-set traps, are brought slowly to the surface to allow the fish time to adjust to pressure differences. Rapidly hauling a fish up from as little as 10m (33ft) can cause it damage and distress.

The techniques listed above have been used at an artisanal level for centuries, and the balance between the needs of the human population and the productivity of the accessible parts of the reef has been maintained. The most damaging technique is the third in the list – sodium cyanide poisoning.

Sodium cyanide is a poison of considerable efficacy, but some animals are much more sensitive to it than others, and those most affected may not be the species sought. Sodium cyanide is commonly used for collecting in reefs around the Philippines, and the technique has allegedly spread to Malaysia and Indonesia. In this method of fishing, the collector dissolves the cyanide in water. The fish are then chased into the coral and the cyanide solution squirted into the region. The fish become stupified and can be collected by hand. They are subsequently taken in containers to an unpoisoned area (upcurrent) and left to recover.

There are two drawbacks with this method of fish capture. Firstly, the fish that are caught fairly quickly, or on the edge of the cyanide cloud, and rapidly recuperate are most likely already destined for ill-health. Their liver and kidneys will have already suffered irreversible damage, the degree of which will depend on the duration of contact with the cyanide solution. Almost every fish stupified enough to be caught in this way will be damaged. At first, they may appear healthy, but after about a month, they will start to show signs of distress, swimming in circles, stopping feeding and becoming so emaciated that their ribs can be seen through the skin. Then they will die. An oddity of the cyanide poisoning symptoms is that, even at their end, the fish have not lost colour.

The second disadvantage in using cyanide is that the fish not collected, as well as the corals, remain in contact with the cyanide long enough to be killed. This is especially serious for the corals, as they are very sensitive to the cyanide. Coral does not regenerate as rapidly as the coral reef fish can repopulate the collected area. Dewey (1979) estimated that the mortality rate of fish at sodium cyanide collecting sites was 75 percent, and that there was a further mortality rate of 20-25 percent of the recovered fishes before reaching the exporting centre at Manilla. Rubec (1986) noted that even seemingly unaffected coral heads in regions that had been cyanided had died within two months. It has further been suggested (Schiotz 1989) that the Crown-of-Thorns Starfish (*Acanthaster planci*) has become more abundant because of collecting by this method.

Although damage has been done in the past, the future looks brighter as a result of close ties that wholesalers have with their collectors. Customers, too, are no longer prepared to buy fish collected by cyanide and this message has gone through the retailers to the wholesalers and thence to the suppliers.

The only reasons for using cyanide in the first place are that it is cheap and less labour-intensive than using nets. Despite the fact that net-caught fish are going to be slightly more expensive, their greater viability allied to the lower level of damage that net-fishing causes to the environment, are compensating factors. Indeed, the lack of cyanide-caught specimens has become an advertising policy for a number of UK-based wholesalers.

It was direct pressure from aquarists, retailers and wholesalers that started the movement in the Philippines away from cyanide and towards nets. It is encouraging that in October 1990, over 10 percent of the cyanide fishermen in the Philippines had changed to using nets. But there is still a long way to go, and the hobbyist must continue to be a driving force.

Right: *Cyanide used to catch fish has killed these corals. This is one reason why this method of catching should be strongly discouraged.*

Above: *A school of recently caught* Pseudanthias tuka *in an outdoor tank. Farming reefs on a sustainable basis benefits the entire aquatic industry.*

Farming the reef

The coral reefs can provide mankind with a production yield far above some terrestrial ecosystems. Taken from various sources and expressed as grams per square metre per year (dry weight), the open ocean gives 125, the continental shelf 250 and agricultural land 600. In dramatic contrast, the figure for a coral reef is 3,500. There ought, therefore, to be no difficulty in regarding a coral reef ecosystem as a sustainable resource of a high order. However, this does not mean that it is infinite; no natural resource is infinite.

Foward planning and enlightened management can provide initiatives whereby the reef can be cropped of fish and corals to the financial benefit of the local population and the ultimate satisfaction of the aquarist. The best people to farm a reef in this way are the local people themselves. They have the advantage of being there all the time and can rapidly detect changes in the same way that an agricultural farmer can know when to let fields go fallow or when to change the crops grown on a particular field to maintain the fertility of the soil. The local people become both guardians and beneficiaries of their local resource, and it is in their own interest to maintain the ecological health of the reef system. The guardian function they fulfil is especially important, as they would prevent the dynamiting or poisoning of their asset by outsiders, and they are most unlikely to destroy 'the goose that lays the golden egg'.

There is also scope for reef expansion that can be most effectively practised on a local basis. For example, off the Bahamas, a research team based in Miami found a most useful purpose for old car tyres. They strapped them up in large bundles and put them close to existing reefs. Surprisingly quickly they became covered with algae and, within a few years, a rich reef invertebrate fauna was present, which, in turn, attracted reef fish.

Even the best-managed and best-intentioned projects can suffer and local depletions can occur, but if the area affected is small and surrounded by a vigorous ecosystem, these deficiencies will soon be made good. It should be remembered, though, that large-scale natural disasters can overwhelm any population. For example, until March 1882 there was a thriving fishing industry off the east coast of North America for the Tilefish (*Lopholatilus chamaelionticeps*). After that March there were no Tilefish to be caught and the industry collapsed and fishing communities were badly affected financially. During March and April millions and millions of these fishes died. One steamer reported sailing for two days through Tilefish corpses. It seemed as if that species had become extinct. About 20 years later, a few were caught and, by 1915, the species had become sufficiently abundant for a small fishery programme to be started in the area. The cause of this dramatic decline was not man-made; but quite natural; the Gulf Stream had moved. The recovery was also natural, but doubtless speedier than it might have been had the disaster occurred in a centre of human interference.

In more recent years, parts of, particularly, the Australian Great Barrier Reef were plagued by the Crown-of-Thorns Starfish (*Acanthaster planci*). The reason for the population explosion is unknown. It has been argued that, as species often undergo natural cycles in population numbers, it was a natural population explosion at the beginning. But then it is possible that it became exaggerated by the scarcity of the corals on which it fed for preference. It is also highly likely that, if the stories are not apocryphal, one 'control' measure greatly increased the population numbers. In some areas, when the starfish were collected, they were cut into pieces and thrown back. Happily for starfish, but less fortunately for the custodians of the reef, each arm of the starfish can regrow into a whole animal.

This seemingly foolish act has a precedent. Towards the end of the last century, the famous oyster beds at Whitstable, on the north coast of Kent in south-east England suffered a plague of Common Starfish (*Asterias rubens*). Common Starfish like oysters as much as humans do. They open the shells by exerting a strong, gentle pull on both valves until the oyster's adductor muscle tires and the shell opens a little bit. The starfish then effectively inserts its stomach and the digestion process starts. The oystermen were so enraged by their loss of livelihood, that they dredged and raked up starfish by the thousand, cut them into pieces and threw them back into the sea as a warning to other starfish. Needless to say, this was not an effective method of control. (The starfish plague did eventually decline, however, and the oyster population slowly built up, though not quite to its former numbers, as pollution later became a limiting factor.) The point of this seeming digression is to illustrate the fact that natural regeneration is possible, but may be slow. The chance of it happening is, however, greatly diminished when natural conditions are altered.

No matter whether the source of depopulations is caused by over-collecting locally, dynamiting reefs for food fish, or explosions of the magnitude of Krakatoa in 1883, if the environment remains unchanged, recolonization will occur. If it can

Below: *The curio trade collects shells in vast quantities. Such indiscriminate collecting is both uncontrolled and wasteful of a natural resource.*

Above: *As the boom in SCUBA diving continues, it is important that divers are properly trained and observe a strict 'look but don't touch' policy.*

occur after Krakatoa, when a large part of an island disappeared, it can occur anywhere. But conditions must remain unchanged, and here is where we have to extend our thinking beyond the reef as an isolated ecosystem.

Conservation and tourism

Although coral reefs encourage tourism, tourism is not good for coral reefs; or at least, it is a double-edged sword. Yes, a reef may attract tourists to the benefit of the local community, but too many tourists walking over the reef will destroy it. Each footstep can break a piece of coral or tread a polyp into oblivion. Too many footsteps, and there is no reef. In some of the more popular resorts, local patches of reef have been destroyed in this way.

The indiscriminate collection of tourists' curios and souvenirs can also have an uncontrolled effect upon the ecosystem that is the reason for the tourists' presence. 'Uncontrolled' is the vital word. Tourists will hardly ever have the longterm awareness of the sustainable bounty of the reef possessed by the local people. Ironically, there are instances of tourists having their souvenir confiscated by Customs and Excise on their return from holiday. In their ignorance they had brought back a species protected under the regulations of CITES (The Convention of International Trade in Endangered Species).

Tourists also bring waste, which must be disposed of in a sensible fashion. Just jettisoning empty beer cans and plastic bags in the sea is not the way to conserve the ecosystem. It can be argued that beer cans and plastic bags can be removed from the reef, but the other form of tourist waste – sewage – must be disposed of with even greater care.

Tourists' feet treading over exposed coral at low tide allowed for, what about the sea-borne threat of SCUBA divers? Here, luckily, the more responsible training schemes inculcate into the divers a 'look but don't touch' policy. Sadly, not all SCUBA divers are responsible but, slowly, this element is being shamed and persuaded into behaving responsibly and becoming a guardian or sympathetic friend of the reef. Formerly, it was a common (although completely incomprehensible and pointless) practice for divers to smash open sea urchins at the end of a dive and enjoy watching the fish gobbling up the pieces. While to many people, sea urchins are spiny and seemingly inanimate reef inhabitants, they nonetheless form a vital element in a complex chain.

Recently, the chaos theory, whereby the consequences of an event cannot be reliably predicted, has gained great credence, especially in fluid systems exemplified by meteorology and ecology. The chaos theory has been expressed simply in sentences like 'the beat of a butterfly's wing can give rise to a tornado'. It is not suggested that smashing open one sea urchin is necessarily going to destroy the reef, but why destroy it unnecessarily? Responsible SCUBA divers don't.

Deforestation and pollution

Corals have algae living symbiotically inside the cells of each polyp. The coral needs them to survive and the algae – the zooxanthellae (see page 33) – need sunlight to survive for themselves and the coral. Far-distant logging operations can destroy this delicate balance. The chain of events works like this: coral reefs occur in warm tropical zones in shallow water, but tropical regions have monsoons. Monsoons shed their water content as rain, in large quantities and in a very short time and all this sudden deluge has to go somewhere. The great advantage of forests – in this case, the aptly named rain forests – is that they, and their soil, act as both a barrier and a sponge respectively to slow down and absorb the deluge. If the forest is no longer there, the water runs straight, and savagely, to the sea. Its force in

Above: *An idyllic view of a tropical paradise where coral reefs abound. This can be preserved for future generations if we start conservation policies now.*

doing this strips off the soil and carries it to the sea. There, as the power of the water current diminishes, the silt is dropped. It makes the water turbid, cuts down light and is deposited in shallow water. Where are the coral reefs? In shallow water. What does coral need to live? Sunlight – which is precisely what coral does not get in some areas owing to deforestation a thousand miles away. A forest cleared in a few months can destroy ten thousand years of coral growth in a couple of monsoon seasons.

Some threats to reefs are global, but not natural. The sea is the final sump of the world for all waste products, and the coastal parts are the first to be affected. All over the world, industry discharges poisonous waste. Not easily detectable, yet insidious in its effect, is discharge of heavy metals, which can never be broken down. The rare metal vanadium, for example, is naturally extracted in minute quantities from seawater by molluscs, which concentrate it in parts of their body for biological reasons. They need it in the same way that we need iron to make our blood. The problem is that the absorbing mechanism will also let in atoms of metals that are poisonous. Some fish, through the food chain, concentrate mercury and cadmium in their tissues in this way, and these two elements are very poisonous.

Conserving the reefs

As it is unlikely that in the foreseeable future these widespread threats will be curtailed, it is up to us to maintain the reef ecosystem in as healthy a condition as possible. To this end some areas have been set aside as marine nature reserves from which nothing should be taken. Those in the Red Sea and in the Caribbean are well known.

Recently, there has been an enterprise in the Philippines called *Bantay Dagat*, which means guardian of the seas. This project is working at several levels and is supported by the Philippine Tourist Department and the Philippine Commission on Sport SCUBA Diving. A media campaign to educate the public about the value of the reefs and the disadvantages of bad fishing practices (dynamiting, cyaniding etc.) has also been launched. Marine parks and sanctuaries are being designated and local people are encouraged to act as watchmen and report abuses to the authorities. Furthermore, those whose livelihoods have been affected are being re-trained. All of this is highly laudable and will help to ensure that reefs remain a valuable resource by limiting damage to them.

With some background protection in such a reef-rich country, there is increased optimism that, at least in that part of the world, a continuing supply of fish and invertebrates will be available to the hobbyist. But the maintenance of this supply depends heavily on the sensible cropping of a renewable resource.

Conservation and the hobbyist

It is in the face of possible catastrophes that collecting activities become less subject to criticism. Yet, it is now that the aquarium trade must play its full part in maintaining reef biodiversity. It is encouraging that this is slowly starting to happen. An obvious contribution is the captive breeding of reef fish. Many species have proved recalcitrant to breeding in the aquarium. At commercially viable prices, only a few species – Neon Gobies, damsels, clownfish and some centropygids – are in trade. Others are being experimentally bred, but the cost has so far proved prohibitive. The hope is that each time another species is bred, the knowledge gained will lead towards commercial production, thereby minimizing collection of these creatures from the wild.

As they have spectacular shapes and colours, giant clams (or, at least baby giant clams) are popular in the home aquarium, but in the wild they are under great threat. They are sought for food by many peoples of the Indo-Pacific region. As the individual clams are slow-growing and the human population is increasing alarmingly, it is not surprising that the giant clams' numbers have been decimated. Young clams were also collected for the aquarium trade which did not help their plight.

Now, however, captive breeding programmes for giant clams have been developed and help the survival of the species in the wild and also maintain their availability for the aquarist. It was about 15 years ago that various centres started the experiments necessary to find out the techniques for the captive breeding. Problems abounded; the basic biology of giant clams was known, but the detail of the larval rearing was unknown territory.

One unexpected problem was finding that the larval stages of a snail parasitize the young clams. The larvae settle between the shell and the mouth and then feed on the mantle, eventually killing the clam. The snails have to be removed manually as soon as they are noticed. Another snail with similar habits can be washed out. All these problems occur on top of the difficulties of captive breeding.

The most frequently bred species are those of the genus *Tridacna*. In this popular genus, the young do not need any feeding. Spawning in adults is stimulated while they are in large mixed groups. The larvae have their own food supply in the form of a yolk sac. So, for several days, there is no feeding problem. The still-mobile young are then inoculated with zooxanthellae algae, which enter into the cells, live symbiotically and produce the food for the growing, settled clam. One centre, in Palau in Micronesia, has usually about 10,000 growing clams for the aquarium trade and for future research in their biology.

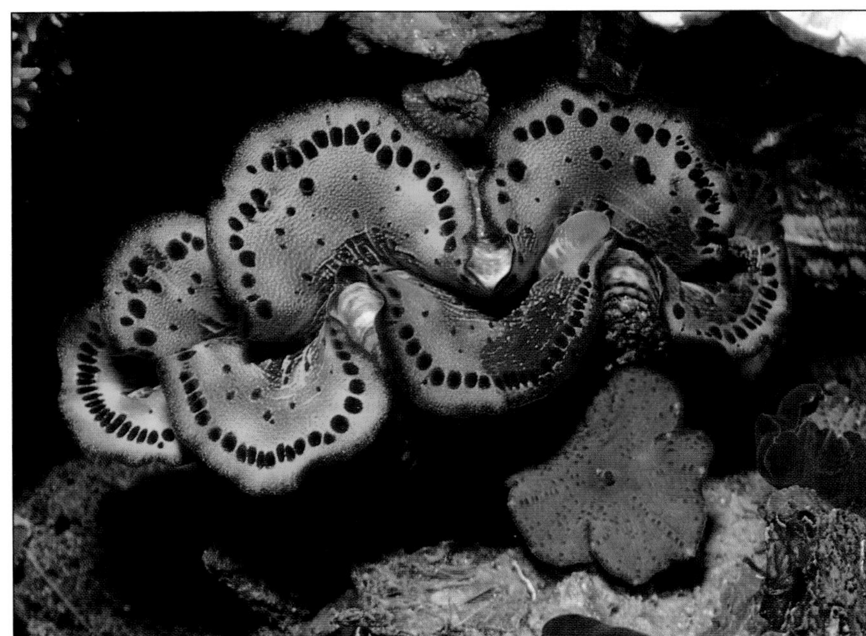

Above: *Giant clams, such as this* Tridacna maxima, *are now being bred in captivity in large numbers. Pressures on wild populations are thus relieved.*

The clams are sold when between one and two years old and are some 5-10cm (2-4in) in length. *Tridacna deresa* and *T. gigas* are popular for filters and *T. crocea* and *T. maxima* are kept because of the bright colours of their mantles. All in all, these ventures benefit both the aquarist and the conservationists, as well as giving employment to the local people.

Because corals grow slowly and are often difficult to keep, their removal is the most conspicuous danger to the reef ecosystem. Unfortunately, in the Third World, where there are reefs, such collecting has been a source of much-needed income to the local people. This problem has been overcome in the Philippines, where irresponsible reef collecting is discouraged. Further, an industry has now been set up to make artificial corals and sponges from fibreglass. The climate lends itself to the manufacture of these fibreglass models, and many of the former reef collectors are employed in their moulding and painting. It is a successful venture, both economically and ecologically. The false corals and sponges are very acceptable to hobbyists, look realistic in the aquarium and, anyway, soon acquire a veneer of natural algae.

One ought to note that many of the farm-raised or captive-bred fish and invertebrates are not, at the moment, as cheap as wild-caught individuals. Because of the high cost of overheads and the expenses of the previous research into breeding techniques, the hobbyist has to pay more to support such programmes. The sensible hobbyist will realize that this is a good investment for the future so that wild stocks remain in the wild, yet are still available to the aquarium trade.

In time, when the techniques are perfected, the aquarist may have no choice but to buy farmed fish. This may happen for one or both of two reasons. Firstly, uncontrolled collecting may exterminate various species in the wild. Secondly, legislation may be introduced to prevent the sale of wild-caught animals. Either way, it is preferable to invest money into a breeding programme, and sooner rather than later. And, when the breeding techniques are perfected, the prices will fall. The future of the hobby is in our hands.

PART TWO

SETTING UP THE AQUARIUM

Planning and preparation have always been the keys to successful marine fishkeeping; long before you make any plans to bring the creatures themselves home, you will have much work to do. You will need not only to make physical preparations, but also to gain a good understanding of what makes an aquarium 'tick'. Once you, as a prospective marine aquarist, have decided what you wish to keep, practical considerations come into force, for there is no doubt that these creatures are special, coming, as they do, from the richest and possibly most varied habitat on earth.

Over recent years, many innovations have made the life of the marine aquarist very much easier, and fish and invertebrates have been enabled to live an increasingly natural and prolonged lifespan within the aquarium. Aquarium design has altered radically over the past 20 years; no more the ugly and primitive iron-framed 'waterboxes'; nowadays, people have come to expect, quite rightly, the aquarium to be an integral part of their homes; aesthetic appeal and practical application have come together in a successful and popular union.

However, a certain amount of understanding is not only desirable, but also absolutely essential; water testing is useless if the results are not clearly understood, and any amount of filtration equipment will fail to support valuable livestock if it is incorrectly installed. Setting up a new aquarium is exciting and all part of the pleasures of fishkeeping, but if mistakes are made at this stage, then the whole system will collapse, leading to unhappiness for you, and an almost certainly worse fate for the livestock! Most fish and invertebrates have made a long and difficult journey for our pleasure. We, as caring marine aquarists, owe it to them to provide the best and most natural environment possible.

Left: *Achieving a beautiful living reef aquarium such as this involves careful planning of all aspects of filtration, lighting and compatibility of stock. With some experience and common sense, the results can be breathtaking.*

Exploring the Options

Why keep a marine aquarium? There are many answers to this question: it is a rewarding challenge; it helps develop a better understanding of natural habitats and their ecology and biology; it can instigate a keen interest in conservation, and it can be generally educational by indirectly helping to teach us about geography and various other subjects. Of course, all these considerations can also be applied to keeping a freshwater aquarium, but it is the diversity of species, their characters and personalities, curious appearances and stunning colours that draws our interest to marine fishes and invertebrates. Many have quite distinctive lifestyles, coexisting in association with other animals. For example, some clownfishes have a close symbiotic relationship with certain anemones. The possibility of housing fishes and invertebrates in the same aquarium is an added attraction and one that is not easily achieved in a freshwater aquarium.

Marine fishkeeping also raises other interesting questions: why are juvenile fishes often a totally different colour and pattern to adults of the same species? Why is it the male seahorse that undergoes pregnancy? Why are the fishes' colours so intense? We already have the answers to some of these questions, but others remain a mystery. Perhaps it will be you who finds out the truth behind a perplexing puzzle.

Meeting the challenge

Do not underestimate the challenge of keeping marine fishes; generally speaking, it is a more complex undertaking than maintaining most freshwater aquariums, and demands a certain amount of dedication, which can be time consuming. It is not just a case of setting up the tank and regarding it as a living ornament in your lounge. This is not to say that freshwater aquarists are not dedicated, but it is much easier to set up a freshwater aquarium without having had any previous experience. In fact, it is a positive advantage, although not essential, to have been a freshwater aquarist before moving on to marines. Many aspects of freshwater and marine fishkeeping are similar. For example, the basic principles of filtration apply to both. However, certain aspects of marine fishkeeping have no direct equivalent in the freshwater world, and new skills must be learned from scratch.

The main challenge arises from the fact that marine environments, and coral reefs in particular, are more environmentally stable than most

Below: *The fish-only aquarium makes a colourful introduction to the hobby for the beginner. There need be no worries about sensitive invertebrates.*

Above: *Local fishermen in Cebu in the Philippines catching ornamental marine fishes using nets. This is the correct way to collect the fish and the first step in the fishes' journey to the aquarist's tank.*

freshwater situations. Coral reefs are so stable that even minute environmental changes can take decades to take effect, whereas in the marine aquarium these same types of changes can happen within a few hours. It is easy to understand that coral reef animals have no mechanism for dealing with such rapid changes, hence the need to work hard at maintaining water quality in the captive environment. Freshwater habitats tend to be very small compared to seas and oceans, are more easily affected by the weather and seasons and are also easier to pollute. Therefore, freshwater organisms have generally evolved into tougher animals, the downside being that there are many critically endangered species and habitats and a faster rate of extinction compared to the situation in tropical marine environments.

The availability of marine fishes and invertebrates has improved with an increase in the numbers of aquarium stores stocking them. Collecting and shipping techniques have generally improved over recent years, with many fisherfolk returning to more traditional methods to catch their fishes. A trend towards sustainable harvesting is giving the industry a better image and is ensuring the livelihood of many fishing villages for the foreseeable future. As the industry develops, it is actually helping to put a value on the reefs that encourages the fisherfolk to manage them sensitively and is ultimately helping to secure their future.

Over time, our knowledge of the reproductive behaviour of marine species has improved to an extent that many species of coral reef animals can now be successfully bred in captivity. Hobbyists and professionals alike have contributed to this knowledge base. Some of the most popular species have been bred in commercial numbers and are now available to marine aquarists. However, there is still much to be learned and the hobbyist is well placed to take on such challenges and help to improve the knowledge base further.

Successful captive breeding programmes will help ensure the future of many species as a kind of 'safety-net' in case of severe habitat degradation in the wild – even though we all hope global damage to this extent will never occur. However, it will always be necessary to import wild stock in order to maintain genetic integrity. In other words, new blood is important to ensure that captive-bred animals are genetically as close as possible to their wild relatives and that there is some element of random selection as would be found in nature. (See page 146-151 for more on breeding marine fishes.)

The systems

In a domestic-size freshwater aquarium, it is possible to establish a natural biological equilibrium using only 'organic' elements, i.e. keeping

Stocking levels

Experienced freshwater aquarists will already be familiar with the theory that the number of fishes that can be comfortably held in a tank of any given volume depends on three things; the amount of dissolved oxygen in the water and its replenishment rate capability, the temperature of the water and what sort of fishes you are keeping. Warm water holds less dissolved oxygen than cold water. However, the whole complex problem can be conveniently calculated by using one of two methods illustrated in this panel, or a combination of both, to make the calculation. Work on the principal that biological filter beds with a volume of one-fifth of the volume of water in the system are generally sufficient.

Use water quality tests to decide when it is safe to introduce new specimens into the aquarium, ideally only introducing one at any given time. This progressive technique will allow your filter to adjust to the extra loading on the system, which occurs each time you add a new animal. It is a good idea to measure the dissolved oxygen level of the water on a regular basis. This should be in the region of 80-90% saturation; a tendency to drop below this range is a good indication that stocking levels are too high. Consult your dealer if in doubt, but usually a little forethought and common sense will prove effective. These are good husbandry guidelines for a newly set-up aquarium, but with increasing experience and new technology the parameters could be altered.

Volume of water for one fish

In volume terms, it is good practice to allow 1cm of fish standard length to 7 litres of water (Equivalent to 1in of fish body length per 4 gallons). This will help to achieve a good standard of husbandry, particularly if you are new to the hobby or if the aquarium is newly established. This is a guideline only and the length of fish to this volume of water can be increased to a degree with experience.

Left: *Since the Yellow Tang* (Zebrasoma flavescens) *is a territorial fish, you should either keep a single specimen or a group of six or more. In this case, you will need a large tank to accommodate them.*

Fish length and water surface

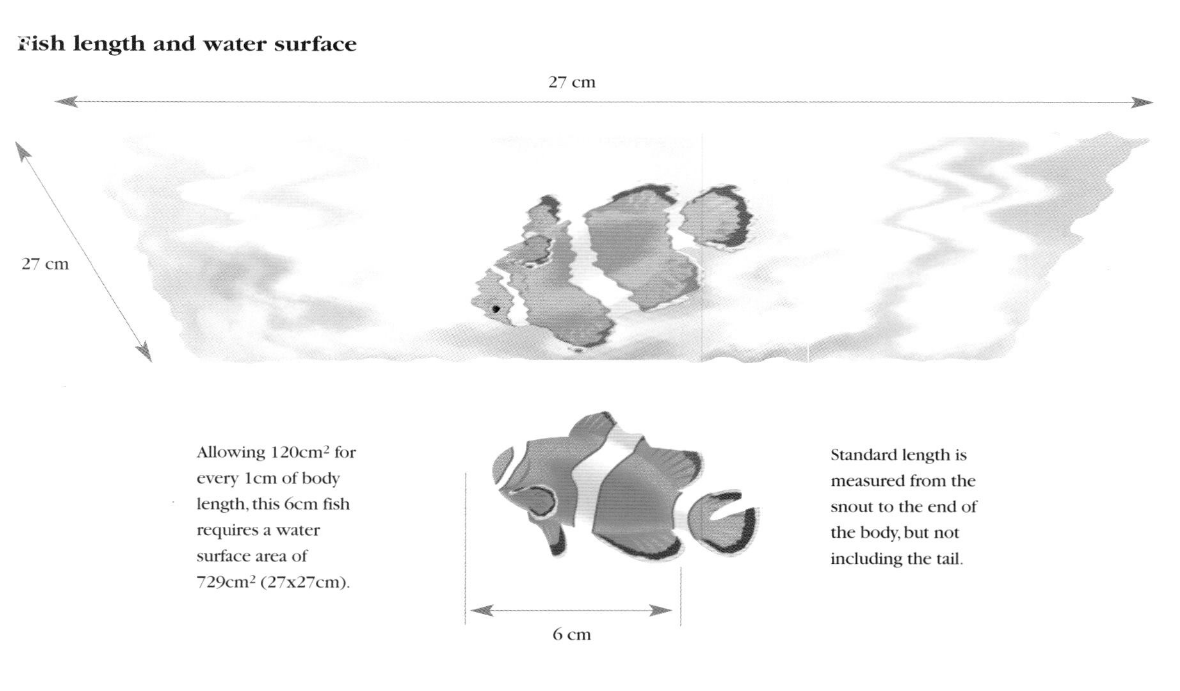

Allowing 120cm^2 for every 1cm of body length, this 6cm fish requires a water surface area of 729cm^2 (27x27cm).

Standard length is measured from the snout to the end of the body, but not including the tail.

Above: *The invertebrate-only aquarium has an aesthetic beauty all its own. In the absence of fish, and their associated waste products, many invertebrates seem to flourish more freely.*

the correct number of aquatic plants and fishes to create a biologically balanced aquarium. Although not totally impossible, it is extremely difficult to achieve a similar equilibrium in the marine aquarium; in attempting to do so, you would first need to combine many years of experience in marine aquarium keeping with an enormous amount of research into reef ecology and biology.

In the sea, the 'waste disposal' problem is solved by the sheer vastness of the water, wave action and the activity of filter-feeding animals, such as sponges, sea squirts and fan worms, etc. At the same time, there is massive bacterial activity on the equally large surface area of rocks, corals and the seabed that serves to 'purify' the water. An aquarium designed to function in exactly the same way would be so large that it would be beyond the scope of the average fishkeeper. Furthermore, such an aquarium would be very susceptible to 'explosive pollution' if its subjects were overfed or a decaying body were to go undetected.

Conversely, logic might suppose that a constantly monitored, automatically controlled, smaller marine aquarium is possible in this 'hi-tech' day and age. This may be true to some extent, albeit at a proportionately large financial cost, but, while theoretically everything may be under control, there are always seemingly unpredictable factors to be considered when keeping live animals in captivity that tend to upset even the best laid plans. Speculation suggests that the animals within such a system could become 'over-protected' by the technological aids and lose their natural resistance to disease should any be inadvertently introduced into the aquarium, or the fishes removed to other, less 'sanitary' quarters. A further drawback with this type of aquarium is that it may not be possible to keep filter-feeding animals, as their food is removed most effectively from the water by the constant action of very powerful filter systems. Efficient removal of vital minerals from the water may also preclude the growth of marine algae in the aquarium.

Marine fishkeeping has in general developed a middle path between these two extremes. An understanding of the natural cleansing processes that occur within the ocean has led to the development of relatively low-cost

Is marine fishkeeping expensive?

At first, it may look as if marine fishkeeping is relatively expensive, but closer examination shows that there is only a small premium to be paid for the privilege of 'going marine'. Marine fishes may individually be more expensive than their freshwater counterparts, but this is because when they are shipped, they must be packed singly, whereas many freshwater fishes can be packed together in large groups. This means that, where marine fishes are concerned, you are mostly paying the freight costs for the water your fishes are shipped in. On the other hand, it is possible, and often desirable, to keep many more specimens in a freshwater aquarium of a given size than you can marines, so the cost for animals can quite easily even out.

The basic equipment requirements are the same for both marine and freshwater aquariums, but at the setting up stage you will need to use a marine substrate that is generally a bit more expensive, plus you will need the essential saltwater that adds a bit of extra expense. Also you may want, or even need, to include additional lighting and it is likely you will want to install extra devices, such as a protein skimmer. The extra items that are not required for freshwater fishkeeping add to the initial cost, but bear in mind that marine fishes are generally much longer-lived than freshwater fishes, and therefore need replacing less often, so on balance the costs need not be too different when spread over time.

Of course, the above refers to a basic system, but there is no limit to the amount you can spend and there are plenty of opportunities to do so. You may want to go for a fish-only system with basic habitat structures and simple economical lighting. Such a system is relatively inexpensive and will cost much the same as an equivalent-sized, freshwater aquarium. Or you may opt for one of the so-called 'total-systems' that has everything necessary, plus extras, which will cost more. Maybe you have a particular interest in hard corals and clams, which are usually extremely expensive, draining your finances dramatically and, in fact, costing you more in animal purchases than it does to set up your aquarium with all its apparatus. Potentially, the 'reef aquarium', packed with living rock and hundreds of invertebrates, plus the dedicated equipment and water treatments often used in conjunction with them, can be the most expensive option. The choice is yours, but one thing you must never do is try to cut corners in order to save money. This will almost certainly result in failure and is therefore absolute false economy.

Below: *Many marine fishkeepers strive to possess a piece of 'living reef', as shown here. The fascinating invertebrates and colourful fish provide a stunning display, but there are pitfalls – especially for beginners.*

Above: *The Electric-blue Damsel* (Pomacentrus coeruleus) *is widely available, relatively hardy and often one of the first choices of the newcomer to the marine fishkeeping hobby.*

Right: *The peaceful Raccoon Butterflyfish* (Chaetodon lunula) *is more suited to aquarium life than many other species in the family. It will benefit from regular feeds of brineshrimp.*

solutions to the equivalent problems in the aquarium. Modern filtration systems – particularly those based on bacterial activity – use natural methods of processing wastes and this is the key to the increasing popularity and success rate of marine fishkeeping around the world.

Complete aquarium set-ups based around efficient, but in essence 'natural' filter systems are discussed in a later chapter. However, armed with a basic understanding of water management, there is no reason why you should not be able to build up an aquarium system from separate components. In fact, this often proves more satisfying, and probably better suits the needs and finances of the average hobbyist. At the very least, doing things 'bit by bit' offers the opportunity to absorb some knowledge along the way. If you buy everything all at once in a single package, you may not need to find out or even understand how and why the system works because it is a simple case of filling it with water and plugging it in. The problem is that if the system develops a fault and fails, you may not be equipped with the essential know-how required to put it right.

Coral reef fishes

For most aquarists embarking on marine aquarium keeping, it is the brightly coloured fishes that provide inspiration. This is admittedly the major area of interest for hobbyists and accordingly takes up a substantial part of this book. The techniques of marine aquarium husbandry are usually learned while keeping a fish-only aquarium and are highly valuable when considering the inclusion of other animals.

Coral reef invertebrates

A wide range of reef invertebrate life can be kept in captivity, and this is a rapidly growing area of marine aquarium keeping. Suitable species include shrimps, sea anemones,

living corals, clams, starfishes and tubeworms, which all do a great job in helping to create a most naturalistic captive environment. A piece of so-called 'living rock' may have tiny polyps or fan worms living on it, along with many other representative life-forms that will further help create the illusion of having a tiny portion of natural reef in your tank. If you research and carefully choose the invertebrates you wish to keep, you will find many of them will happily coexist with fishes. Indeed many fishes and invertebrates have naturally close associations in nature, as we shall see in later sections.

Alternatively, you may wish to establish an invertebrate-only aquarium, allowing you to study the lifestyles of these creatures without the worry of problems caused by predatory fishes. Most tropical invertebrates are every bit as colourful as the fishes and will reward the patient observer with intriguing behaviour patterns.

Coldwater marine fishes and invertebrates

It would not be fair to assume the above selection of tropical marine life presents the whole picture. Fishes and invertebrates from coldwater and temperate water regions can also be kept in captivity, sometimes with fewer demands. One advantage of tackling this aspect of marine fishkeeping is that, very often, collecting your own specimens is not only free, but also

Above: *Clownfishes are happiest living amongst the tentacles of a sea anemone, where they are protected from being stung by the mucus coating on their skin. Observing this relationship is a source of endless fascination.*

Right: *A tropical octopus makes an ideal subject for an invertebrate species aquarium. Given time, they can become quite tame. Be sure to provide plenty of hiding places and pollution-free water.*

usually a very enjoyable activity – depending on how near you live to suitable collecting sites. Be aware of laws and regulations, as many coastal areas are nature reserves and it may not be legal to collect from such locations.

Exploring your local seashore can be a useful lesson in conservation and it is likely you will want to do your best to preserve these natural habitats. With this in mind, always take care to replace any rocks you have moved as they maybe home to animals you are not interested in collecting. Always take litter away and dispose of it in the correct manner. Also, only collect animals you are sure you can look after throughout their normal lifespan. It is no longer regarded acceptable to return fishes back into the wild if they grow too large for your aquarium, as there are very serious concerns about the risk of introducing unnatural diseases, etc., into the natural habitat by doing this.

Rockpool animals naturally live in conditions that are ever-changing and therefore they tend to be very hardy and ideally suited to the rigours of captivity. However, during hot summer months, the temperature may rise too high for all but the hardiest of rockpool creatures. They can be kept at relatively low cost, but they are generally not as colourful as their tropical relatives.

The colder and more stable conditions found offshore mean that keeping animals from such locations is a bit more demanding and will probably require the addition of an expensive chilling system. (See page 78-79 for details of temperature control in the marine aquarium)

Reaping the rewards

Whatever form of marine fishkeeping you decide to involve yourself in, the rewards are really quite self evident. You will enjoy a great sense of achievement. Even when things go wrong, you will learn by your mistakes and feel satisfied when you have solved your problems. There is still much to learn about the marine environment and you, as an aquarist, are ideally placed to observe a tiny bit of nature, all of which has relevance in science and conservation. Recording your observations puts you in the enviable position of being able to disseminate information for the benefit of others.

At the very least you can sit, watch and enjoy the fascinating and curious lifestyles of your aquarium subjects.

Below: *If you find the colours of the tropical marine aquarium a little too bright, the subdued tones of coldwater marine species may be more appealing. The display can be equally impressive.*

Selecting a tank

There are a number of constraints that require careful consideration when choosing a suitable aquarium tank for marine use. A little forethought is required when deciding the size, shape and design of the tank, as well as the materials to be used in its construction.

Tank construction

Saltwater is highly corrosive and abrasive, which means the chosen tank must not include any metal in its construction, or any other material that could release toxins into the water. This also applies to all associated equipment used to maintain the aquarium. Even some plastics can present a problem, as seawater can strip potentially dangerous surface chemicals off items such as pipework. Food-grade materials are safe to use, but to be certain it is always best to use equipment manufactured especially for the aquarium hobby. Fortunately, all-glass and acrylic aquarium tanks are readily available and are totally safe for marine fishkeeping.

If it is absolutely necessary to use equipment with metal parts, such as some aquarium hoods, you must apply three or four coats of protective polyurethane varnish before use. Saltwater spray can also be damaging to objects close to the aquarium, so these will require protection also. Always check that the varnish you use is safe for pets.

Hobbyists can choose from a wide variety of shapes and sizes of commercially available tanks, although the rectangular style is the most common. This long, shallow, 'letter-box' design may not always be the most aesthetically appealing, so tank manufacturers have become more adventurous and creative, although not all their designs are practical for some areas of marine fishkeeping

Selecting tank size and shape

When considering the size of an aquarium, remember the principal that 'large is good, but bigger is better'. The larger the water volume, the more inherently stable it can be in terms of water quality. The same rule applies to the filtration area if it is to be included in the tank. So, although it is possible to establish a marine aquarium in a relatively small tank, always opt for the largest you can accommodate and afford.

Regarding shape, it is important to remember that tall, narrow tanks have less surface area than wide, shallow ones. Marine fishes and invertebrates require a high level of oxygen (O_2), which can only be absorbed into the water at its surface. Potentially dangerous carbon dioxide (CO_2) is also dissipated into the atmosphere at the water surface. So, the larger the surface area is, the more efficient this gas exchange will be. Inefficient gas exchange will mean that the system can support fewer animals. Always bear this in mind when deciding the shape of your tank. It is no accident that the standard, rectangular aquarium remains the most practical and popular choice.

Unusual shapes are commercially available both in glass and acrylic, although there is greater variety in the latter due to its more flexible properties. Cylinders, corner units and hexagonal tanks are just a few that may appeal and are suitable, providing you consider the rules of gas exchange. One shape that offers interesting viewing aspects along with an acceptable surface area in relation to depth is the cube.

Water is heavy and aquariums are expected to

Left: *Fishkeepers today have a wide choice of aquarium shapes and sizes. The curved tank shown here is one option, but the basic criteria remain the same; the tank should have a large surface area and be able to accommodate all the vital life-support equipment.*

Buying a tank

When buying any type of tank, it is worth checking the following points:

- Regardless of material, all edges should be smooth to avoid risk of injury.
- Check for cracks, splinters and other blemishes that could weaken the material.
- Make sure that all sides of the tank have been cut accurately so that all edges are flush without undesirable overhangs.
- In a glass aquarium, the silicone beading used to bond the sides together should be smooth and neat without any bubbles or air pockets.
- In acrylic tanks, it is important that the bonded seams do not have any bubbles or air pockets.

contain a remarkable weight. Both glass and acrylic are very strong materials and, providing the aquarium is well constructed, are ideally suited for the job, although each has its advantages and disadvantages. The final choice will be a matter of personal preference. Glass is more brittle than acrylic and therefore more likely to break if not looked after correctly, but it does not scratch as easily as acrylic, which may require special polishing from time to time. Acrylic has superior light-transmitting properties that give a much clearer view and it is less reflective than most types of glass, especially where thicker materials are necessary. Glass is still somewhat cheaper than acrylic.

If you intend to upgrade your system with new accessories at a later date, make sure it will be capable of accommodating these new items. For example, a protein skimmer often requires extra 'headroom' in an aquarium; this is something that could be easily overlooked when deciding on the initial system. Similarly, extra room above the tank could be required if lighting is to be upgraded.

Above: *A successful marine aquarium will allow each of the inhabitants to establish its own territory within it. This means providing plenty of safe retreats.*

As a starting point, choose a tank no smaller than 90cm long x 30cm wide x 40cm high (36x12x16in). A tank this size will hold approximately 114 litres (25 gallons) of water. This has a good surface area and will allow for a number of small fishes or invertebrates, or a compatible mix of fishes and invertebrates, to establish themselves within their own space. As long as each fish has a space it can retreat to, it will not feel threatened and will settle more easily, and generally be more visible.

Space for territories

Another consideration is the territoriality of some species. In the relatively confined space of an aquarium, many fishes will not tolerate others of the same species, or even close relatives. An example would be angelfishes, particularly

Above: *Bear in mind that you will need easy access to the aquarium for feeding the fishes. A large tank such as this is very impressive, but could be difficult to maintain and expensive to run.*

those in the genus *Pomacanthus*, that will aggressively fight with other angelfishes and sometimes with similarly shaped species. This often happens because there is not enough space for more than one fish to establish a territory, and the least dominant fishes are continually encroaching on the most dominant individual's space. Even small species, such as many damsels, are so territorial, particularly when they are guarding a nest site, that they will attack virtually any other fish in the aquarium. In many species, the males are intolerant of each other and will fight relentlessly, often to the death.

The same can also apply to many invertebrates, especially crustaceans. Even aggression amongst corals is known. Researching the natural history of the species you intend to keep and reading material by experienced fishkeepers will help you to determine which species you can and cannot keep together in one aquarium.

Siting the tank

When a tank measuring 90x30x40cm (36x12x16in) is filled with decorative material, substrate and water, it will weigh about 114kg (250lb) and thus become an immovable object. You must therefore consider where the tank will be situated before you set it up.

Because it is so heavy, site the tank on a firm base, which is in turn evenly supported on a strong floor. Try to arrange an even distribution of weight across floor joists. The aquarium stand should have a solid, perfectly flat top on which to place the tank – particularly where all-glass tanks are concerned. You can cushion the tank against any unevenness in the stand with a material such as expanded polystyrene, cork or special foam sheets available at aquarium dealers. However, such underlay will only compensate for minor irregularities; any major twist or warp in the supporting surface will stress a filled tank and result in breakage. The same principles apply if you decide to install the tank into a dividing wall, or onto a shelf or cabinet.

The aquarium will need lighting equipment and pumps and, if it is to house tropical marines, heating apparatus, so be sure to site the tank near to an electricity supply. Also bear in mind that water and electricity do not mix, so plugs and sockets must be a safe distance from splashing, or protected in some other way. Ideally, the electricity supply should be above and away from the water surface level.

It is not a good idea to site the aquarium close to a window because, even though it may be a tropical setup, sunshine through glass can seriously overheat the water, making accurate temperature control very difficult. Putting the tank in a bright conservatory or sunroom can cause similar problems. Obviously this situation would be even more critical where coldwater or temperate fishes are concerned. Avoid placing the aquarium too close to radiators for the same reason. Also, excessive light falling on the tank could encourage unwanted growths of algae. Should you wish to grow any of the popular macro-algae, it is best to use artificial lighting systems, over which you have control.

To avoid disturbances from external sources, try to place the aquarium away from anything that may cause stressful vibrations in the tank, such as doors opening and closing. Conversely, some aquarium equipment may be noisy, so consider other members of the household who may enjoy watching TV, or are trying to sleep on the other side of a partitioning wall.

Wherever the aquarium is situated, always make sure there is room for the correct installation of the equipment you want to use and that there is good access for essential maintenance.

Below: *Stands usually have feet that can be adjusted by screwing them up or down. Ensure that the stand is level before placing the aquarium on top.*

Left: *Seat glass tanks on a layer of polystyrene or a foam mat to even out imperfections in the base board. A small piece of grit can cause a fine fracture.*

Siting the aquarium

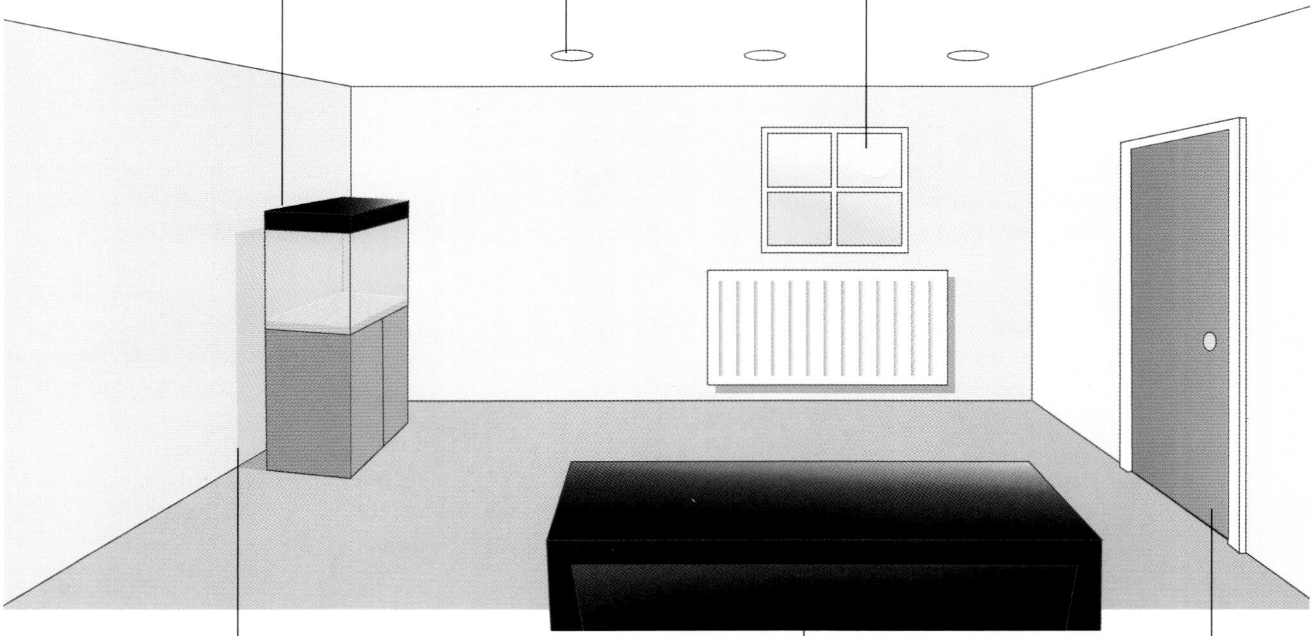

Space around and behind the aquarium is essential for maintenance and cables or pipework. Space beneath the aquarium can be used for storing food or equipment.

If possible, fit a dimmer switch to the main room light. This will eliminate any sudden light changes that will shock the fish

Heat from sunlight and radiators can affect the aquarium. In this room, direct sunlight will only reach the tank for a small part of the day.

Electrical sockets should be nearby but not directly underneath. Make sure any cables fall below the wall socket to prevent water from reaching the plug.

Vibrations from audio equipment such as TVs or stereos can disturb fish. Make sure any such equipment is not too close to the aquarium.

Doors opening and closing suddenly can stress fishes. The aquarium in this room is positioned where the fish can see the door at a safe distance.

Temperature Control

The water in a marine aquarium must be maintained at a reasonably constant temperature if fishes and invertebrates from tropical coral reefs are to survive. Animals collected from your local coast can be maintained at the temperatures that occur naturally where you live. In some places, measures to cool down the tropical aquarium may be required, particularly during hot summer months.

Types of heating equipment

Various forms of heating have been developed over the years. However, the most popular method of heating aquarium water is by means of small, individual electric immersion heaters combined with a thermostat control, commonly known as heaterstats. These units are generally protected inside a glass sleeve, although you can also buy more rugged types made from materials such as titanium. Some external, canister-style power filters also incorporate a heating system, but be sure to check these out carefully as most are only safe for use in freshwater systems because the elements and thermostat connections could corrode in saltwater. Undergravel heating cables controlled by an external thermostat are also available.

Heating equipment may also be incorporated within the water treatment compartment (or sump) of a built-in 'total system'. This can make more efficient use of your heater, as it is heating a smaller body of water at any one time. For larger systems there are heating elements housed in a sleeve that can be plumbed directly in the pipework of the water circulation system.

In large fish rooms it would probably be more efficient to heat the space around the tanks. Gas central heating and thermostatically controlled fan heaters are good for the job, as are fuel-burning heaters. However, bear in mind that any form of fuel-burning system must have good ventilation to keep up the oxygen supply to it and to the air around the tanks and also to vent off fumes, which could be harmful to aquarium animals.

To measure the temperature, you can use any type of aquarium thermometer, as they all tend to be made either from glass or a suitable plastic. You can also choose from a variety of digital electronic thermometers for aquarium use.

Controlling and conserving heat

In a standard aquarium heaterstat, the built-in thermostat controls the supply of electricity to the heating element by sensing the temperature of the water. This sensing is achieved by means of a bimetallic strip that bends and straightens, making and breaking contact as the temperature changes, or by microchip circuitry. Microchip thermostats are normally a separate unit from the heating element and temperature control is achieved by a probe in the water that sends a message back to the thermostat, which in turn regulates the power to the heating element. Large, ready-

Heaterstats are available calibrated in °C or °F, or both scales side by side.

Above: *Combined heaterstats are easy to adjust by turning the knob at the top until you reach the desired temperature. Some units have a light to indicate whether it is on or off. Make sure you can see it.*

A combined heater and filter

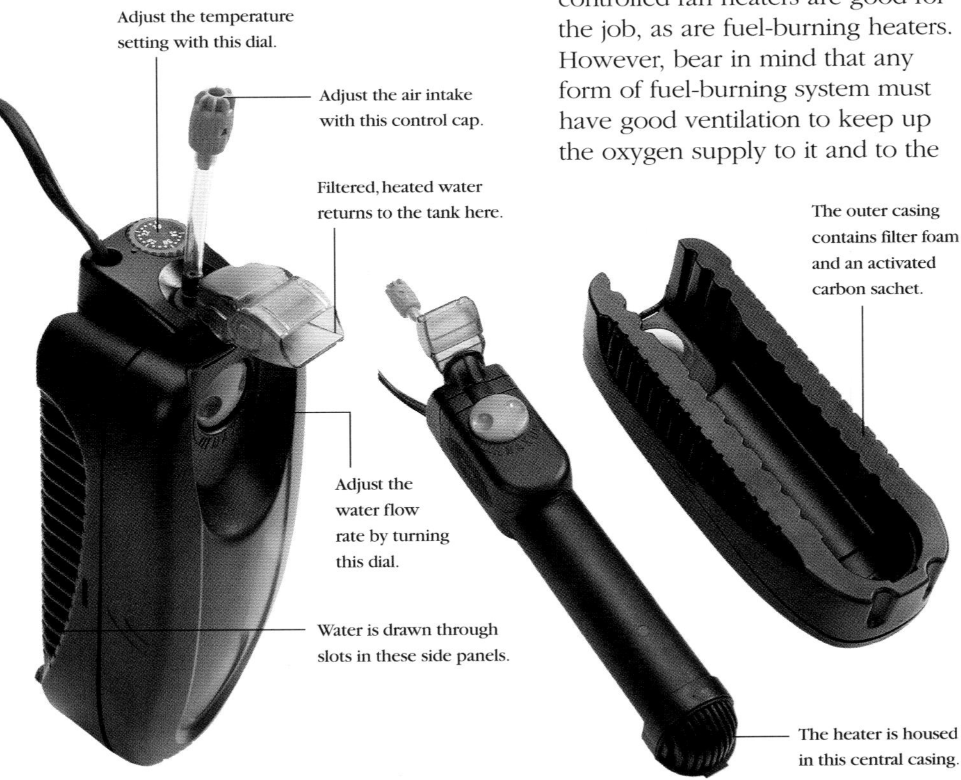

What size heaterstat?

Allow about 10 watts per 4.54 litres (1 gallon) of water content. A 90x30x38cm (36x15x12in) aquarium has an approximate volume of 110 litres (24 gallons) and would therefore require 240 watts of heat. A smaller heater would be sufficient if the room is permanently heated. Following the guidelines described above, a single 250-watt heater should suffice, but two separate 150-watt heaters would be better and afford some margin for error or heater failure. Always keep a spare heaterstat handy in case of failures.

built complete systems often use these high-tech thermostats, but they are not so widely used in the average home aquarium.

For most tropical marine aquariums, the ideal temperature is around 75°F (24°C). The familiar heaterstats are usually factory preset to this temperature, but can be adjusted to a few degrees above and below this level if necessary.

External thermostat units can be either analogue or digital. Analogue units are set manually, but digital models allow you to programme a variety of temperature parameters and often have automatic features, such as emitting an alarm if the temperature gets too high or too low. Some include a display that records the maximum and minimum temperature reached in a time period, as well as showing the current temperature. Such digital units can offer the degree of control and accuracy that will provide extra protection for aquarium subjects and peace of mind for you, the aquarist.

Computerized aquarium systems that can control temperature along with a variety of water quality testing features from a single unit are also available. Such equipment often includes software and connecting cables to link with a personal computer, allowing you to plot trends and store other information.

To avoid stressing the fishes, always adjust the water temperature very slowly and gradually, particularly if you are lowering it. Fishes are less tolerant of a sudden drop in temperature than they are of a rise, and such adjustments could trigger a disease problem. Allow time to elapse between each small adjustment before rechecking the temperature and making any further changes. Once the water has reached the required temperature, a relatively small amount of electricity is needed to maintain it at that level. The larger the aquarium is, the slower the rate of heat loss from it.

Any type of heater must be able to maintain the desired water temperature without having to run constantly; for example, in a 136-litre (30-gallon) aquarium in a normally heated room you should allow 2 watts per litre of heating (about 10 watts per gallon). Most aquarium heaters are manufactured in standard ratings, usually in steps of 50 or 100 watts. If you are using heaters inside the tank, it is more efficient to split the total heat requirements between two heaterstat units positioned at opposite ends of the tank. This will help maintain an even temperature distribution throughout the aquarium. It will also safeguard against sudden drops in temperature if one heater fails, as it is less likely that two will malfunction at the same time.

Below: *Various types of thermometers are available for aquarium use, including easy-to-read liquid crystal types that stick to the outside surface of the tank. A digital model is shown being used on page 119.*

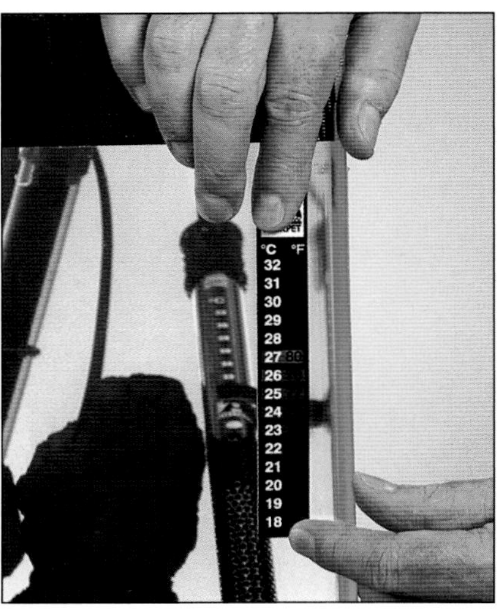

Some external thermostats are fitted to the aquarium with metal clips. Remember the dire warnings about the dangers of metal in contact with saltwater and the resulting toxic effect on aquarium inhabitants, so make sure all fastening clips are waterproof. Better still, use the more advanced microchip thermostats that can be placed anywhere within reach of the aquarium because they operate with a remote sensing probe.

To conserve heat and reduce costs, particularly in cold climates, you can insulate the room where the aquarium is situated, or even the tank itself. Heat rises in water, as it does in air, so fitting a condensation tray over the tank (even a 'double-glazed' one) will go a long way to reduce heat loss through the top of the tank. Of course an aquarium hood will help even further.

Cooling the water

In some situations, particularly in tropical countries, it may prove necessary to cool down your marine aquarium. This could be particularly important if you want to keep live corals, which do not do well in prolonged higher-than-normal temperatures. Water pumps and lighting produce heat and could take temperatures too high. In such cases you will need to install a chilling unit into the system. There are a number of such devices on the market for various applications, but it is far better to invest in one designed and manufactured for marine aquariums. These chillers are never cheap; do not be tempted to risk an undersized unit in order to save money, because you will discover that this can be a false economy. Consult your dealer or the manufacturer to make sure you obtain the correct size and type of chiller for your system.

Lighting the Aquarium

Not surprisingly, sunlight is more intense on a coral reef than over a tropical jungle river, where vegetation and debris dredged up in the water flow filter out much of the light. It therefore follows that the lighting requirements of an anemone or leather coral are very different from those of an Amazonian discus fish or Asian *Aponogeton* plant.

Lighting in a fish-only aquarium is really down to personal taste. Two fluorescent tubes will usually suffice, with perhaps a third, blue lamp for night viewing. However, if there are invertebrates in the tank, lighting becomes far more important. Many corals, anemones and molluscs rely on algae known as zooxanthellae for food. As well as good water quality, the main requirement of zooxanthellae and macro-algae, such as *Caulerpa*, is high-intensity light at the correct wavelength. In fish-only systems with relatively low light intensities, zooxanthellae will not grow. In a reef aquarium, the correct lighting is therefore of paramount importance and this usually means using metal-halide lamps.

There are two key elements that together contribute to the suitability of a particular tube or lamp for a given marine aquarium setup. Understanding these factors will help you to choose the best lighting system for a fish-only tank or a reef aquarium with invertebrates.

Light intensity

There is a common misconception that the intensity of aquarium lighting is measured in watts, whereas in fact wattage is the amount of power required to make a lamp work and is standard amongst most fluorescent tubes. For example, a 60cm (24in) tube is usually 18-20 watts, a 120cm (48in) tube is usually 36-40 watts, etc.

So if the power into a lamp is measured in watts, how do we refer to the intensity, or brightness, of a light source? The answer is in 'lumens', which are measured with a lumen meter. You may also see light intensity quoted in terms of lux – the number of lumens falling onto each square metre of surface.

The intensity of a lamp is usually indicated on the packaging. Most fluorescent tubes rarely exceed 5,000-6,000 lumens, and some are far lower. On the other hand, metal-

Below: *This stunning aquarium recreates a reef gorge, penetrated by a sparkling shaft of sunlight. The right lighting not only benefits the animals, but also enhances the overall display.*

Above: *Shining a beam of white light into a glass prism produces a very clear spectrum of colours, from violet, through blue, green, yellow to red. The prism literally 'splits' the beam to reveal the colours that make it up.*

Light intensity

Sunlight over a reef
The average recorded sunlight over a reef is 20,000 lux at a depth of 10-15m (33-50ft).

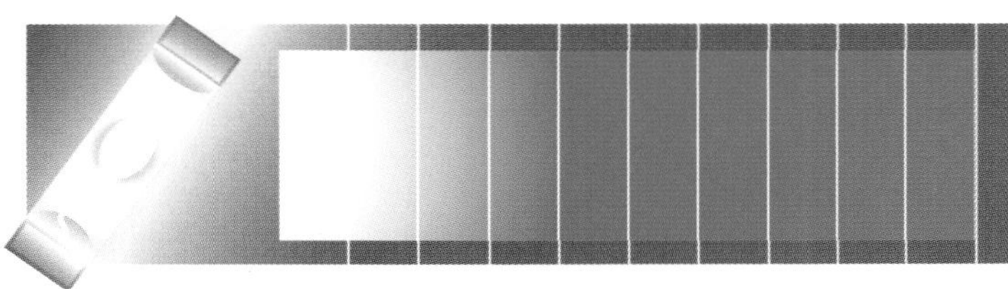

Metal-halide lamps
A 150-watt metal-halide lamp produces 10,000 lumens.

Fluorescent tubes
A 25-watt white triphosphor tube produces about 1,600 lumens.

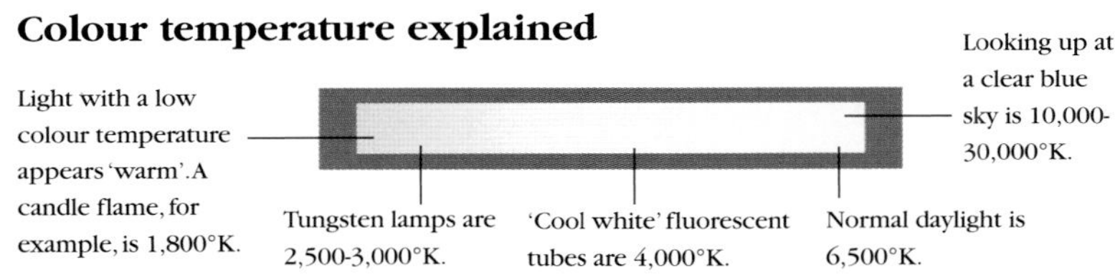

halide lamps commonly emit in excess of 10,000 lumens, so it is easy to see that you would need many fluorescent tubes to replicate a three-lamp metal-halide unit.

Light intensity also depends on the efficiency of the lamp and it is difficult to achieve high levels of light intensity with fluorescent tubes. This is especially true in deeper tanks, where the light from most tubes fades very quickly. However bright any type of lamp may be, if it cannot penetrate through the upper water layers of an aquarium and provide the correct intensity for reef animals it is obviously of little use in a reef aquarium. A lux meter can measure whether clams, corals and other light-sensitive invertebrates are receiving the correct intensity of light, giving a reading of the light intensity at a particular point in the aquarium. If you buy a good-quality aquarium tube or lamp, the manufacturer will have done the hard work for you.

Another factor to bear in mind is that without sufficiently high light intensity, the marine aquarium may attract low-light algae, such as dark green and red varieties, that can smother corals and inhibit the

Colour temperature explained

Light with a low colour temperature appears 'warm'. A candle flame, for example, is 1,800°K.

Tungsten lamps are 2,500-3,000°K.

'Cool white' fluorescent tubes are 4,000°K.

Normal daylight is 6,500°K.

Looking up at a clear blue sky is 10,000-30,000°K.

Sunlight over the reef

Normal daylight measured at the water surface has a colour temperature of about 6,500°K.

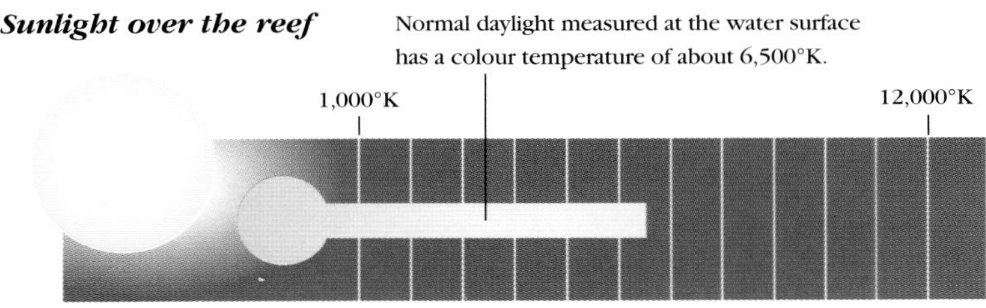

Metal-halide lamps

These can produce light with a colour temperature of 10,000°K and even higher.

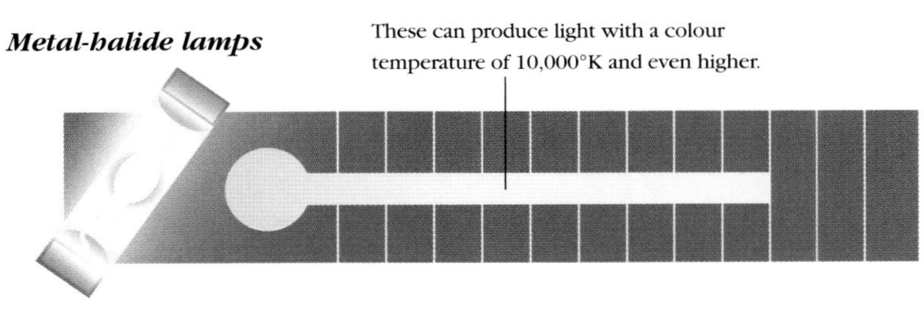

Fluorescent tubes

A white triphosphor fluorescent tube produces light with a colour temperature of about 9,500°K.

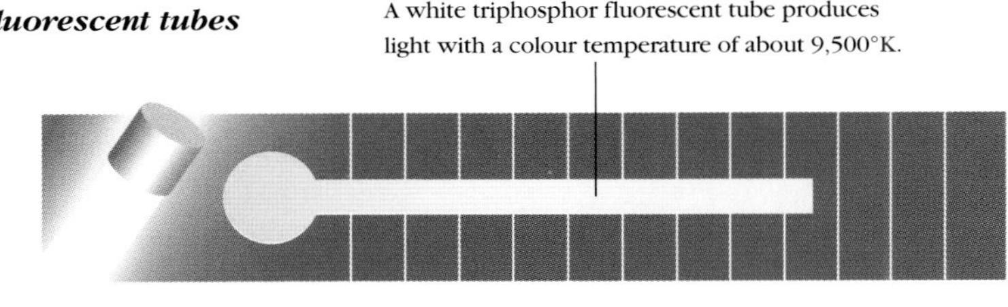

How light is lost in the aquarium

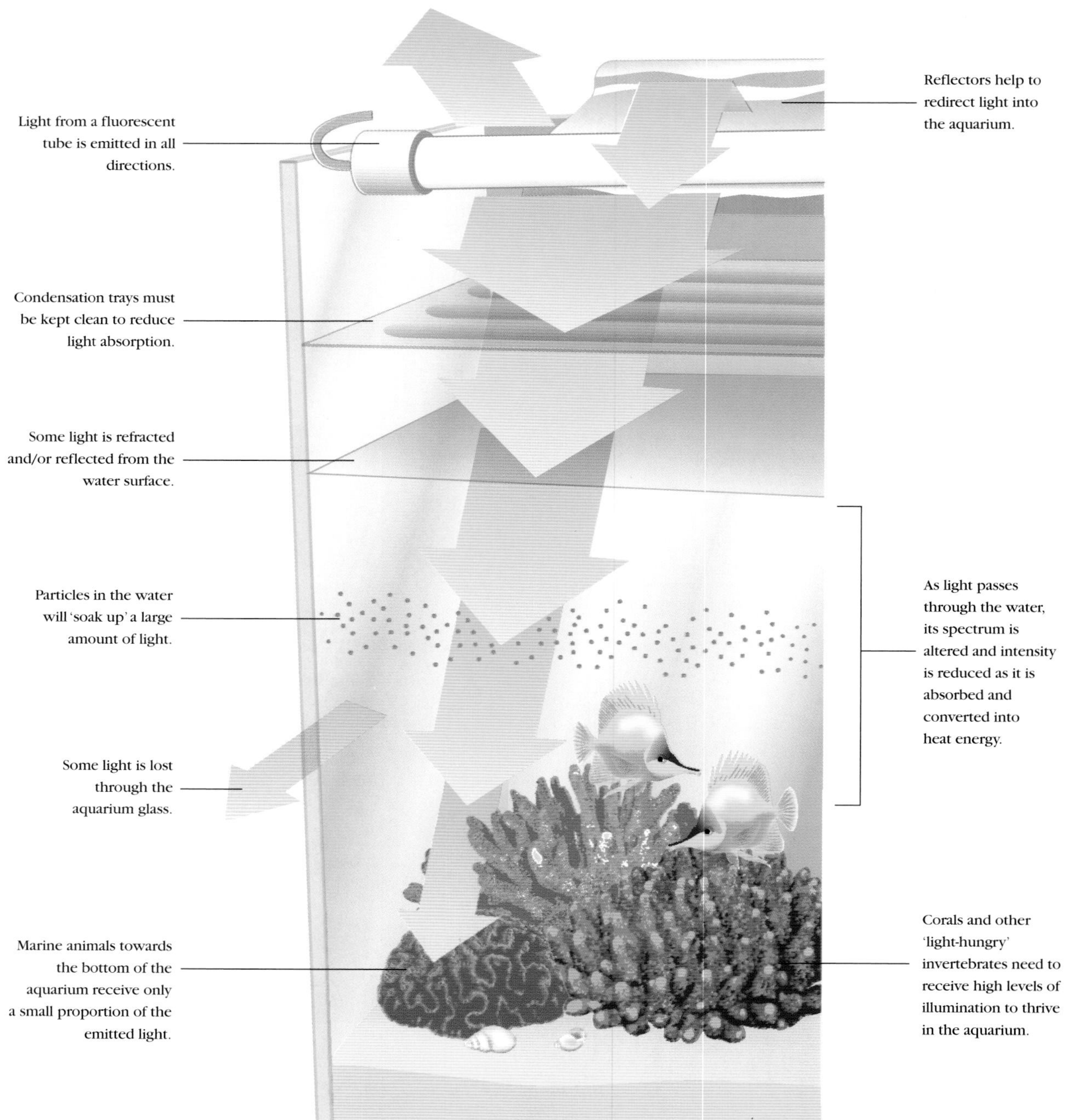

growth of zooxanthellae. Furthermore, not only do you need enough light output, it must also be of the correct 'colour'.

Colour temperature

Any type of lamp, whether metal-halide or fluorescent, appears to give off light in a particular colour. In fact, the colour we perceive is made up of many different colours, each with their own spectral wavelengths. This is called the 'colour temperature' of the lamp and is measured in degrees Kelvin (°K). The higher the Kelvin rating, the more white and 'cool' the light appears. A low Kelvin rating produces a 'warm' appearance, usually predominantly red or yellow, but why should this be and why is it vital to understand?

As we see in a rainbow, light is made up of a spectrum of colours ranging from violet to red. Seawater is an efficient light filter, and different colours are filtered out at different depths. The first to go is red light, which penetrates only the very upper layers of the reef. This is followed by orange and yellow, both of which are also filtered out in the upper layers of the water. The most penetrative light colours are green and blue. This is why many fish that appear bright red in an aquarium, and are easy prey in shallow water, are actually rendered almost black in deeper water, as

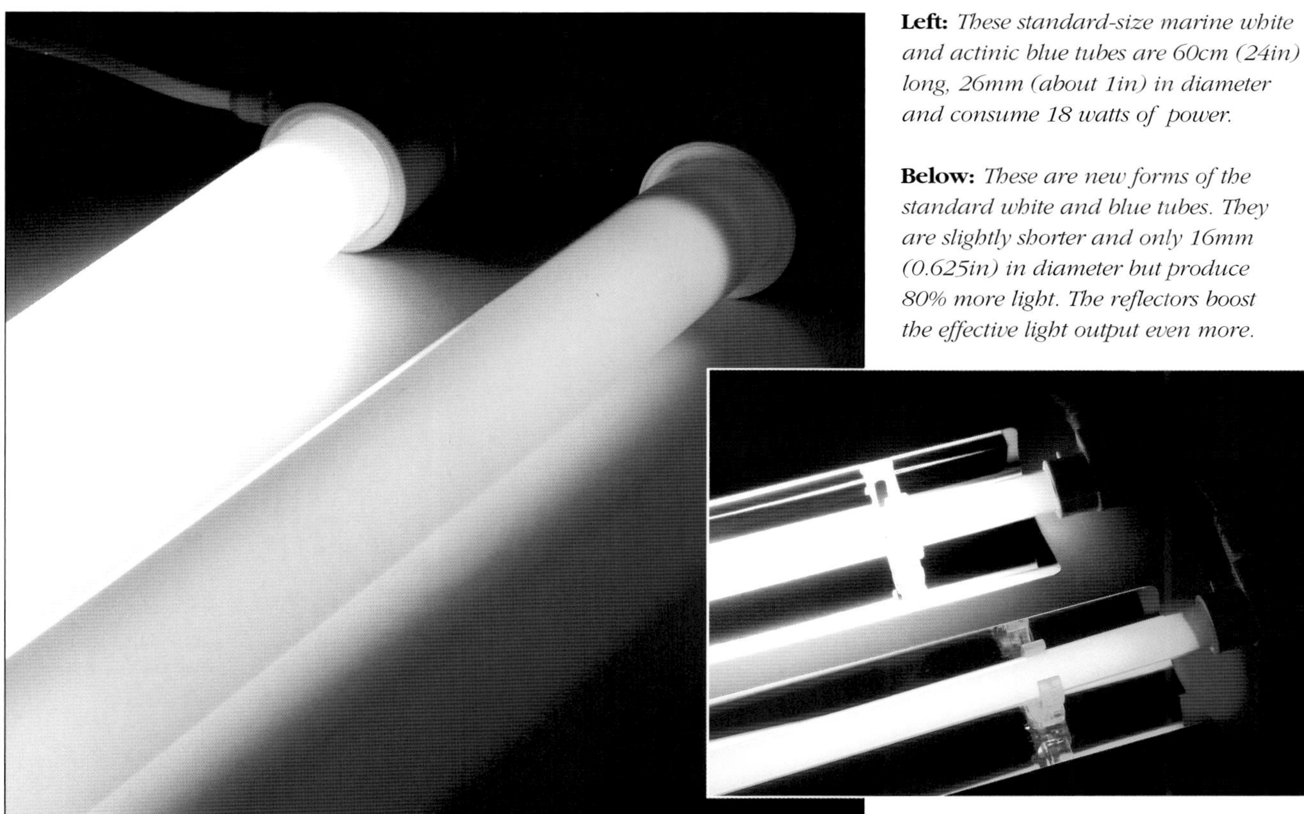

Left: *These standard-size marine white and actinic blue tubes are 60cm (24in) long, 26mm (about 1in) in diameter and consume 18 watts of power.*

Below: *These are new forms of the standard white and blue tubes. They are slightly shorter and only 16mm (0.625in) in diameter but produce 80% more light. The reflectors boost the effective light output even more.*

anyone who has dived off a reef will have noticed. For example, a fire shrimp that is bought for its vivid red coloration in the aquarium, actually blends into the dark background in its natural reef environment.

The output of the various wavelengths of light (and therefore the strength of light in the different colour 'bands') produced by a lamp is also referred to as its spectral power distribution. You will usually see coloured graphs and diagrams on lamp packaging to reflect this.

Fluorescent lighting

The fishkeeping hobby has come a long way since the early days, when tungsten (incandescent) lighting was the norm. The first fluorescent lamps were not designed with the fishkeeper in mind; more often than not they originated from office lighting or, as in the case of Gro-Lux tubes, from the horticulture industry.

The first major breakthrough in fluorescent lighting for aquariums came with the advent of the triphosphor lamp, which concentrates its light output in the

Spectral power distributions

Light is made up of many wavelengths and the balance of these produced by a light source affects its overall 'colour'. It is possible to measure which wavelengths are present and at what strengths. This is called its spectral power distribution. The graphs shown below compare the output of two light sources set against the sun's complete spectrum. Wavelengths are in nanometres (nm) – billionths of a metre – and the vertical scale reflects comparative output at points along the spectrum.

White triphosphor fluorescent tube

These spectral output curves show that this type of fluorescent tube produces useful levels of light at a wide range of wavelengths, providing bright illumination for all creatures in the aquarium.

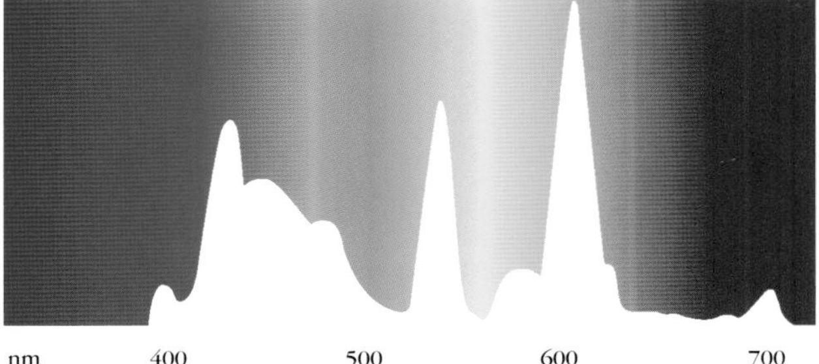

Blue actinic 03 fluorescent tube

This tube is 'strong' in the blue area of the spectrum, especially in the so-called 'actinic' range peaking at 420nm, which is vital for zooxanthellae to thrive. It also supplies some UV for a fluorescent effect.

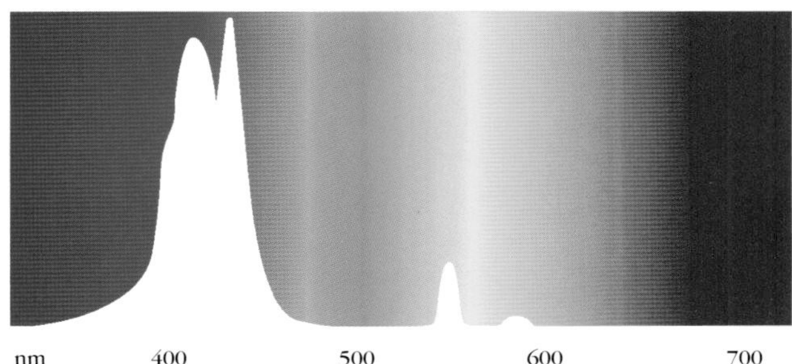

Above: *A metal-halide unit suitable for a marine aquarium. The 150-watt lamp produces an intense light at 14,000°K to simulate a tropical reef.*

Metal-halide lamp

Metal-halide lamps generate a wide output with high levels at 400-480nm (good for zooxanthellae) and 550nm (to simulate sunlight).The volume of the curves in the spectral output shown below indicates a bright lamp.

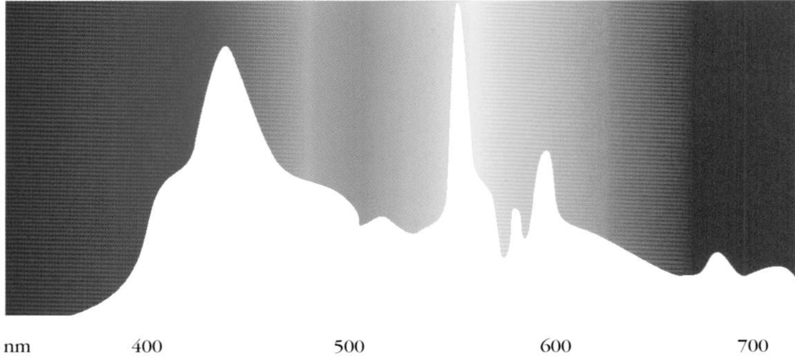

key areas of the spectrum essential for invertebrate and macro-algae growth. The spectral distribution of the lamp allows for the fact that various colours are filtered out at varying rates in seawater and compensates accordingly.

Furthermore, the lamp retains its spectral qualities until the end of its life. This is particularly important if you are using fluorescents for invertebrate aquariums, as most lamps lose part of their spectrum over a short period of time, while still emitting light. To the human eye they do not appear to have changed at all, but the deteriorating health of any corals in the aquarium often indicates a reduction in the effectiveness of the lamp.

In addition to using triphosphor tubes, many aquarists use blue ones designed specifically for night viewing. Actinic blue tubes (which may be more expensive) produce ultraviolet light, essential to many types of invertebrate, as well as an attractive blue colour for night viewing. When selecting actinic tubes, be sure to buy the 03 type, which gives off a more suitable wavelength than the similar 05 actinic tube.

The efficiency of fluorescent tubes can be greatly enhanced by using polished aluminium reflectors in the hood of the aquarium. They reflect light from the rear and top of the lid back towards the tank, increasing the effectiveness of a light by up to 50%.

Metal-halide lighting

There have been significant advances in our understanding of the light intensities and colour spectrums required by corals, and it is widely accepted now that metal-halide lamps are essential in order to maintain many coral species.

Unlike fluorescent tubes, metal-halide lamps offer a range of high-intensity outputs with hardly any size difference. The most common halide lamps are 150 watts and 250 watts, although 400-watt lamps are now available for very deep aquariums.

In addition to the high-intensity output they afford, metal-halide lamps are now available at Kelvin temperatures far better suited to the reef aquarium than used to be the case. It is now common practice to use lighting with a temperature of between 10,000 and 14,000°K. These high-Kelvin lamps create a beautiful rippling effect in the aquarium and greatly enhance the appearance of the inhabitants, as well as supplying the correct light needs for zooxanthellae to flourish.

Metal-halide lamps are usually suspended from the ceiling or a wall bracket, at least 30cm (12in) from the water surface in the aquarium, as they give off a tremendous amount of heat. The other disadvantage is their high cost, although the price of lamps and units is falling all the time.

Before you decide to keep hard corals, clams and other invertebrates that require high light levels, assess whether you are prepared to invest in the correct lighting. If the answer is 'no' then consider keeping a fish-only aquarium until funds are available to buy a metal-halide lighting system. Never buy delicate corals without having the correct lighting in place to maintain them and allow them to grow.

The photoperiod

The final piece in the lighting jigsaw is the length of time the lighting is left on, known as the 'photoperiod'. There are no hard and fast rules about this, as every aquarium differs slightly in its requirements. Once again, the best way is to learn from nature and try to replicate life on the reef in your aquarium.

Left: *This small reef aquarium benefits from the illumination provided by two lamps suspended above it. The light has encouraged a mangrove plant to grow and spread its leaves above the water.*

Around the equator, the period of sunlight is about 12 hours each day, whereas in tropical latitudes (up to about 20° north and south of the Equator), full sunlight is only experienced between about 9am to 3pm (i.e. six hours). As a starting point, if you are using fluorescent tubes, try setting your lighting period to about 12 hours. A blue lamp or one of the less bright lamps should come on one to two hours before the main lighting and go off one to two hours after it has been turned off. This will create a rudimentary feeling of dusk and dawn and avoids stressing nervous fish in the aquarium.

If you are using metal-halide lamps, try starting with a photoperiod of about eight hours, again with blue lamps that come on before the main lights and remain on after the halides have been turned off for the day.

The latest and most sophisticated artificial lighting combines metal-halide with fluorescent lighting units. It includes a programmable timer and a special 'moonlight' lamp that matches the cycle of the moon.

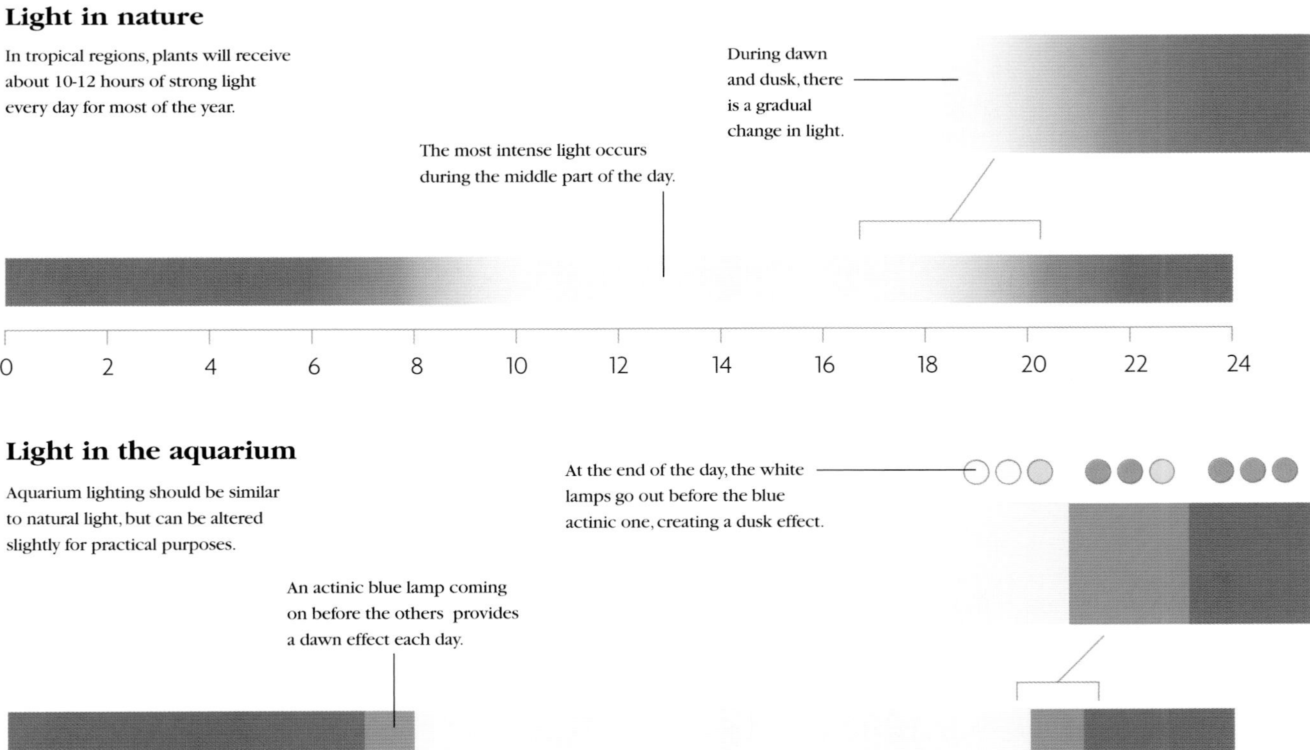

Water - Simulating the Real Thing

A shroud of mystery has surrounded marine fishkeeping as a hobby ever since it began. Many people are still fearful of attempting what, to them, appears to be nigh impossible, and the main problem seems to be maintaining the necessary water quality. To quote Stephen Spotte, one of the leading exponents of water management techniques, success depends on 'how well you control the inevitable changes taking place in seawater ....the water, you see, is everything. It's as simple as that'. You can deduce from this that we are waterkeepers as much as fishkeepers. In fact, you could almost say that if the water is well looked after, the fishes will look after themselves.

The composition of seawater

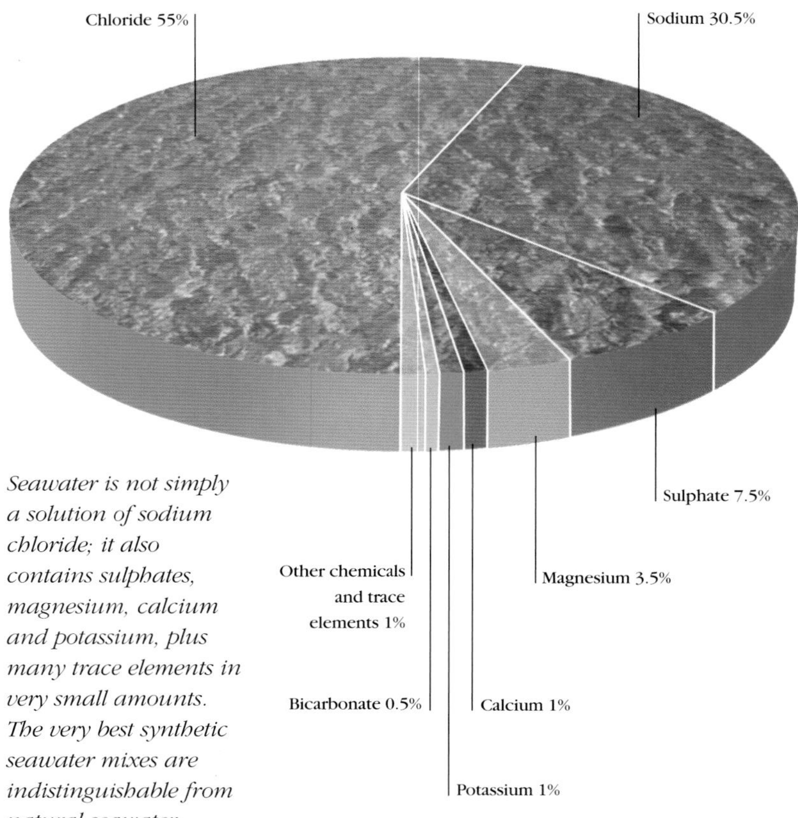

Seawater is not simply a solution of sodium chloride; it also contains sulphates, magnesium, calcium and potassium, plus many trace elements in very small amounts. The very best synthetic seawater mixes are indistinguishable from natural seawater.

Natural seawater

As 71% of the Earth's surface is covered by seawater, you might expect it to be one of the most convenient commodities to obtain. Unfortunately, it is not often suitable for the domestic marine aquarium, for several reasons.

For most aquarists it is totally impractical to make regular trips to the coast to collect and transport large quantities of natural seawater. Secondly, relatively few marine aquarists have the luxury of living in the tropics and being able to collect local water. For most, collecting cooler local water and converting it to 'tropical water' can present a number of problems. Warming up natural seawater could cause plankton either to die off, creating potentially toxic conditions, or rapidly multiply and use up vital oxygen. In addition, coral reef fishes are unlikely to have the natural means to fight off disease pathogens that occur in water from other parts of the world. Should you wish to establish an aquarium to house fishes from your local shores, then it is acceptable, but not always convenient, to use seawater from the same locality.

Another important point to consider is the difficulty of finding a source of unpolluted natural water. The increasing volume of seagoing commercial traffic and effluent from industrial activity around the world means that coastal waters are not likely to be entirely pure, to say the least!

It is clear from this that using natural seawater in a home aquarium can generally create more problems than it is worth.

Synthetic seawater

The best way of providing suitable water for the marine aquarium is to use an artificial mix that is carefully balanced and combined with good quality tapwater so that the final composition approximates as closely as possible to natural seawater. These commercially available mixes of dry salts, minerals and essential trace elements are sterile and should be manufactured from scientific-grade materials, so that there is no risk of inadvertently introducing diseases and other problems into the aquarium. Also, because you only purchase the dry mix and add it to freshwater when needed, it is very convenient in terms of carrying and storing.

Modern mixes are so exact in their formula and manufacturing process that you no longer need to use up an entire package at once in order to produce a given volume of water with the desired specific gravity (or density) and correct chemical composition. These days you can use up part of a package and still be sure of obtaining the correct chemical composition regardless of what specific gravity you wish to attain. (Reseal partly used bags and store in a cool, dry

Above: *These sea whips and seafans are thriving in clean, unpolluted water. You are unlikely to have access to a supply of such pure water and are best using a synthetic alternative.*

place.) This offers a great deal of flexibility and is an ideal solution for preparing small amounts of seawater for partial water changes. This is the medium your fishes and invertebrates have to live in, so quality is essential.

Below: *Seawater contains a high level of dissolved salts, and marine life is adapted to thrive in this salty environment. Keeping marine creatures successfully in an aquarium is made easier today by using synthetic mixes that reflect the natural balance of the sea.*

Preparing synthetic seawater

To start with, you must carefully follow the manufacturer's directions. It is best to prepare the synthetic seawater in advance of setting up the aquarium so that it is ready to use. It is very important that the salts have dissolved fully before use to avoid ending up with an incorrect specific gravity. You may find the dissolve time differs from one brand to another, but in any case, you must keep regular checks on the specific gravity by using a marine aquarium hydrometer throughout the operation. It is always best, and quicker, to dissolve smaller amounts of the salt mix at a time, rather than a large heap, and to provide strong aeration. During the initial setting up, you can carry out the mixing directly in the aquarium, as there will be no animals in it, of course. However, all subsequent mixes will have to be prepared in a separate container. As always, ensure that the receptacle in which you mix the salt is made from non-corrodible materials.

The following guidelines will help you achieve the best results.

1 It is normal for water authorities to treat domestic tapwater in order to make it safe for humans. Unfortunately, the chemicals used are not safe for aquatic animals. Chloramines are commonly used for this purpose. The more traditional use of chlorine was relatively easy to deal with, as vigorous aeration would dissipate it into the atmosphere. This is not so easy with chloramines. Fortunately, on the other hand, aquarium treatments are now available to remove these and help make tapwater safe.

In some areas there is a risk of fertilizers, such as phosphates and nitrates, getting into water supplies from farms, particularly after heavy rainstorms. Water authorities usually do their best to deal with this problem, but there is evidence that some quantities do get into the system. Also, many cities still have lead piping in their water supply systems, so phosphorous is added to stabilize the lead. All these chemicals are undesirable in the aquarium because, being fertilizers, they are very effective at promoting undesirable hair algae and certain slime bacteria.

If you are unlucky and find these harmful chemicals in your water supply, then you will have to invest in nitrate- and phosphate-removing resins, or a reverse osmosis unit, which will filter out, albeit very slowly, a wide variety of chemicals and minerals. Activated carbon is also useful for removing chlorine and several other chemicals from water. Of course, all tapwater must be treated before it is used to make synthetic seawater, whether it is for a complete fill or just for topping up with freshwater after evaporation loss, once the aquarium is fully functional.

2 As already stressed, only use glass, plastic or other non-metallic containers for preparing seawater. Polythene or polypropylene containers made for use with food or home brewing are good, but beware of any made from recycled plastics, such as refuse bins, as these may release harmful toxins.

Fill the container with the required amount of water and mark a line on the outside to indicate the depth of water. This will help you be accurate when making further mixes in the future, and save time.

3 Ideally, make up the seawater 24-48 hours in advance to allow for complete dissolving. Add the dry salt mixture to the water a small amount at a time, apply vigorous aeration and keep a regular check on the specific gravity. The salts usually dissolve better in warm water and, as marine aquarium hydrometers are calibrated for use at around 75°F (24°C) water temperature, you will be more accurate if you can place an aquarium heater into the mixing container. This also means the water will be at the correct temperature when it is added to the aquarium.

Below: *The correct specific gravity (S.G.) is indicated when the chosen value coincides with the miniscus (water surface level). It is easy to see in the coloured section on the stem.*

4 Once you have the mixed water in the aquarium, turn on pumps, filters and heaters to ensure a thorough mix at the desired temperature. After a few hours, make a final specific gravity test. If all is correct, leave the aquarium running to continue maturing before introducing any livestock.

5 It is very difficult to assess the exact volume of water in an aquarium that is already furnished with rocks and other forms of habitat, so measure the amount of water used when filling the aquarium for the first time and make a note of it for future reference. This information may one day be very useful in calculating, for example, the exact amount of medication required to treat a disease outbreak.

Specific gravity

You will have noticed the term 'specific gravity' mentioned several times already. To clarify, it is simply the ratio of the density of any liquid compared to that of distilled water, which has a specific gravity of 1. Seawater is greater in density and contains far more dissolved minerals, so its specific gravity (S.G.) is higher than 1. (The concentration of total solids dissolved in a specified amount of water can also be expressed in terms of salinity, i.e. grams/litre. The table shows the relationship between specific gravity and salinity.)

The salinity of seawater varies from one location to another. For instance, the Red Sea is more saline than the open ocean because it is non-tidal and has a high rate of evaporation. The Dead Sea is the most extreme example, as it has the highest salinity of any sea anywhere in the world and no fishes can live in it at all.

The salinity/specific gravity of water has an effect on the fishes living in it, and here we come to one of the fundamental differences between freshwater and seawater fishes in terms of their basic biology.

Osmoregulation in marine fishes

As part of their regulation of osmotic balance, marine fish must drink water to replace that lost from the body. This creates a salt overload that must be eliminated via the kidneys and gills.

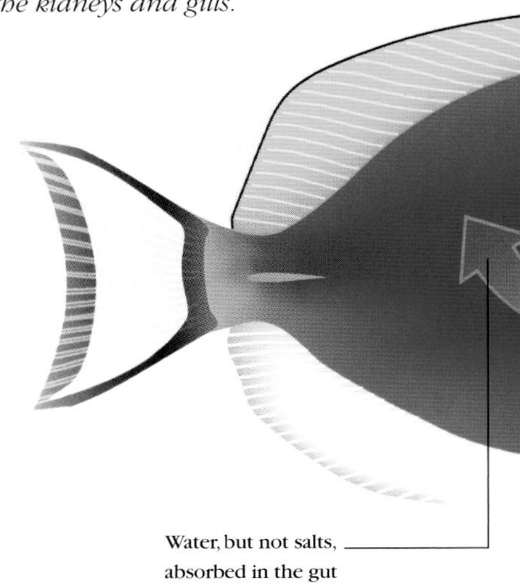

S.G. and salinity

Specific gravity varies with temperature. When mixing salt, always take the water temperature into account; the warmer the water in the aquarium, the more salt will be required.

15°C	Salinity	25°C
1.022	30 gm/l	1.020
1.023	32 gm/l	1.022
1.025	34 gm/l	1.023
1.027	36 gm/l	1.025

Osmoregulation in freshwater fishes

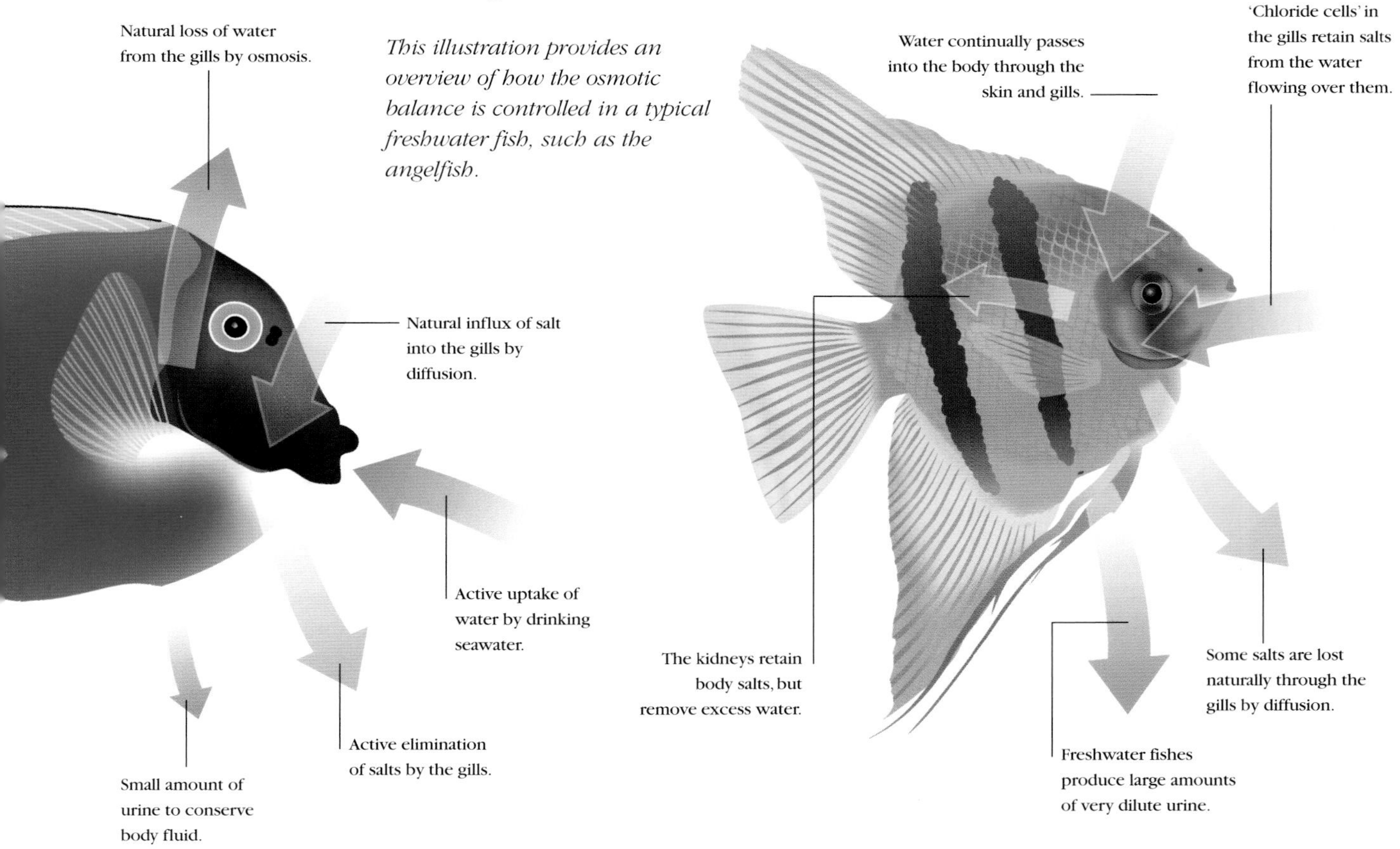

This illustration provides an overview of how the osmotic balance is controlled in a typical freshwater fish, such as the angelfish.

Natural loss of water from the gills by osmosis.

Natural influx of salt into the gills by diffusion.

Active uptake of water by drinking seawater.

Active elimination of salts by the gills.

Small amount of urine to conserve body fluid.

Water continually passes into the body through the skin and gills.

'Chloride cells' in the gills retain salts from the water flowing over them.

The kidneys retain body salts, but remove excess water.

Some salts are lost naturally through the gills by diffusion.

Freshwater fishes produce large amounts of very dilute urine.

A freshwater fish is surrounded by water that is less dense than its body fluids. Due to a phenomenon known as osmosis, water is absorbed into the body and the fish must excrete water constantly so that it does not burst. The marine fish faces the opposite situation, in that it constantly loses water to its surroundings and must therefore drink copious amounts of water and excrete only salts.

Variations of S.G. can occur in the aquarium as a result of evaporation. Only pure water is lost during this process, so evaporation losses must only be made good with freshwater and not a prepared salt mix. To top up evaporation loss with saltwater will result in the aquarium water becoming progressively more dense, and dangerously so if this incorrect practice is continued on a regular basis. Cover glasses over the tank (or condensation trays) will prevent water loss through evaporation, as well as helping to conserve heat.

The control of salinity can be utilized as an aid to disease prevention. Many disease pathogens, particularly external crustaceans and protozoans, cannot survive in low salinities and it has become common practice to maintain marine aquariums at a specific gravity of 1.022, and in some cases as low as 1.018. Most fishes can tolerate these levels and actually seem to benefit from them because of less demanding osmotic pressure. However, many invertebrates will not do well below 1.022. If you think about it, the crustaceans you keep as tank subjects are close relatives of the crustacean parasites you are trying to prevent by reducing the salinity, so it stands to reason a low specific gravity will not be to their liking.

The pH of water

The pH of water is a measure of its acidity or alkalinity. It is measured on a logarithmic scale; values below 7 are acidic while values above 7

Above: *Tapwater is treated with chemicals such as chloramine to make it safe for drinking. These are harmful to marine creatures and should be removed.*

are alkaline (7 being the neutral value). Seawater has a higher pH than most freshwater and domestic tapwater and should be maintained at 8.3. If you are keeping a temperate marine aquarium, then 7.9 is acceptable in many cases. A falling pH usually indicates an increase in carbon dioxide production because of a build-up of organic debris over time, and that the water's buffering capabilities (its ability to resist pH changes) is declining. Regular tank maintenance and partial water changes will go a long way to keeping the pH stable.

Sudden changes in pH are dangerous to fishes and many invertebrates, especially if the trend is upwards. In most cases it is the change in pH that fishes experience when they are moved from one aquarium to another without sufficient time to acclimatize that causes severe stress and often death. When introducing a new fish, it is vital to check the pH of both the water the fish is in and the water it is being moved into and, if necessary, make several checks in between until equalization has been achieved.

Monitoring water quality

Coral reefs are amongst the cleanest and most stable environments in the world and the fishes and invertebrates that live on them thrive on it accordingly. It follows that these same animals are naturally intolerant of environmental change and poor water quality. The environmental pressures on the relatively small body of water contained within an aquarium are enormous and perfect conditions are difficult to maintain without care and dedication. In the main this is because stocking levels are higher pro rata than found in the wild and the resulting metabolic waste matter has a profound impact on water quality. Consequently, elaborate filtration systems have been developed over the years to help maintain the kind of water quality that coral reef organisms would experience in nature.

Regular monitoring of water quality is essential. This is particularly so when the aquarium is first established, because the various initial biological processes are very unstable, making conditions impossible to support fishes and other marine animals. A clear understanding of the nitrogen cycle is essential here. In simple terms, this naturally occurring process involves the breakdown of the extremely poisonous metabolic by-product ammonia (NH_3) into less dangerous but still toxic nitrite (NO_2), which in turn is broken down into relatively harmless nitrate (NO_3). In the natural environment, nitrate is absorbed by plants as a primary nutrient and incorporated

How pH is measured

Water (H_2O) is made up of positively charged hydrogen ions (H^+) and negatively charged hydroxyl ions (OH^-). The pH level is a measure of the ratio of these two ions in a body of water. Acidic water has more hydrogen ions; alkaline water more hydroxyl ions. Neutral water has an equal number of both.

Water molecule

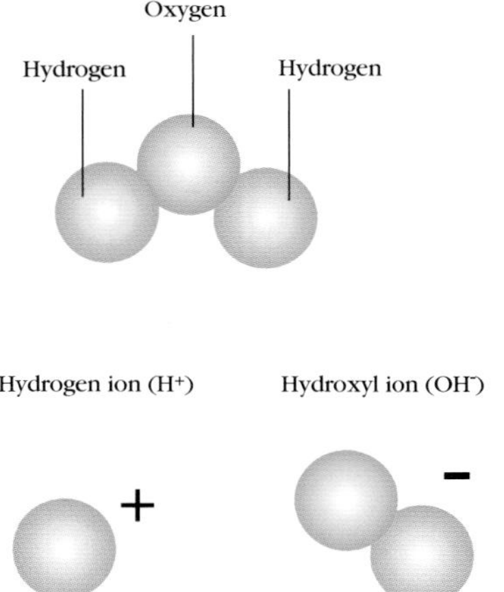

The pH scale is logarithmic, meaning that each unit change in pH, say from 7 to 8, is a ten times change. A change of two units from 7 to 9 is a hundred times change, and from 7 to 10 reflects a thousand times change. This is why a sudden change in pH is very stressful and harmful to fish.

pH 9: 100 times more alkaline than pH 7.

pH 8: 10 times more alkaline that pH 7.

pH 7: neutral.

Left: *Test the water regularly to monitor the pH level, which in a marine tank should remain fairly stable. Some tests involve adding chemicals to a measured sample and comparing the colour change to a printed chart.*

Right: *The final stage of testing the pH, showing a correct reading of between 8.0 and 8.4. When you compare the sample colour against the card, follow the directions; not all tests are the same.*

Nitrate poisoning

Nitrate and other related toxic build-ups are generally observed in the following symptoms. (Of course, many of these symptoms could be attributable to other causes, but if these have been eliminated, consider the possibility of nitrate poisoning.)

In fish Loss of appetite, general deterioration in condition, susceptibility to disease, loss of colour and vitality, unusual changes in behaviour, death through no obvious cause.

In coral invertebrates Unwillingness to display full potential, inability to attach to rocks, unusual discharges, general 'shrinking', untimely death.

In crustaceans Loss of appetite, changes in behavioural patterns, inability to shed exoskeleton, sudden death.

Above: *Tooth Corals are highly sensitive to nitrate.*

into plant tissue. This is eaten by herbivorous animals that are themselves eaten by carnivorous animals. And so this conversion cycle of nitrogen-containing compounds keeps turning. (See page 93 for details of the nitrogen cycle and biological filtration.)

So, in addition to regularly measuring pH and specific gravity, you should be keeping a close check on ammonia, nitrite and, to a lesser degree, nitrate levels in your aquarium. Nutrients in the water supply from agriculture can also be monitored. Although these nutrients, such as phosphates and nitrates, naturally occur in minute quantities in seawater, excessive amounts are definitely unwelcome. Testing the alkalinity will provide an indication of your water's buffering capabilities. All these tests will help you evaluate the efficiency of your filtration system and to determine your schedule for carrying out partial water changes. In addition, the regular measurement of dissolved oxygen will be very useful, especially as an indicator to whether you are overstocking your aquarium with livestock.

Outside of essential monitoring, there are also tests available for other reasons. For example, should you decide to use ozone in your system, it will be useful to test for residual ozone and for redox potential (see page 102 for more details). Another example is testing for copper in your aquarium water when using it as a treatment for certain parasitic infections. It is important to maintain the correct level throughout the course of treatment and, as it is difficult to calculate the volume of water in a furnished tank accurately, using a test kit will allow you to determine the correct dosage without knowing that volume.

Water testing is a vital part of good management aimed at keeping aquarium conditions stable. Since modern technology has provided the means to monitor water quality, it would be foolish, and false economy, to ignore these facilities.

Obtaining accurate test results

- Commercial viability has meant that some test kits (e.g. nitrate tests) cannot be 100 percent accurate, so provide for a degree of allowance.
- All reagents are highly toxic; store them safely out of the reach of children and animals.
- Liquid reagents are usually only viable for a limited period of time; discard them after their 'use-by' date.
- Always follow manufacturers' instructions very carefully to achieve the highest possible accuracy. It is particularly important to adhere strictly to standing or development times.
- Record all results in an aquarium log to help give an overall picture and to identify possible longterm problems.
- Always take tests at the same time of day to establish a base from which to compare unusual readings.
- Where possible, use the same manufacturer for all your test kits. They are far more likely to inherit the same characteristics and be easily comparable.
- Be sure that the scales of measurement are clearly marked and have broad ranges where small amounts may make all the difference.
- If a test indicates remedial action, be sure that you understand all the options available and their consequences; drastic actions usually give drastic results – but not always the desired ones!
- Prolong the life of test kits by storing them in a cool, dark place. Colour charts left exposed to light for long periods will fade, leading to inaccurate or impossible comparisons.

Filtration Systems

As we stated right at the outset, the key to successful marine fishkeeping is maintaining good water quality. Here, we look in detail at aquarium filtration systems and how they help to provide healthy conditions for a wide range of marine creatures.

The nitrogen cycle

The nitrogen cycle is an extremely important biological process on the reef – and in all ecosystems, for that matter. It is an important purification system, but it is more than that, because it is also the source of primary food production, without which nothing on earth would survive. Disturbances to this process caused by pollution from human waste and chemicals are putting a serious question mark over the future of our world, because in many places not even the vast exchange of ocean water is capable of diluting these substances.

Below: *The superb reef aquariums often seen in retail outlets are an inspiration to potential marine fishkeepers. But to maintain a display like this successfully, you need a first-class filtration system.*

Likewise, nothing will survive in the marine aquarium without proper utilization of the processes within the nitrogen cycle.

The nitrogen cycle is basically the removal of nitrogenous compounds that gradually build up in the aquarium water, starting with free ammonia (NH_3) and ionized ammonia (NH_4+). Fishes and invertebrates produce ammonia as a waste product from their metabolic processes. This is added to the ammonia produced by bacteria 'working on' other waste materials in the aquarium, such as uneaten food and faeces. Ammonia is highly toxic to fishes and invertebrates; if it is not removed, or converted into other less harmful substances, your aquarium subjects will soon perish. Fortunately, in Nature's Grand Plan, a substance that is poison to one living organism is food for another and, thus, there is a natural way of dealing with ammonia removal.

Aerobic (oxygen-loving) bacteria, such as *Nitrosomonas* species, convert ammonia to nitrite (NO_2), a slightly less toxic substance, but one that is still dangerous to fishes and invertebrates. A second group of bacteria, such as *Nitrobacter* species, transform the nitrite to nitrate (NO_3), which is a much safer substance but one that can still cause some problems if allowed to build up too much. It is not fully understood to what level nitrate can cause problems for aquarium subjects, although it seems to be detrimental to delicate fish species and some invertebrates. The important thing is that nitrate does not occur on the natural coral reef other than in the smallest quantities, so we should not make compromises but strive to keep it to an absolute minimum in the aquarium. Nitrate is a primary nutrient for algae and the mainstay of primary food production right at the beginning of the food chain from which all other living organisms benefit.

It is worth noting that many species of undesirable algae may flourish with the presence of excess nitrates, as well as phosphates.

By the process of denitrification, anaerobic, or oxygen-hating, bacteria convert nitrate into free

How the nitrogen cycle works

The nitrogen cycle is a term applied to the continuous process of the generation and disposal of nitrogenous compounds within the aquarium. The initial wastes are toxic, but are sequentially made safer until they are eventually eliminated from the cycle.

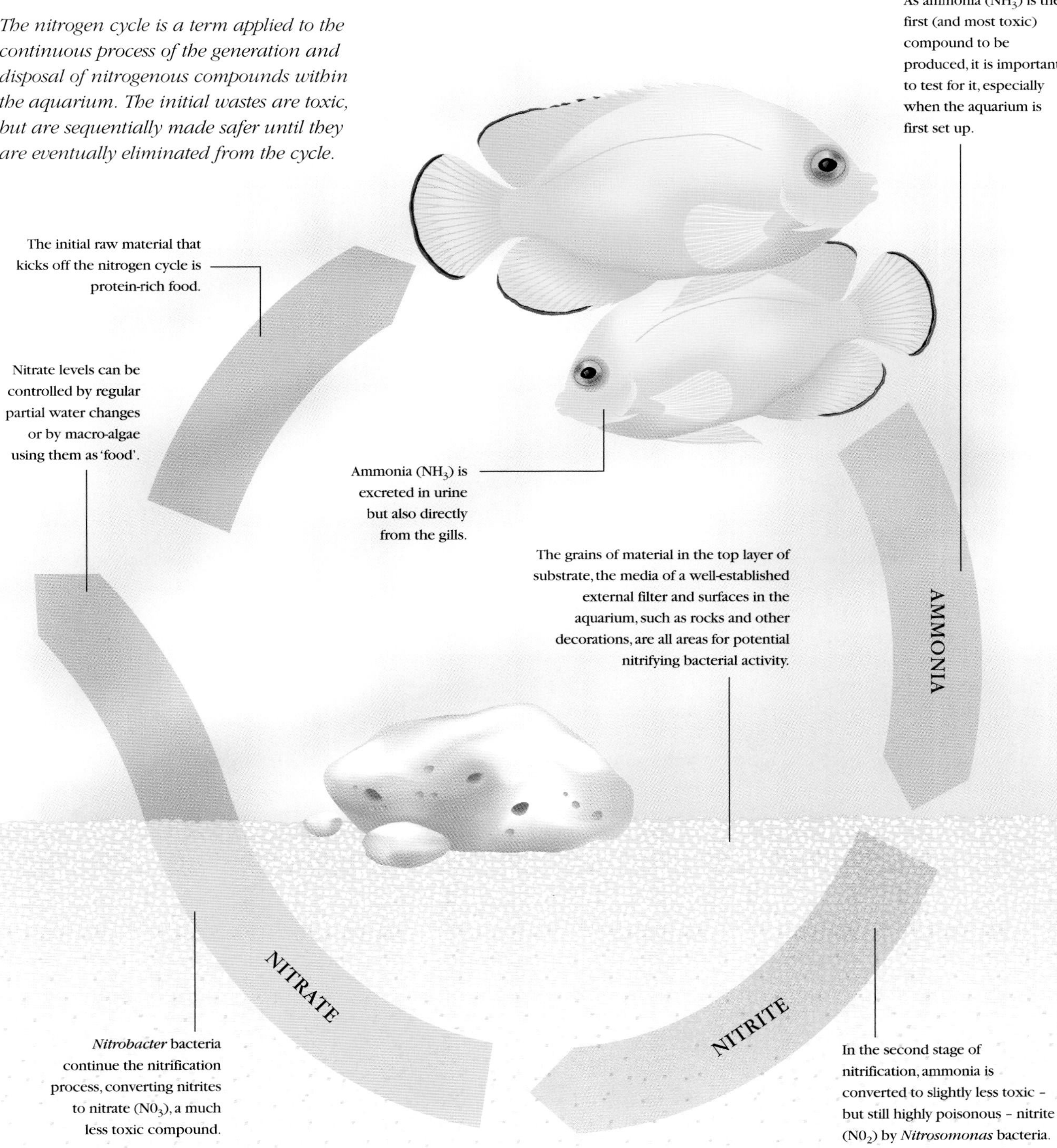

atmospheric nitrogen, which is naturally vented from the aquarium. The conditions that allow this are often found in porous material such as living rock, where pockets of oxygen-deficient water can be trapped, promoting the growth of anaerobic bacteria. The same thing can happen in the bottom levels of substrate, but here the gases can get trapped, including potentially dangerous sulphur (the gas with a pungent smell like bad eggs). However, herein lies a paradox, since if we are to provide ideal conditions for the complete removal of nitrogenous compounds, then it appears we must provide two sets of conditions for opposite types of bacteria to flourish.

Filtration systems

The purpose of the aquarium filtration system is to remove as much 'dirt' from the water as possible. As well as visible dirt and sediments stirred up by the actions of fishes and other tank inhabitants, the water will contain invisible dissolved nitrogenous and other organic compounds (waste products

Simulating nature

Environmental conditions on a healthy coral reef are pristine and extremely stable, which is largely due to the vast expanse of ocean water that dilutes nutrients and organic chemicals. On a more localized level, a number of processes contribute to the general health of the reef and its water quality. Understanding these processes will help you provide the best artificial means of carrying out similar functions in the aquarium and enable you to appreciate the differences between the natural and the captive environment.

It would be great to be able to gather everything from a suitably sized cube of reef and transplant it into a home aquarium, along with all the animals and algae that were living in that space. You might think that this would provide a perfect equilibrium between all the life forms and the biological processes needed to sustain them. Alas, this is not the case – for several reasons.

To begin with, waste materials and other pollutants build up to toxic levels very rapidly in the small volume of water in an aquarium, which is one reason why large systems can be easier to manage. Secondly, a tank does not benefit from the continual water exchange that occurs in nature. Thirdly, the general biological loading in an aquarium far exceeds that found in the equivalent area on the reef. Not only are there more animals present, but also the food levels are much higher. For example, food is generally made available to aquarium subjects once or twice a day in relatively large quantities that create spot loadings, whereas on the reef, a set level is available at all times.

To deal with some aspects of such 'bioloading', aquarists can use similar strategies to those found in nature, but for others purely artificial methods are needed. This panel compares the problems and the solutions in both the natural and captive environment – an interesting analysis for marine fishkeepers.

NATURE

Mechanical filtration Sediments and detritus become trapped in certain areas of the reef structure, where animals will feed on it and break it down to a form that other organisms and bacteria can utilize. Sand plays a very important role in the process of trapping detritus. Sea cucumbers, worms and many other organisms associate themselves with the sand bed environment and feed off the materials that settle there. New sand is continuously created by boring worms and by parrotfishes that bite off chunks of coral rock and grind it up to extract algae. The resulting sand falls to the seabed.

Gaseous exchange Oxygen (O_2) is taken in from the atmosphere at the water surface (or air-to-water interface). Waves help the process by increasing the surface area and allowing more oxygen to be absorbed. Oxygen is distributed through the water column by wave action and currents. Carbon dioxide gas (CO_2) is released into the atmosphere at the air-to-water interface.

Water movement The back and forth swell of the sea combined with currents and countercurrents, creates powerful movement. This is important because it cleanses the reef structure, prevents sediments from settling, particularly on delicate corals, and delivers food to filter-feeding animals.

Biological filtration All solid surfaces throughout the porous structure of the reef provide space for bacteria to colonize. Nitrifying bacteria feed on the ammonia waste (NH_3) from marine organisms and convert it first into nitrite (NO_2) and then into nitrate (NO_3). Denitrifying bacteria convert nitrate into nitrogen gas (N_2). All these bacteria are part of the nitrogen cycle. Huge populations of sponges, sea squirts and clams filter the water directly and contribute greatly to its clarity.

AQUARIUM

Mechanical filtration Most aquariums cannot sustain the level of natural organisms necessary to deal with sediments and other debris. Water must be passed through a suitable filter medium, such as sponge or floss, to filter out fine solid particles.

Gaseous exchange As in nature, gas exchange occurs at the water surface. You can improve its efficiency in the aquarium by using a protein skimmer, which bubbles copious amounts of air through the water and ensures good water circulation within the aquarium.

Water movement Small submersible pumps, such as powerheads, can be used to create currents in the aquarium. This will help distribute oxygen and prevent debris from accumulating in one place. Timers and wavemakers can introduce a random pattern to the water currents.

Biological filtration All solid surfaces within the aquarium provide space for bacterial colonization, including porous material used to create habitats. In most cases, special biological filtration units that harbour beneficial bacteria are situated outside the aquarium.

Protein skimming is a filtration process unique to aquariums that relies on the natural affinity of dissolved organic substances to stick to the surface of air bubbles in water.

NATURE

Chemical filtration Certain bacteria and other organisms are capable of utilizing organic chemicals and are effective in removing such substances from the water. The calcareous coral rock is also able to adsorb certain chemicals. Water exchange also serves to dilute harmful chemicals.

Sterilization Natural ultraviolet (UV) radiation from the sun helps to reduce the pathogen and suspended algae spore count in the open sea, although it is really only effective in very shallow water. Tropical electric storms produce ozone that, in combination with surf, is a useful sterilizing agent. High-energy surf itself has sterilizing properties.

Alkalinity and pH The vast expanses of calcareous material (coral rock), good oxygenation and the buffering power of the oceans' saltwater ensure that alkalinity and pH levels remain constant.

AQUARIUM

Chemical filtration Since the aquarium cannot benefit from the massive water exchange found in nature, regular partial water changes are necessary to dilute the accumulation of undesirable chemicals. Activated carbon and other chemically active media are used to remove dissolved pollutants.

Sterilization Ozone and ultraviolet light radiation produced by special equipment can help to reduce, or eliminate, disease pathogens and algae spores in the aquarium.

Alkalinity and pH In the aquarium, various natural processes act to reduce the pH, alkalinity and calcium levels. For example, a general build-up of carbon dioxide produced from metabolic functions and the breakdown of organic waste will in time cause a lowering of pH. Ageing water, along with increasing levels of dissolved organic carbons, have a profound effect on its buffering capabilities and reduce alkalinity and calcium levels. Quite often there is a relationship between pH, alkalinity and calcium levels, and shifts in their concentration can occur at the same time. However, a drop in pH, for example, does not always mean there will be a drop in alkalinity at the same time. Good oxygenation, regular water changes and the frequent addition of calcium, either chemically or with a calcium reactor, will help to maintain desirable levels in the aquarium.

Below: *As aquarium water passes through a UV sterilizer, waterborne organisms (good as well as bad) are killed by the UV rays. The longer their exposure, the more effective the results.*

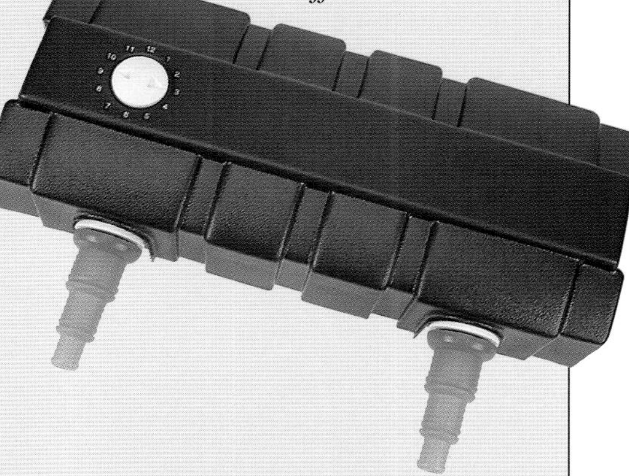

Below: *An overhead view of a very large reef aquarium. Intense lighting systems and complex filtration equipment can simulate conditions found on the reef.*

and their decomposition) and certain chemicals, such as phenols, that discolour the water, all of which must be removed.

Many types of filters are used in the aquarium hobby, ranging from simple air-operated box filters to highly sophisticated water purification systems. Filters vary not only in their design but in their mode of operation; some provide simple mechanical straining, while others exert a chemical or biological influence on the water flowing through them. Some filter designs perform all three functions.

In addition to these 'standard' filter types, many of which find a ready application in both freshwater and marine aquariums, certain water treatment systems are used more or less exclusively for marines. These include algae scrubbers, protein skimmers, ozonizers and ultraviolet sterilizers. We shall discuss the operation and merits of these water treatment methods later in this section. First we will look at the options open to the marine aquarist among the standard types of filters.

A fluidized bed sand filter

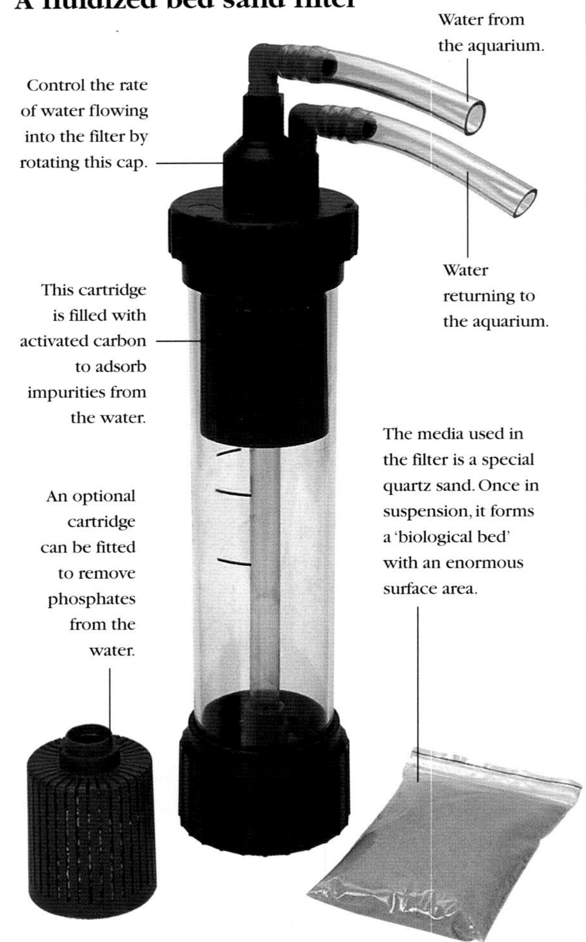

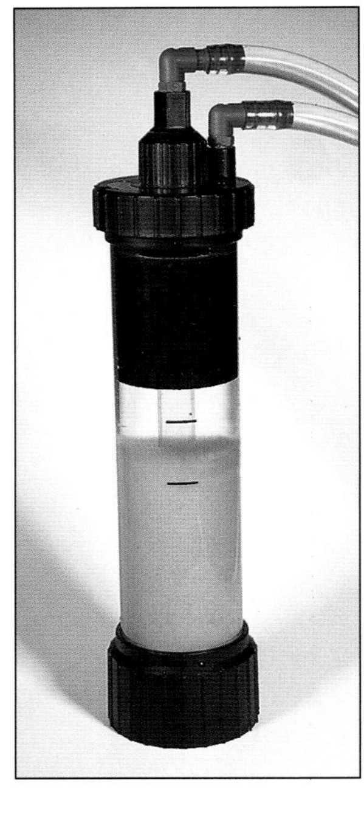

Above: *When in operation, the sand's moving biological bed is held in suspension (the two lines show the upper and lower levels of the medium). A valve in the unit prevents sand siphoning back into the pump if the power fails.*

Biological filtration

Biological filtration is by far the most important type of filtration; without it, keeping a marine aquarium just would not be viable. All the biological processes that occur in the aquarium also exist in the wild, but the natural marine environment also benefits from the cleansing action of the sea, which disperses and dilutes nutrients and other potentially harmful chemicals. In the closed confines of an aquarium, fishkeepers must provide an efficient system to purify the water. By making use of the nitrogen cycle, biological filtration provides a natural and effective means of removing ammonia-based wastes from the aquarium.

Certain bacteria that live on virtually any solid surface (although they are more positively attracted to calcareous material) perform biological filtration. Passing oxygenated water over these bacteria helps to maintain an efficient population. To improve this efficiency further, all sorts of filters have been designed that either draw, push or percolate water through a variety of media, such as gravel, sand, open-cell sponge and plastic balls, etc. The more surface area available for bacteria to colonize, the greater the quantity of water that can be filtered. The aim is to provide the right conditions for aerobic bacteria to thrive.

Providing the necessary oxygen-rich environment for *Nitrosomonas* and *Nitrobacter* bacteria is easy. Agitating the water increases its surface area, boosting the oxygen saturation. As the water travels around the aquarium's circulatory system, the oxygen content is depleted by living organisms within the tank, including the aerobic bacteria. When it is returned to the tank from the filters, the water is relatively low in oxygen and renewed agitation will help to disperse carbon dioxide (CO_2) and absorb fresh oxygen to continue the cycle. If this were to stop, the colonies of beneficial bacteria would die and the water would rapidly become polluted.

In a newly set up aquarium, bacterial colonies in the biological filter will take time to become established and, until the colony has 'matured', there will be little control over the rise of ammonia and nitrite levels. At this stage, the aquarium is unable to support fishes and invertebrates.

Nitrosomonas and *Nitrobacter* colonies do not appear from nowhere; conditions have to be right for them. For example, there must be some ammonia present. There are many additives available that will provide food for the bacteria and help get the process underway, otherwise it could take many months for anything to happen. Adding some 'living rock' will also speed up the process, because it will have its own bacterial colonies. Make sure there are no animals living on the rock that would succumb to ammonia poisoning. Another method is to 'seed' the filters with material from an established aquarium.

It has been a common practice to use relatively tough fishes such as damselfishes to provide the necessary ammonia in order to 'kick-start' the nitrifying bacteria colonies. However, this is a serious act of cruelty and if the fishes actually survive the ordeal it is only due to extremely good luck.

Patience is definitely a virtue and, in fact, essential if you are to establish a marine aquarium successfully. Careful monitoring of ammonia and nitrite levels will indicate when it is safe to introduce the first inhabitants, and from then on regular nitrite testing will tell you whether your aquarium water continues to be safe or not. Remember that you must build up the full population capacity of the tank over a reasonably long period of time, ideally several months, so that the filter bed can keep in step with the increasing levels of waste materials it has to deal with.

The inevitable build-up of nitrate is best kept under control by carrying out regular partial water changes. If your mains tapwater supply contains a high level of nitrate, then treating it with nitrate-reducing resins will be particularly useful. Some modern 'total systems' include hi-tech modules for creating the ideal conditions for both aerobic and anaerobic bacteria.

Fluidized bed sand filters

The most significant recent development in biological filtration for the average domestic marine aquarium is the fluidized bed sand filter. This is a vertical tube containing a layer of fine, evenly sized and shaped quartz sand grains. A controlled flow of water from the aquarium is injected into the base of the tube and forces the sand into a steady tumbling motion, hence the term fluidized bed. As the sand remains in suspension and completely surrounded by water, it means that the entire surface of each particle is available for colonization by bacteria, allowing an enormous area for biological activity and great efficiency. Water returns to the aquarium from the top of the tube. As these sealed units are fitted inline in the water circulation system, they can be placed anywhere around (outside) the aquarium without the risk of floods. Another great advantage is, because of their efficiency, they are small compared to other filter designs.

Trickle filters

Also popular are the so-called 'total systems' that use plastic balls as the biological filtration medium. These are often referred to as trickle filters because water from the aquarium literally trickles in a thin layer over the plastic surfaces, providing highly oxygenated water to the bacteria. One downside to this system is that it can become extremely active in nitrate production because of the large populations of bacteria it can support. Trickle filters are not necessarily always part of a 'total system' and can be stand-alone units.

'Total systems' can also include mechanical and chemical filtration modules, heaters, protein skimmers and all manner of ancillary equipment, all conveniently fitted in a sump, which is most popularly housed in a cabinet beneath the aquarium.

Wet/dry filters

In some trickle systems, the filter material is partly submerged in water and these are commonly known as wet/dry filters. Water still percolates through the upper section of the medium in the usual fashion, but the submerged section can provide areas of still water and, in time, anaerobic conditions can occur to allow some denitrification to take place.

The plenum

This is basically a porous plate that fits tightly to the tank's sides about 2.5cm (1in) off the base. It is covered with a layer of 'live' sand approximately 5cm (2in) thick, or in many cases two layers of different-sized gravel and sand, separated by a mesh screen to prevent mixing. The sand is called 'live' because this biological filter works by culturing all manner of sand-dwelling organisms that would be found in such a situation in nature. Small sandhopper shrimps and other

The plenum system

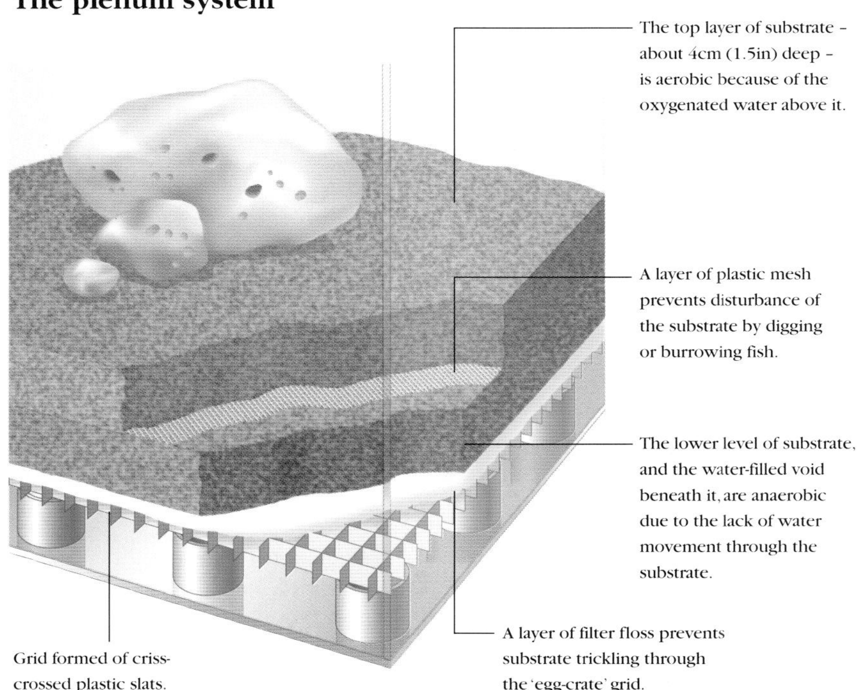

The top layer of substrate – about 4cm (1.5in) deep – is aerobic because of the oxygenated water above it.

A layer of plastic mesh prevents disturbance of the substrate by digging or burrowing fish.

The lower level of substrate, and the water-filled void beneath it, are anaerobic due to the lack of water movement through the substrate.

A layer of filter floss prevents substrate trickling through the 'egg-crate' grid.

Grid formed of criss-crossed plastic slats.

An external canister filter

Shut-off taps allow you to disconnect the filter without water spillage.

These plastic tubes carry water to and from the aquarium.

The electric water pump is housed in the top part of the filter.

The incoming water passes upwards through the filter media, packed in a plastic basket inside the canister. Water flow must be maintained at all times to prevent the media turning anaerobic (without oxygen), as would occur rapidly following a power failure.

Typical filter media

This filter floss traps any small particles, giving the water a final polish before it returns to the tank.

Activated carbon adsorbs chemical compounds and any yellow coloration.

Filter floss 'separator'

Ceramic pieces harbour colonies of aerobic bacteria that 'purify' the water.

This block of open-cell sponge holds back any large particles in the flow.

minute crustaceans, along with a variety of worm species and all the various bacteria, will maintain a healthy substrate.

With the plenum arrangement, good water movement and oxygenation occur above the substrate, whereas a stagnant state is created below, with no oxygen or water movement. Little water actually passes through the substrate from one condition to the other, but nutrients and chemicals are drawn over the substrate material in a state of flux, causing very efficient reduction of all unwanted elements.

The plenum is most commonly used in 'natural systems' where as little, if any, filtration equipment is used to maintain biological equilibrium. However, they are occasionally included in wet/dry filter systems.

Mechanical filtration

During mechanical filtration, particulate matter is removed from the aquarium water by straining it through a suitable material. The most common materials are open-cell foam (other foams can be toxic), filter floss or matting made from Dacron, spun nylon or some other manmade fibre.

Mechanical filters of any type will only remove particles that are suspended in the water column and therefore are transported to the medium; particles trapped in the substrate or rocks cannot be removed by this method. Strong water movement and, if possible, alternating currents will go a long way to preventing sediments from settling. However, regular gentle stirring of the substrate will always be necessary to bring debris into suspension so that mechanical filters can do their job.

Power filters utilize one or more types of filter media. The internal submersible types normally contain a foam block and also provide extra beneficial water movement. On the other hand, the larger external canister types usually contain two or more materials, as well as creating extra water movement. Some models of external canister filter have separate compartments where the first in line will contain, for example, small ceramic tubes that act as a prefilter to trap large particles, while the next compartment contains foam or matting to collect the finer particles. Another compartment could be used for chemical filtration.

In 'total systems' that are normally incorporated into a sump below the aquarium, water is percolated through a mat prefilter and then an open-cell foam block to facilitate mechanical filtration.

Diatom filters use diatomaceous earth as the medium to filter out the smallest of particles to create excellent water clarity. This diatomaceous earth is an extremely fine powder that provides an ideal barrier for preventing very fine particulate matter from passing through. Such filters are so effective that they can clog very quickly and therefore require regular maintenance. The most popular type is an external canister, usually made of clear glass, and powered by an integral water pump.

Protein skimmers remove organic compounds (proteins) that dissolve in seawater and therefore cannot be extracted by physical straining. In a protein skimmer (also known as a foam fractionator) air is bubbled into a water column whose uppermost surface is open to the atmosphere. These dissolved organic compounds attach themselves to the air bubbles and rise to the water surface, forming a protein-laden foam. The foam is then forced up into a collection cup, where it collapses into a dark brown liquid (skimmate) that can be flushed to waste. There are many types of protein skimmer available, employing different techniques for introducing the air into the water flow (airstone, venturi or turbo air injectors) with varying water/air flow paths (co-current, counter-current or triple-pass). For a protein skimmer to be efficient, a large quantity of small air bubbles must be kept in turbulent contact with the water for as long as possible, producing a concentrated skimmate. Protein skimming can be enhanced by injecting ozone instead of air into the water flow.

Chemical filtration

Filter media that remove chemicals can play a vital role in filtration.

Activated carbon Over time, dissolved organic carbons (DOC) and phenols, etc., build up and give the water that tired and aged yellow look. The traditional way of removing them from aquarium water is by means of activated carbon, which adsorbs these elements onto its surface. Activated carbon is basically wood carbon that is 'activated' by being baked at a high temperature to open up tiny pores in the particles and to make the surface of the carbon more 'attractive' to certain substances. Only highly activated carbon is suitable for use in the marine aquarium because of standard carbon's tendency to lower pH rapidly. Carbon also clogs quickly, which can result in concentrated leaching of all the substances it has adsorbed back into the water, with potentially dangerous consequences. For this reason, it must be replaced with a fresh batch every four to six weeks. Activated carbon is most commonly used in a canister filter

An advanced protein skimmer

This advanced skimmer maximizes the contact time between the tank water and a constant stream of fine air bubbles. Protein wastes stick to the bubble surfaces and can be collected and removed as the bubbles collapse.

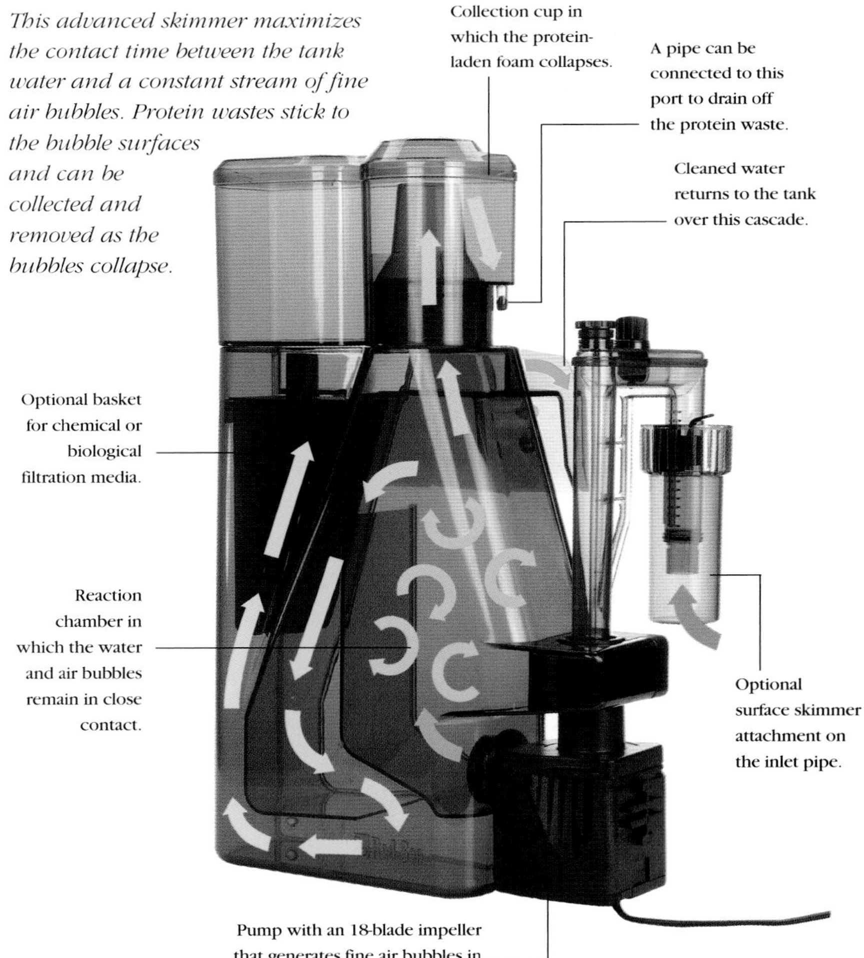

Anatomy of a protein skimmer

This graphic shows the working principle of a protein skimmer using a counter-current flow of water and air bubbles.

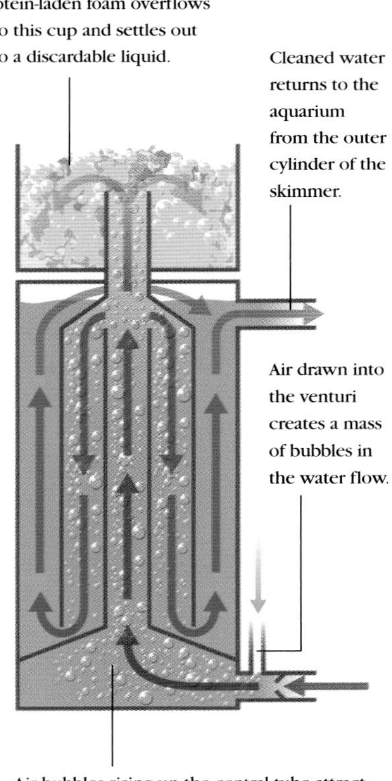

Above: *The pitted surface of a piece of living rock is home to encrusting algae, a wide range of tiny animals and aerobic and anaerobic bacteria that can help to keep the water clean.*

or, as in 'total systems', contained in a filter bag in the sump.

By their very nature, any types of chemical filtration must be taken out of action whenever the aquarium needs to be dosed with medicines and certain other water treatments.

Living rock as a natural filter

Using living rock as a means of filtering water is becoming increasingly popular. As we have seen, living rock is populated by aerobic bacteria, and probably even by anaerobic bacteria. In addition, there may also be organisms such as sea squirts and sponges that are very efficient filter-feeders and excellent water conditioners. There may also be a variety of algae growing on the rocks. Good water flow amongst the rocks will mean they can become effective biological filters.

Algae as natural filters

Being plants, algae will take up nutrients from the water and, along with light, use them in the photosynthetic process. The removal of nitrates and phosphates by this method is particularly useful. Algae scrubbers are external units used for culturing macro-algae to absorb unwanted nutrients, including carbon dioxide, and to produce oxygen. Water from the aquarium is passed through the scrubber continuously. The algae must be harvested on a regular basis in order to remove such nutrients from the system completely and to provide space for fresh growth. If harvesting is not carried out, the algae culture could crash, causing all the nutrients to be put back into the aquarium system in potentially dangerous concentrations. These systems require plenty of light to function efficiently. When working well they are very effective, as can be seen at one very large public aquarium in Australia, where algae scrubbers are the main form of filtration.

The most popular way of using algae for this purpose is to grow them in the display aquarium. However, they must still be harvested regularly for the same reasons given above.

On a healthy coral reef, algae are not immediately evident, due to the continuous grazing of herbivorous animals. For example, the *Caulerpa* species that often grow very long in a marine aquarium are usually only seen as short stumps on the wild reef. If you prefer this kind of algae-free appearance, then an external algae scrubber in a sump or a tray above the tank would be the best approach.

Do not attempt to use these 'natural' methods as the sole form of filtration for your display marine aquarium unless you are a very experienced marine aquarist with a complete understanding of all the biological processes. As we have seen, overall conditions in the aquarium are not entirely as they are 'in nature'.

Other types of water purification

The above types of filtration will enable you to maintain a well-balanced aquarium. However, you may wish to go one step further in achieving superb water quality or, perhaps, you intend to keep certain animals that demand more exacting water conditions. Here we look at some items of equipment designed to help you make such improvements.

Reverse osmosis filter

If you have concerns about the quality of your tapwater, then a reverse osmosis (RO) unit will help. This is a very efficient means of

How reverse osmosis works

Water has a natural ability to 'even out' the compounds within it and spread dissolved salts and minerals. Reverse osmosis, a form of mechanical filtration, is the forced opposite of 'natural' osmosis shown here.

In 'natural' osmosis, water in a dilute solution flows into a concentrated solution through a partially permeable membrane.

In reverse osmosis, water is forced through a fine membrane, leaving dissolved salts and minerals behind.

The membrane is so fine that only water molecules can pass through, thus producing pure water.

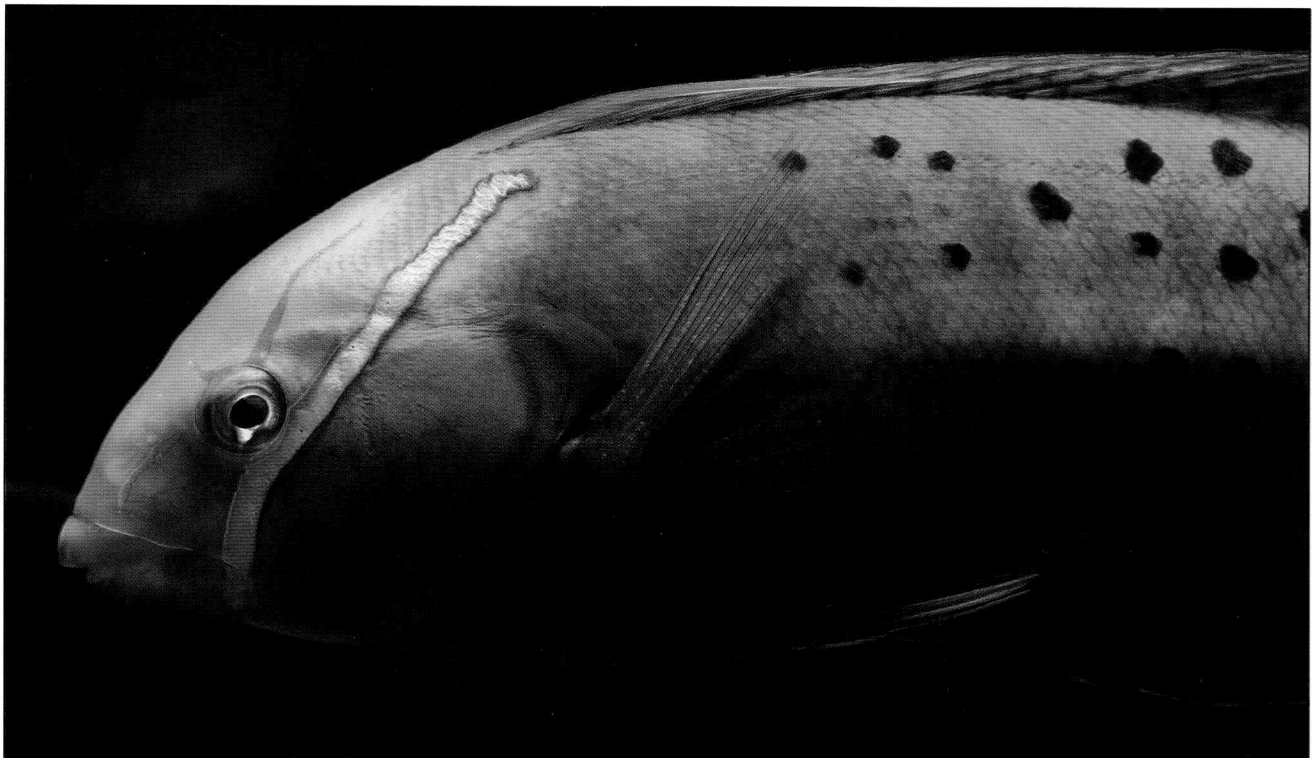

Above: *Impressive fish such as this African Clown Wrasse* (Coris formosa) *can grow up to 20cm (8in) in a tank with an efficient filtration system.*

removing all manner of salts and minerals and even metals from your mains water supply. It works by forcing water through a membrane in order to remove the various substances. Due to its high efficiency, the membranes can quickly clog and must be replaced regularly. This makes RO units quite expensive to operate over time, as the membranes are not cheap. The other downside is that only a portion of the water finds its way through the membrane, while 80-90% goes to waste. However, this wasted water is treated by a carbon block cartridge within another chamber on the unit and can be used for other purposes, even making a good cup of coffee. Try not to waste water unnecessarily. The upside is that you can have water for topping up that is so pure it is close to distilled quality.

Ultraviolet light sterilization

Ultraviolet (UV) light is capable of eliminating algae spores and bacteria that are freely suspended in the water and sometimes cause cloudiness. A germicidal-grade lamp can also destroy disease pathogens, but is only effective on pathogens with a free-swimming stage that may find their way through the UV unit, so do not rely on it for total disease control. Bear in mind that UV light is dangerous to the eyes, so NEVER look directly at the lamp without eye protection.

The UV sterilizer consists of a UV lamp fitted inside a sealed clear quartz sleeve, mounted within a water jacket. Aquarium water fed into the outer jacket is sterilized as it flows from one end to the other. The efficiency of sterilization depends, among other factors, on the length of time the water is exposed to the UV light. The effectiveness of the lamp can be optimized by prefiltering the water mechanically before passing it through the sterilizer. This prevents organic material and suspended matter from obscuring the quartz sleeve and thus lessening the effect of the UV rays. Even so, the lamp

How a UV sterilizer works

Aquarium water can be sterilized by passing it through a UV unit. The water hose connectors are translucent so that you can see the 'glow' of the UV lamp when in operation, a safety measure to make sure you do not open the unit and damage your eyesight.

Water flows though this outer glass tube.

The fluorescent tube in the middle produces ultraviolet light with a wavelength of 253.7 nm. This UVC is harmful to living tissue.

This quartz sleeve encases the tube but allows UV light to pass through.

has a definite useful lifespan; used continually, most lamps will require replacement every six months. After this period, the lamp may still appear to be functioning, but in fact the UV light is no longer able to penetrate the quartz sleeve.

Using ozone

Ozone (O_3) is an unstable form of oxygen (O_2). The extra atom of oxygen readily separates from the molecule and oxidizes toxins and other compounds in the aquarium water. This oxidizing action makes ozone an effective disinfectant; it will kill bacteria, disease pathogens, algae spores and other free-swimming microorganisms that come into close contact with the gas. Ozone is used by many large public aquariums as part of their overall water quality management systems.

Ozone is formed by passing air (ideally dried) over an electrical discharge in a device known as an ozonizer, converting some of the oxygen in the air to ozone. The ozonized air is then passed through a special water/ozone contact chamber or a protein skimmer. Providing this is made from ozone-resistant materials, it makes an ideal ozone reactor. Since ozone is harmful to the aquarium inhabitants, it must only be applied in a separate vessel, never directly into the aquarium. Ozone-treated water should be passed through a carbon filter before being returned to the tank in order to remove any residual ozone or any harmful byproducts of excessive ozonization. It is advisable to use an ozonizer together with a redox (or ORP – oxidation reduction potential) controller. A probe in the aquarium monitors ozone concentration in terms of the redox potential of the water and switches on the ozonizer only when the water conditions require it.

As you might imagine, ozone is a dangerous gas and must be used with the utmost care. Always follow the manufacturer's instructions to the letter. Ozone is also capable of damaging a wide range of materials, such as rubber piping and pump diaphragms, and excessive levels can also make plastics turn brittle.

Ozone and protein skimming

Froth carrying organic waste overflows into a collecting cup at the top of the unit.

The waste can be drained from the base of the cup through this tube.

A check valve prevents water siphoning back into the ozonizer. Renew it regularly.

A probe hanging in the tank measures the redox potential of the water and regulates the amount of ozone produced by the ozonizer.

Ozone passes through this tube and into the water flow through a venturi device.

The ozone generator uses a high-energy electrical discharge to bond an extra atom to oxygen molecules to create ozone (O_3).

Nitrate and phosphate filters

As we have seen, there are several ways of eradicating nitrates and phosphates. In anaerobic conditions, certain bacteria can use nitrate, and algal filters use nitrate and phosphate as important nutrients. Wherever there is an excess of these substances, another way is to run either tapwater or aquarium water through a canister filled with special resins. Some are designed specifically for nitrate and others for phosphate. These resins often require dangerous chemicals to recharge them, so in a domestic situation it is best just to replace the resins once they are spent.

Another word of warning regarding the high efficiency of some resins: they can sometimes act so fast that the result is an extremely

Above: *Activated carbon placed in a compartment on top of the collecting cup prevents any excess ozone entering the atmosphere.*

Calcium reactors

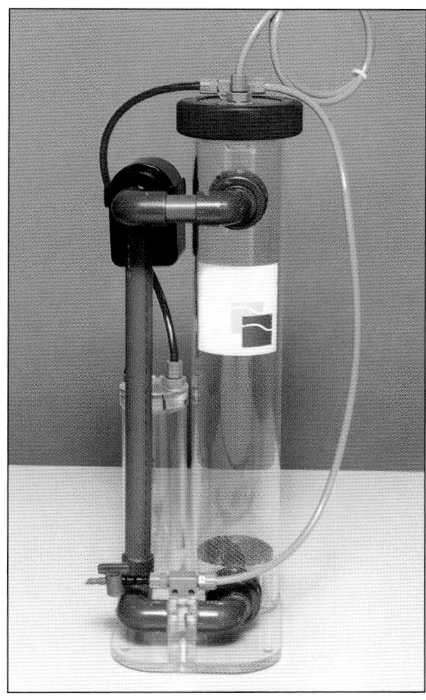

Above: *For invertebrates it is essential to maintain the correct hardness, alkalinity and pH levels. A calcium reactor such as this (shown without media) will provide a simple means to do this.*

rapid change in environmental conditions, which could put your aquarium subjects into a state of shock. We know that some polyp animals, such as corals, turn white after losing their symbiotic algae due to the use of some resins. Exercise extreme caution when using these materials.

Calcium reactors

A calcium reactor is not a filter, but it is included here because it is normally used in tandem with a filter system. Invertebrates need calcium carbonate in order to grow their skeletons or shells, and regularly take these elements out of the water. As water ages and its calcium buffering capabilities diminish, the pH has a tendency to drop. This can cause metabolic problems for fishes and invertebrates, such as respiration difficulties. Therefore, it is important to maintain the correct pH (8.3 for reef animals). A calcium reactor can help to achieve this. The apparatus is usually a sealed container made from, say, acrylic, and filled with calcareous material such as aragonite. Aquarium water is delivered to the unit fairly slowly via a bypass system from the main filtration. The system is injected with carbon dioxide because its acidic nature slowly dissolves the more alkaline aragonite and thus charges the water with calcium. The carbon dioxide is used up in the process, so there is little risk of excess building up in the aquarium.

Another way of maintaining hardness and alkalinity is to drip-feed calcium water into the aquarium. Some total systems have automatic dosing equipment fitted to the filter sump for this purpose.

Bear in mind that regular partial water changes will do a great deal to help maintain pH, etc. If your mains tapwater is of good quality, nitrate and phosphate levels will be kept low.

Below: *Where the aquarium is housed in a cabinet, it makes good sense to assemble the water treatment equipment in one convenient place – out of sight but accessible for maintenance tasks.*

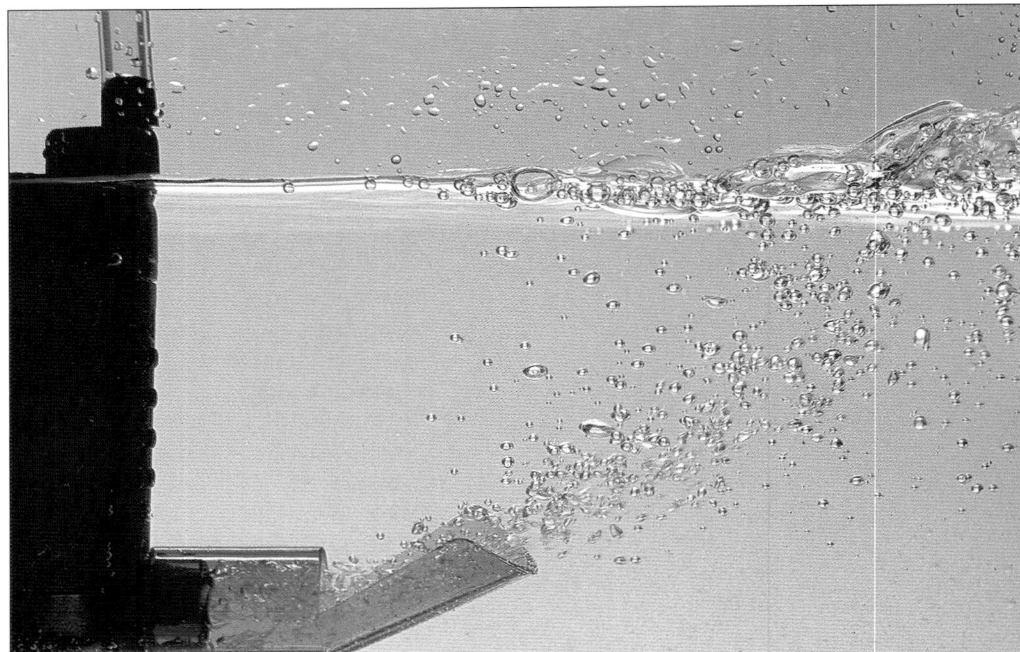

Left: *To simulate tidal flows in the aquarium, install powerheads at the surface and at varying levels in the water. Remember to guard their intakes. This powerhead is fitted with an air intake to inject extra aeration at, or near, the water surface.*

Nutrients, minerals and trace elements

Bear in mind that some types of filters – protein skimmers, ozone and UV sterilizers – are capable of either removing or completely destroying certain nutrients, as well as important minerals and trace elements in the water. Furthermore, the metabolism of organisms will make use of all these substances, causing a depletion in the aquarium water. This is another good reason for regular water changes, but it is also likely that you will need to add specially prepared supplements. These are readily available and there is a wide variety to deal with different situations, such as iodine, strontium and even vitamin deficiencies. It is not always easy to test for such deficiencies, so regular dosing is a necessary part of your routine tank maintenance.

Water movement

Water movement plays an essential role in the good management of the marine environment, as it distributes vital oxygen and helps to prevent stagnant areas where detritus can build up. Equally important is its effect on metabolism. All solid objects in water, including living organisms, are surrounded by a layer of stagnant water, almost like a membrane. In water with a strong flow, this 'membrane' is very thin, whereas in still water, this stagnant layer thickens and can impede metabolic processes. Strong currents can be created in the aquarium by adding extra pumps; small powerheads are ideal for this purpose. Randomly alternating currents can be achieved by using two or more powerheads controlled by a wavemaker, or by a series of timers, to simulate wave action on a natural reef. The result is that the aquarium water is thoroughly oxygenated and detritus is kept in suspension so that the filters can draw it out, thus maintaining the good health of the aquarium's inhabitants.

Using filters with medication

The treatment of disease in the marine aquarium can be complicated by the presence of sophisticated filtration systems. Activated carbon will adsorb many medications, and protein skimmers are also effective in removing such substances. In these circumstances, it is useful to have a separate hospital tank to which infected animals can be transferred for treatment. If several animals are infected simultaneously, or you are worried about stressing the animals too much by moving them, you will have to treat them in the main aquarium and turn off the chemical filtration for the duration. In any case, do remember that invertebrates in general are intolerant of many chemicals, including copper, so read the instructions carefully to make sure that the medications you use are safe with these animals. (See also pages 152-159.)

Filter-feeding animals

Many invertebrates are filter-feeders that require their food to remain in suspension. Some filters will draw this food out of the water column quicker than the animals can feed on it completely. In these cases, you may have to turn off the filtration for a while, which is not always ideal. Alternatively, you could spend time individually targeting the relevant animals at feeding time by delivering food directly to them via, say, a drinking straw or pipette. Alternating surge currents often have the effect of keeping such foods in suspension for a longer period before it is drawn out by filters and, therefore, may be a better solution to the problem.

Below: *Make sure that filter-feeders can obtain sufficient food before the filtration system removes it from the aquarium.*

Creating Habitats

Newcomers to marine fishkeeping may be forgiven for thinking that decorating the tank with substrate and rocks, etc. is done solely for aesthetic purposes. However, in modern marine aquariums, these items play an integral role in maintaining water quality and providing the fishes and invertebrates with habitat to live in or on. Generally speaking, these materials require thorough cleaning, or curing, before use and must be prepared well in advance of setting up the tank.

When you come to decorate the aquarium, always work from the bottom up. First put in the rockwork or living rock directly on the tank base and then build up the substrate on top. An obvious statement perhaps, but if you intend to use biological filters, such as a plenum system (see page 97), that are often situated below the substrate, then you have to make sure these are fitted before any other work is carried out.

The substrate

In the case of a tropical marine aquarium, coral sand and gravel are the only real choices if you wish to establish a 'natural' look. Where temperate systems are concerned, you could use soft beach sand, gravel or small pebbles, or a combination of these materials.

Sand on the reef is mostly produced by animals such as boring worms and parrotfishes, which crunch up coral to extract tiny organisms and algae. Their crunching activities are so thorough that they eventually excrete fine sand that falls to the seabed. Coral gravel is created by wave action, whereby the coral is broken and the fragments are slowly worn down. In nature, myriad organisms, such as worms and crustaceans, some microscopic, live in the sand and keep it clean and aerated to a certain depth. In the aquarium, too, these organisms can become very useful when the sand is allowed to become 'live'.

Above: *Coral gravel and sand (shown here) are the most suitable and easily available substrates for a marine aquarium. They not only look right but also help to maintain a stable pH and high buffering capacity.*

Rocks suitable for a tropical marine aquarium

Rocks for a temperate marine aquarium

This collection of rounded cobbles, pebbles and stones can be used to recreate the weathered rocks found along temperate shores. Use different-sized stones together in the aquarium for a more natural effect.

For more dramatic aquascapes, you can safely use pieces of slate. They are ideal for making caves, but make sure they are firmly positioned so there is no risk of collapse.

Below: *Scooter blennies* (Petroscirtes temmincki) *spend most of their time 'scooting' around the base of the aquarium in search of food. These generally shy fish will feel at home on a coral gravel substrate.*

Choosing rocks

Apart from deciding how to set out the tank, you must choose the correct materials to put into it. Once again, remember the importance of water quality control and choose from the wide range of calcareous and inert substances available. Fortunately, there is no difficulty in obtaining materials such as lava rock, ocean rock and so-called 'live rock' for use in the tropical marine aquarium. Where temperate or coldwater marine tanks are concerned, you could use a wider variety, such as sandstone, granite, some slates (grey is safe) and limestone. Whichever you decide on, you must examine the pieces before use to make sure there is no evidence of metallic-ore veins in the rock. Ores have occasionally been found in tufa and volcanic lava rock, in particular.

How you design the habitat in your aquarium is largely a matter of taste, but it is worth taking a bit of time to consider the needs of the animals you want to keep. Fishes certainly need somewhere to go at night, unless they are nocturnal and the reverse applies. Shrimps and other crustaceans need overhanging ledges to get under, and some fishes, such as lionfishes, often hang upside-down under ledges. Territorial animals, as the name implies, must be able to establish their own territories, whilst cruising species, such as triggerfishes, batfishes and angelfishes, need a reasonable amount of open space. By including caves, crevices, ledges and arches along with plenty of swimming space, you will be able to cater for a wide range of needs.

Living rock

The term 'living rock' refers to rock that has been collected from the wild and kept damp whilst in transit,

Building a lava rock cave

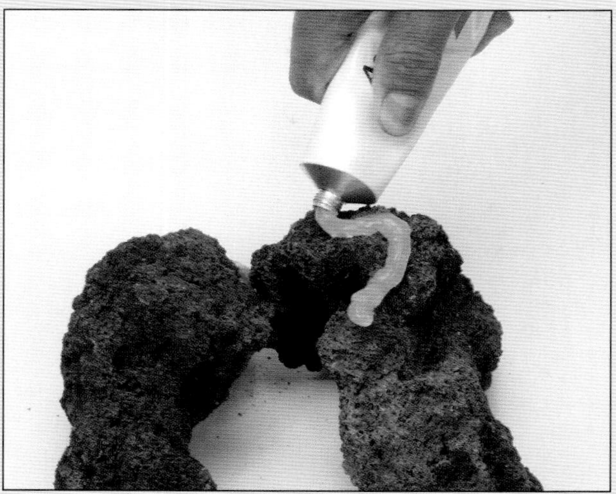

1 Once you have selected a few rocks, use the largest pieces for the base and apply sealant to the highest points or those that will touch the next segment.

2 Firmly press the 'roof' of the cave onto the siliconed areas. Depending on the shape of the cave, you may need to position the structure at an angle to dry.

3 Fill any gaps with silicone and smooth the join with a wet finger. These areas should be hidden in the finished cave, although you can cut excess sealant away.

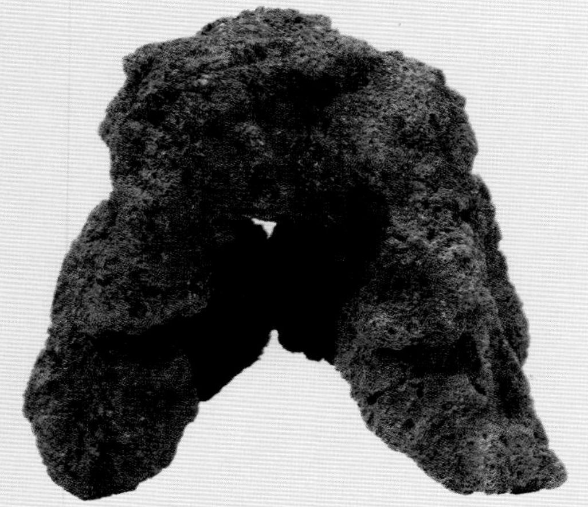

4 Leave the finished cave to dry for a few days and trim off any excess silicone sealant to improve the appearance. The cave is then ready for use in the aquarium.

so that any organisms attached to it will, hopefully, remain alive. The pieces popularly regarded as the best quality are generally coated in pink coralline algae. This rock is the ideal medium for building habitat and the bonus is that it may bring with it an array of invertebrate life, algae and on rare occasions, the odd small fish, or a young growth of coral. Often eggs and larvae will be hidden within holes and crevices, and eventually emerge as a pleasant surprise to the aquarist. Of course, it can work the other way round, and undesirable animals, such as certain types of predatory crab or mantis shrimps, appear as if from nowhere.

Living rock is expensive because it is heavy and costs a lot to ship, so filling the entire aquarium with it could be prohibitive. If this is the case you could build a base of, say, ocean rock and then strategically place choice pieces of live rock around the structure. If you choose rock with a similar appearance to living rock, with time, the two types of rock will start to blend in with each other as algae and invertebrates spread themselves around the aquarium.

Good-quality living rock has excellent qualities for helping achieve and maintain optimum water conditions, so much so that some very experienced marine aquarists use it as the only form of filtration and water conditioning in

their aquariums. However, this type of rock needs to be properly looked after right from the time it is collected, otherwise organisms will start to die. If this happens, you may end up with a nasty, foul-smelling lump that requires some urgent curing before it is placed in the aquarium. In this event, keep the rock in a separate, well-aerated container of saltwater at the correct temperature and specific gravity, preferably with filtration. Check it every day and if you find any decaying patches on the rock, scrub them away thoroughly with a small, stiff brush. Only when the decay has halted and there is no longer a nasty smell can you introduce it into the tank. Fortunately, the majority of living rock is either of good condition or the collectors and importers have already cured it before sale, but it is always safer to check first.

Collecting living rock is becoming more controlled in certain countries and may be banned in future, so some enterprising collectors and dealers now seed other types of rock in aquaculture-style systems and 'grow' them on until they look just right for sale.

Left: *Notice the macro-algae, pink encrusting calcareous algae and small polyp animals on this living rock. It will also support a range of tiny crustaceans, plus worms and beneficial bacteria.*

Below: *The fully established tropical marine aquarium soon becomes the ambition of most hobbyists. Catering for the needs of all the animals is a prime consideration if it is to be achieved.*

Above: *Models of corals moulded in resin are incredibly lifelike and will soon take on the patina of realism as they become covered in algae and detritus in a marine aquarium. They are the only choice if we are to conserve the real thing in the wild.*

This synthetic seafan looks surprisingly realistic, and its elegant sweeping form will contrast well with more upright shapes.

Coral

Living hard corals (also called stony corals), the reef-building corals, are controlled by C.I.T.E.S. (Convention for the International Trade in Endangered Species) but licenses to import them can be obtained. Clams (*Tridacna* spp.) are also controlled, but soft corals, anemones and other polyp animals are not. Commercial coral propagation farms now exist and it is far more appropriate to buy pieces that have originated from such sources whenever possible. Many aquarists have successfully propagated their own corals and swapping pieces with fellow enthusiasts is quite common. You can also obtain artificial coral 'skeletons' moulded in resin that soon take on a more realistic appearance in the tank.

Adding corals and related animals to the marine aquarium will help create a stunning and realistic environment, and is not as difficult to achieve as it was some years ago. However, hard corals are still not for the inexperienced and you should begin with other, tougher, related polyp animals. One thing you must always keep in mind is that certain species of fishes will eat corals and other invertebrates, even those found on living rock, so some forethought will be required when considering what mix of animals you wish to keep.

Marine algae

Some authorities have had the notion that coral reefs should more accurately be called algae reefs, as the sheer mass of algae on a reef is quite enormous. Apart from the more recognisable types of macro-algae that grow on one substrate or another, there are the zooxanthellae that live within the tissues of corals, particularly hard corals, and clams. It is because of these algae that corals can only survive in areas of very strong sunlight. Like other plants, zooxanthellae need adequate levels of light to photosynthesize.

By including macro-algae in the reef aquarium, you can provide the plant element that many aquarists miss if they have moved from keeping a freshwater aquarium to setting up a marine tank. Macro-algae can be not only attractive, but also very useful for marine fishes that like to graze, such as herbivorous surgeonfishes. The algae derive much of their nourishment from waste products in the aquarium water, but you may have to supplement their needs by adding trace elements, fertilizers and even extra carbon dioxide, which is perhaps the most important nutrient for plants. One drawback of achieving a lush growth is that it may suddenly 'crash', releasing toxins into the aquarium water as it dies back. To avoid this, harvest your algae periodically. Macro-algae, especially some of those in the genus *Caulerpa*, are capable of rapidly taking over the tank, as their daily growth rate is quite phenomenal when conditions are right.

Below: *Red algae is a fairly unusual aquarium decoration, but it provides an excellent focal point in the display tank, as well as a food source for some herbivorous species. Monitor its progress carefully, as it can spread rapidly.*

Building up a Marine Display

In this chapter we consider the stages involved in setting up a basic marine aquarium using separate pieces of equipment to achieve the three main types of filtration, i.e. biological, mechanical and chemical, along with heating and lighting. (This so-called customized system differs from a total system that incorporates integral filters, heating and lighting and which is purchased as a single unit. Total systems may also include a variety of water management aids, such as a protein skimmer, calcium reactor, UV sterilizer and denitrifying unit.) Our customized aquarium includes some living rock and a compatible selection of fishes and invertebrates (shown being added in the next chapter, starting on page 126).

Our setup will feature an externally fitted fluidized bed sand filter for biological filtration, an external protein skimmer for removing organic and chemical waste, and an external power filter to help remove particles in suspension and to improve water movement. As some of the equipment is to be situated outside of the tank, make sure there will be room on the stand (or along the back panel of the tank) to accommodate them. Lighting will be provided by fluorescent lamps and for heating we will use two small thermofilters without their foam-filled filter 'jackets' in place. For decoration, we will have a coral sand substrate and a seascape built up using pieces of living rock. Some hardy polyp animals will be included along with other invertebrates and, of course, some fishes. This system is easy to set up and not too expensive, but it will provide the means of managing good water quality and a wide variety of animals. Even if you choose to install a more sophisticated system, you will find that much of the practical information is still relevant.

Advanced preparation

It is useful, as discussed earlier, to prepare your saltwater mixture in advance of setting up the aquarium. If living rock is to be immediately introduced at the setup stage then it will not be appropriate to make the initial saltwater mix directly in the tank. However, if living rock can be introduced a few days later then it will probably be more convenient to mix the saltwater in the aquarium. Remember that subsequent water changes must be

Siting the aquarium

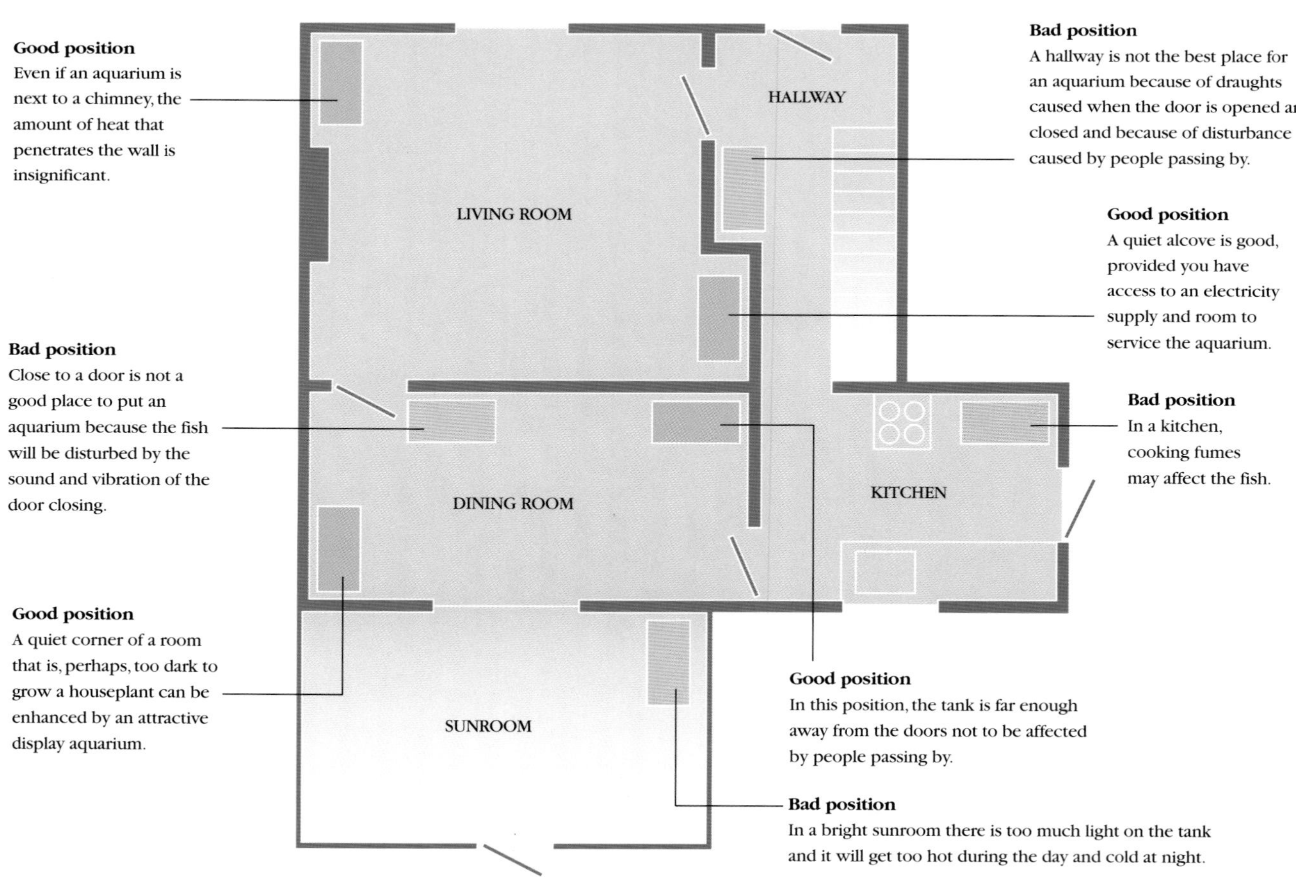

Good position
Even if an aquarium is next to a chimney, the amount of heat that penetrates the wall is insignificant.

Bad position
A hallway is not the best place for an aquarium because of draughts caused when the door is opened and closed and because of disturbance caused by people passing by.

Good position
A quiet alcove is good, provided you have access to an electricity supply and room to service the aquarium.

Bad position
Close to a door is not a good place to put an aquarium because the fish will be disturbed by the sound and vibration of the door closing.

Bad position
In a kitchen, cooking fumes may affect the fish.

Good position
A quiet corner of a room that is, perhaps, too dark to grow a houseplant can be enhanced by an attractive display aquarium.

Good position
In this position, the tank is far enough away from the doors not to be affected by people passing by.

Bad position
In a bright sunroom there is too much light on the tank and it will get too hot during the day and cold at night.

made with water that has been prepared in another container. Also make sure any rockwork you plan to use in the display (not the living rock) and substrate are sufficiently cleaned before the designated setting-up time.

Preparing the site and tank

It is a good idea to make a checklist of items you will be requiring and the jobs you will have to carry out. Use the list to make sure that everything is at hand before you start setting up. Choose a site for your tank that is near to an electric power point and easily accessible, not only during the setting-up stage, but also for maintenance afterwards. For safety's sake, fit an RCD circuit breaker. Make sure your work area is free of clutter.

Just to recap on a couple of points already made. Make sure your tank stand or cabinet is strong enough to take the weight of your aquarium when it is full of water and, likewise the floor must also be strong enough. If possible, make sure the whole system is supported directly on floor joists as opposed to inbetween them.

Good commercially made aquariums should have been pre-tested for leaks. However, if you have any doubts, test the tank by placing it on a suitable strong, flat surface somewhere outside your house. Fill it with water and should you find a leak, return the tank to the shop where you bought it.

If you are happy with your tank then you can start the setting up process. Remember to locate your aquarium away from bright sunlight and heating radiators. Also make sure there is plenty of room to accommodate the different pieces of equipment around the outside of the tank. Place a foam rubber mat or a sheet of expanded polystyrene equal to the area of the aquarium's base on top of the stand or cabinet to help support the tank evenly. Then sit the tank on top of that.

Pumps, filters and heater

Now is the time to arrange where you are going to place any pumps required for running the fluidized bed sand filter and skimmer, as well as the external power filter and heater units. Do not plug any equipment into the electricity supply at this stage. Pumps need to be positioned at the back of the tank where they can be easily connected to the apparatus, whilst the intake and return pipes for the external power filter can be placed at opposite ends along the back wall of the tank. Position the heater units on the back glass near the corners using the suckers supplied with them, making sure that the element does not get covered by any substrate and that there will be good water flow around them.

Place the fluidized bed filter and skimmer wherever is convenient, although, if possible, situate them at opposite ends of the tank. Some models will need to be stood on top the aquarium stand, whilst others have attachments for hanging on the side or back glass of the tank (as here). Fluidized bed sand filters are usually pressurized so they can be sited anywhere providing the hoses are long enough and the associated

1 In all but the smallest of aquariums, it is best to use two heaters placed at opposite ends of the tank to ensure even heat distribution and as a safeguard against one heater failing.

2 Place the return pipe from the external power filter at one end of the tank and try to arrange it so that it can easily be hidden by your habitat.

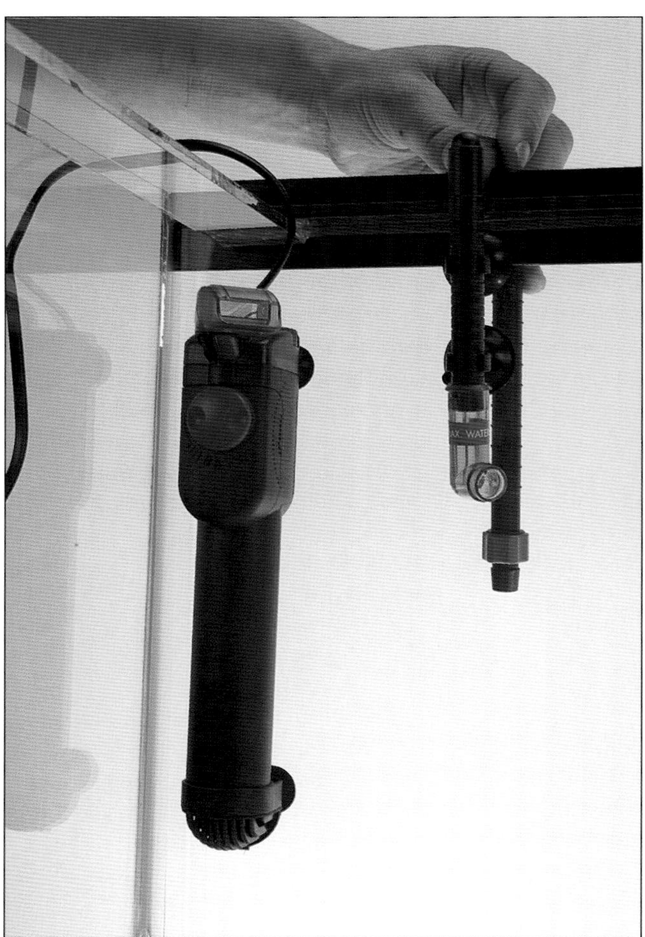

3 Place the inlet filter pipe from the external filter at the opposite end of the tank from the return pipe to provide the most efficient water circulation.

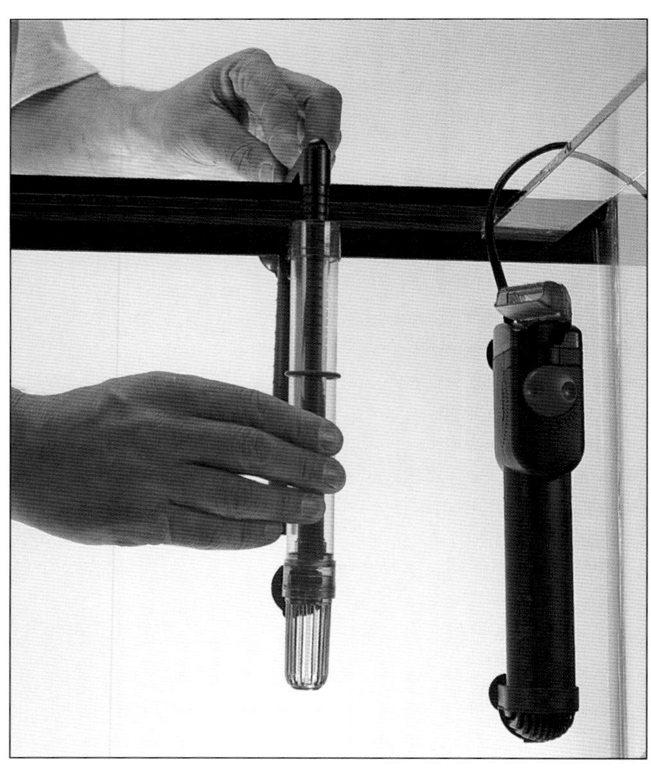

4 Connect hoses to the external power filter. Take care to fit these securely so that they do not come apart when the filter is running under full pressure – otherwise water in the tank ends up on the floor!

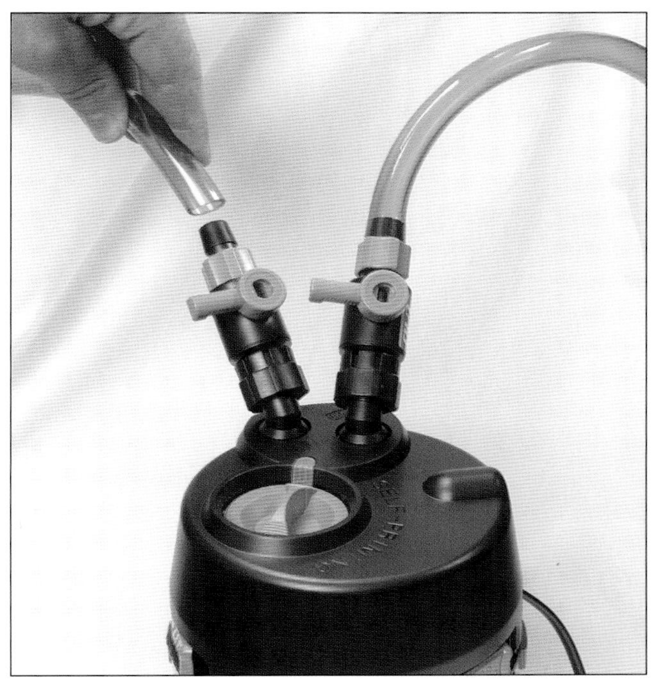

5 Connect the hoses to the external power filter securely, making sure they are not tangled and, if necessary, mark them IN and OUT.

6 If you choose to place your display aquarium on a cabinet, then it is easy to hide away external equipment such as this power filter.

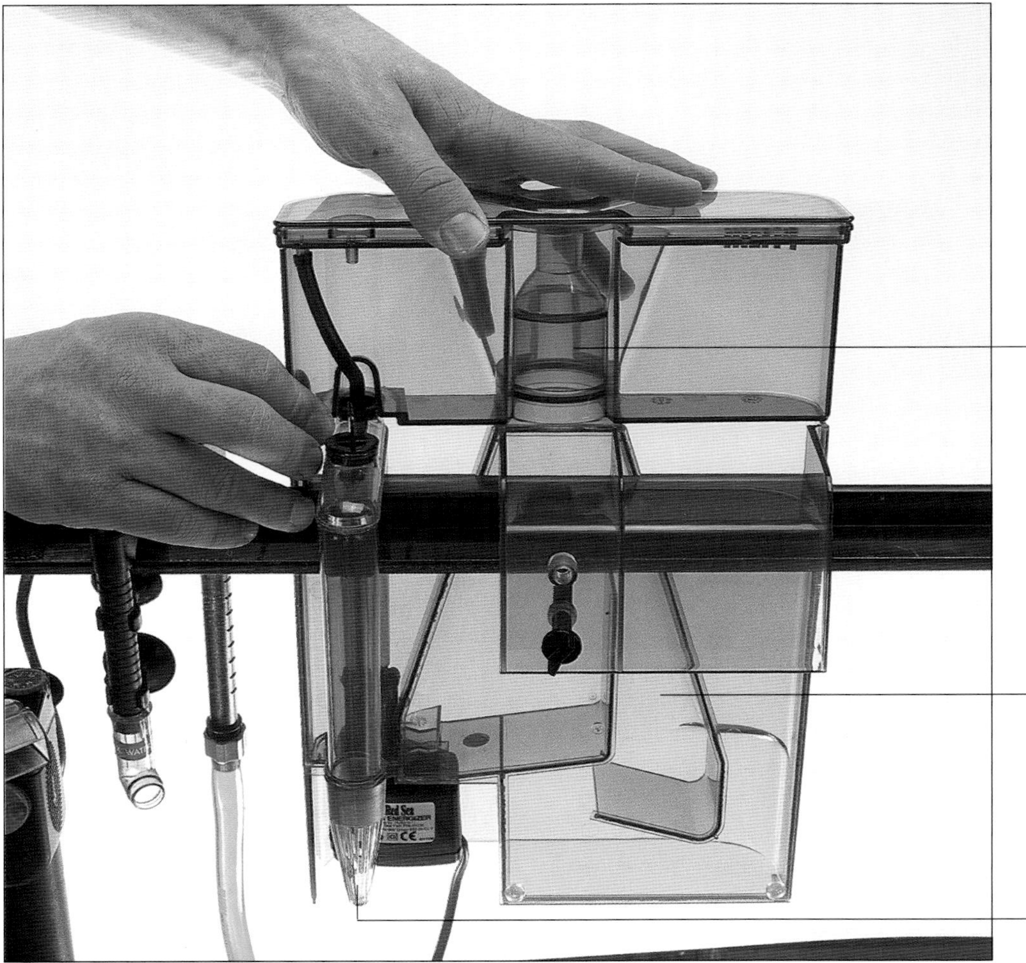

7 There are several designs of protein skimmer available. This one needs to be hung on the back panel of the aquarium. Make sure you provide easy access to such equipment for regular cleaning.

Protein waste sticking to the surface of the collapsing bubbles collects here and can be discarded.

The convoluted pathway provided by these baffles maximizes the contact between the air bubbles and the flow of water as it moves upwards.

Water is drawn into the skimmer from the tank through this inlet tube and comes into contact with a stream of air bubbles created by a Venturi device within the skimmer.

8 This aquarium makes use of a fluidized bed sand filter for biological filtration. This particular unit is driven by a small submersible water pump. Attach this by suckers inside the tank on the back glass.

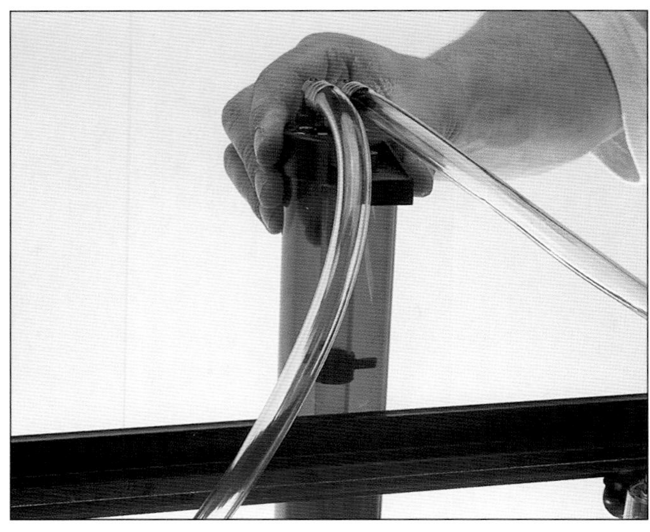

9 Hang the fluidized bed sand filter on the outside of the back glass and connect it to the internal pump with a hose. Always make sure that the chamber containing the sand is fitted in a truly vertical position.

Below: *Here is how the aquarium looks with the heating and filtration equipment fitted. For safety, remember to avoid tangling up electrical cables and situate connections away from water and splashes.*

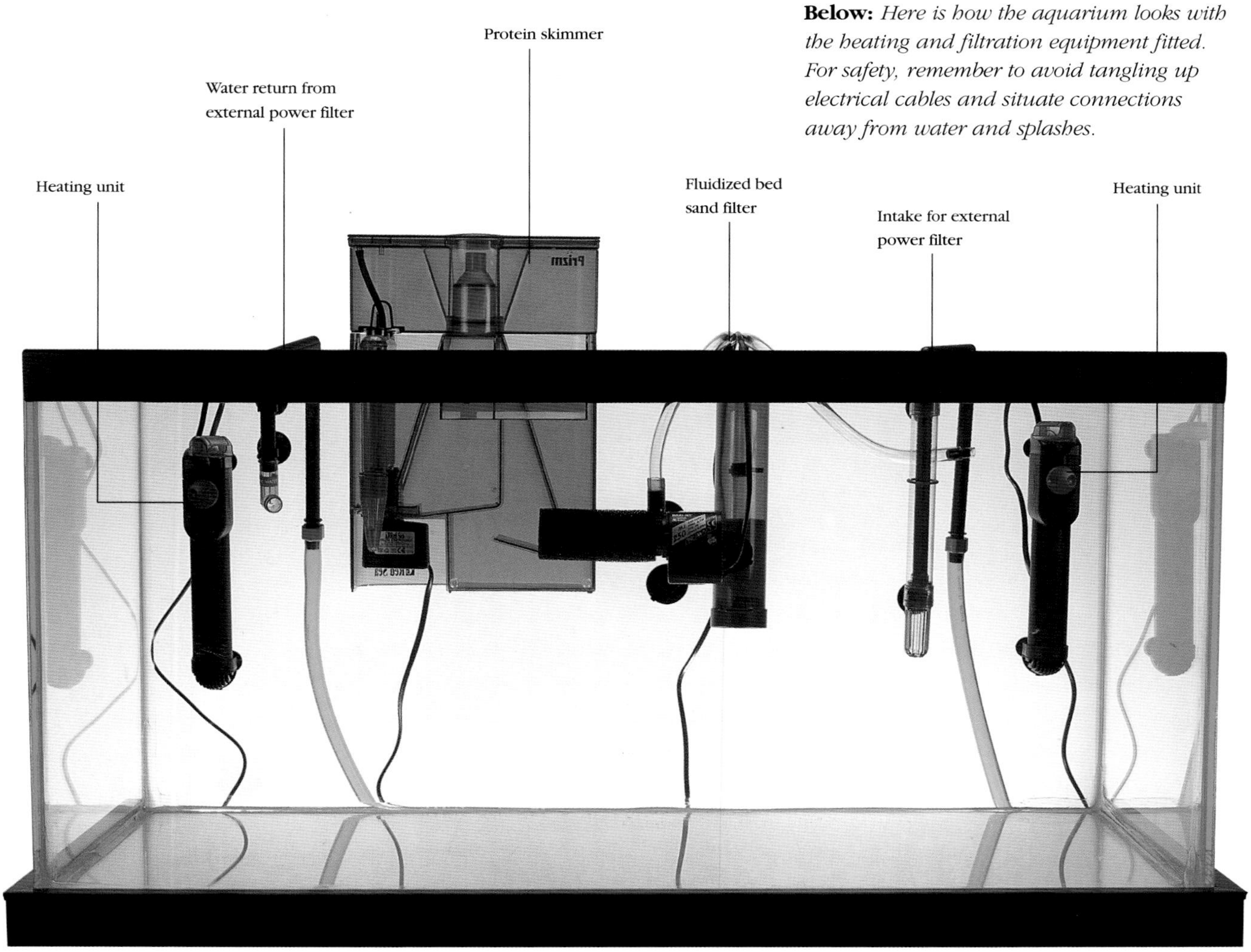

Heating unit

Water return from external power filter

Protein skimmer

Fluidized bed sand filter

Intake for external power filter

Heating unit

pump is powerful enough to maintain the correct throughput of water through the unit. Protein skimmers are not pressurized, however, and must be placed so that the correct operating water level is no lower than that of the aquarium, otherwise they will overflow. Connect up to the pumps by following the maker's instructions carefully.

The habitat

In this setup the habitat will be serving two purposes, one to provide cover and territory for the inhabitants and, secondly, to hide the equipment you have installed. If you are on a limited budget and cannot afford to create your habitat entirely from living rock then use some cheaper inert rock for constructing the base features. Check with your aquarium dealer to find out what is available. It is likely that this base rock will require washing before use. It is also a good idea to place each piece in a pan of boiling water for a few minutes at a time to sterilize them before arranging them in the tank.

It will be your own artistic abilities that govern how you arrange your rock, but some knowledge of natural reefs and an idea of what animals you want to keep will help. Be sure to provide plenty of crevices, caves, overhangs and perhaps archways for the inhabitants to take up residence in. Also keep in mind that any pieces of living rock being added later will need sites to fit into.

If you have no budgetary constraints it is far better to create your habitat from living rock only, as this will improve the water conditioning and natural filtering properties of the tank.

Adding living rock

Providing you have a supply of previously matured saltwater available to hand that has the

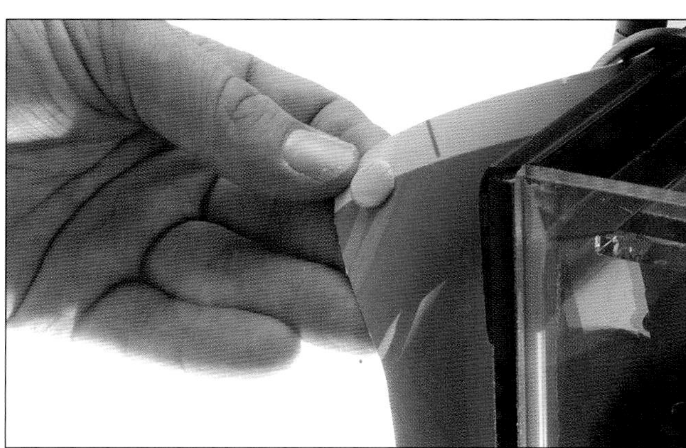

10 Fit a background to the outside of the back glass to hide the equipment. Blue is the best choice, as the colours of fishes and invertebrates stand out well against it. Black can also be used to good effect.

11 Add the first pieces of living rock directly onto the tank floor. Place them carefully so that you can build up a stable display. In this setup we are using high-quality living rock only and have opted not to include any form of base rock or other decor.

12 Create the habitat in a way to provide plenty of retreats for the inhabitants and to hide pieces of equipment placed internally. However, leave open swimming space for those fishes that require it. It is vital that the rock is not allowed to dry out.

13 The best substrate for this aquarium setup is coral sand. Spread it around the base of the tank and against the rocks to give the appearance of the habitat rising up from within the sand.

correct temperature, specific gravity and pH of 8.3, you can introduce your pieces of living rock to complete the habitat. In this case it is important your water is added immediately after placing your rocks and laying the substrate. As this rock includes living organisms it is not good practice to subject it to the harsh environment of new, unmatured saltwater. If you only have newly mixed saltwater available at the setting up stage, then it is important to wait until the aquarium is fully operational before adding the living rock.

The substrate

The substrate is the next thing to install into the aquarium, and in this case we are using coral sand. Ideally, introduce enough to cover the base of the tank to a depth of about 2.5cm (1in). This is equivalent to about 4.5kg (10lb) per $30cm^2$ ($1ft^2$); any deeper and you will run the risk of anaerobic conditions developing in the lower layers.

It is likely you will need to wash the substrate before use and this is best done in advance of starting the setting-up process. The best, and quickest, way is to wash a small amount at a time in a fine mesh hand net. Hold the net over a bucket and run water through from a tap or hose until all the detritus has been flushed out of the sand. Dispose of the waste by whatever means you have available, but it is advisable to avoid clogging the trap in your sink. When you are happy that all your sand is clean you can spread it over the base of your tank and around your habitat to give the impression that the rocks are rising out of the substrate.

Adding the water

If you have already matured the water in another aquarium then it is simply a case of carefully pouring it into the tank. It is a good idea to pour the water onto a rock or into a container placed on the substrate to avoid the sand being moved out of place. You will now need to connect the pumps for the fluidized bed sand filter and protein skimmer to the electricity supply and switch on in order to fill their chambers and start circulation. Carry this out in full accordance with the manufacturer's instructions. The water level in the aquarium will drop a little and will need to be topped up. Now switch on the power filter and the heater.

If you do not have pre-matured water ready you will have to mix a new batch in advance of setting up. When mixing, the temperature should be at the normal aquarium operating level of 24°C (75°F), as the salts will dissolve more readily. A thermometer stuck to the outside

14 *Attach the readout unit of a digital thermometer to the outer glass and place the probe in the water, ideally some distance away from the heating units.*

A sturdy plastic container is ideal for storing and transferring saltwater. Do not use metal containers.

15 *Because this setup includes living rock, it is important to add matured saltwater, i.e. from another established aquarium. New saltwater can harm the many tiny invertebrates already living on the rock. Pour the water gently onto the rocks to prevent displacing the sand substrate.*

of the mixing container is good for making a quick reference, but to be accurate it is best to use a glass thermometer that reads directly from the water. Once you are certain the salts have completely dissolved take a specific gravity reading using a hydrometer. If it is low, add more salts and continue doing this while taking further specific gravity tests, until the S.G. is 1.022-1.023. Remember, once the aquarium is fully operational and has animals living in it, you must never mix saltwater directly in the tank again. Always perform this task in a separate container.

When you are happy all is correct, add the water to the aquarium and connect up the heating and filtration.

Installing the lights

The lighting canopy must be made from non-corrosive and non-toxic materials and be large enough to accommodate two white 10,000°K fluorescent tubes and one blue actinic 03. It is also important that the canopy can have sections cut out of it to allow filter fittings, hoses and cables to be routed through. A wooden hood laminated with plastic, or painted with several coats of polyurethane varnish, is ideal. Any control gear for the lamps must be situated away from water and splashes.

It would be useful to connect the power cables for the lights into a remote control box or power strip with the pumps and heaters so that

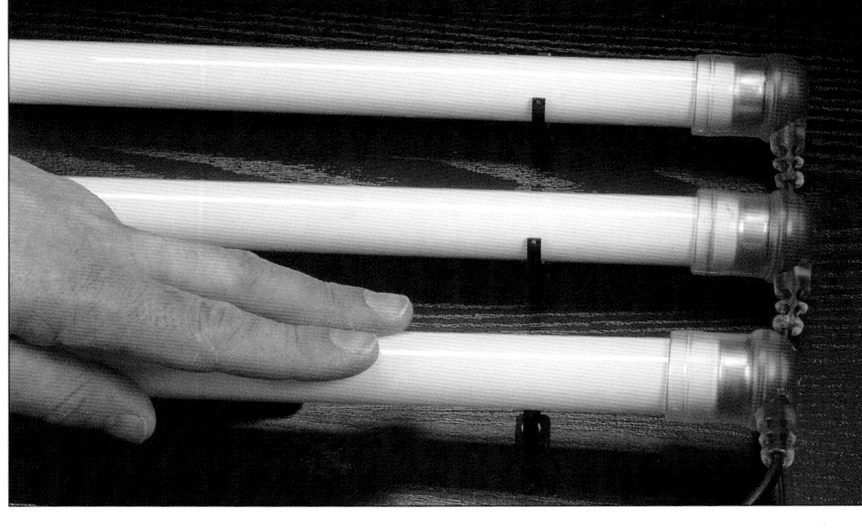

16 *When using fluorescent tubes it is important they are secured properly into the hood by clips designed for this purpose. Do not use metal clips.*

17 *Space out the tubes in the hood so that they provide the best light coverage within the aquarium and there is good air circulation between them to prevent overheating. Reflectors (not shown) fitted around each tube can boost the light reaching the water.*

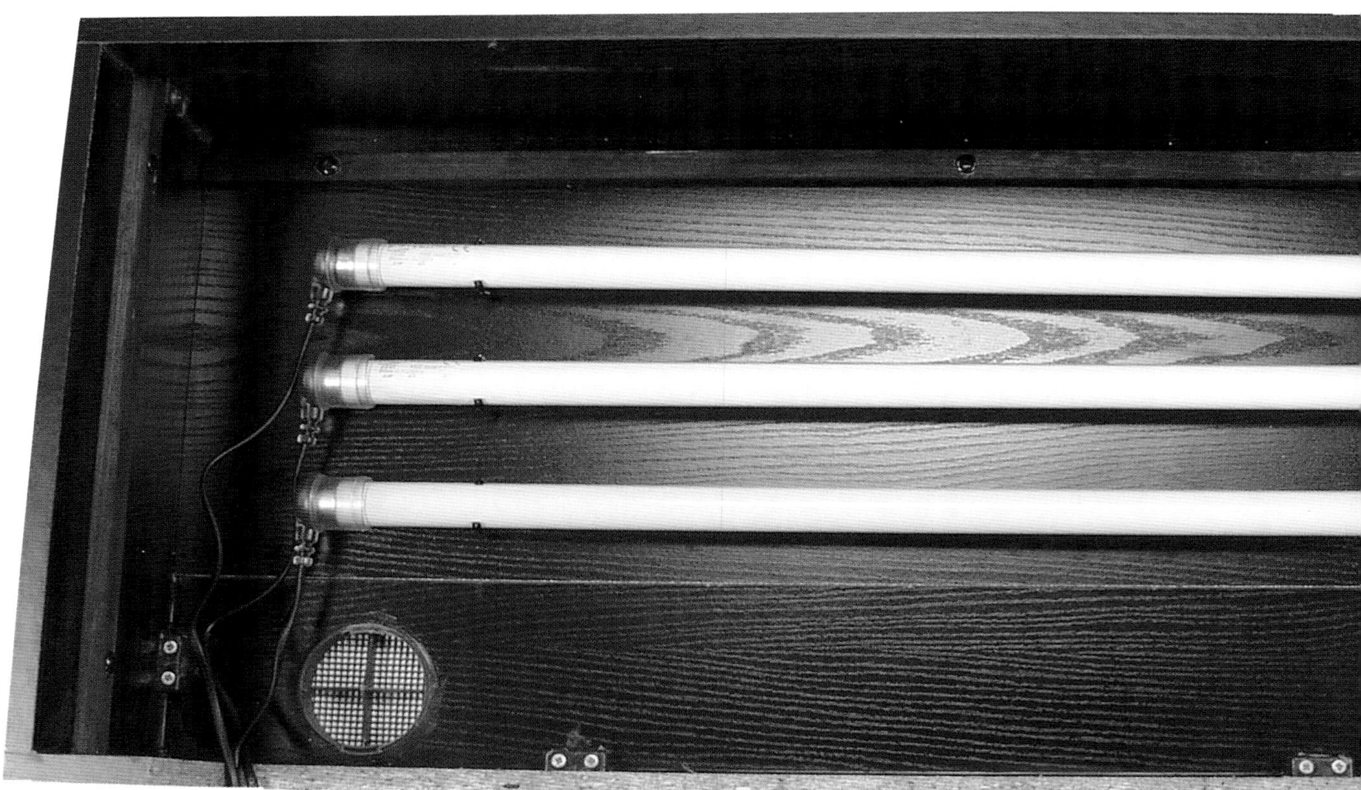

there is only one cable running to the electricity supply socket. Some controllers have on/off switches incorporated for each of the various appliances connected to them and are protected by cutout functions in case of equipment faults.

Maturing the filters

Even though there are no animals in the aquarium at this stage it is good to have the lights on for the normal photoperiod, i.e. 12 hours per day, as this will help the maturation process, and is essential once the living rock has been introduced.

It is absolutely critical that you do not introduce any more livestock into the aquarium until the filters have matured. This means you must wait and be patient until there is a large enough population of nitrifying bacteria to deal with ammonia and nitrite. As living rock is included in this setup that may have the bacteria already living on it, the process could be faster than in other arrangements. However, you must now make daily tests for ammonia and nitrite levels using aquarium test kits until the readings show clear for both. It is likely you will not see any evidence of ammonia or nitrite right away, but this does not mean the coast is clear, as the levels will build up gradually, with ammonia peaking first. Be patient and wait until you have had several consecutive days of clear readings before considering adding livestock. When you are certain that all is clear make a 20-25% saltwater change to dilute the resulting levels of nitrate.

The coldwater aquarium

More or less the same criteria apply to setting up a coldwater or temperate marine aquarium. The main difference being that a heating system is not required.

Of course, the substrate and habitat will be different to a coral reef setup and will be made up of materials more common to the locations where your choice of fishes and/or invertebrates are naturally found. As suitable animals and some habitat materials for such aquaria are not so commonly found in the aquarium trade, it may be a case of collecting your own. If this is the situation for you, remember to look out for nice pieces of rock with plenty of life on them and treat them as living rock. Be aware, though, that many species of seaweeds, particularly wracks and kelps, do not do well in small tanks and should be avoided. When collecting, especially during the warmer months, make sure you transport your specimens home in insulated containers to prevent overheating. Provide aeration if you can by investing in a battery-operated airpump. Also, be sure not to transport predator with prey in the same container to reduce the risk of arriving home with less specimens than you collected. For this reason you must research your animals to decide exactly what you will be able to keep together.

Rockpool animals are subjected to frequent changes in temperature and other water conditions due to the to-and-fro movement of the tides and the subsequent exposure to the sun. Therefore, these animals are generally hardy and are most suited to life in the aquarium. However, if your choice is fishes

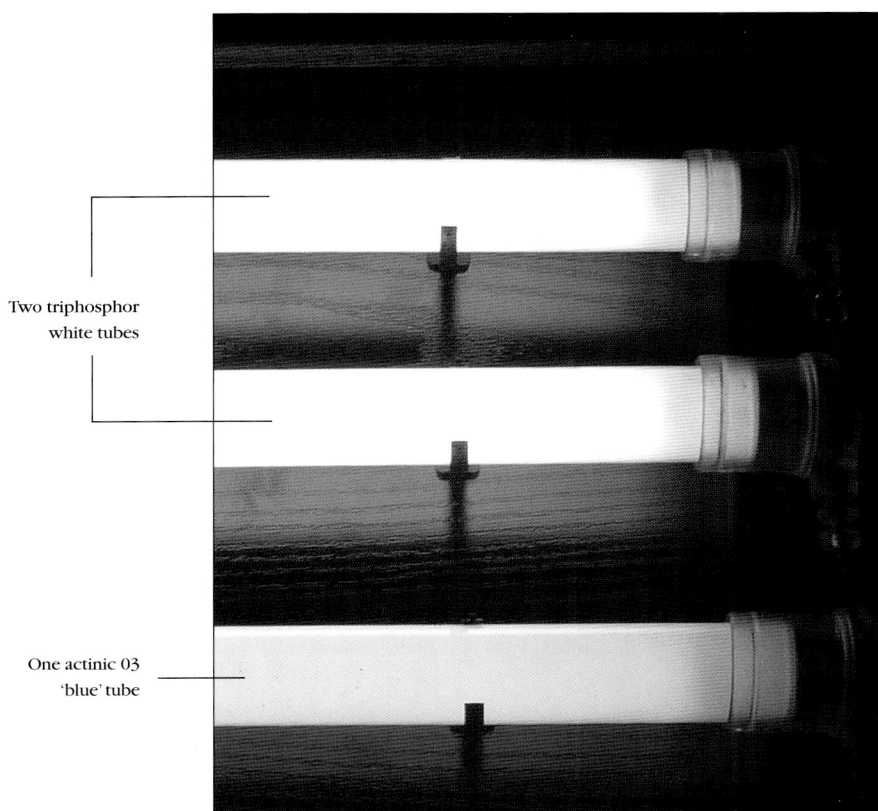

Two triphosphor white tubes

One actinic 03 'blue' tube

18 Connect the heating and filtration equipment to the electricity supply and turn them on. However, it is vital that you monitor water quality and do not introduce any livestock until ammonia and nitrite levels have been zero for several days.

Check that all the heating and filtration systems are functioning properly during the maturation period.

Without fish and invertebrates in the aquarium, the skimmer will not be producing any protein waste.

The living rock is likely to have a coating of beneficial bacteria that will break down any ammonia present in the water and help to start up the biological filtration process.

that are found in open water where conditions are cooler, then you will most likely have to consider incorporating a chiller into your system, which ultimately can make a coldwater marine aquarium far more expensive to set up and run than a tropical one.

Otherwise, you can use exactly the same type of tank, filtration, protein skimmer and lighting as you would for a tropical marine aquarium to establish a successful coldwater marine system.

Alternative options

Should you find the setting-up arrangement described above unsuitable, you could fit the fluidized bed sand filter, protein skimmer and heater units into a sump, which could be hidden inside a cabinet. In this case, fit an overflow from the aquarium to the sump and a pump in the sump to return water to the aquarium.

To improve water movement, extra pumps, such as small powerheads, could be installed in the aquarium and hidden behind the habitat. Alternate currents can be achieved by controlling these pumps from an electronic surge unit. Further improvements can be made by directing the flow from one or two pumps directly at the living rock.

You may also want to consider including an UV (ultraviolet light) sterilizer to help maintain excellent water clarity. The UV light disrupts living cells and can be effective against some bacteria and parasites.

PART THREE

MARINE FISH AND INVERTEBRATE CARE

Once suitable 'life-support' arrangements have been made, you can look forward to the next and, arguably, most enjoyable task: that of selecting and looking after suitable livestock. Although a pleasurable pastime, it is not always easy, and you will need to exercise great care, especially if you are just embarking on the hobby.

Buying on impulse is a common route to disaster, so always plan your purchases in advance. Try to see fish, in particular, feeding before you take them home and always make sure that all livestock is 100 percent healthy; decline offers of sick or ailing stock, which may be for sale at cheaper rates.

The key to long-term success is correct, regular maintenance. Neglect this at your – and your livestock's – peril! Maintenance should be seen as an enjoyable task and a chance to learn about and improve the aquarium environment. If you have a sensibly stocked aquarium with a good, well-balanced feeding regime, you should rarely encounter problems with diseases. It is wise to be prepared, though, and a basic range of medicines, as well as a quarantine tank, is strongly recommended.

With any luck, and having provided the optimum conditions, you may witness the greatest compliment the creatures can pay you. The excitement of seeing fishes spawn for the first time in your tank can be tremendous, and the fry of some species, such as anemonefishes, are not exceptionally difficult to raise. Coral may divide and multiply or even colonize spontaneously.

Remember that your charges rely entirely on you for their well-being and deserve the best possible care, and in return you will be rewarded with a colourful, fascinating and trouble-free display for many years.

Left: *The close relationship between clownfish and anemone is one of the most endearing scenes of the marine aquarium, but such a harmonious arrangement will not last long without your dedicated care and attention.*

Choosing Fishes and Invertebrates

Having taken all possible care to set up the tank and provide the ideal conditions, do not ruin your painstaking preparations by choosing unsuitable animals for your aquarium. Several factors must influence your choice; their compatibility, both with their own kind and unrelated species; their feeding requirements; their tolerance of captivity; their appearance and even their cost. It is, therefore, very important to research thoroughly all the species you would like to keep .

Obtaining healthy stock

Observe fishes and invertebrates carefully before buying them. They should be alert and free from any sort of damage. Avoid fishes that look thin, or have pinched stomachs, as they often have trouble recovering. Freshwater fishkeepers are used to seeing their healthy fishes swim with erect fins, but many marine fishes naturally keep their fins down, so this is not necessarily a sign of ill-health. With invertebrates, it is more difficult to tell whether they are in good condition or not. In the case of corals (ideally attached to rock), anemones and other polyp animals, look out for tissue damage or even decay. The same applies to sponges, but with crustaceans and starfishes it is usually a case of making sure all their limbs are intact. Sea urchins should not be showing any signs of shedding their spines. Generally speaking, it is worth avoiding any invertebrates that appear to be shedding unusual mucus-like substances, unless you know for sure that this is a normal trait in that species.

Stressed fishes will often produce excessive skin mucus that usually has the appearance of white slimy patches. Avoid these fish, even though the temptation may be to transfer them to your own tank, where conditions are much better.

Many tropical marine fishes and invertebrates are brilliantly coloured, which is what makes them particularly attractive as aquarium subjects. Make sure their colours are as they should be and avoid specimens with an unnaturally dull appearance or any with poorly defined markings. Cloudy or swollen eyes, ulcerations and abnormal swimming or instability are bad signs. In particular, look out for signs of scratching or unusually high respiration, as these indicate parasite infections or other possible ailments, as well as toxic water conditions.

Some species, particularly those caught directly from the wild, may take a while to start feeding in captivity, so it is worth asking if you can observe them eating before you buy. Most aquarium dealers will not have any problem with this. However, one problem arising from this is the risk of the food being regurgitated or the fish defecating in the transit container on the way home and causing an ammonia problem. If the journey is short the risks may be negligible, but if it takes more than half an hour to get your subjects home, then refrain from transporting them until they have been purged. Once you have seen the animal feed, it is worth leaving a deposit and arranging to collect it the following day. For these reasons it is always worth developing a good relationship and level of trust between yourself and your chosen dealer.

Continually using the same source for your fishes and invertebrates will help to ensure a consistent quality of livestock and service. Always listen to the recommendations of other aquarists before trying new dealers. If you obtain specimens from a variety of sources it will often be difficult to

Below: *Starfishes should have all their arms intact and be firm to the touch. Always examine potential additions to the aquarium from all angles to ensure that they are healthy and undamaged.*

Above: *Buying from a reputable dealer should ensure that you obtain good stock. Nevertheless, you should always examine fish carefully and reject any specimens with cloudy eyes, wounds, hollow bodies or swimming difficulties.*

Right: *When faced with the wide range of fishes to choose from at the aquatic store, you should know what to look for, so that you only buy healthy stock. Avoid buying fish simply because you like the look of them; they might not be compatible.*

trace where a problem may have originated and therefore you will not be able to alert the relevant people, or expect any one source to take responsibility.

The journey home

Once you have obtained your chosen specimens you will be taking them, presumably, on the final stage of their journey from natural habitat to aquarium. Assuming they have survived all the traumas of capture, air travel and several changes of aquarium conditions, you must make sure that their introduction into your aquarium is as stress-free as possible.

The best, and standard, way of transporting most fishes and invertebrates is in plastic bags filled with one-third aquarium water and two-thirds air. If your journey home is a long one, explain the situation to the dealer so that you can arrange for oxygen to be injected into the bag instead of air. If the weather is cold, or very hot, you may be able to buy or borrow an insulating polystyrene shipping box to transport your animals.

Whilst in transit, never subject your fish to bright light, but keep them calm in the dark. The plastic bags should be wrapped in paper or

Adding fish to your tank

1 Once caught from the dealer's tank and bagged up, fish are usually placed into a brown paper bag. Being in dark surroundings usually calms them down and prevents undue stress occurring during the journey home.

2 Equalize the transport water with that in the aquarium by floating the unopened bags in the tank, preferably with the lights off as this will help the fishes or invertebrates stay calm during this process.

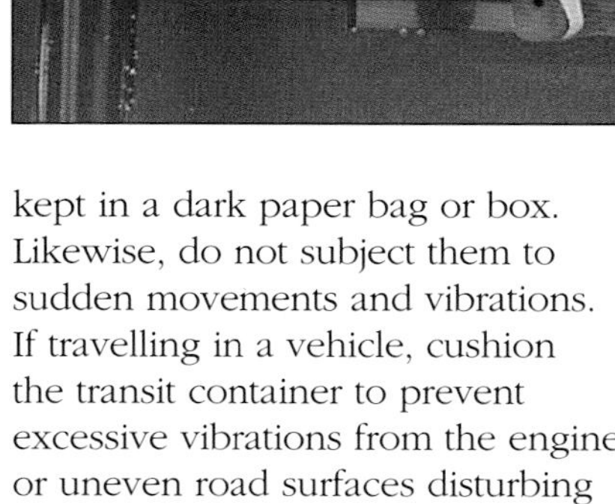

3 After the bags have floated for 15 minutes you can open them and start gradually mixing in some tank water as described in the main text. Doing this will equalize differences in pH, specific gravity and 'fine tune' the temperature before release.

kept in a dark paper bag or box. Likewise, do not subject them to sudden movements and vibrations. If travelling in a vehicle, cushion the transit container to prevent excessive vibrations from the engine or uneven road surfaces disturbing the animals.

Introducing the animals

Continue to keep the new animals in dimly lit conditions throughout the introduction process. Unpack the bags and float them in your aquarium for approximately 15 minutes to allow any differences in temperature to equalize. If you have had a long journey, there is a risk that the pH of the water in the transit bags will have dropped. Sudden changes in pH are dangerous to marine animals, so gradually mix the transit water with the aquarium water until equalisation has been achieved. There are two ways to do this. You could open the floating bags and introduce a small amount of aquarium water at a time until the bag is full, making sure it does not sink, then pour two-thirds back into the tank and repeat the process. By the time you have filled the bag a second time, you should find that the pH, specific gravity and temperature have all equalized. Nevertheless, you must take some tests to be absolutely certain before releasing the animals.

Alternatively, you could transfer the animals into a receptacle such as a very clean bucket, and then drip-feed water from the aquarium into the bucket via a length of airline with a valve on the end. Continually monitor conditions until equalization is achieved and it is safe to transfer the animals into the aquarium.

Left: *A pair of cleaner shrimps. All kinds of invertebrates require the same type of careful treatment as marine fishes when being introduced to the aquarium.*

Above: *Avoid placing individual corals and anemones too close to each other and never touch their living tissue with your fingers as you position them, as this may cause serious damage to the animals.*

Left: *The same careful approach applies to living rock, algae and corals. Take care not to damage other invertebrates when placing new items into your habitat formation. Place them onto the rockscape in stable positions to prevent other tank inhabitants from easily dislodging them.*

To avoid further stress on the fishes and invertebrates you should carefully balance the need to acclimatize them with the length of time it takes to do so. Carefully monitoring respiration will indicate to some degree the level of stress a fish is experiencing, but it is much more difficult to assess with invertebrates.

As living rock actually includes living organisms, it is necessary to acclimatize it to your aquarium in exactly the same way you would with fishes and invertebrates. The same also applies to macro-algae.

Quarantining new stock

If you are not certain about the health of new animals, it may be advisable to quarantine them in a tank designed for this purpose before introducing them to the aquarium. Always maintain such a tank to the same standard as your main aquarium. Despite the best intentions, it may be argued (with some degree of logic) that any extra transference of animals from one situation to another can cause stress. The extra quarantining stage may be an example of this and will require that you acclimatize the animals in the usual ways when transferring them. Careful handling of healthy stock from a reputable dealer will reduce the number of occasions where quarantining is necessary.

The first days

After the animals have been successfully introduced into the aquarium, leave them with the lights off, but not in total darkness, for about an hour. After this the lights can be turned on in stages, and it is often a good idea to offer a very tiny amount of food. For many animals, eating when in a new situation is what is known as a displacement activity and the fact that food is available helps them to settle. Imagine being thrown into a totally new environment and discovering there is no evidence of a food source, you would certainly feel stressed, as the most powerful survival instinct is to eat. Obviously, the presence of healthy living rock will provide a number of suitable food items in the form of microorganisms and algae. However, some fishes may not feed for a couple of days while they are settling in and, in most cases, this will not cause undue harm. The

Yellow Sailfin Tang - a hardy fish ideally suited to this type of aquarium setup.

The living rock habitat supports its own community of living organisms, but also provides retreats for other aquarium subjects and a base for adding live corals, anemones and other sessile creatures.

Below: *The finished aquarium, including the initial livestock. Only introduce one fish or invertebrate at a time, unless they are small enough to allow more – please use good judgement! Always monitor the water quality before making any further introductions to avoid overburdening the filter system and in turn stressing the animals.*

most notable exceptions to this are surgeonfishes and seahorses, which must keep eating virtually constantly.

Whether you are introducing animals to a newly set up aquarium or an established system, add only one fish at a time to avoid overloading the capabilities of the biological filtration. Gradually the bacteria population will catch up with the extra loading and you will be able to make another addition. For corals and other invertebrates, you can count a cluster of polyp animals on a rock as the equivalent of one animal, providing it is not a massive piece. In fact, invertebrates can be added in pairs at weekly intervals.

It is worth bearing in mind that any animals known to exhibit particularly aggressive territorial behaviour are best introduced last of all. If established in the tank any earlier, these animals could mercilessly attack newcomers that are introduced after them.

Compatibility

To avoid unwarranted aggression, choose your aquarium subjects in terms of their compatibility with one another. This will require some research before drawing up your species 'wish list'. If you are not sure, it is best to avoid mixing fishes that have big mouths with ones that are small enough to be swallowed. Conversely, do not include crustaceans with large claws in a community of delicate animals. Employing some forethought and common sense, and providing a variety of habitat features with a good amount of open swimming space will usually ensure that the aquarium inhabitants can find sufficient escape routes and retreats should a skirmish break out.

Compatibility guide

It is important to consider the compatibility of both the fishes and invertebrates you intend to keep together in the same aquarium. Nature seems cruel when you think about a large predatory fish eating a smaller species, which in turn may eat a yet smaller fish or invertebrate; or the fact that certain invertebrates are quite capable of devouring fishes. Sadly, tank inmates do not necessarily become docile and domesticated in the home aquarium, where food is more easily available, so food chain trends continue.

If you are not certain about the normal lifestyle of a species, it is best to use the guideline that if one fish is bigger than the others in the aquarium and has a large mouth, then the chances are that the smaller fishes will be eaten. Groupers, lionfishes, anglerfishes and moray eels are typical of those that fall into this category. Likewise, invertebrates with large claws are potentially going to do some serious damage, and anemones with powerful stinging cells can easily catch slow, weak-swimming fishes, such as seahorses.

Less obvious threats are butterflyfishes that eat the stinging cells of corals, filefishes that often bite out the eyes of less robust species and triggerfishes that have jaws adapted to eating spiny sea urchins. Another consideration is that when a fish that naturally lives in a shoal is kept as an individual, it may change its defence tactic by becoming aggressive and territorial because it can no longer rely on the safety of numbers. The best line of defence against predation in the aquarium is to read about the lifestyles of the animals you are interested in before obtaining them.

To avoid other types of aggression, it is a good idea to learn how to tell sexes apart. In the case of damselfishes, for example, males that have established a nestsite will fiercely fight with one another, and other fishes that get too close for that matter, whilst females are happier living together out in the water column. Male damsels often have colour in their fins, but the females' fins are transparent.

Below: *Many species, such as this Red Reef Lobster, are nocturnal and rarely seen during the day.*

Lifespans

Our knowledge of marine fishkeeping is increasing all the time, but it is still difficult to give any accurate guidance concerning the projected lifespan of aquatic animals kept in aquarium conditions. Nor has there been a great deal of research into the longevity of the same species in the wild. That said, many species originally thought to live for only, say, a couple of years in captivity have now been found to survive much longer, thanks to advancements in aquarium technology and husbandry. Often in the past, it was fishes in public aquariums that had the longest lifespans, presumably because they fared better in the generally larger systems. Today, however, marine aquarium hobbyists are finding that their species often live as long and occasionally longer than those kept in large exhibits.

Feeding Fishes and Invertebrates

Providing the correct diet for many of the marine species kept in the aquarium was once a major problem, but these days you can choose from a wide variety of foods, and new technology in manufacturing and processing means that most species can be catered for. A greater knowledge of the natural history and biology of invertebrates also means that it is no longer such a difficult task to sustain them in the aquarium. Needless to say, there are still species that are regarded as impossible to feed successfully. For example, several species of marine angelfishes only feed on specific sponges that are not readily available to the aquarist, and although these fishes may accept other types of food, their digestive systems are not designed to deal with them. In such cases, the fishes derive no nourishment and over several weeks, sometimes months even, they will slowly die of starvation. Sometimes a single species can cause confusion because it has developed different feeding strategies according to the location it lives in. For instance, the Regal Angelfish, *Pygoplites diacanthus*, was once believed to be impossible to keep in the aquarium due to its highly specialized feeding habits. However, that was the situation for specimens originating from within its Pacific Ocean range. It was discovered that the Regals living in the Red Sea had naturally developed a more varied diet and were therefore better suited to life in the aquarium.

In recent years the aquarium industry has taken a hard look at its practices and has done much to inform hobbyists and dealers alike of those species regarded as difficult and therefore better off left in the wild, resulting in reduced demand. In general, it is another case of doing some homework to learn as much as you can about the species you would like to keep in an effort to avoid making unnecessary mistakes.

Below: *Angelfishes, such as this Blue-faced Angelfish, have strong mouthparts that are ideal for grazing on encrusted sponges and algae. However, they may prove difficult to feed in captivity.*

The food pyramid

A clear understanding of the food pyramid, or food chain, and where the species you want to keep are placed within it, will be very useful. It can be very complex but, in essence, there are plants, algae and phytoplankton at the bottom of the pyramid, with herbivorous animals situated above them in the scheme of things and carnivorous animals further up. The apex predators are situated right at the top of the pyramid. The plants are primary providers of nourishment and all species in the pyramid derive some benefits from them. This is because herbivorous animals that are directly nourished by plants are eaten by carnivorous species, allowing them to be indirectly benefited. Finding out where fishes and invertebrates fit into the scheme of things will help you make better informed choices for your aquarium. For example, it is no good mixing most triggerfishes with sea urchins, as urchins are the natural diet of these fishes. Likewise, you will see that groupers and lionfishes are predatory carnivores that will eat virtually any fish, or crustacean in some cases, that they can fit into their enormous mouths.

Furthermore, if you are hoping to establish lush macro-algae growth then you will have to avoid keeping herbivorous species such as surgeonfishes in the same aquarium.

The food pyramid

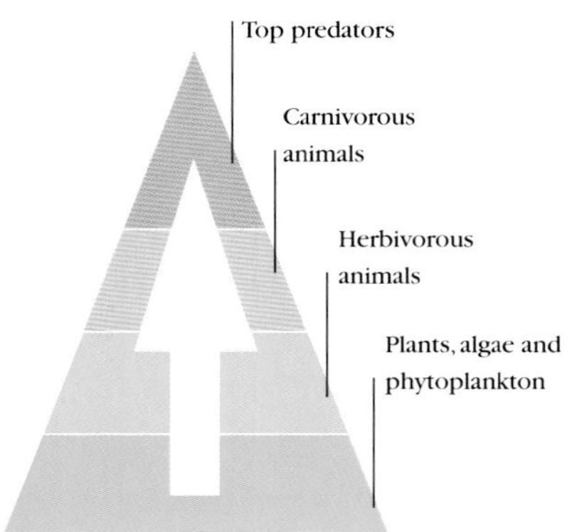

Above: *Feeding relationships can be conveniently shown as a food pyramid, with plants at the bottom leading up through herbivores to top carnivores.*

Feeding strategies

Marine fishes and invertebrates employ a wide variety of feeding strategies, and you should take these into careful account for the well-being of your aquarium subjects. Some species will readily take food in the open water column, but many have jaws and teeth modified for grazing algae or tiny microorganisms from the rock surfaces. Parrotfishes have gone one stage further; they actually bite off portions of rock, crush it, extract the algae from it and then excrete it, thus adding fresh sand to the substratum.

Predators usually employ an element of surprise and adopt one of two strategies; either they ambush their prey, as many moray eels do, or, like groupers and lionfishes, they often stalk it.

Plankton is most evident at dusk and animals that feed on such organisms, including polyp animals such as corals, take particular advantage of this. Corals and many other polyp animals derive their main nourishment from the photosynthetic processes of the zooxanthellae algae that live within their tissues, but they will also extend their tentacles in the evening to catch planktonic animals (zooplankton). Filter-feeding invertebrates continually take in and pump out water in order to extract microorganisms, phytoplankton or sometimes even organic debris as their food source.

Generally speaking, marine fish fit into one of three main feeding groups: the open-water feeders, the grazers, and the specialist feeders. Many species are surprisingly adaptable in the aquarium, but it is still sensible to understand their natural behaviours. In the main, fish in the open-water category are easy to cater for and the grazers are not too difficult either. However, you must pay special attention to the specialist feeders, which can include predators, filter-feeders, all the polyp animals such as corals and anemones, and even those species with a nocturnal lifestyle that only feed after dark.

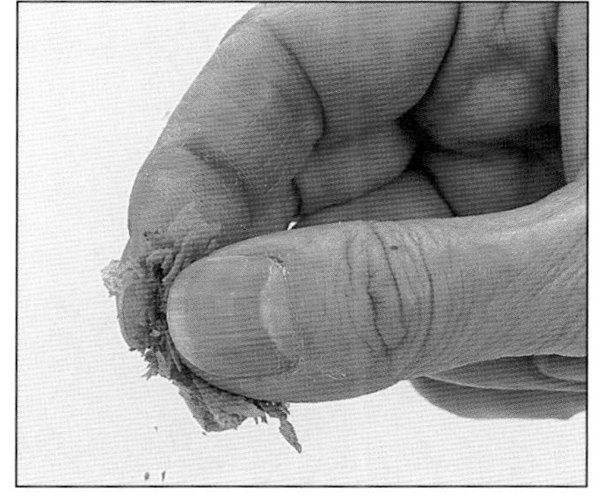

Above: *When feeding flake food, it is safer to offer only small amounts, crumbled between your fingers. Excess feeding will lead to an unnecessary strain on the biological filtration system.*

Flakes and granules

Flake foods fall slowly through the water and are ideal for most midwater and upper water level species.

Mixed flakes satisfy the nutritional needs of most marine fish.

Brineshrimp flakes. Initially, you may have to mix them with live or frozen brineshrimp to tempt the fish.

Granular food. This sinks quickly for the benefit of bottom-dwellers.

Freeze-dried foods

Based on fresh natural foods, most freeze-dried portions can be stuck onto the interior glass panels at any level.

Tablet foods. Excellent for sticking on the tank glass.

Freeze-dried river shrimp. These can be fed to medium-sized fish such as triggerfishes.

Freeze-dried krill are accepted by lionfish and groupers.

Freeze-dried brineshrimp look less natural and may not tempt shy feeders.

Sources of food

Here we examine the advantages and disadvantages of foods available for marine aquarium animals.

Prepared foods

Research continues into suitable foods for use in marine aquariums and the many advances to date ensure there is now a wide variety available for a number of applications.

Dried foods, such as flakes and pellets, are excellent and convenient to use as part of a staple diet for the wide range of species that will readily accept them. They are also first-rate conditioning foods, as they usually contain added vitamins and other

Frozen foods

Whole cockle. This natural food is accepted by all marine fishes.

Marine mix is a mixture of various natural marine invertebrate and fish meats.

Shrimp. Many wild-caught foods are irradiated to destroy disease pathogens.

Small fish make excellent 'one-gulp' food for larger fishes.

Krill. A nutritious food for larger fish; break up for small fishes.

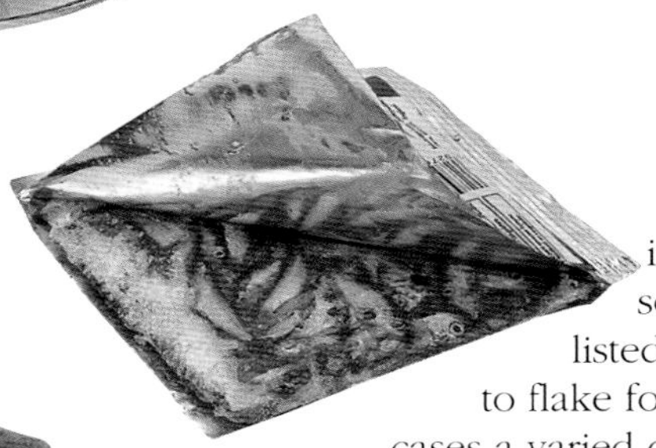

Above:
Frozen foods are sold in single slabs (break off pieces as required) or in individual push-out 'servings'. Thaw frozen foods before offering them to fish.

beneficial substances that are often missing in frozen foods as a result of processing. Freeze-dried shrimps and worms are also convenient additions to diets. Liquid preparations are also available that provide suspended food particles for filter-feeding animals, but for more specific requirements you may want to make your own by blending fish, shrimp and perhaps some flake with water in a food processor.

Prepared dried foods have few disadvantages apart from the fact that, in general, predators and other specialized feeders will not be interested in them. However, it is important to offer some of the foods listed below in addition to flake food, as in most cases a varied diet will improve the well-being of your animals.

Fresh foods

It would be easy to assume that because marine animals take their food from the sea, obtaining seafoods from a fishmonger would be ideal for aquarium fish. In some cases this is true, as small whole fishes, prawns and cockles, for example, are good fare for carnivorous species. The advantage of these fresh foods is that they will contain their original goodness in terms of vitamins and certain beneficial minerals. On the other hand, their main disadvantage is that they could introduce disease pathogens that infect your animals, particularly if they have come from a location where your fishes and invertebrates do not naturally occur. In this instance, your animals will have little resistance to such ailments. It could be argued that strong, healthy animals should be able to ward off such illnesses, but in reality there is no guarantee.

To reduce the risk of infection from fresh foods, it is worth removing the guts from fish and shrimps, but this also means you are removing some very nutritional items. Soaking fresh seafoods in freshwater for half an hour or so before use also helps to kill off marine parasites that may be on the food. However, neither of these techniques will offer any form of guarantee, so to be more certain you should boil and then freeze these foodstuffs before offering them to your aquarium subjects.

Frozen foods

Many types of frozen foods are produced commercially specifically for aquarium use and these can provide the bulk of the diet for many species. Small fishes, squid, krill, mysis and other shrimps, algae, clams, cockles and mussels, worms, plankton and eggs from fishes, crabs and lobsters are all now available in frozen packs from aquarium stores. Generally, these frozen foods have been irradiated with gamma rays to sterilize them and eliminate the risk of introducing diseases. The other advantage is they can be stored for several months in a freezer and pieces broken off as required.

But there is a serious disadvantage in that the irradiation and freezing processes destroy important vitamins. If possible, therefore, it will be necessary to add some dried prepared foods to the diet and/or soak the food with liquid supplementary vitamins on a regular basis before feeding it to your animals. Such vitamins should be available from your dealer.

Live foods

There are several different types of live foods available to aquarists, although most are particularly suited to freshwater fishes. Those, such as black worms *(Tubifex)*, bloodworms and water fleas *(Daphnia)*, that will not live for long in the marine environment should only be fed to marine fishes and invertebrates as long as you are sure they will all be eaten in less than a minute. Otherwise, you run the risk of polluting your aquarium water as the live foods you have offered die off. The likes of black worms originate from freshwater ponds that are often polluted, so they must be kept in good-quality, running water for several days to flush out any potentially toxic substances

Above: *Feeding live brineshrimp is an ideal way of encouraging shy fish to feed. Set up your own hatchery to be sure of a regular supply of this valuable food.*

Gamma irradiation

Gamma irradiation is a method by which food potentially containing harmful microorganisms can be made safe for fish to consume. Gamma rays are a form of electromagnetic energy, similar to microwaves. Whereas microwaves have sufficient energy to move molecules and thus create heat, gamma radiation has more energy and can therefore discharge electrons. The resultant 'freeing' of electrons from atoms, known as ionization, makes them available as part of a chemical reaction that can disrupt DNA. This is the fundamental mechanism by which microorganisms are killed, thus preventing disease passing from frozen food to the fish.

Hatching brineshrimp eggs

1 You will need the following equipment: brineshrimp eggs, two or three empty clear plastic bottles, a small airpump with airline, some marine salt (as used in your aquarium) and a fine net.

2 In one of the bottles, mix one litre of water with two heaped teaspoons of marine salt. Add a small pinch of brineshrimp eggs. Adding too many eggs will not increase the 'harvest'; excessive newly hatched brineshrimp will simply die quickly, polluting the water. Drop in the airline attached to the airpump and switch it on. The bubbles will circulate the eggs.

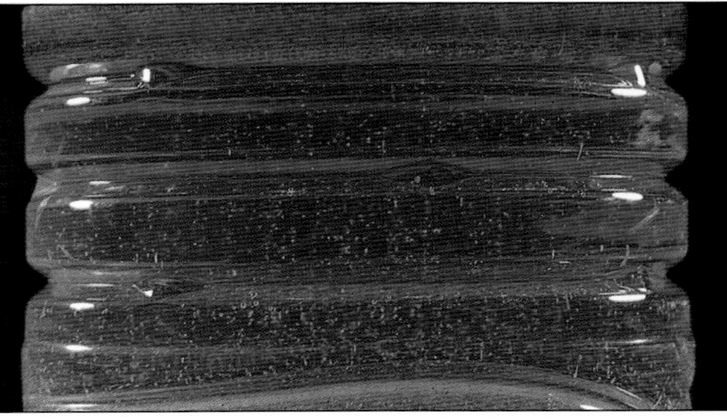

3 Stand the bottle in a dark place and keep the water at 21-24°C (70-75°F). Depending on the temperature, the eggs should hatch in 24-48 hours.

Ease of feeding in the aquarium

Group	Easy	Reasonable once feeding	Difficult	Difficult, need livefoods
Angels		✓	✓	
Basses	✓			
Blennies	✓	✓		
Butterflyfishes	✓	✓	✓	✓
Cardinals		✓		
Catfishes	✓			
Clownfishes	✓	✓		
Damsels	✓			
Eels	✓			
Filefishes			✓	
Gobies	✓			
Jawfishes		✓		
Lionfishes		✓		✓
Seahorses			✓	✓
Squirrelfishes		✓		✓
Surgeons	✓			
Tangs	✓			
Triggers		✓		
Wrasses	✓			

Feeding for groups with multiple entries depends on species.

Above: *Tangs and many angelfishes appreciate a green supplement, such as blanched lettuce or spinach. Trap the leaf between two halves of an algae magnet and let it sink to the bottom.*

before you use them as food. Treating them with a general bactericide may also help.

By far the most popular and readily available live foods for marine aquariums are brineshrimp *(Artemia)*. Many aquarium stores have regular supplies of adult brineshrimps for sale and these make an excellent and nutritious treat for a large number of species. Brineshrimp eggs are also readily available and are very easy to hatch in a well-aerated saline solution. Special hatcheries can be bought for this purpose, but it is easy to make your own, using any clean container made from non-corrosive and non-toxic materials. The base should be narrower than the top, i.e. a wedge or funnel shape. As the egg cases generally float after hatching, it is much easier to drain the shrimps from the bottom of a container with such a shape. To make life even easier, you can also buy decapsulated brineshrimp eggs. As the name suggests, the outer case has been removed from the eggs. The newly hatched nauplii stages are ideal for filter-feeding invertebrates and planktivorous fishes, such as damselfishes in the genus *Chromis*. They are also a good food for small juvenile fishes. However, since brineshrimps lack calcium, they should not be offered as the sole food to fishes such as seahorses and pipefishes that require quite high levels of calcium in their diet. Mysis shrimps are much better in such circumstances.

Live mysis shrimps have become increasingly available in aquarium stores over recent years. Mysids are small saltwater shrimps, although larger than brineshrimps, and can be found in most parts of the world. You can collect your own from places such as sea walls, where they often congregate in huge numbers, and then keep them alive in their own well-aerated and filtered tank until they are required. To avoid introducing potentially harmful microorganisms with these shrimps, once again it is worth medicating them with a general bactericide suitable for use in a marine aquarium and with crustaceans.

Vegetable foods

As we have seen in the food pyramid, all species derive benefits from eating plants, either directly or indirectly. Therefore, it is essential that you include vegetable matter in the general marine diet. Culturing algae in the aquarium is probably the best way to provide this food. If this is not practical then you must provide it by other means. Vegetable flake foods are available and make a good alternative, while species such as surgeonfishes and angelfishes often seem happy to take fresh lettuce. Lettuce is largely made up of water, but it is a great source of a large number of vitamins. Spinach is also good, but blanch it first with boiling water or freeze it before use in order to break down its cellulose, which fishes cannot digest. Feed spinach sparingly, however, as its leaves contain small traces of arsenic. Always wash fresh vegetables thoroughly, as they may

Vitamin sources in foods

Food	Vitamin
Algae	A, B_{12}, C, E
Beef	A, B_2, B_6, B_{12}, C, K
Crustaceans	A, B_2, B_6, D, K
Daphnia	D, K
Earthworms	D
Egg yolk	A, B_{12}, D, E
Fish meat	B_2, B_6
Fish eggs	C
Fish liver	A, D
Lettuce	A, C, B_2, B_6, B_{12}, C, E, K
Mealworms	D
Mussels	B_2, B_6, B_{12}
Shrimps	D, K
Snails	D
Spinach	A, B_2, B_6, C, E, K
Tubifex	D
Water plants	A, C, K
Wheatgerm	E
Yeast	A, B

have agricultural pesticides on them that could prove fatal to your animals.

A balanced diet

Understandably, most of the research on fish nutrition has been centred on species raised in captivity for conservation purposes or on foods for humans – trout bred on fish farms, for example. It seems logical that many of these findings will also apply to other fishes in captivity, including ornamental marine fishes.

Such research has shown how vital it is to provide a diet containing the right balance of carbohydrates, proteins and fats to provide energy and to build body tissue. As we have seen, this has led to the production of high-quality prepared foods for a wide range of fishes, and should influence all our decisions about suitable diets. For example, it is clear that fishes need a ready supply of so-called 'essential' amino acids (the building blocks of proteins) for normal growth and healthy development. These requirements are species dependent and vary with the age of individuals. Deficiency in any particular essential amino acid produces characteristic symptoms, ranging from reduced growth rate to death, in extreme cases. Although it is possible to add these amino acids to the diet in a 'free' form, many fishes cannot make use of them in this way. The best approach is to provide a varied and well-balanced diet.

Research into nutrition also shows that fishes require highly unsaturated fatty acids to maintain good health. One vital reason for this is that such fats enable the delicate membranes throughout a fish's body to remain flexible and fluid at relatively low temperatures. It is particularly important to prevent fats in fish foods from becoming rancid, i.e. oxidized, as this will cause specific health problems.

It is also important to remember the vital role that minerals and vitamins play in diets. Although needed in only very small amounts, vitamins act as catalysts to activate the nutritional processes. Some vitamins are manufactured in the fish's body, while others must be constantly available in the food. No single type of food provides all the essential vitamins, but all foods contain some vitamins. Thus, there is an added bonus in offering a varied and balanced diet in that a wide range of vitamins will become available. Vitamin groups may be fat soluble (A, D, E and K) or water soluble (B and C). Vitamin B is a collective name for a group of vitamins known by individual names and/or numbers, such as B_1 (Thiamine), B_2 (Riboflavin), B_6 and B_{12}, the last one of which is the very useful vitamin responsible for encouraging animals to eat. The table shows the vitamin content of some foods, although please note that not all those listed are useful for marine aquarium animals.

Feeding methods

The well-tried formula of feeding 'a little and often' is suited to a large number of marine fishes and invertebrates, as many feed in this manner in the wild. There is one proviso to this feeding technique and that is to take the utmost care

Possible symptoms of vitamin deficiency

If fish are not provided with a balanced diet, they can become ill and may eventually die. Below are some symptoms that may result from a lack of various vitamins. If these symptoms appear, examine diet and water quality as possible causes.

Vitamin	Symptom of deficiency
A	Loss of appetite, eye and gill problems, loss of weight and slow growth.
B_1	Muscular wasting, poor growth, loss of balance.
B_2	Eye problems such as a cloudy or bloody appearance. Poor growth and anaemia.
B_6	Loss of appetite, excessive body fluid, bloating, fits.
B_{12}	Anaemia, poor growth.
C	Reduced vividness of colour, eye diseases, deformed growth.

Right: *This Decorated Dartfish* (Nemateleotris decora) *is a midwater feeder and has no problems in capturing food such as this fragment of thawed-out shrimp as it falls through the water.*

Feeding invertebrates

FEEDING TYPES	SUITABLE FOODS	QUANTITIES AND FREQUENCY OF FEEDING
Hunters Large crabs, lobsters. Large univalve molluscs, e.g. Queen Conch, octopus, squid, cuttlefish, Nautilus.	Small whole fish, shellfish meat, defrosted whole shrimps, prawns. Flaked food tucked into fish meat to supply essential trace elements.	Feed once a day. Remove uneaten food after one hour. Quantities depend on the size of the animal, e.g. 30cm (12in)-diameter octopus needs 2-3 large shrimps, or one 5-6cm (2-2.4in) fish.
Opportunists and scavengers Small crabs, shrimps. Horseshoe crabs. Cowries, sea slugs. Starfishes, sea urchins, sea cucumbers	Small pieces of fish, shellfish meat, shredded prawn, mysis shrimp, brineshrimp, cockles, mussels. Algae.	Feed once a day at most. Remove uneaten food after one hour. These animals require little food and may subsist on the leavings from any fish in the tank.
Filter feeders and self sustainers Sponges. Seapens, soft corals, sea whips, seafans, anemones*, jellyfish, hard corals. Flatworms. Fanworms, tubeworms, featherduster worms. Barnacles. Clams, scallops, oysters. Crinoids. Sea squirts.	Liquidized fish, shellfish meat or mussel blended with salt water from the aquarium. Newly hatched brineshrimp nauplii. Algae, pulverized or as a suspension. Live rotifers. Prepared plankton food.. Liquid feed. Vitamin supplements.	Feed once a day at most; filter feeders are better underfed than overfed. Under intense lighting, many corals and clams need little if any supplementary food. One drop per day per animal of a good liquid feed is sufficient. Switch off filtration for half an hour to prevent premature removal of food.

*Anemones are classified here as filter feeders, but will accept small pieces of food once a fortnight.

not to give so much that uneaten food is continually left to pollute the water. Always remove uneaten food as soon as the animals have stopped feeding, either by netting it or siphoning it out. Regular nitrite testing will indicate whether water quality is declining due to uneaten food being left in the aquarium, or if an animal has died unnoticed. This practice will reassure you that the biological filters in your system are working efficiently or alert you to a problem if they are not.

If a newly acquired fish shows no interest in feeding, it may be helpful to add vitamin B_{12} directly to the aquarium water in the hope that the fish will take it in and it will trigger the urge to eat. Suitable vitamin supplements for this purpose are available. Squid has a

Above: *To prevent green foods becoming stuck in filter inlets, secure them to the aquarium glass using a sucker and clip. Discard uneaten food.*

powerful odour in water and many species may find it irresistible, so it is worth offering small pieces of this to finicky eaters, making sure you remove it again if not taken.

In the case of predators that are normally used to eating living food, it may be necessary to 'train' them to take more convenient and safer dead foods. This can be done by impaling a strip of fish, squid or prawn onto the end of a transparent plastic or glass rod with the idea that the fishes see the food but not the rod. By trying to simulate swimming movements, it is often possible to entice such fishes into feeding by this method.

Never forget the needs of any animals with nocturnal feeding habits. However, once nocturnal animals have become used to their aquarium surroundings, they will often adapt to feeding during the daylight hours, making it much easier on the aquarist.

Most free-swimming invertebrates tend to graze continually, scavenge or wait for an opportune moment to feed. However, the sessile (non-moving) species, such as corals and anemones, do not need constant attention where feeding is concerned. Polyp animals that contain photosynthetic zooxanthellae algae derive much nourishment from byproducts of photosynthesis. Anemones can be fed small pieces of prawn or fish every couple of weeks, but corals usually only require the occasional feeding of a plankton substitute. If filter feeders, such as fanworms, clams and sponges, are present in the tank, offer a suitable suspension food a couple of times a week, plus regular offerings of newly hatched brineshrimps. Any corals sharing the same aquarium may also benefit from these feeds.

Left: *The extended polyps of* Dendrophyllia *sp. are much like tiny anemones. These corals are best fed live foods in the aquarium.*

Should you go on holiday, you must arrange for a totally trustworthy fellow hobbyist, relative or neighbour to look after your aquarium and feed its subjects while you are away. Unlike freshwater aquarium fishes, which can survive for relatively long periods without food providing they are in a healthy condition to start with, the majority of marine aquarium fishes must be fed on a regular basis regardless. Do not use holiday food blocks in the marine aquarium, as they could pollute the water if uneaten because the fishes find them too unfamiliar. It is far better to make up the correct amount for each feed due while you are away and store it in separate packages in a freezer so that whoever is looking after your aquarium does not accidentally overfeed. This person should also be given some basic training in looking after the life-support system of your aquarium and the phone number of a friendly expert or two in case of emergencies.

Below: *The mixed aquarium is truly a thing of great beauty and appeal. Correct and careful feeding is one of the keys to success in the marine hobby.*

Regular Maintenance

Being able to see the fruits of your labour is a great pleasure and it is entirely up to you how much time you spend on maintenance. Once your aquarium is completely up and running, the time taken by routine maintenance is relatively small, yet it is something you can still enjoy.

Routine checks

There are several checks that you should make on a regular basis. First and foremost are daily temperature checks, along with a 'head count' of your aquarium subjects. Counting fishes is best done at feeding time, when they tend to be the most visible, although some invertebrates may be more difficult. Over time, you will develop an 'eye' for what is right and wrong, so that you can tell almost instinctively if any animals are more than just missing. Do your best to locate them and immediately remove any that have died. If an animal dies and the cause is unlikely to have been old age, you must try to discover the reason and take action accordingly. Marine fishes and invertebrates are generally sensitive to disturbances and the potential stress they cause, so do your best to use your eyes rather than searching around the tank with your hands. In other words, keep your physical intrusions to an absolute minimum. Some species are capable of jumping, so if an animal is not evident in the aquarium, it is worth looking on the floor, especially if the tank is not covered.

As the aquarium gradually becomes more established, its subjects will settle down into their natural behavioural patterns. If you take time to observe the animals' normal activities, you will soon be able to recognize any irregularities that may be early indications of trouble.

In a fully established aquarium, you should check pH weekly, making sure it remains stable at around 8.3 – but no higher – and no lower than 8.1. If it starts to drop, adjust it by adding buffering materials (see page 90-91). The situation may require some water renewal, especially if the pH continues to drop after you have attempted to adjust it. Siphoning off debris from the substrate on a weekly basis will go a long way in preventing a decline in water conditions, especially pH. Most of this debris is likely to be organic, so as it breaks down it will be releasing carbon dioxide into the water and affecting its buffering capabilities.

Take a specific gravity reading once a week and test for ammonia and nitrite levels once every two weeks. It is also a good idea to keep a check on the nitrate and phosphate levels weekly. Fishes generally appear to have a higher tolerance of nitrate than many invertebrates, and experienced marine aquarists have suggested 40mg/litre is an acceptable upper limit. However, it is always best not to make any compromises and try to keep nitrate levels below 5mg/litre.

It is important to carry out regular partial water changes. Do not change too much at any one time as it may cause a sudden drift in environmental conditions and cause some stress to the animals. Around 10% change each week is good, although smaller amounts on a daily basis would be more efficient, but far less convenient, for most aquarists. As already discussed elsewhere, never mix new supplies of saltwater directly in the tank once there are living organisms in it. Occasionally, it may be necessary to top up due to evaporation loss. As only water evaporates, leaving the salts behind, you must only top up using freshwater. Always use the best quality freshwater available to you for this purpose.

Below: *Observe your aquarium closely and regularly for signs of trouble. You can then take remedial action before a crisis occurs. Routine maintenance should be a pleasure, not a chore.*

How your aquarium matures

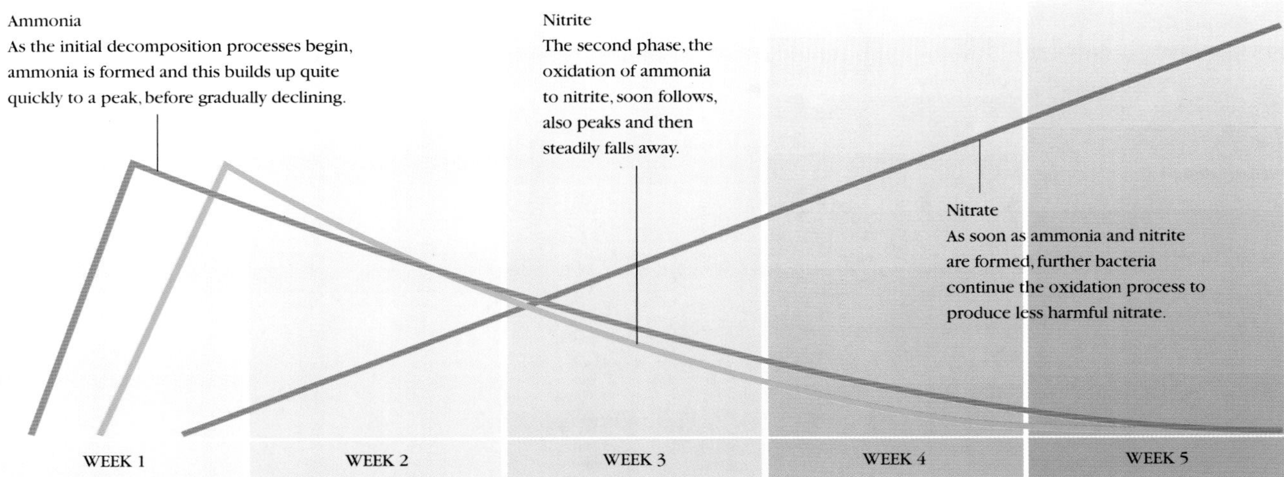

Practical tips for a healthy aquarium

Choose healthy stock and quarantine all new additions, provided that you keep the quarantine tank up to the standard of your main tank. Avoid stressing the fish in any way.

Do not hope to keep all the fishes that you like the look of; bear in mind the feeding habits of different species, their compatibility with fish of the same or different species and their eventual mature size.

Do not use any metal objects in the aquarium. Purists even remove the inside half of magnetic algae-scrapers when they are not using them.

Remove uneaten food at the earliest opportunity; any water siphoned off during this process can be filtered through a fine cloth and returned to the aquarium. Acclimatize fish to any new food over a period of time.

Learn to recognize symptoms of impending water problems: frothy, cloudy, yellowing and smelly water are all signs of deteriorating conditions in the aquarium.

Do not neglect regular partial water changes. Changing 20-25% of the water in the aquarium each month is an average guide, but an invertebrate tank may require more frequent changes to keep it in good condition.

Top up evaporation losses with fresh water, not saltwater.

Make all changes to the aquarium water gradually. For example, after siphoning off 20-25% of the tank water for a water change, add the new water slowly over a period of at least half an hour. Remember to turn off powerheads or other motorized filters that may be left 'high and dry' when the water level is low.

Keep cover glasses clean. Salt spray soon renders them opaque, which prevents the full light intensity reaching right down into the water.

Check that the water flow rate from filters remains high. Clean external mechanical filters and replace both the filter medium and activated carbon frequently – at least once a week if necessary. Wash filter media in aquarium water to avoid killing any bacterial colonies.

You can check the efficiency of activated carbon by adding a few drops of a dye, such as methylene blue, next to the filter inlet. If clear water emerges from the outlet, the carbon is still working; if blue emerges, the carbon needs replacing.

Empty the collecting chambers of protein skimmers regularly.

Isolate taps in the hoses to external filters to lessen the risk of spillages when cleaning filters.

After cleaning external power filters, make sure that the hoses are tightly attached – a filter pump will just as easily empty a tank as filter it!

After a period of time, algae will grow all over the tank. Remove it from the front glass with a non-metal scraper; nylon and plastic scourers are very effective. Excess algae scrapings may be fed to fish in less algae-covered tanks. There is no need to remove algae from the remaining panels, as the fish will graze on it. Thin out excessive growths, as a sudden 'algae death' could cause pollution.

When treating fishes with disease remedies, follow the manufacturer's recommendations. Most treatments are designed to be added to the whole aquarium, but remember that copper-based cures will kill most invertebrates in the tank. (This is one reason why it is more difficult to keep fishes and invertebrates together. A practical ratio would be 80% invertebrates to 20%, or even fewer, fishes.) If necessary, remove sick fishes and treat them separately from the main tank. Do not mix medications. Sterilize all equipment after use and do not share a net between two tanks.

Emergency measures

Occasionally things can go wrong. If a heater fails, causing a serious drop in temperature, it is a good idea to float plastic bottles filled with hot water in the aquarium, taking care that the displacement of aquarium water does not overflow. If you own an enamel pan, you could also heat up some aquarium water and return it to the tank very carefully and gradually. In the meantime, either repair the heater or replace it with a new unit – the latter being the most likely course of action.

On the other hand, should your heater's thermostat stick in the 'on' position, causing the temperature to rise, switch off power to the unit and apply extra aeration. In a reverse of the method described above, you could fill plastic bottles

A typical maintenance schedule

Task	Frequency (new tank)	Frequency (old tank)
Check ammonia and nitrite levels.	Every day for a week when first animals are added. Then every week up to week 8.	Daily for 2/3 days when new animals are added. Then monthly or when needed.
Check nitrate.	Every week (to week 8).	Monthly or when needed.
Check pH level.	Every week.	Every week.
Check specific gravity.	Every week (to week 8).	Monthly; after all water changes and when needed.
Partial water change:		
Lightly stocked tank.	Every month.	Every month.
Heavily stocked tank.	Every two weeks.	Every two weeks.
Empty protein skimmer cup and clean interior of protein skimmer.	As needed.	As needed.
Clean cover glass/ reflector and remove algae. Check airstones.	As needed.	As needed.
Rinse/replace filter media. Cut filter sponge in half and clean alternately.	Every month.	Every month.
Top up evaporation losses with freshwater.	As needed.	As needed.
Check for dead fish, signs of disease, bullying and abnormal behaviour.	Daily.	Daily.
Check equipment, temperature /flow rate.	Daily.	Daily.

Phosphate test

1 *Add 5 drops of the phosphate reagent to a 5ml sample of tank water and shake gently to mix.*

Testing for ammonia, nitrite and nitrate

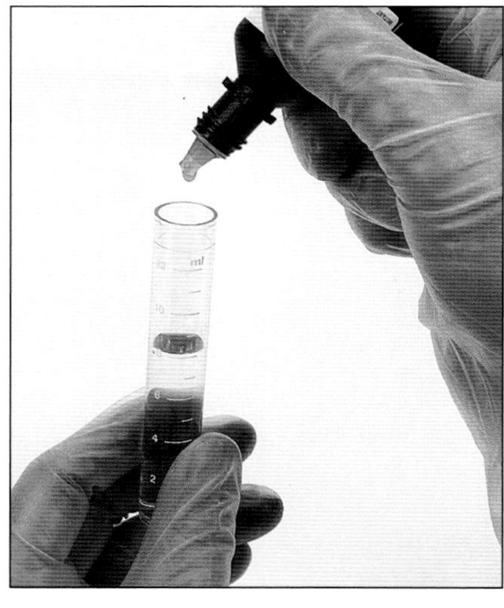

Above: *Testing the water involves adding chemicals to a measured sample and comparing the colour change to a printed chart. Some tests involve adding two or three chemicals in stages. Allow the correct time period to elapse between adding reagents. If recommended, wear protective gloves when using chemicals, as they may cause skin irritation.*

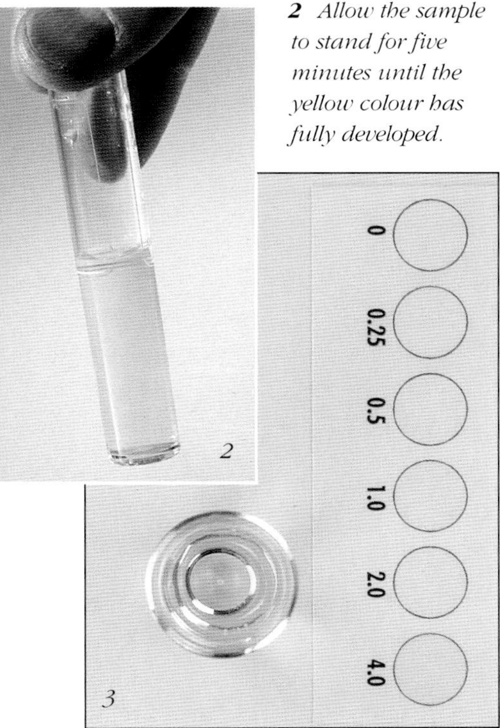

2 Allow the sample to stand for five minutes until the yellow colour has fully developed.

3 Place the tube on the printed chart and look down the length of the tube to compare the colour of the solution.

Carbonate hardness (KH) test

1 Add the KH reagent a drop at a time to a 5ml sample of tank water and gently swirl the tube to mix. Count each drop of reagent.

2 Initially, the sample turns blue.

3 As more reagent is added, the water sample turns yellow. Continue counting the drops added until the yellow colour is stable. Each drop added from the beginning of the test represents 1°dH, which is equivalent to 17.5mg per litre of carbonate.

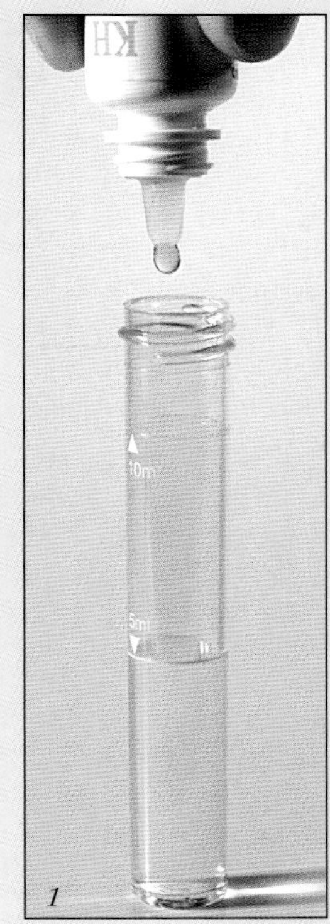

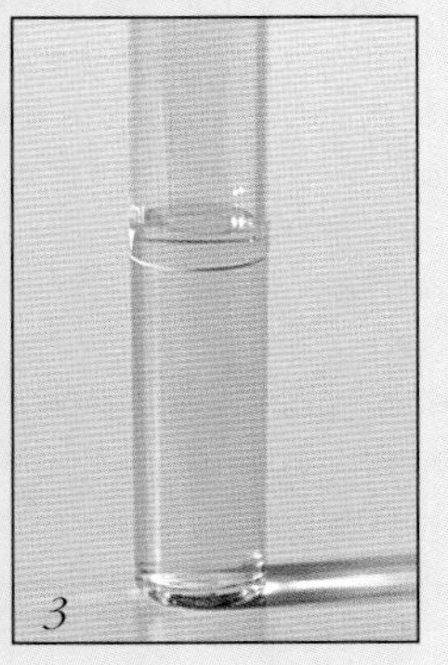

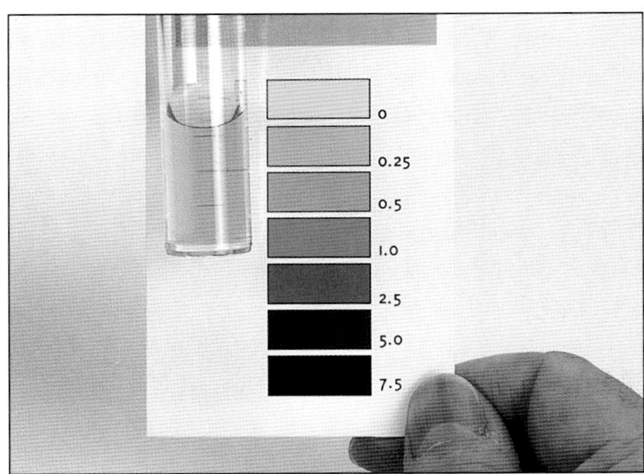

Left: *When testing for ammonia, the aim is to achieve a reading of zero. Not until this reading is consistently at the lowest possible value, is it safe to introduce any fish into the aquarium. Test the water regularly.*

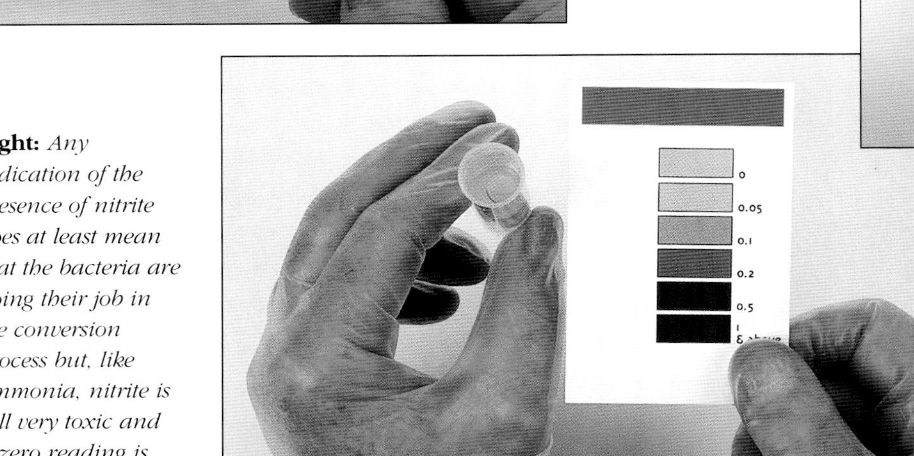

Right: *Any indication of the presence of nitrite does at least mean that the bacteria are doing their job in the conversion process but, like ammonia, nitrite is still very toxic and a zero reading is what you need.*

Above: *With some original nitrate already present in the mixing water, readings are likely to be high. Although some species can tolerate nitrate, do not allow it to exceed 10mg/litre. Here, the reading is very low.*

with ice in order to reduce the temperature gradually.

Should your electricity supply fail, such as in a power cut, the relatively large body of water in the aquarium can act as a heat reserve and will take a while to cool down. Lagging the tank with insulating material will help if there is concern that the power outage will last a long time. If you have other means of heating water, you could use bottles as described above. It is more critical to keep the filters running and to provide extra aeration. If the nitrifying bacteria die off due to a lack of oxygenated water, you will be back to 'square one', running the serious risk of deadly ammonia build-up. In such an event, one or two battery-powered airpumps would be very valuable investments and could maintain both water movement and the filter system until power is restored.

Back-up systems are worth considering. To avoid disaster from a sticking thermostat, you could connect a second one in line to the power supply. The idea is to set the second thermostat at a couple of degrees higher than the first, so that if the main one sticks, the other one will still turn off the heater and prevent an unwanted temperature increase. Otherwise, you could install two units as a precaution against one failing and causing a temperature drop. A further refinement would be to install a buzzer alarm to announce trouble; battery-operated buzzer alarms are available to indicate power failures.

Look on the bright side

Finally, remember not to look on routine tasks as chores to be avoided; most of them should be part of the pleasurable task of providing your aquarium subjects with the care and attention that they undoubtedly deserve. They will repay you in the best manner possible – with a living picture of beauty and colour that is both entertaining and educational. As a hobbyist, this is the reward for your hard work and dedication.

Dissolved oxygen test

Regularly checking the dissolved oxygen content of aquarium water indicates whether the system is overstocked with animals. Over time, animals grow and certain invertebrates will reproduce and increase the demand for oxygen. Excess waste will result in larger populations of nitrifying bacteria in the filters, which will also add to the demand for oxygen. Use the test shown here to record the oxygen level in mg per litre.

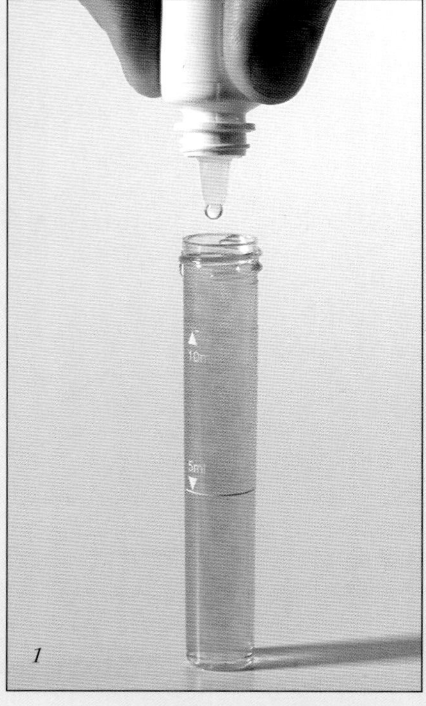

1 *Stabilize the oxygen content with the first reagent, then add eight drops of the second (shown here), forming a cloudy precipitate.*

2 *Add five drops of the third reagent and mix. The solution turns clear yellow.*

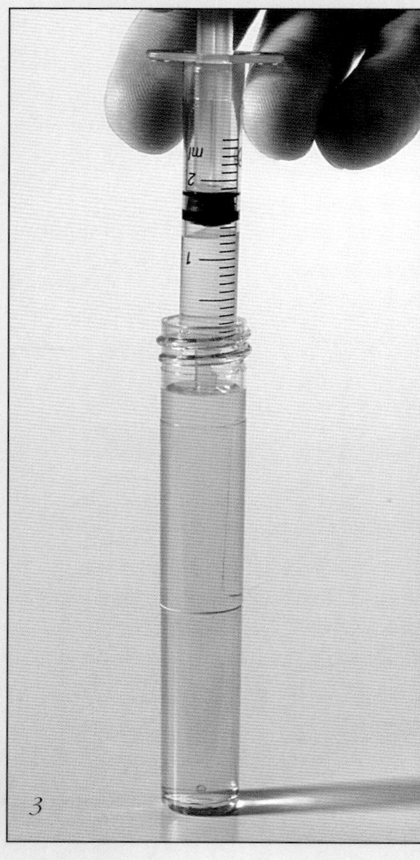

3 *Use the syringe to remove liquid down to the 10ml mark on the test tube.*

4

4 Pour the 10ml of yellow solution into a small beaker for the next stage of the oxygen test.

5

5 Add five drops of a fourth reagent to the yellow solution in the beaker, which turns black.

6

6 - 8 Gently swirl the black solution until it is an even colour. Add the final reagent a drop at a time until the black solution is colourless. Each drop added is equivalent to 0.5mg/litre of oxygen in the sample of tank water.

7

8

Breeding and Rearing

The art of breeding marine fishes and invertebrates in captivity is still regarded as being in its infancy. However, well over 100 species have now been bred in aquarium conditions and some of these are actually available commercially, yet only a few years ago this would have been thought impossible with most species. Successfully breeding and rearing a species must be the ultimate achievement for any marine aquarist. The results of such achievement are very important for the future of the hobby and for conservation. The knowledge gained from such experience will in time help to reduce the demand for wild-caught specimens and help the conservation of natural habitats. Just as importantly, this information could be used to teach those who are currently collecting for the aquarium hobby to set up breeding stations as an alternative means of income should the demand for wild stock diminish. To breed the popular species in their natural countries of origin would be far more cost effective than attempting the same on a commercial level in, say, northern Europe, because the ideal natural seawater would be available, as well as the correct foods, good sunlight and perfect temperature. The infrastructure for packing and shipping already exists and very little else is required, apart from knowledge.

There are tried and tested methods for breeding and rearing some marine species, but there is still a great deal of experimentation to be done for most. Some species may require a more radical approach and perhaps aquarists will need to employ a certain amount of creative license to attain success. For example, one of the earliest successes in breeding and rearing clownfishes back in the 1950s involved offering a combination of foods, including powdered silkworm cocoons, to rear the fry. What on earth made that person think of using silkworm cocoons?

Breeding strategies

Marine fishes and invertebrates employ various methods of reproduction. There are egg-scattering species, egg-depositors, mouthbrooders and even

Anemonefishes - egglayers

Anemonefishes are amongst the most popular of marine aquarium fishes and, although not the hardiest, they are probably the most likely to breed in a home aquarium. The Common Clown Anemonefish, *Amphiprion ocellaris*, has been bred in captivity over and again since the early 1950s and has fascinated even novice marine fishkeepers with its characteristic breeding behaviour.

Selecting pairs

Finding a true, viable pair of Clown Anemonefishes is easier than almost any other species. Because they all start life as males, with the largest, most dominant eventually turning into a female, you can obtain any two fishes with a very strong likelihood of ending up with a true pair.

Breeding strategy

In nature, Clown Anemonefishes live in association with any one of three anemone species: *Heteractis magnifica*, *Stichodactyla gigantea* or *Stichodactyla mertensii*. However, in the aquarium they will occasionally strike up a symbiotic relationship with other anemone species. They normally live in a close-knit group around their anemone, where the female rules over a sexually active male and a number of sexually inactive males that live on the periphery of the anemone. Should the female die, the active male will change into a female and the next attendant male in line will become sexually active. When spawning, they clean an area of rock, usually close to their anemone's trunk, to deposit the eggs. The male aggressively protects the nest site and cares for the eggs by fanning them to prevent detritus settling. Occasionally the female helps, but generally spends her time feeding.

The eggs are orange in colour because of the yolk sac they contain. Just before hatching at six to seven days, the large eyes of the embryos are clearly visible. On hatching, which occurs in the evening just after dark, the larvae first drop to the bottom, but quickly make their way up into the water column. These larvae remain in the plankton for 8 to12 days, but then settle near the reef substrate, close to anemones, and begin to develop their juvenile form and colour.

In the aquarium, clown anemonefishes seem to spawn readily without the presence of an anemone or attending males.

Rearing the larvae

The larvae are attracted to light, so soon after hatching they can be collected from the surface by shining a torch to gather them in one place and then very gently scooping them out into a plastic container. Do not use a net. Transfer them into the rearing tank. At this stage, the larvae are only about 3mm (0.125in) long and transparent, other than their eyes and a few tiny spots. They still have their yolk sacs.

Ideally, the sides of the rearing tank should be blacked out and there should be a cover with a central hole through which some light can be directed. This will ensure the larvae stay centred and do not crash into the

Left: *Both the male and female Common Clownfish clean the site upon which the batch of eggs will be laid – a practice shared by all clownfish species.*

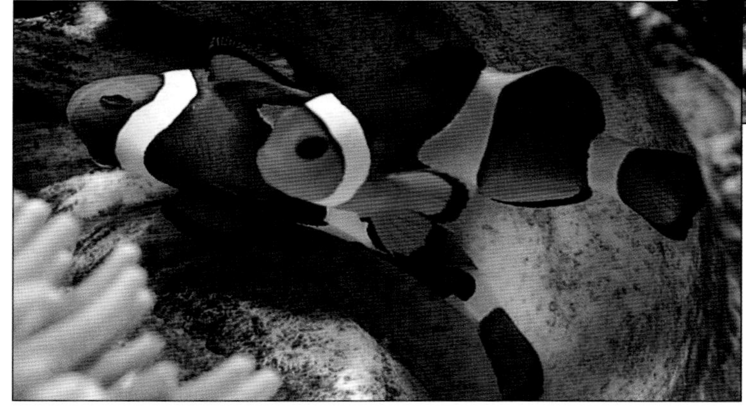

Right: *After the female has laid a line of eggs, the male passes over them and fertilizes each new row immediately. In this way, almost all the eggs are successfully fertilized.*

Above: *Although it is nearly always the male that attends the eggs, the female takes an occasional interest, as shown here. At six days old, the silvery eyes of the unhatched larvae are visible.*

sides of the tank and damage themselves. It may be useful to add a mild fungicide to the water as a precaution. No substrate is required. Filtration is not essential for the first few days, but should you wish you could use a small air-driven sponge filter with minimal water movement.

The larval fishes rapidly use up their yolk sacs, so other food must be ready and available to them, lest they quickly starve. The rotifer *Brachionus plicatilis* is the most readily available, and most suitable, for rearing larval anemonefishes. To ensure there is plenty to satisfy the larvae, drip-feed the rotifers into the tank at a slow but steady rate. When metamorphosis occurs at 8-12 days – the stage at which the yolk sacs are used up and the larvae begin to look like tiny fish – offer a wider variety of foods. It is at this time that aquarists have the most problems with rearing the fry, and this is believed to be due to nutrition. While continuing to give rotifers, also offer some newly hatched brineshrimp, as well as a mixture of liquidized mysis shrimps and marine flake food. It is also worth increasing the filtration and water movement a little. At around 20 days, the juveniles will be more recognizable as young anemonefishes and you can wean them off rotifers in favour of more conventional foods. You can now keep them in a more standard marine aquarium setup, but at this stage it may be necessary to transfer some of them into another tank to provide more space for efficient growth.

The above sequence reflects only one breeding strategy for these fish; clown anemonefishes have been bred and reared successfully in a variety of tank arrangements.

A clownfish (anemonefish) breeding tank

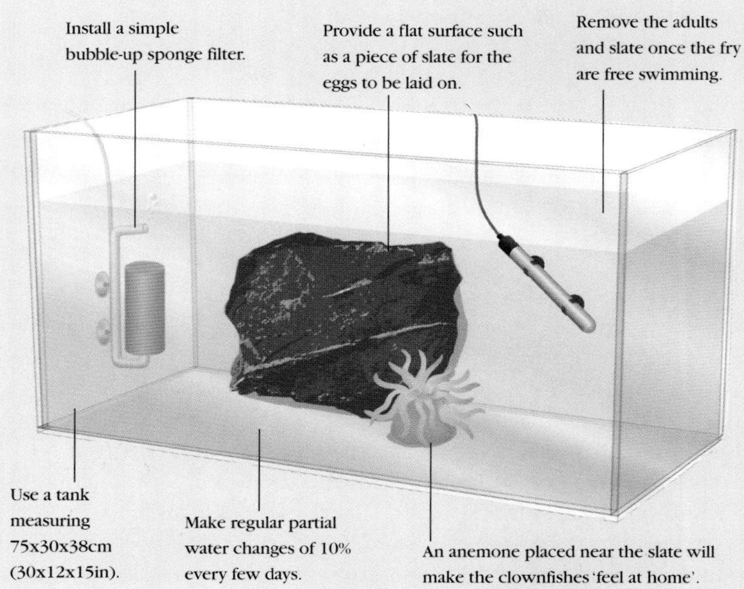

Cardinalfishes - mouthbrooders

Many cardinalfishes are popular with marine aquarists, but there is one that has captured a great deal of interest in recent times – the Emperor, or Banggai, Cardinalfish, *Pterapogon kauderni*. This species was only discovered relatively recently and appears to be very restricted in its distribution, being found at only a couple of locations around the Banggai Islands off the coast of Sulawesi in Indonesia. Because of its limited distribution, there has been some concern that collecting for the aquarium hobby will impact on the wild population, so breeding the fish in captivity is a worthy initiative. Fortunately, they reproduce readily in the aquarium and it is hoped that in the near future all specimens offered for sale will be captive bred.

Selecting pairs

It is sometimes possible to acquire proven pairs, but in general it is difficult to be certain of the sexes. It is best to obtain a small group and hope that there is a male and female among them and that pairing occurs.

Breeding strategy

Freshwater aquarists will be familiar with mouthbrooding cichlid species, and these cardinalfishes reproduce in a very similar manner. Eggs are produced and fertilized in the normal way for egglayers, but are then taken into the mouth of the male for incubation. Even after hatching, the juvenile fishes remain in the mouth for protection from predators. Because the juvenile fishes are afforded this extra parental care, they are better equipped to fend for themselves when they become free swimming. Since it is not necessary for these cardinalfishes to invest energy in producing large numbers of eggs, their broods are quite small. When the juveniles emerge from their parent's mouth they are tiny, fully formed replicas of the adults. Banggai Cardinals live in association with long-spined sea urchins *(Diadema* sp.*)* and the newly emerged juveniles head straight for the urchins to spend their early days living amongst the spines for protection.

Rearing

It is not essential to keep sea urchins in order to rear this species successfully, but if they are not available it is advisable to separate the juveniles from the adults, at least until they have grown larger. Some enterprising aquarists use artificial urchins with good results. It has been noted that juvenile Banggai Cardinals will sometimes protect themselves in anemones if urchins are not present in the aquarium.

In nature, young Banggai Cardinals feed on zooplankton and small bottom-dwelling invertebrates, so newly hatched brineshrimp and very finely chopped mysis shrimps, etc., are good foods for these relatively large juveniles. As they grow, you can offer them larger food particles.

The great thing about breeding this, and similar, species is that the entire operation can be carried out in an aquarium as small as 90 litres (20 gallons). This is due to the very small brood sizes and the fact that you can easily separate adults from juveniles by using a partition that allows a flow-through of aquarium water.

Below: *The challenge of breeding the Banggai Cardinalfish adds another dimension to the fishkeeping hobby.*

pouchbrooders. Egg-scattering species, which include basslets and angelfishes, are probably the most difficult to deal with, but definitely not impossible, especially where relatively small species are concerned. Clownfishes, damselfishes and gobies are all well known egg-depositors and their breeding behaviour, particularly that of the clowns and damsels, is very similar to that of some freshwater cichlids. The mouthbrooding jawfishes and some cardinalfishes are also similar to many African cichlids. Potentially, it is these marine mouthbrooders that present the easiest opportunities for captive breeding. For example, the fascinating Banggai Cardinalfish *(Pterapogon kauderni)*, is currently very popular with marine aquarists and reproduces frequently in the home aquarium.

Large species are often not practical contenders for captive breeding due to aggressiveness toward their own kind in confined spaces. Also, fish such as surgeonfishes require something in the region of 4.5m (15ft) of water depth in order to carry out their intricate courtship routines and are unlikely to reproduce in most captive situations.

In the case of invertebrates, some lay, or carry, eggs, while others simply divide in order to multiply. Crustaceans are often cannibalistic right from birth, making them difficult to rear, but corals multiply readily, providing water conditions are just right. However, in very basic terms, it seems that when dealing with clownfishes and some damsel and cardinalfishes, all that is required is a male and female, and breeding will regularly occur.

Basic requirements for breeding
Firstly, you must thoroughly research the species you wish to try breeding in your aquarium. It is important to find out all you can about the natural history of the species in order to get their habitat and water conditions right, as well as providing the correct types of food, and so on.

In the course of a great number of tropical marine breeding projects, it has been discovered that the special water conditioning power that living rock seems to possess can go a long way to help induce breeding behaviour. In fact, many of the most successful projects have been carried out with minimal equipment and have relied upon a simple biological filter, such as a fluidized bed sand filter, living rock, a single fluorescent lamp, regular partial water changes and heating where needed. Of course, in most cases, such breeding setups only need to support little more than a pair of fishes, so the biological loading is at a minimum. The important thing is that water quality must be optimum for the species in question if there is to be any chance of breeding them.

Space in the breeding aquarium is important for many species. Obviously, if the species is physically large it will require corresponding amounts of space. Also, some species operate as a harem, where a single male will service a number of females, either in a group, such as in the Lyretail Anthias *(Pseudanthias squamipinnis)* or the male visits a number of females in turn spread over an area of reef, as in certain species of Dwarf Angelfish, *Centropyge*. Available space becomes more of a problem when rearing juvenile fishes. Once fry have been produced, it is usually best to attempt rearing them in a separate tank from the parents. As the young fishes grow, it is also possible that you will have to separate them further into even more tanks to prevent overcrowding. If you are this successful, you should have in mind what course of action you will take to maintain such a large number of young fishes and how you will dispose of them if it is not practical to keep them all.

There are several other points worth considering to increase the chances of successful breeding. For instance, the influence of moon phases or season may be particularly important. Temperature, fluctuations in salinity and food availability are also likely triggers for one species or another. As we have seen, a good knowledge of the natural history of the fishes you wish to breed is extremely useful, and you should adjust the operation of your tank accordingly.

Selecting suitable pairs of fishes
Obtaining a suitable pair to breed from can sometimes be difficult, for

Seahorses - pouchbrooders

There is increasing concern for seahorse conservation, which suggests that as many attempts at captive breeding as possible would benefit them. On the other hand, seahorses are so difficult to keep, due to their continuous need for live foods and their susceptibility to various diseases, that only aquarists with a history of breeding other marine species successfully should attempt them. Seahorses do not possess a stomach and therefore have to eat continuously in order to derive any nourishment, devouring thousands of tiny shrimps during the course of a day.

Wild-caught seahorses that mated before capture often release young in the aquarium shortly after being introduced. In these cases, both adults and offspring find it difficult to deal with anything other than large quantities of live foods. However, should any captive-born seahorses survive to reproduce themselves, the subsequent generations seem better able to thrive on a combination of live and frozen foods and are more resistant to diseases.

Seahorses are so fascinating that aquarists will always want to keep them, but it is best not to try breeding them until you have first had plenty of experience with other marine species.

Selecting pairs

Whenever possible, only acquire specimens that have been bred and reared in captivity. It is very easy to distinguish males from females, as the males possess a pouch, which causes the body line from the belly to curve smoothly and gradually to the tail. Females, which do not have a pouch, are acutely angled from the belly to the tail. It appears that seahorses are monogamous – i.e. they keep the same partner for life – and it is possible to select a true pair in some species by observing their daily ritual greeting at sunrise.

Breeding strategy

Seahorses are unique in that it is the male that becomes pregnant and gives birth to the young. Breeding can be linked to the lunar cycle and it is known that most, but not all, species perform a ritual greeting at the start of each day. This is believed to help reinforce pair bonding and to help maintain synchronization between egg production by the female and the male's ability to accept them into his pouch.

The female produces eggs just as in other fishes, but she transfers them to the male's pouch after elaborate courtship. He indicates his readiness to accept the eggs by making muscular contractions of the pouch. Once the eggs are inside and fertilized, the pouch functions in a similar way to a womb, where hormones and calcium are supplied directly to the developing embryos. The hormone prolactin promotes enzyme activity that breaks down the outer layer of the eggs to produce 'placental fluids'. However, essential nutrients are provided from within the eggs. Development can take 10-42 days, depending on the species and water temperature. When the juvenile seahorses are fully developed they emerge from the pouch as miniature versions of their parents. The female is continually producing eggs and it is likely that another transfer to the male's pouch will occur later on the 'birthday'.

The males only produce sperm to fertilize the eggs seasonally, which means that when their partners are not receptive, the females often abort eggs, dropping them onto the substrate.

Rearing the young

Rear young seahorses in their own tank, allowing plenty of space for growth. As they need to feed on a large amount of shrimps, it is understandable that they produce a great deal of waste matter. Because of this, it is best to use a bare tank with no substrate to facilitate regular siphoning of faeces and other detritus. This really has to be done religiously before every feeding session and you must replace the resulting loss of water with a fresh batch of seawater. An external canister filter containing mature biological media is ideal for maintaining water quality, but cover the inlet (taking water from the tank to the filter) with

A seahorse breeding tank

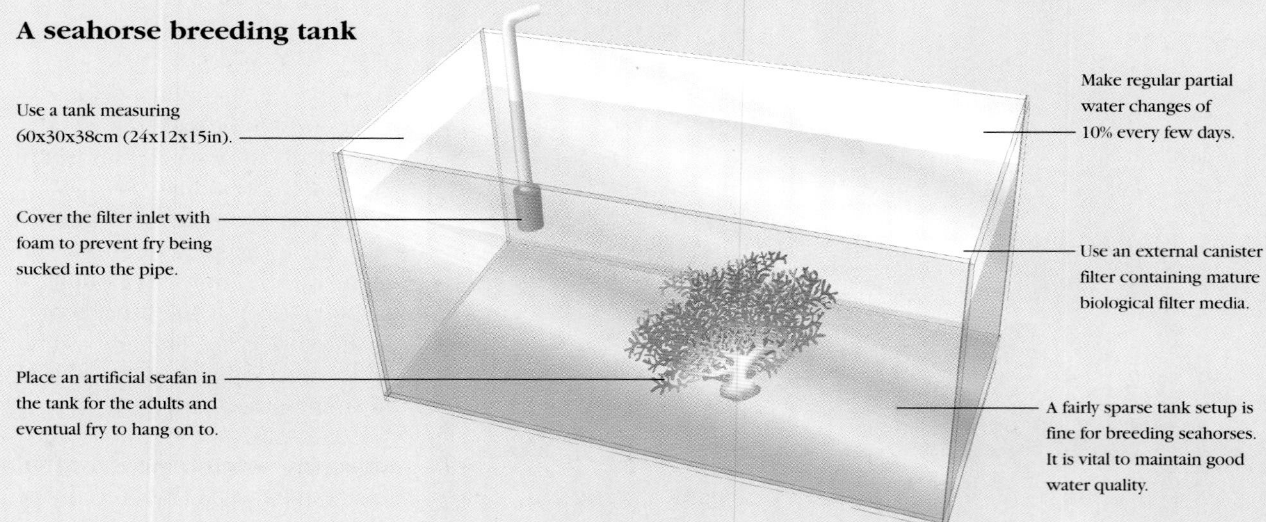

Right: *Seahorses require specialized care and feeding in the aquarium. Breeding them and raising their fry is a mission for aquarists with plenty of experience.*

foam to prevent any fry being sucked into the pipe. Seahorses need to anchor themselves by wrapping their prehensile tails around a suitable holdfast, so provide, for example, some plastic plants with fine stems and branches or a resin-moulded seafan.

A continual supply of live food is essential for newborn seahorses. Newly hatched brineshrimp can be used, but as they do not provide calcium – and seahorses have a high calcium requirement – many aquarists feed the brineshrimp a vitamin- and calcium-enriched food before offering them to the developing seahorses.

As is the case with many other marine fishes, it appears that correct nutrition becomes critical when the juveniles are 12 days old. Mysid shrimps are an excellent food for both growing seahorses and adults, so it is vital to encourage the young to take these as soon as possible. At first, offer finely chopped mysids while continuing to offer live brineshrimp. As the seahorses become interested and start taking the mysids from the bottom of the tank, reduce the amount of brineshrimps being offered and, with luck, you will eventually train the juveniles to take only the more beneficial mysid shrimps. Until they are adult and able to take them whole, you can offer growing seahorses larger pieces of shrimp. Remove any uneaten food regularly and to achieve success, offer these creatures at least four feeds a day.

a number of reasons. To start with, fishes offered for sale are often juveniles that have completely different coloration and patterns from the mature adults of their species. Secondly, in many species, the sexes have no easily distinguishable features, and thirdly, a large number of marine fish species change sex during the course of their lifetime. Clearly, you need all the relevant information about your chosen species before you can ensure that you have a true pair. And as we have seen, it may not be a simple case of acquiring just a pair of fishes because some species need to be part of a harem to mate and reproduce successfully.

Health and general condition are also very important when selecting suitable candidates. Conditioning a fish can be achieved over time, but it is still worth fully screening any specimen required for a breeding project before you acquire it. Of course, it may be possible to obtain pairs, or groups, that have already proven to be breeders, but such opportunities are still quite rare.

Dealing with offspring

Before embarking on any breeding project for the first time, you must be aware of the specific requirements of the resulting larvae and juveniles. Newly hatched fishes make up a large proportion of natural food for other fishes, so it is easy to understand the importance of rearing them in their own tank. In many species, the parents will eat their young once they have become free swimming, making it difficult to rear the offspring in the tank the eggs were laid in. However, it is equally important that the water the fry are transferred to is identical to that in the breeding tank to prevent shock.

Providing suitable foods for hatchling fishes can sometimes be difficult and time consuming. The majority of marine fish larvae are much smaller than those of freshwater fishes and cannot even cope with newly hatched brineshrimp. As the young fishes grow, however, brineshrimp can become a useful part of the diet later on. In most cases, rotifers are a more suitable first food. Rotifers have to be cultured using certain types of algae for their food. Fortunately, rotifer- and algae-culturing kits, complete with instructions, are now available to make the situation a little easier.

Because marine fish fry are generally so small, they can be easily filtered out by water circulation systems. Strong water movement can also pose the risk of fatal damage to these delicate baby fishes, as they could be easily swept against rocks and other solid objects. In some cases, filtration is not required in the first stages of rearing, but if it is necessary, then small air-driven sponge filters are the most suitable.

Meeting the challenge

So, you want to take the next step towards breeding your own marine fishes! There is an enormous number of species to choose from, most with very little or no information available to help guide you. To start things off, it will be best to gain some experience by working with species that have already been bred successfully in the aquarium.

Success is not always achieved at the first attempt, so persevere until you find the best way. The techniques described here are only suggestions that have worked for some aquarists, but there is a great deal yet to learn and easier methods just waiting to be discovered. You may be the one to do it.

Basic Health Care

The general health and longevity of animals in the marine aquarium has improved greatly in recent years, and this trend should continue as more is discovered about husbandry. It is likely that poor health and even death are the result of bad water management. Incorrect diet, bad handling and anything that may cause stress could trigger ill-health. Stress is a serious cause of reduced efficiency in the animals' immune system.

In their natural habitats, marine organisms live in extremely stable conditions, but in the comparatively unstable environmental conditions found in the aquarium, they are more likely to succumb to parasitic attacks or microbial diseases. Aquarium subjects are at their most vulnerable when in transit and on first being introduced into a new tank. The stress they experience during this period is often enough to cause illness. However, once completely settled, and providing conditions are at optimum, most species will build up a strong resistance to many ailments.

Minimizing the risks

As we have seen, stress is the main catalyst for poor health, and the three main causes of such stress are poor water conditions, poor diet and direct exposure to disease pathogens. We have discussed ways of minimizing the stresses of transportation and introduction to a new aquarium, providing the correct diets and maintaining optimum water quality. Now we will look at the procedures for quarantining. If you are not certain that your dealer has sufficiently quarantined animals before sale, you will no doubt find this practice beneficial.

Keeping fishes in a lower than normal salinity can help prevent infections from certain parasites. (More information on this can be found on page 89.)

The value of quarantining

All new aquarium subjects must be screened for diseases and other ailments. Hopefully your dealer has already quarantined them, which will make the screening process easier. If you are absolutely certain that your new purchases are in top condition, you might risk introducing them directly into your main aquarium, but remember, if diseases are inadvertently transferred then all your established animals will be at risk. It is far better to keep your new animals in a separate tank for at least three weeks. 'Quarantine' actually means 40 days, as this period has been deemed sufficient for pathogens to run their course and allow for effective treatment. While in their quarantine tank your livestock can take time to settle into your particular water conditions and get used to some of your husbandry routines, such as feeding times and so on. Hopefully, the final move into the main aquarium will then be less of an ordeal.

The quarantine tank should be simple. There is no need to include any substrate or habitat other than somewhere for the animals to retreat into for security. A clay flowerpot is good for this purpose. Otherwise, the water quality must be as good as that in your main aquarium, with pH, specific gravity and water

Setting up a quarantine tank

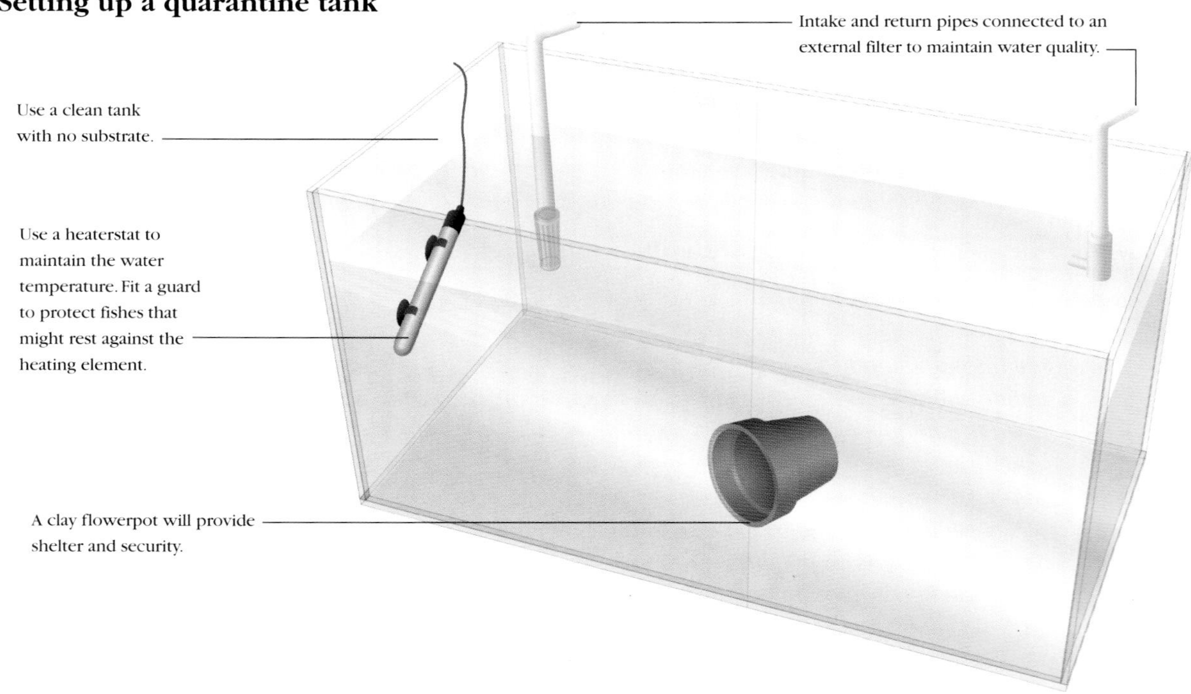

Treating what you cannot see

Left: *Fungal threads, or hyphae, intertwine and form a network deep into a fish's tissue.*

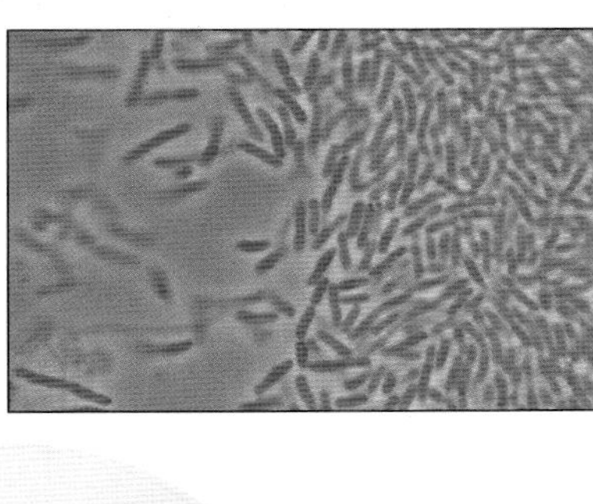

Below: *A microscopic view showing stained, rod-shaped bacteria.*

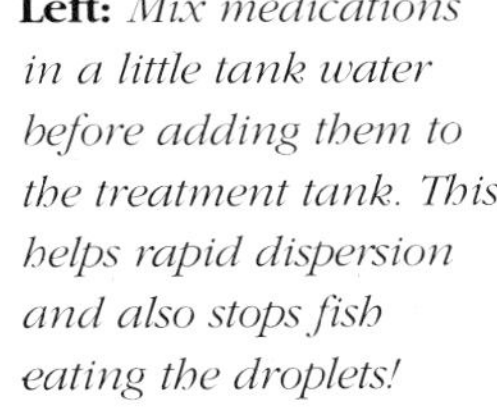

Left: *Mix medications in a little tank water before adding them to the treatment tank. This helps rapid dispersion and also stops fish eating the droplets!*

Amyloodinium (Marine Velvet parasite) cycle

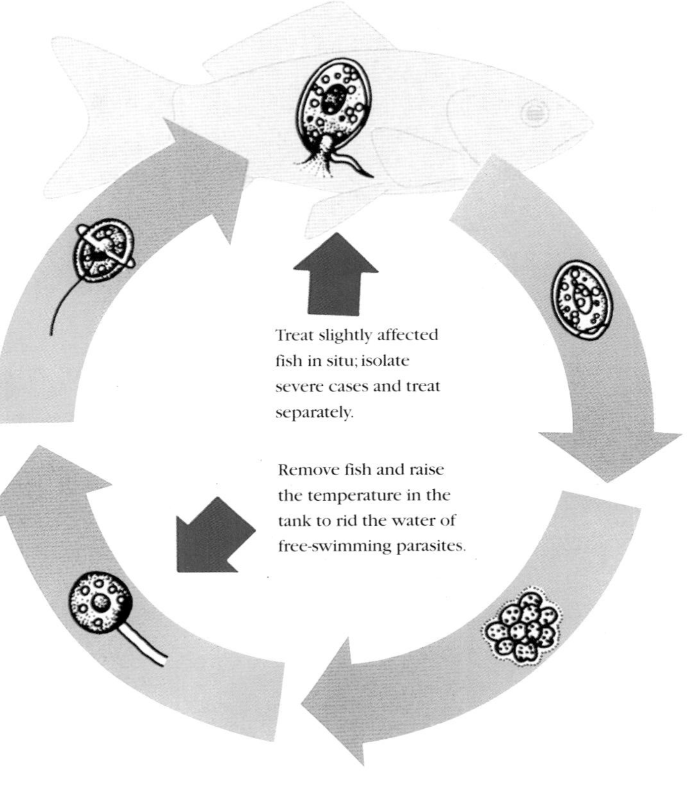

Above: *In this typical parasitic life cycle the adult stages attach to the fins, gills and skin. Mature forms fall away and undergo division to produce spores that infect new fish hosts.*

temperature exactly the same. As it is unlikely that many animals will be held in quarantine at any one time, there will be little loading on the filter, so a small external canister filter should be able to provide all the biological, mechanical and chemical filtration necessary. If any treatment turns out to be necessary then chemical filtration must not be included in the system.

Organics in the water will often impede the effectiveness of some treatments, so keeping the quarantine tank spotlessly clean is important. Once a quarantine tank has been set up, it is wise to keep it running whether there are subjects in it or not, and to be ready for any eventualities. This means you will have to maintain the bacterial population in the biological filter by ensuring there is a suitable food source.

While your animals are in quarantine take time to check for damage or any lesions that are, or could become, infected. Where fishes are concerned, look for unusual white spots or other blemishes that are obviously not part of their normal markings. The same goes for behaviour; listlessness, lack of interest in food and abnormal swimming can all indicate there is something wrong. You will almost certainly observe higher than normal respiration, but this will not be unusual for the first few hours. If gill rates are still high on the second day, this could indicate a problem. Carrying out such observations is infinitely easier in an uncluttered quarantine tank.

Having said all that, do not regard quarantining as an absolute guarantee against all problems, because the latent effects of stress can sometimes, albeit rarely, take three months or more to manifest themselves.

Recognizing ailments

Loss of appetite is a good indication that something is wrong and that further investigation is necessary. Observing feeding habits on a daily basis is very useful. It is another good reason to ask your dealer if you can see the animals you are interested in feeding before you purchase them. When fishes have been caught from the wild with chemicals such as cyanide, irreparable damage can be done to their digestive systems and, although they can look in good health otherwise, they will slowly starve to death.

External parasites are among the easiest ailments to recognize, because they are often clearly visible and the infection is accompanied by vigorous and continual scratching on rocks and substrate. Do not be too alarmed at very occasional scratching because it may only be the fish trying to dislodge a bit of

Parasites

Parasites abound in the natural world, from single-celled protozoan forms to larger creatures, including worms and crustaceans. They all depend on a host animal for survival and many have complex life cycles. Understanding this is the key to tackling them at a vulnerable stage.

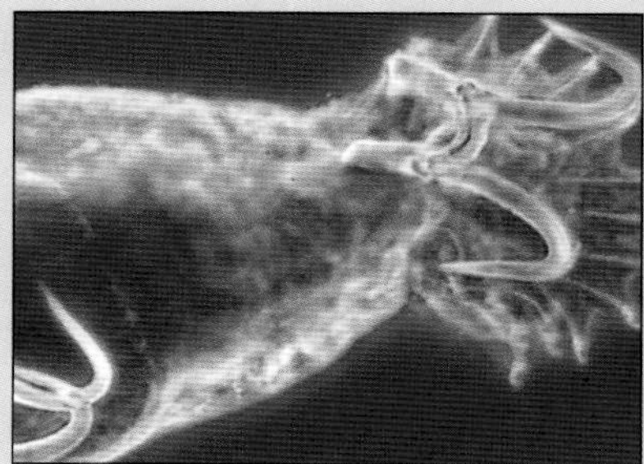

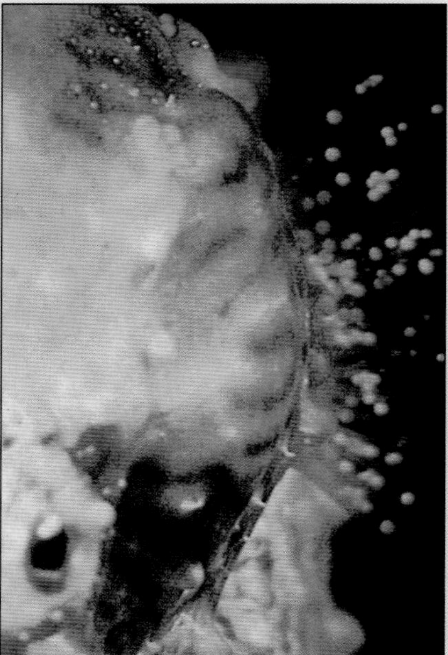

Left: *A Florida Seahorse showing white/grey tumorous masses – a sign of a Microsporidian infection. Spores are ingested by fish, usually when they cannibalize a previous fish host.*

Below: *The 'head' of a cestode worm parasite, with its tiny 'jaws' that severely damage the host's gut wall. Heavy infestations impede digestion.*

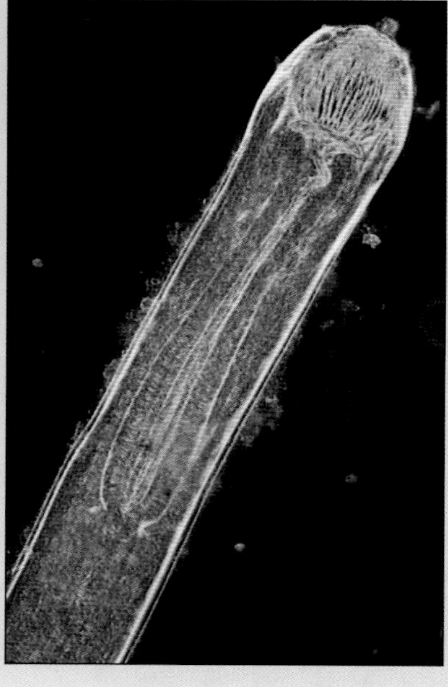

Above: *These ferocious-looking hooks are used by this Dactylogyrid parasite to attach itself to the fish's skin. Proprietary remedies are effective.*

Right: *Another Dactylogyrid parasite attached to the gills of its fish host. Heavy infestation causes breathing problems, so take prompt action.*

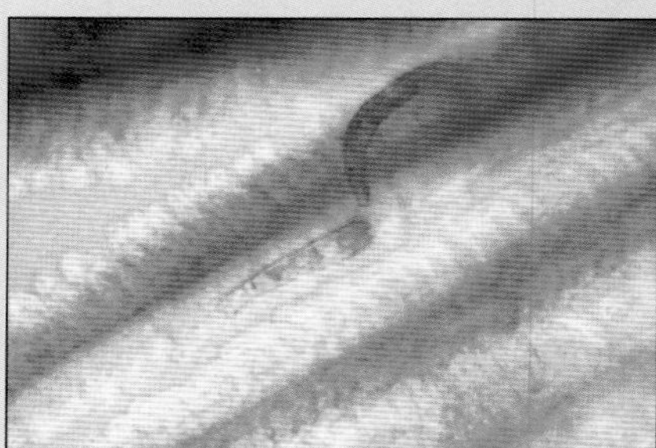

debris it has picked up, or some other minor irritation. Likewise, bacterial infections are generally clearly visible because they commonly appear as reddening around the bases of fins and tail, or on a wound. It is the internal ailments that present the most difficulties in identification, although some will offer a visible sign through red ulcerations appearing from beneath the scales. Generally, the only way to tell that there may be something wrong internally is through a change in the animal's behaviour.

Often, internal ailments are recognized too late to do anything about them and the animal dies, or sometimes it is kinder to put it out of its misery humanely. Postmortem examination will be useful in these cases in order to determine whether you need to take any action to protect your other aquarium subjects. To preserve a dead fish for later examination, freezing is the best option. Although freezing can damage tissue, it is best to do so as soon after death as possible, otherwise the processes of decay can change the nature of the body so much that accurate diagnosis becomes impossible.

However, a word of caution is necessary here. Do not be too quick to jump to potentially wrong conclusions, as poor water quality and certain toxic situations can cause similar symptoms to a number of diseases. Some toxic conditions can cause a reddening of the fins and ulcerations and also scratching, whilst sluggish behaviour, lack of appetite, scratching and abnormal swimming could all be symptoms of other water quality problems. Always eliminate water quality from your investigations before deciding on any course of medication for diseases. (See the panel on pages 158-159.)

Treating ailments

If disease breaks out in your aquarium you will have to make one of two choices: whether to treat the entire aquarium or to remove the infected individual and treat that one alone. There are other factors to consider as well, such as whether there are invertebrates in the aquarium that cannot tolerate the medications you will be using and, whether the same medications are going to be harmful to the bacteria in the biological filter. Should you opt for transferring individuals into a treatment tank remember that, although conditions should be very similar, proper acclimatization procedures must still be observed.

Numerous reliable remedies are available for marine aquarium use; they are the result of prolonged research programmes. Be sure to follow the manufacturer's directions for their use to the letter. Copper is a widely used substance for treating

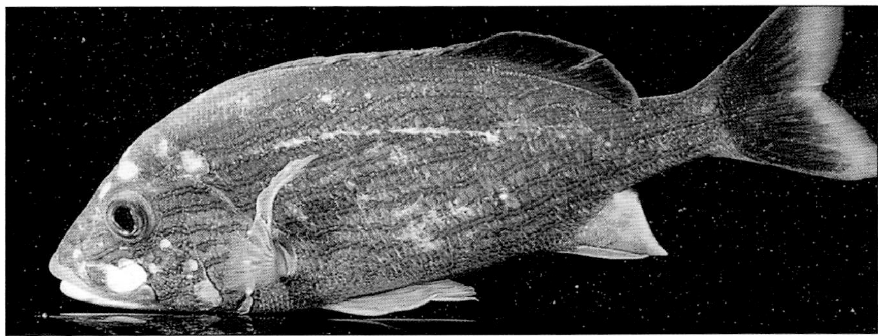

Above: *A Blue-striped Grunt with Head and Lateral Line Erosion (HLLE). Holes develop and enlarge in the sensory pits around the head and down the lateral line. Try a vitamin A supplement and Metronidazole baths as directed.*

an array of parasitic infections, but it does have drawbacks. Firstly, it cannot be used where invertebrates are being kept, and some species of fishes, notably surgeonfishes, sharks and rays, do not tolerate it either. Secondly, its effectiveness can be nullified by certain water treatment additives, which can eliminate non-chelated copper from the water. (Chelated metallic ions are bound with an organic molecule.) The power of copper-based remedies will also be diminished by calcareous materials in the aquarium system; it may be necessary to increase the dose in tanks where coral sand is used, for example. Use a copper test kit to be certain that you are maintaining the correct dosage level during the treatment.

As a general rule, use only one type of medication at a time. Although it is true that some work well – or even better – together, it is also possible that a combination of ingredients can produce a substance that is toxic. If in doubt, ask your dealer for advice. In general though, always restore normal water conditions before beginning another course of medication.

Antibiotics

In some countries antibiotics can only be obtained with a veterinary prescription. Antibiotics can be very effective when correctly used, but they are capable of destroying the beneficial bacteria in your filters and so are better administered in a treatment tank. One particularly effective way of giving antibiotics is with food. You could soak food in the medication for a period before use, but there will always be wastage in terms of the antibiotics washing out when put into the aquarium water. Commercially made medicated foods where the antibiotics are fixed into the food during manufacture are more effective than home-mixed ones.

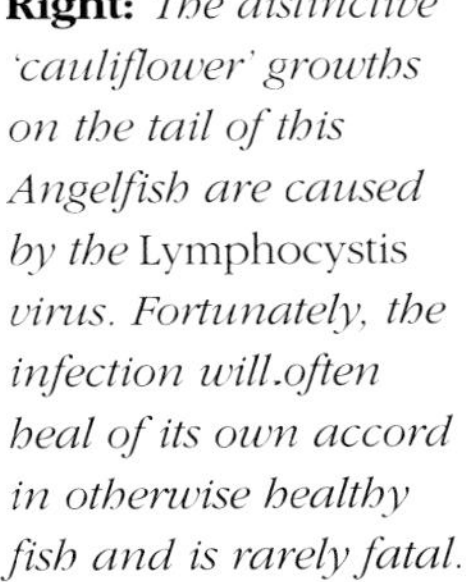

Right: *The distinctive 'cauliflower' growths on the tail of this Angelfish are caused by the* Lymphocystis *virus. Fortunately, the infection will often heal of its own accord in otherwise healthy fish and is rarely fatal.*

Below: *A Squirrelfish suffering from skin ulcers and 'dropsy', both of which are clear symptoms of a severe bacterial infection. Treat with antibiotics. Large ulcers may also need 'packing' to seal the breach in the osmotic barrier.*

Right: *The osmotic shock caused when a marine fish enters freshwater kills pathogens – they take up water so fast that they 'pop'. However, freshwater baths are also stressful to the fish and should be carried out with great care. Monitor the progress of the fish continuously and remove it at the first sign of distress.*

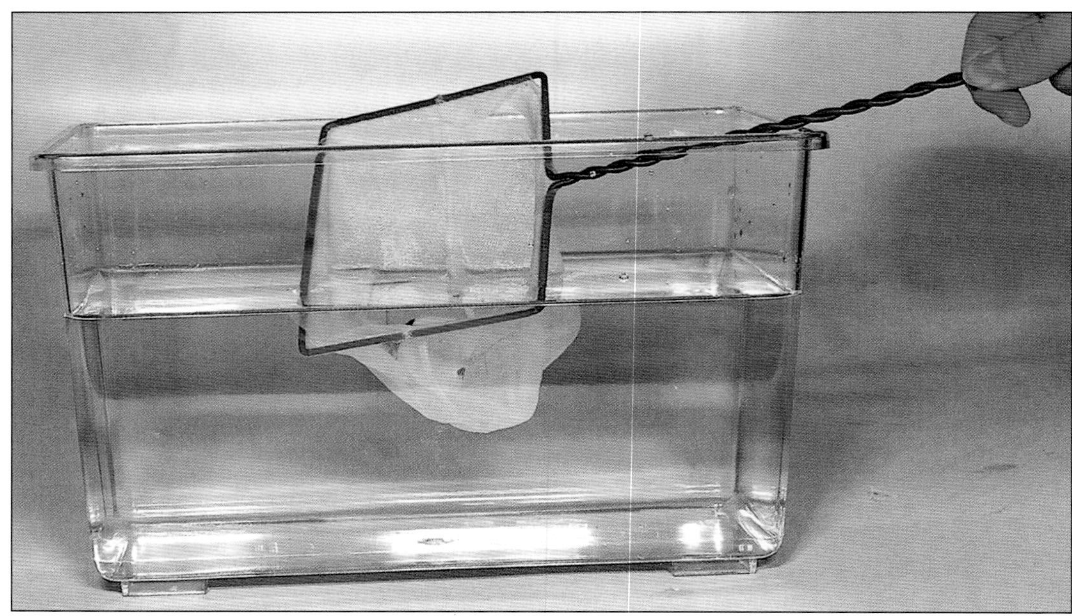

Freshwater baths

Some large public aquariums give freshwater baths to incoming specimens as a routine part of their quarantine protocols. It could be argued that this treatment subjects the animals to stress over and above that caused by capture and transportation. However, it is known to be effective for the control of many parasites, although the level of effectiveness can vary according to different species' tolerance of this kind of treatment. Accordingly, different species are held in freshwater baths for varying lengths of time. For example, a snapper might be able to withstand 10-15 minutes in freshwater, but a butterflyfish may only be able to take 1-2 minutes. Basically, a fish must be removed as soon as it starts showing discomfort and its respiration rate has risen to a level that causes concern. A useful indicator is to approach the fish with your hand and if there is absolutely no response, remove the fish from the bath and return it to normal conditions as quickly as you can.

To avoid sudden shocks when giving marine fish a freshwater bath, make absolutely sure that the temperature and pH of the water the fish is coming out of is the same as the bath and also the eventual display aquarium.

Sterilizers

Exposure to germicidal UV light may eradicate some parasitic organisms, or at least keep their numbers low, but unless the parasites have a free-swimming stage and can actually be drawn through the unit, its effectiveness will be negligible. The same limitation applies to using ozone and even diatomaceous earth filters used for stripping out microscopic matter from the water.

Diseases of invertebrates

The diseases and other ailments of invertebrates are still poorly understood. It is known that parasitic infections occur, as well as bacterial and fungal ones. Recognizing these infections is not always easy, but look for excess mucus production, decaying tissue and discoloration, as these may all be indications of health problems. Treatment is not easy either, because without an exact knowledge of the ailments, it is impossible to treat them accordingly. Very short freshwater baths have been tried with varying results, but have been found to be particularly useful for polyp animals attached to rocks, such as corals, before they are introduced into the aquarium for the first time.

Sudden deaths in the aquarium

Every now and then, fishkeepers may experience a setback for which there appears to be no cause or obvious reason. The worst of these is the dreaded 'wipe-out'. This phrase is singularly descriptive: one day all is progressing well and the next, everything is dead. So swift is

Disposing of fish humanely

At some point in your fishkeeping career, you may find it necessary to dispatch a fish because of illness or old age. If a sick fish is beyond saving, the best thing is to dispose of it humanely. If you can bring yourself to do it, the quickest method is to sever the spinal cord behind the head with a sharp knife. Alternatively, obtain the fish anaesthetic MS222 from a veterinary surgeon or pharmacist and leave the patient in a solution of this for several hours. Never flush a fish down the lavatory, throw it on the floor or place it alive in the freezer. Freezing affects the capillary blood vessels just under the skin, causing the fish great pain before it loses consciousness.

such a disaster that there is little opportunity to spot any signs of the impending catastrophe. Authorities who have made prolonged studies of the phenomenon report that before it occurs, fishes will behave oddly – hiding, breathing differently, apparently hanging in the water, rapidly jerking back and forth or darting erratically around the aquarium. Foam appearing at the water surface has also been observed. Furthermore, it seems that a fish can be removed with some aquarium water and placed in a separate container and survive, while those left in the aquarium die. Sometimes it is only one species, or very closely related species, that are affected. This phenomenon is now referred to as 'toxic tank syndrome' and appears to be caused by the build-up of species-specific toxic proteins. The problem is particularly prevalent with freshwater fishes in aquarium stores, where shipment after shipment of the same species is placed in the same tank for display. Fortunately it can be less of a problem for marine fishes, as protein skimmers seem to be effective in stripping out these toxins, which is another good reason for installing one.

In a newly set-up aquarium where the biological filters are being matured, another cause of sudden 'wipe-outs' can be attributed to the naturally excited and impatient aquarist who decides to introduce several animals as soon as an acceptable nitrite reading has been taken. This action overloads the capabilities of the biological filter system, causing a rapid increase in ammonia levels and the aquarium animals to die. In this case, the phenomenon is known as 'new tank syndrome'. Only ever introduce one animal at a time to avoid this.

It is more difficult to determine the cause of a sudden 'wipe-out' in long-established systems. Apart from the possible reasons already discussed, it is worth investigating the potential of accelerated bacterial activity producing toxic conditions (particularly those involved in the ammonia conversion process). Excessive algae spores could also present problems. Any increase in bacteria populations, possibly as a result of too much organic waste material accumulating, could cause a significant drop in oxygen levels. It should go without saying that such incidents would be seriously detrimental to fishes and invertebrates, and, potentially, the bacteria in your filters. In general, the continuous use of an efficient biological filter allied to protein skimming will prevent such problems arising in the first place.

Below: *Such a display of healthy invertebrates is the result of careful attention to aquarium conditions. Always choose healthy specimens, be sure to supply their nutritional needs and provide adequate lighting.*

Detecting and treating health problems

Symptoms	Cause	Treatment
Gills affected, breathing difficulties, mouth kept open. Fish listless, not eating. Eyes may become cloudy. Triangular spots on body (with apex towards rear of fish).	*Benedenia*, a trematode parasite similar to *Dactylogyrus* gill fluke.	Proprietary remedies and anti-parasite treatments are effective. Follow instructions and check for incompatibility with invertebrates. Consider giving a freshwater bath – with extreme care.
Body swellings that may be either localized or spread over larger areas. Secondary infections may occur if swellings burst. (See also 'dropsy'.)	Bacterial infection – caused by various bacteria. Other bacterial conditions are described below.	Use copper-based remedies and then medicated food. Follow veterinarian's or manufacturer's instructions for use when giving medicated foods.
Opaque areas on the skin, especially on the dorsal surface of the body.	*Chilodonella*, a single-celled parasite that attacks skin around a wound or ulcer. May spread to the gills and cause asphyxia.	Antiparasite treatments are effective. Requires a host fish, so an uninhabited aquarium will be free of the parasite within about five days.
White spots 2mm (0.08in) in diameter appear on body and fins. Fish scratch against rocks. Breathing may become rapid if gills are affected.	*Cryptocaryon irritans*, parasite causing 'saltwater ich'. One-celled parasites penetrate the outer layer of skin. Secondary infection may follow.	Copper-based remedies or other anti-parasite remedies are effective; follow instructions carefully. Check for incompatibility with invertebrates.
Thin white slimy faeces. Rear part of body may be swollen.	Diarrhoea. Poor diet, insufficient roughage or rotten, unclean fish meat given as food.	Raise tank temperature to 28°C (82°F). Do not feed for two days then give plenty of roughage foods such as shrimp, water fleas, etc.
Pronounced swelling of body accompanied by erect scales.	'Dropsy' often resulting from a bacterial infection. Similar to dropsy in freshwater fishes.	Consult your veterinarian. If caught in time, the most effective treatment involves giving suitable antibiotics to the affected fish and its contacts.
One or both eyes protrude from the socket. Eye disorders also connected with other ailments.	Exophthalmus or 'pop-eye'. In one eye, the cause may be TB; in both eyes, chronic or acute bacterial infection. Possibly parasites.	No definite remedy, but antibacterial and antiparasite treatments may be effective. Affected fish do not appear too distressed by the condition.
Edges of fins ragged; tissue between rays gradually disintegrates.	Finrot. Bacterial infection often aggravated by poor water conditions.	Copper-based remedies and antibiotics may be effective if used early, otherwise surgical trimming may be necessary. Improve aquarium conditions.
White tufts of cotton-wool-like or threadlike growths on body. (See also *Chilodonella*.)	*Saprolegnia* fungus. Usually affects fish with mucus deficiencies, open wounds or other skin ailments. Encouraged by excess organic matter in water.	Immediate partial water changes can be effective, as are malachite green remedies, temporary freshwater baths and antibiotic treatment. Wipe away fungal growth.
Rapid breathing and gaping gills, without other external signs found in *Oodinium* and *Cryptocaryon*.	Gill trematode parasites, such as *Dactylogyrus* and other species. Tiny wormlike 1mm (0.04in) flukes grip with disc of hooks.	A formalin bath (3ml per 4.5 litres/ gallon of 37% formaldehyde) for 15-30 minutes, followed by treatment as for *Oodinium* and *Cryptocaryon*.

Right: *This clownfish has a tumour on its lower lip. The condition is untreatable but rarely fatal. It does not appear to cause the fish any distress.*

Symptoms	Cause	Treatment
Fish emaciated, although eating normally. Fins ragged, scales raised in groups. Colours fade, eyes may protrude. Balance problems. The symptoms can be very similar to tuberculosis.	*Ichthyosporidium*, an internal fungal disease. Complex infection cycle may involve direct spread of fungal spores or through eating crustaceans carrying spores. Infection spreads through body and damages internal organs.	No effective cure known, but raising the water temperature to 28-30°C (82-86°F) and feeding medicated foods may help.
Cauliflower-like growths appear on the body and fins over a period of several weeks.	*Lymphocystis*, a viral infection. Affected fishes may eventually waste away or recover spontaneously.	Improving conditions often induces self-healing. Treatment of viral infections is always uncertain.
Tiny, dustlike white spots on body and fins. Fish scratch against rocks. Gills may be inflamed. Rapid gill movements, breathing affected.	An infection by the single-celled parasite *Oodinium ocellatum* – known as coral fish disease. Infection cycle involves formation of cysts on tank floor that release new batches of free-swimming parasites.	Proprietary remedies and antiparasite treatments are effective, but follow the manufacturer's instructions carefully and check for incompatibility with invertebrates, corals, etc.
Dull eyes and rapid breathing. Fish dash and whirl about and usually die from exhaustion.	Poisoning by paint fumes, tobacco smoke, metals in water, poisons secreted by other fishes.	Immediate partial water changes, with a total water change as a last resort.
Fish cannot control its position in the water.	Swimbladder trouble, often caused by chilling.	Isolate fish in warmer water. Feed medicated foods.
Fish emaciated, but may still be eating normally. Fins ragged, scales raised in groups, colours fade, eyes may protrude. Similar to *Ichthyosporidium*. Usually only individual fishes affected, although others may succumb over a longer period.	*Tuberculosis*. Bacterial infection. Difficult to diagnose accurately because the collective symptoms include some seen in other diseases.	Antibiotics may bring temporary relief. Isolate sick and dying fish; otherwise, cannibalism will occur and may spread the disease to other fishes in the aquarium.
Discoloured skin, loss of appetite, open ulcers, vent and junction of body and fins inflamed.	Ulcer disease, an infection with *Vibrio* bacteria.	Consult your veterinarian, who may treat the affected fish with antibiotics. Also consider using medicated foods.
Wounds	Perhaps caused by bullying in the aquarium, accidental damage or mishandling when transferring fishes, etc.	General antibacterial treatments, antibiotics or medicated foods. Povidone iodine can be applied to the affected area with a cotton bud.

PART FOUR

TROPICAL MARINE FISHES

Although nearly three-quarters of the earth's surface is kept covered by salt water, relatively few marine fishes are kept in the aquarium, and of these, the vast majority are tropical species. Nevertheless, such is the appeal of this small group of fishes that the marine fishkeeping hobby has flourished and continues to attract an ever-growing number of enthusiasts around the world.

The most striking tropical marine fishes are native of the coral reefs and coastal waters, where collection is quite easy. Fishes from the deepest waters usually grow too large for the aquarium, and also present too many collection and transportation problems. The majority of suitable fishes come from the Indo-Pacific Oceans, the Caribbean area of the Northern Atlantic Ocean, and the Red Sea.

The fish featured in this section should all be readily available to the home aquarist. Although not an exhaustive survey, it does provide a typical illustration of each of the more commonly kept families of tropical marine fishes. If you cannot find the specific fish you are looking for, similar species will usually provide enough useful data.

Many species have been omitted on the grounds that they have proved extremely difficult or impossible to keep in the home aquarium. Others are, or are likely to become, the subject of various import bans in some countries. Appendix Two on pages 380-381 lists some of those species still currently available but not recommended for the aquarist, and you may have to make a decision, based on conscience and practicality, as to whether or not to keep these species.

Left: *The exotic beauty of the Queen Angelfish is undeniable and typifies what attracts many people to the marine fishkeeping hobby. Chosen wisely, fish such as this can thrive in captivity and give pleasure for many years.*

Family: ACANTHURIDAE

Surgeons and Tangs

Family characteristics

Members of this family are characterized by their high profile and laterally compressed, oval bodies. In addition, they have very sharp 'scalpel-like' erectile spines on the caudal peduncle (hence the name 'Surgeons'), which are used during inter-territorial disputes and in defence. The dorsal and anal fins are long-based and the eyes are set high on the head. The scales often end in a small protruberance, giving a rough feel to the skin. In their natural habitat these fishes may grow up to 400mm (16in), but aquarium specimens usually attain only half the size, if that, of their wild counterparts.

Although there are no drastic colour changes between juveniles and adults in most species, the Caribbean Blue Tang (*Acanthurus coeruleus*) has a yellow juvenile form. Since the adult colour occurs at no predetermined age or size, small fishes can show adult coloration while larger specimens retain their immature colours. When the change occurs, the body is the first area to show the blue adult colour, followed by the caudal fin. Thus, for a period there is an intermediate stage; which has a blue body with a yellow caudal fin.

Although external differences between the sexes are normally rare, some darkening of the male's colours during breeding is quite usual. Size is not a reliable indication of the sex of the fishes; sometimes the male is larger, sometimes the female. The pelagic (free-floating) eggs that result from the typical ascending spawning actions of two fishes (or a group of fishes) take a long time – possibly months – to pass through the planktonic stage. This means that, although spawning in captivity may occur, rearing the fry may prove to be much more difficult.

Diet and feeding

Surgeons and tangs need to be fed several times each day, especially if there is insufficient algal growth for them to browse upon. In fact, algae are such an important element of their diet that you should not introduce them into an algae-free aquarium.

Young fishes grow very quickly and will starve if denied ready nourishment. Although many species are herbivorous, others will eat small animals too, which means that once they have become accustomed to feeding in captivity they will take many of the established dried, frozen and live foods.

Aquarium behaviour

Surgeons and tangs live in shoals around the coral reefs of the world. In the aquarium, however, they forsake this gregariousness and will quarrel among themselves, unless you provide a suitably spacious tank. Established species often resent new fishes introduced into the aquarium; smaller fishes may well get off with a warning but similarly sized fishes may suffer attacks. Young surgeon and tang specimens, whose scalpels are, fortunately, not as dangerous as those of adults, mount threatening motions against newcomers, but, thankfully, these displays are generally shortlived.

All members of this family are somewhat prone to Oodinium and White spot infection, especially in less than perfect water conditions. Unfortunately, the copper-based medications that are used to treat such infections generally preclude the suitability of these fishes in mixed fish and invertebrate aquariums (see *Health Care and Disease Treatment*, pages 144-159).

SCIENTIFIC CLASSIFICATION AND THE HOBBYIST

It is most unfortunate that scientific classification does not necessarily correspond to that used by the hobbyist. The academic, scientific system has to deal with all known organisms in a universal way. There has to be as little uncertainty as possible so that scientists of different nations, speaking different languages, all know which organism is under discussion or being talked about. The hobbyist, by contrast, deals with a small and eclectic sample of the world's fauna and flora and this is reflected in his or her terminology, which suits that localized interest. There is nothing wrong with this attitude because it has evolved to satisfy and cope with their needs and enables enthusiasts to communicate with each other. But only within limits. For an English-speaking hobbyist to communicate with precision to another whose native tongue is not English there has to be resort to scientific names. That species you may know as the Harlequin Tuskfish is not going to evoke any response from a Russian speaker, nor even, necessarily, from an Australian. However, *Lienardella fasciata* (this species' scientific name) has a universality that transcends native languages. Hence the important need for the scientific classification.

Unfortunately, although scientific classification has the advantages of being universal and having reference points, this does not mean to say that there is universal agreement. Indeed, there are some areas that are the subject of particular scientific dispute. For example, a series of 'very similar' fish known by only a handful of specimens from just a few sites over a wide area may belong to a single widespread but variable species, or be specimens of many, closely related species; only further study could decide and later information may change the early conclusions.

Acanthurus achilles

Achilles Tang; Red-tailed Surgeon

☐ **Distribution:** Pacific.

☐ **Length:** 250mm/10in (wild), 180-200mm/7-8in (aquarium).

☐ **Diet and feeding:** Will accept the usual protein foods, such as gamma-irradiated frozen foods (*Mysis* shrimp, plankton, krill, etc.) and live brineshrimp, plus algae and other greenstuff, such as blanched lettuce and spinach. Shy grazer.

☐ **Aquarium behaviour:** Normally peaceful, but very delicate. Compatible with most fish, but may fight at first with other members of its own family. Do not add to tank until the first fish are established.

☐ **Invertebrate compatibility:** Not recommended.

The brown body is offset by yellow-red baselines to the dorsal and anal fins. The white marking on the gill cover behind the eye and the dull white patch on the chest are shared by other members of the family, but the feature that positively identifies this fish is the teardrop-shaped orange-red area on the caudal peduncle, in which the scalpels are set. Like most members of the family, this is a beautiful fish, but young specimens do not have nearly as many red markings as the adults.

Below: Acanthurus achilles
Members of the Acanthuridae family are easily distinguished by their oval shape. Apart from one or two species – many like this Achilles Tang – are brilliantly coloured, with beautiful body patterns.

Acanthurus coeruleus

Blue Tang

☐ **Distribution:** Western Atlantic.

☐ **Length:** 300mm/12in (wild), 150mm/6in (aquarium).

☐ **Diet and feeding:** Mainly algae. Bold grazer.

☐ **Aquarium behaviour:** Small specimens may become bullies if established in the aquarium ahead of other fishes, but this tendency generally decreases with time.

☐ **Invertebrate compatibility:** Not recommended.

Young fishes are yellow with blue markings around the eye. As they age, the fish develop narrow blue lines, the adult fish being darker blue than the 'almost adult' fish. The scalpels on the caudal peduncle are ringed with yellow or white in mature fishes.

Above: Acanthurus coeruleus (adult)
In adulthood, the Blue Tang may lose its territorial nature and become slightly more sociable. Its dark blue coloration defies the bright yellow of the juvenile.

Below: Acanthurus coeruleus (juvenile)
The young fish is bright yellow with blue-rimmed eyes – not to be confused with Zebrasoma flavescens *(see page 169). Small specimens can be quite aggressive.*

Acanthurus glaucopareius

Goldrim Tang; Powder Brown

☐ **Distribution:** Mainly the Pacific Ocean, but is sometimes found in the eastern Indian Ocean.

☐ **Length:** 200mm/8in (wild).

☐ **Diet and feeding:** Algae. Bold grazer.

☐ **Aquarium behaviour:** Normally peaceful.

☐ **Invertebrate compatibility:** Not recommended.

It is fairly easy to identify this fish by the white area on the cheeks. Yellow zones along the base of blue-edged dorsal and anal fins may extend into the base of the caudal fin. A yellow vertical bar crosses the caudal fin.

Below: Acanthurus glaucopareius
The markings on this fish are extremely fine. There is some justification in defining it as a Powder Brown as the colour patterning is similar to that of the Powder Blue Surgeon, Acanthurus leucosternon. Acanthurus glaucopareius *is easily distinguished by the white cheek patches, however. It is a fairly easy species to keep in the aquarium, being generally quite peaceful, but should not be kept with invertebrates.*

Above: Acanthurus leucosternon
One of the most familiar of all surgeonfishes, the Powder Blue Surgeon is a firm favourite with hobbyists. It is best kept on its own (as any two will fight) and needs plenty of room, excellent water conditions and sufficient vegetable matter in its diet.

Acanthurus leucosternon
Powder Blue Surgeon

☐ **Distribution:** Indo-Pacific.

☐ **Length:** 250mm/10in (wild), 180-200mm/7-8in (aquarium).

☐ **Diet and feeding:** Protein foods and vegetable matter. Bold grazer.

☐ **Aquarium behaviour:** Keep only one in the aquarium. Dealers usually segregate juveniles to prevent quarrels developing.

☐ **Invertebrate compatibility:** Not recommended.

This is a favourite surgeon among aquarists. The oval-shaped body is a delicate blue; the black of the head is separated from the body by a white area beneath the jawline. The dorsal fin is bright yellow, as is the caudal peduncle. The white-edged black caudal fin carries a vertical white crescent. The female is larger than the male. In common with all surgeons, it requires plenty of space and optimum water conditions.

Acanthurus lineatus
Clown Surgeonfish; Blue-lined Surgeonfish; Pyjama Tang

☐ **Distribution:** Indo-Pacific.

☐ **Length:** 280mm/11in (wild), rarely above 150mm/6in in the aquarium.

☐ **Diet and feeding:** Algae. Bold grazer.

☐ **Aquarium behaviour:** Small specimens can be quarrelsome. Keep only one per tank or, alternatively, try keeping several together, rather than a pair, if the aquarium is large enough, on the assumption that there is safety in numbers.

Acanthurus sohal

Zebra Surgeon; Majestic Surgeon

- **Distribution:** Red Sea.
- **Length:** 250mm/10in (wild), 180mm/7in (aquarium).
- **Diet and feeding:** Algae. Bold grazer.
- **Aquarium behaviour:** Small specimens can be quarrelsome; keep only one per tank.
- **Invertebrate compatibility:** Not recommended.

Above: Acanthurus sohal
This striking fish is not a common sight in aquatic dealers' tanks, but its beautiful body lines make it very noticeable when it does appear. As with other surgeonfishes, young specimens can be quarrelsome.

This smart fish is similar in body shape to *A. lineatus*. Its blue-edged, blue-black fins add an outline to the pale body, and the scalpels are marked with a vivid orange stripe. The upper part of the body and head are covered with a series of parallel dark lines. A rare but beautiful fish.

- **Invertebrate compatibility:** Not recommended.

The yellow ground colour of the body is covered with longitudinal dark-edged, light blue lines. The pelvic fins are yellow.

Right: Acanthurus lineatus
This is one of the species of the Acanthuridae family that has a split level of coloration; there is a lighter area to the lower body with decorative parallel longitudinal lines above. Like other surgeonfishes, it appreciates some coral or rockwork to provide welcome sheltering places. Ideally, keep only one of these fish in an aquarium (unless you have a very large tank for several), as small specimens, in particular, can be very quarrelsome.

Naso lituratus

Lipstick Tang; Lipstick Surgeon

☐ **Distribution:** Indo-Pacific.

☐ **Length:** 500mm/20in (wild), 200mm/8in (aquarium).

☐ **Diet and feeding:** Protein foods and greenstuff. Bold grazer.

☐ **Aquarium behaviour:** Normally peaceful.

☐ **Invertebrate compatibility:** Not recommended.

The facial 'make-up' of this fish is quite remarkable; the lips are red or orange and a yellow-edged, dark brown-grey mask covers the snout and eyes. The front of the narrow dorsal fin is also bright yellow. The basic colour of the dorsal fin varies according to geographical origin of the fishes; Hawaiian specimens have a black dorsal, while in those from the Indian Ocean the dorsal is orange. The two immovable, forward-pointing 'scalpels' on each side of the caudal peduncle are set in yellow patches.

Paracanthurus hepatus

Regal Tang

☐ **Distribution:** Indo-Pacific.

☐ **Length:** 250mm/10in (wild), 100-150mm/4-6in (aquarium).

☐ **Diet and feeding:** Algae. Bold grazer.

☐ **Aquarium behaviour:** May occasionally be aggressive towards members of the same species.

☐ **Invertebrate compatibility:** Not recommended.

The brilliant blue body has a black 'painter's palette' shape marking, but the most striking feature of this species is the bright yellow wedge section in the caudal fin. The dorsal and anal fins are black-edged, and the pectoral fin is yellow-tipped.

Right: Paracanthurus hepatus
The striking black markings on the blue body and its yellow caudal fin make positive identification of the Regal Tang very easy. This is one of the few members of the Acanthuridae family that can generally be kept safely in the company of its own species.

Below: Naso lituratus
The extremely well-defined facial markings of the Lipstick Tang are quite remarkable – worthy of any beautician's salon! The remainder of the streamlined fish is no less attractive, with a lyre-shaped caudal fin and double scalpels set in vivid patches.

☐ **Invertebrate compatibility:** Not recommended.

It is unusual to find a marine fish of a single colour, but the vividness of the bright yellow makes up for any lack of pattern. This species can be distinguished from juvenile forms of *A. coeruleus* by the absence of blue around the eyes, although a more obvious guide is the difference in shape of the head and mouth.

Zebrasoma flavescens
Yellow Tang

☐ **Distribution:** Pacific Ocean.

☐ **Length:** 200mm/8in (wild), 100-150mm/4-6in (aquarium).

☐ **Diet and feeding:** Algae. Bold grazer.

☐ **Aquarium behaviour:** Highly territorial. Keep either a single fish or a group of six or more per large tank.

Below: Zebrasoma flavescens
The long snout of this species enables it to graze effortlessly on luxuriant growth of algae. In common with Paracanthurus hepatus, *the Yellow Tang can be kept in a shoal, provided that enough space is available in the aquarium.*

Zebrasoma veliferum

Striped Sailfin Tang

☐ **Distribution:** Indo-Pacific, Red Sea.

☐ **Length:** 380mm/15in (wild), 180-200mm/7-8in (aquarium).

☐ **Diet and feeding:** Protein foods and greenstuff. Bold grazer.

☐ **Aquarium behaviour:** Normally peaceful, but may be aggressive with large fish. Young fish are more adaptable and so do better in captivity than adults.

☐ **Invertebrate compatibility:** Not recommended.

The main feature of this species is the large sail-like dorsal fin and almost matching anal fin; both are patterned. Coloration of both fins and body may be variable in shades

of brown overlaid with several vertical bands.

Below: Zebrasoma veliferum
This juvenile lacks the facial markings of the adult fish. The typical tang body shape is clearly visible. Juveniles do better than adults in captivity.

Above: Zebrasoma xanthurum
This incredibly beautiful fish is generally imported close to full adult size and you will need an appropriately large tank to accommodate it.

Zebrasoma xanthurum

Purple Sailfin Tang; Emperor Tang

- ☐ **Distribution:** Indo-Pacific, Red Sea.
- ☐ **Length:** 200mm/8in (wild).
- ☐ **Diet and feeding:** Protein foods and greenstuff. Bold grazer.
- ☐ **Aquarium behaviour:** Normally peaceful.
- ☐ **Invertebrate compatibility:** Not recommended.

The body colour may vary from purplish blue to brown, depending on the fish's natural habitat. A number of dark spots cover the head and front part of the body. The caudal fin is bright yellow.

Family: APOGONIDAE

Cardinalfishes

Family characteristics
Cardinalfishes are generally slow-moving, often nocturnal fishes that hide among coral heads during the day. However, at the approach of a net, they can move very fast! They are usually found on coral reefs, but some frequent tidal pools and one species enters fresh water.

Unusually for a marine fish, the two separate dorsal fins are carried erect. This feature, together with the large head, mouth and eyes, is a characteristic of the family.

Reproduction is by mouthbrooding. The male generally incubates the eggs, although in some species this task is undertaken by the female. In other species within the family, both sexes share the responsibility.

Diet and feeding
Once acclimatized to aquarium conditions, cardinalfishes will eat most live and other foods (but never flake food). Do not keep them with fast-swimming boisterous fishes or they will lose out in the competition for food. It is a good idea to feed cardinalfishes late in the evening, since this will suit their nocturnal lifestyle and may result in a greater willingness to accept new foods.

Aquarium behaviour
Hardy fishes that should be acclimatized gradually to the bright lights of the main aquarium. Cardinalfishes are an ideal choice for the beginner.

Apogon maculatus
Flamefish

- **Distribution:** Western Atlantic.
- **Length:** 150mm/6in (wild), 750mm/3in (aquarium).
- **Diet and feeding:** All foods. Shy feeder.
- **Aquarium behaviour:** Prefers a quiet aquarium with fishes of a similar disposition.
- **Invertebrate compatibility:** Ideal for the invertebrate aquarium.

Left: Apogon maculatus
The strikingly coloured Flamefish is much slimmer than the more common Pyjama Cardinalfish, Sphaeramia nematopterus. *Like the latter, it is a nocturnal species by nature, and prefers to share its aquarium with less boisterous fishes. It will usually settle well to aquarium life once established.*

This bright red fish with two white horizontal lines through the eye is very easy to identify. It has two dark spots on the body, one below the second dorsal fin and the other on the caudal peduncle (although faint at times). It is a nocturnal feeder and, although shy, usually settles down well in captivity.

Sphaeramia nematopterus
Pyjama Cardinalfish; Spotted Cardinalfish

- **Distribution:** Indo-Pacific.
- **Length:** 100mm/4in (wild), rarely seen above 75mm/3in in the aquarium.
- **Diet and feeding:** Most foods, but not flake.
- **Aquarium behaviour:** Do not keep with larger boisterous species, which would upset the tranquil lifestyle of these fishes.

Above: Sphaeramia nematopterus
The body shape of this fish might be reminiscent of the freshwater tetras, although it boasts an extra dorsal fin and much larger eyes.

- **Invertebrate compatibility:** Ideal for the invertebrate aquarium.

This fish has three distinct colour sections to its striking body, each dissimilar to the next, almost as if it had been assembled like an 'identikit'. The large head section, back to the first of the two dorsal fins, is yellow-brown in colour. A dark brown vertical band joins the first dorsal fin to the pelvic fins. A spotted paler area covers the rear of the fish. The large eyes indicate a naturally nocturnal behaviour. It may be necessary to acclimatize this species with live foods, but, once settled in the aquarium, it will eat well. However, do not offer flake food. This fish was formerly known as *Apogon orbicularis*.

Family: BALISTIDAE

Triggerfishes

Family characteristics
Members of this family have acquired their common name from the characteristic locking and unlocking mechanism of the first dorsal fin. This fin is normally carried flat in a groove, but it can be locked into position by a third ray, thus preventing the fish from being eaten or withdrawn from a crevice in which it has taken refuge.

Triggerfishes are relatively poor swimmers. They achieve propulsion by undulating wave motions of the dorsal and anal fins, the caudal fin being saved for emergency accelerations when required. The pelvic, or ventral, fins are absent in most species, or are restricted to a single spine or knoblike protruberances.

Body coloration can range from the dull to the psychedelic. The patterning around the mouth is typically exaggerated, probably to deter rivals or predators. The teeth are very strong and often protrusive – ideal for eating shelled invertebrates and sea urchins. You should not keep triggerfishes with invertebrates in the home aquarium. Also take care that they do not nip your fingers!

Reproduction takes place in pits dug in the sand within the territory of one of the female fish. These territories, in turn, are all enclosed within the dominant male's greater territory. The eggs, presumed to be demersal (i.e. heavier than water), are released either in an ascending swimming action or over a preselected site.

In the sea, triggerfishes live alone and are intolerant of similar species in the aquarium. They may adopt peculiar resting positions, headstanding or even lying on their sides.

Diet and feeding
Triggerfishes are greedy feeders, accepting anything that is offered. Natural foods taken by the bottom-feeding species of the family include echinoderms such as starfishes and sea urchins, which they devour complete with the spines. Triggerfishes consume the Crown-of-Thorns Starfish in a specific manner – they first blow the starfish over so that its spines are out of the way and then eat the soft unprotected underbelly. Species that occupy the middle and upper waters of the tank take plankton and green foods. Suitable aquarium foods include frozen foods, chopped earthworms and live river shrimp.

Aquarium behaviour
The behaviour of triggerfishes in the aquarium varies from peaceful to unaccommodatingly aggressive, depending on the species. Fishes rest in crevices or caves at night, and so it is advisable to aquascape the aquarium to allow for this. Do not be surprised, however, if the fish take advantage of your thoughtfully provided refuges when you try to net them! In nature, they favour underwater cliff faces; this is especially so in the Caribbean species.

Balistapus undulatus

Undulate Triggerfish; Orange-green Trigger; Red-lined Triggerfish

☐ **Distribution:** Indo-Pacific.

☐ **Length:** 300mm/12in (wild), 200mm/8in (aquarium).

☐ **Diet and feeding:** Corals, crustaceans, molluscs, sea urchins. Bold grazer.

☐ **Aquarium behaviour:** This is the most aggressive triggerfish of all; keep it out of aquariums that contain invertebrates and most fish. Using its powerful jaws, *B. undulatus* is in the habit of picking up lumps of coral and distributing them elsewhere in the aquarium. However, despite its aggressive behaviour and potential size – in a large tank it will grow to about 300mm/12in – it is a rewarding fish to keep, becoming quite tame and enjoying a lot of fuss from its owner.

☐ **Invertebrate compatibility:** This species must not be kept with invertebrates, unless they are destined to be its food!

This species was first discovered in 1797 by the Scottish explorer Mungo Park. In the wild, it is found over a wide area of the Indo-Pacific, although not around Hawaii. The body coloration of this fish – always striking – can vary quite markedly, as its common names suggest. Indian Ocean variants have orange tails, while Pacific specimens have orange-rayed green caudal fins. Males are larger, with no orange banding on the head. Several large spines are arranged in two rows on the caudal peduncle.

Balistes bursa

White-lined Triggerfish; Bursa Trigger

☐ **Distribution:** Indo-Pacific.

☐ **Length:** 250mm/10in (wild), 150mm/6in (aquarium).

☐ **Diet and feeding:** All foods. Bold.

☐ **Aquarium behaviour:** Unsociable towards other Triggerfishes. Aggressive in general to other fishes.

☐ **Invertebrate compatibility:** No.

The red and yellow lines on the head joining the eye to the pectoral fin and the snout to the pectoral fin are the principal clues to the identification of this fish. An area of

Above: Balistapus undulatus
It is easy to understand why this fish is popular, but its striking coloration, and potential tameness should be considered along with another of its traits – it is very aggressive.

Right: Balistes bursa
The coloration around the mouth, together with the lighter body colours, accentuates and apparently enlarges the actual size of the mouth – a good deterrent against would-be predators.

light blue runs below the horizontal line from snout to vent. The fins are virtually colourless. Males are larger and more colourful than females.

Balistes vetula

Queen Triggerfish; Conchino; Peja Puerco

☐ **Distribution:** Tropical western Atlantic.

☐ **Length:** 500mm/20in (wild), 250mm/10in (aquarium).

☐ **Diet and feeding:** Crustaceans, molluscs, small fishes, usual frozen foods, etc. Bold; will take good-sized pieces.

☐ **Aquarium behaviour:** Do not keep with small fishes. Although peaceful with other species, it will quarrel with its own kind.

☐ **Invertebrate compatibility:** No.

Dark lines radiate from around the eyes and there are striking blue facial markings. The tips of the dorsal fin and caudal fins become filamentous with age, especially in the male, which is larger and more colourful than the female. This beautifully marked species may become hand-tame in captivity.

Right: Balistoides conspicillum
With its spectacular spotted markings, the Clown Trigger is an unmistakable fish. Balistoides conspicillum *is a bold, but also aggressive species, so do not keep it with small fishes.*

Below: Balistes vetula
A characteristic of triggerfishes is that many will become hand tame in time. Exercise care when hand feeding, however, for their slightly protrusive teeth are very sharp. Try impaling pieces of food on a cocktail stick before offering them to the fish – it will be safer than hand feeding.

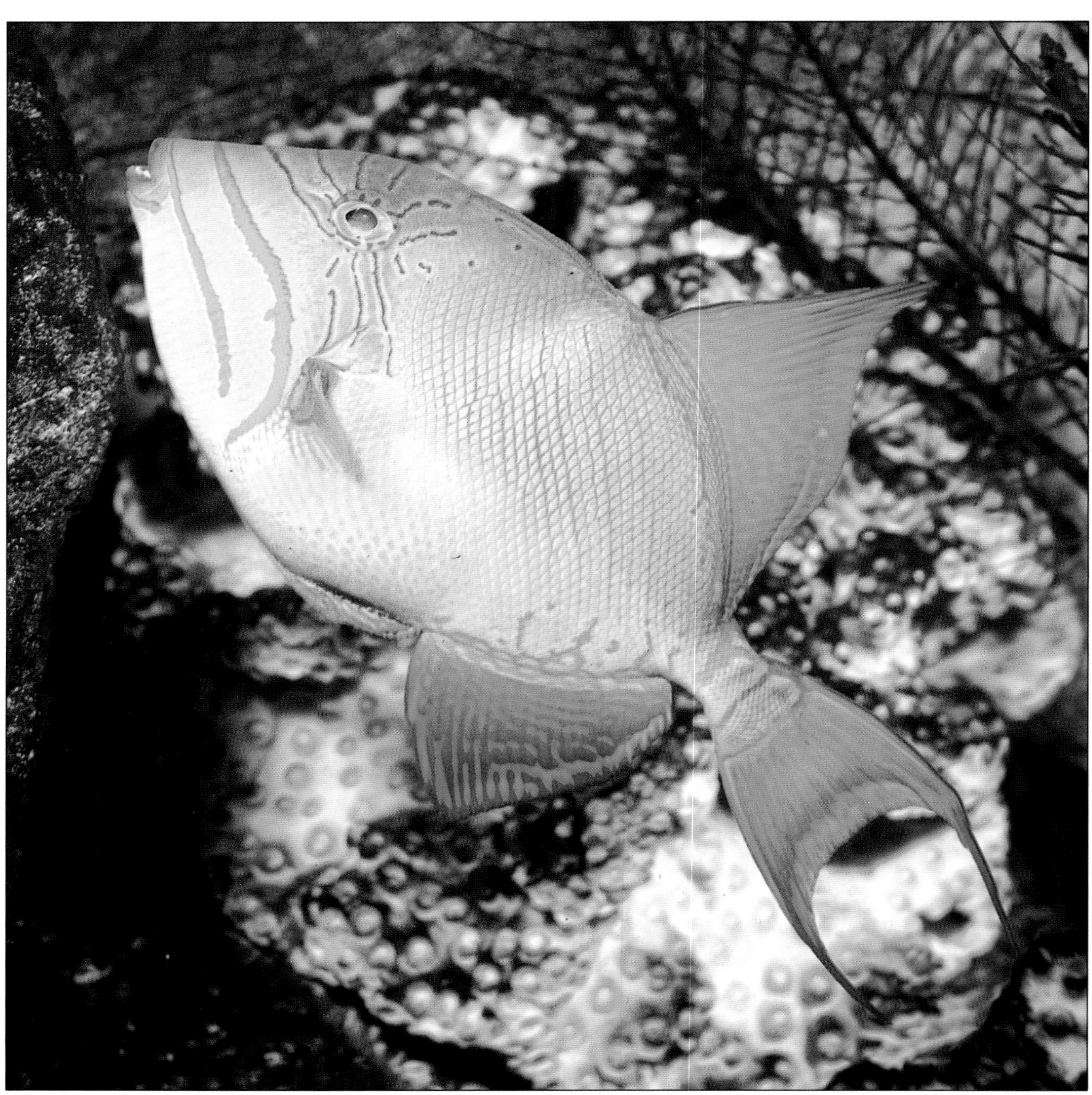

Balistoides conspicillum
Clown Trigger

☐ **Distribution:** Indo-Pacific.

☐ **Length:** 500mm/20in (wild); 250mm/10in (aquarium).

☐ **Diet and feeding:** Crustaceans, molluscs. Bold.

☐ **Aquarium behaviour:** Aggressive. Do not keep with small fishes.

☐ **Invertebrate compatibility:** No.

This is a stunningly beautiful and easily recognizable species, with its large white-spotted lower body. The 'brightly painted' yellow mouth may serve to deter potential predators, while the disruptive body camouflage may assist species recognition. Both the dorsal and anal fin are basically pale yellow and the caudal fin is dark edged. The pectoral fin is clear.

Melichthys ringens
Black-finned Triggerfish

☐ **Distribution:** Indo-Pacific.

☐ **Length:** 500mm/20in (wild), 250mm/10in (aquarium).

☐ **Diet and feeding:** All foods. Bold grazer.

☐ **Aquarium behaviour:** Peaceful. A very gentle triggerfish.

☐ **Invertebrate compatibility:** No.

The body is brownish and the fins are black, but it is the white lines at the base of the dorsal and anal fins and the white-edged caudal fin that distinguish this species.

Below: Melichthys ringens
Although not usually imported in great quantities, the Black-finned Triggerfish is certainly worth waiting for.

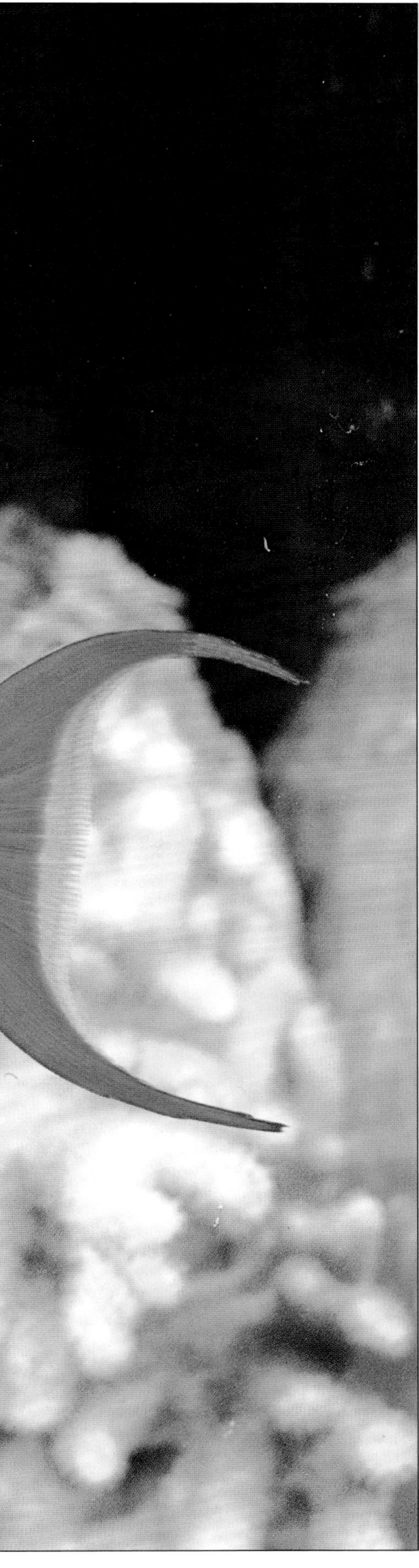

Above: Rhinecanthus aculeatus
Whether used for camouflage, species recognition or as a deterrent, the exaggerated patterns of the Picasso Trigger make it easy to distinguish from other members of the family.

Left: Odonus niger
This species is very colour variable, depending on the collection area; accordingly, it has also occasionally been called the Blue Triggerfish or the Green Triggerfish.

Odonus niger
Black Triggerfish

☐ **Distribution:** Indo-Pacific and Red Sea.

☐ **Length:** 500mm/20in (wild), 250mm/10in (aquarium).

☐ **Diet and feeding:** All foods. Bold.

☐ **Aquarium compatibility:** Fairly sociable and relatively peaceful.

☐ **Invertebrate compatibility:** No.

The body coloration of *O. niger* can vary from blue to green from day to day. The red teeth are often quite conspicuous. Propulsion is achieved by undulations of the dorsal, anal and caudal fins rather than by body movements.

Rhinecanthus aculeatus
Picasso Trigger

☐ **Distribution:** Indo-Pacific.

☐ **Length:** 300mm/12in (wild), 230mm/9in (aquarium).

☐ **Diet and feeding:** Crustaceans, molluscs, 'sea meat' foods. Bold.

☐ **Aquarium behaviour:** Aggressive towards members of the same species and towards other fish of the same size.

☐ **Invertebrate compatibility:** No.

The 'avant garde' colours of this fish make it a popular species. A number of diagonal white bars slant upwards and forwards from the anal fin. The mouth and jawline are accentuated with colour and a blue and yellow-brown stripe across the head connects the eye with the pectoral fin base. This fish may emit a distinctive whirring sound when it is startled.

Family: BLENNIIDAE

Blennies

Family characteristics
Bluntheaded, elongate and constantly active, Blennies make a cheerful addition to the aquarium, although they should be kept in a species tank rather than in a community collection. They naturally frequent inshore waters, hiding in any handy cave or crevice, not always bothering to follow the tide out to sea. Provide suitable living quarters in the aquarium by arranging rockwork to form plenty of hiding crevices and 'observation posts'.

The dorsal fin is long and there are cirri (hairy, bristle-like growths) above the high-set eyes. The skin is slimy, hence the alternative name of slimefishes.

Male blennies tend to be larger and more colourful than females. During breeding, the male may undergo changes in colour during both the pre- and post-spawning periods. One member of the family, the False Cleanerfish, lays its eggs in any handy shelter – empty shells are particularly acceptable – and the eggs are guarded by the male.

Diet and feeding
Blennies are completely omnivorous, eating everything from algae to small fishes and bits of large ones! They will even take dried foods with apparent relish.

Aquarium behaviour
Some blennies are very territorial and aggressive to any other fishes; *Ophioblennius* is a typical case that should not be kept with any fish less than twice its size.

Aspidontus taeniatus

False Cleanerfish; Sabre-toothed Blenny; Cleaner Mimic

☐ **Distribution:** Indo-Pacific.

☐ **Length:** 100mm/4in (wild).

☐ **Diet and feeding:** Skin, scales and flesh – preferably from living, unsuspecting victims! Sly and devious.

☐ **Aquarium behaviour:** Do not keep with other fishes.

☐ **Invertebrate compatibility:** Ideal.

Using its similarity in size, shape and colour to the true Cleanerfish, *Labroides dimidiatus*, this fish approaches its victims, which expect the usual 'cleaning services'; instead they end up with a very nasty wound and a little bit wiser. Easily distinguished by its underslung mouth, which gives it a shark-like appearance. Because of its predatory nature, this species is not recommended for inclusion in the aquarium under any circumstances. It is featured here primarily as a warning, so that you can avoid it.

Below: Aspidontus taeniatus
This fish should be kept on its own in an aquarium; it uses its coloration to mimic the true Cleaner Wrasse, Labroides dimidiatus, *and denude its unsuspecting victims of lumps of flesh! It can be distinguished by its underslung, sharklike mouth.*

Ecsenius bicolor
Bicolor Blenny

☐ **Distribution:** Indo-Pacific.

☐ **Length:** 100mm/4in (wild).

☐ **Diet and feeding:** Frozen marine foods and algae. Bottom-feeding grazer.

☐ **Aquarium behaviour:** Shy with larger fishes; needs hiding places.

☐ **Invertebrate compatibility:** Ideal.

The front half of this fish is brown, the rear orange-red. During spawning, the male turns red with white bars. The female's breeding colours are light brown and yellow-orange. After spawning, the male becomes dark blue with light patches on each side of the body.

Above: Ecsenius midas
When swimming, the Midas Blenny is rather reminiscent of a tiny Moray Eel, although the two are totally unrelated. E. midas *is a fish full of character that seems almost completely fearless once settled into a new home, even in the face of much larger fish. Food is definitely top of its list of priorities.*

Ecsenius midas
Midas Blenny

☐ **Distribution:** Red Sea and Indian Ocean.

☐ **Length:** 100mm/4in (wild).

☐ **Diet and feeding:** Will accept most marine frozen, live and flake foods quite readily.

☐ **Aquarium behaviour:** Can be territorial, but is usually peaceful.

☐ **Invertebrate compatibility:** Ideal.

This endearing fish requires plenty of holes into which to retreat and use as vantage points to observe the rest of the aquarium scene. *E. midas* is an ideal beginner's species, which does well in fish-only and invertebrate aquariums.

Below: Ecsenius bicolor
The rearmost body colour of this shy fish is often hidden, since it spends much of the time in the many hiding places you will need to provide in the aquarium. Given time, however, this endearing fish becomes more confident.

Ophioblennius atlanticus
Redlip Blenny

☐ **Distribution:** Tropical western Atlantic.

☐ **Length:** 120mm/4.7in (wild).

☐ **Diet and feeding:** Frozen marine foods and algae. Bottom-feeding grazer.

☐ **Aquarium behaviour:** Territorial, and it chases everything.

☐ **Invertebrate compatibility:** Ideal.

Keep the Redlip Blenny in a community of hardy fishes and provide plenty of hiding places for it in the aquarium.

Left: Ophioblennius atlanticus
Very common off the West Indies, the Redlip Blenny varies in colour from very dark, as here, to almost white.

Petroscirtes temmincki

Striped Slimefish; Scooter Blenny

☐ **Distribution:** Indo-Pacific.

☐ **Length:** 100mm/4in (wild).

☐ **Diet and feeding:** Algae, small animals. Bottom grazer.

☐ **Aquarium behaviour:** Can be kept in small groups of the same species.

☐ **Invertebrate compatibility:** Ideal.

The body shape is that of a typical blenny, with the eyes set up high on the head. There are no cirri. The coloration is black with white blotches, plus bright blue spots on the head region. Males have an elongated 'flag-shaped' dorsal fin with which they signal to attract females and deter rival males.

Left: Petroscirtes temmincki
The unattractively named Striped Slimefish is nevertheless endearing.

Above: Salaria fasciatus
It is a pity that blennies are so keen on hiding away in caves and under rocks, for it is only when they emerge into more open areas that you can see their body colour patterns, long finnage and cirri – crestlike growths above the eyes.

Salarius fasciatus

Banded Blenny

☐ **Distribution:** Indo-Pacific.

☐ **Length:** 100mm/4in (wild).

☐ **Diet and feeding:** Small animal foods and algae. Bottom grazer.

☐ **Aquarium behaviour:** Requires plenty of hiding places.

☐ **Invertebrate compatibility:** Ideal.

The elongate body is covered with mottled light and dark brown vertical bands, extending into the long-based dorsal fin. The eye patterning – radiating stripes around the rim – is a particular feature.

Family: CALLIONYMIDAE

Mandarinfishes and Dragonets

Family characteristics
Mandarinfishes and the related dragonets are small, mainly bottom-dwelling species that often bury themselves in the sand during the day. Sometimes they will perch on a firm surface not too far away from the aquarium floor.

Sexing these fish is fairly straightforward, males having longer dorsal and anal fin extensions and brighter colours than females. Some reports indicate that fertilization – at least in some species – may be internal. The eggs are scattered in open water, and are normally described as pelagic (in contrast to so-called demersal eggs, which are deposited on a surface). Although this behaviour has been observed in aquariums, no fry have yet been raised.

Avoid buying badly emaciated specimens: they usually fare very poorly.

Diet and feeding
Members of this family feed predominantly on small marine animals, such as crustaceans, that live among the debris on the seabed. An established aquarium with a good population of micro-organisms, and the occasional supplement of rotifers or brineshrimp nauplii, is therefore essential for these fishes.

Aquarium behaviour
Mandarinfishes should be kept singly or in matched pairs. They are ideally suited to a quiet aquarium containing fishes of a similar disposition. Seahorses make suitable companions. Avoid bare tanks housing large fish, as these very rarely provide the best conditions for the comfort and welfare of these species.

Synchiropus picturatus
Psychedelic Fish

☐ **Distribution:** Pacific.

☐ **Length:** 100mm/4in (wild).

☐ **Diet and feeding:** Small crustaceans and algae. Shy bottom-feeding grazer.

☐ **Aquarium behaviour:** Likely to be intolerant of their own kind. May be better able to cope with livelier tankmates than *Synchiropus splendidus*.

Left: Synchiropus picturatus
The bold-patterned Psychedelic Fish is an attractive subject for a quiet tank.

☐ **Invertebrate compatibility:** Ideal.

The basically green body is adorned with lemon-edged, darker green red-ringed patches. This species is found in the Philippines and Melanesia. It is less common than *S. splendidus*.

Synchiropus splendidus
Mandarinfish

☐ **Distribution:** Pacific.

☐ **Length:** 100mm/4in (wild).

☐ **Diet and feeding:** Small crustaceans and algae. Shy bottom-feeding grazer.

Above: Synchiropus splendidus
The Mandarinfish is more common and more gaudily coloured than its relative. Like S. picturatus, *it prefers a quiet tank.*

☐ **Aquarium behaviour:** It is best kept in a quiet aquarium away from larger, more lively fishes.

☐ **Invertebrate compatibility:** Ideal.

This fish has much more red in its coloration – in random streaks around the body and fins – than *S. picturatus*. Males usually develop a longer dorsal spine. It is said that the skin mucus of *Synchiropus* species is poisonous, a fact often signalled in gaudily patterned fishes.

Family: CHAETODONTIDAE

Butterflyfishes

Family characteristics

Due to their close similarity, butterflyfishes and angelfishes (Pomacanthidae, see pages 242-261) were once classified as one group. Although there are now sufficient differences for them to be considered separately, both families continue to share a great deal of common ground.

Butterflyfishes possess an oval body that is extremely laterally compressed. These features, together with the terminal mouth, provide a strong clue as to their natural habitat of coral heads, where their thin-sectioned bodies can easily pass between the branches. Their amazing colour patterns camouflage vulnerable parts of their bodies and assist in species identification.

There appear to be no external differences between the sexes, although at breeding times the females may become noticeably swollen with eggs. Recorded observations of spawning activity in the wild are fairly scarce, but most reports indicate that the majority of species ascend the water column in pairs or small groups and release eggs and sperm simultaneously. Some species have been seen to engage in a 'chasing' ritual, whereby the female is pursued by a male around the lower water layers. In response to being nudged by the male, the female releases eggs, which the male fertilizes as they pass by him. In all cases, the eggs then float briefly until they hatch. The larvae then feed and develop in the planktonic layers for several months before migrating back down to the reef floor. Reports of aquarium spawnings are extemely rare and, as yet, no larvae of any species have been reared successfully.

Diet and feeding

Most members of the Chaetodontidae family are grazing fishes that feed on algae, sponges and corals; some are omnivorous, however, and include small and planktonic animals in their diet. You may need to feed young fishes several times a day with live brineshrimp. Larger fishes should be offered a variety of marine fare, including live brineshrimp and *Mysis* and frozen foods of a suitable size. Sponge-based frozen foods may prove very popular with some species. It is a good idea to witness all butterflyfishes feeding confidently before purchasing.

One or two species have evolved long snouts for reaching even further into crevices for food.

Aquarium behaviour

Although very attractive, these fishes are not suitable for inexperienced fishkeepers. They can be difficult to maintain in captivity, particularly the algae- and sponge-eating species, and some have proved impossible to sustain (see pages 380-381). These species are easily upset by small changes in water quality, usually showing any dissatisfaction with aquarium life by going on hunger strike; one day they are quite content with the diet you provide and the next day they simply will not touch it.

Juvenile specimens may be far easier to acclimatize to aquarium life and subsequently do much better in the long term. Ensure that the aquarium has sufficient retreats and hideaways to give the fishes some form of security.

Butterflyfishes vary tremendously in their tolerance (or intolerance) of members of their own, or similar, species. Most are fairly peaceful, but it is always wise to make sure of this before buying them. Living corals and sea anemones will not last long in the same aquarium with butterflyfishes.

Butterflyfishes may undergo colour changes at night; the usual transformation is the appearance of darker splodges over parts of the body.

Chaetodon auriga

Threadfin Butterflyfish

☐ **Distribution:** Indo-Pacific, Red Sea.

☐ **Length:** 200mm/8in (wild), 150mm/6in (aquarium).

Left: Chaetodon auriga

Juvenile Threadfin Butterflyfishes do not have the long filament from the rear of the dorsal. Adults from the subspecies C. a. auriga *from the Red Sea may lose the eye-spot on the dorsal fin (though it remains in Indo-Pacific specimens). Like other butterflyfishes, it is not safe with invertebrates.*

☐ **Diet and feeding:** Crustaceans, coral polyps and algae in the wild. Offer suitable live and frozen foods in the aquarium. Grazer.

☐ **Aquarium behaviour:** Peaceful, but shy.

☐ **Invertebrate compatibility:** No, not to be trusted.

A black bar crosses the eye, and the mainly white flanks are decorated with a 'herring-bone' pattern of grey lines. The anal, dorsal and front part of the caudal fin are yellow. The common name of this species refers to a threadlike extension to the dorsal fin. *C. auriga* can be weaned on to food of your choice by gradual substitution.

Chaetodon chrysurus
Pearlscale Butterflyfish

☐ **Distribution:** Indo-Pacific.

☐ **Length:** 150mm/6in (wild).

☐ **Diet and feeding:** Crustaceans, vegetable matter. Grazer.

☐ **Aquarium behaviour:** Peaceful.

☐ **Invertebrate compatibility:** No, not to be trusted.

The scales on this species are large and dark-edged, giving the fish a lattice-covered, or checkered, pattern. The main feature is the bright orange arc connecting the rear of the dorsal and anal fins; a repeated orange band appears in the caudal fin. The fish's habitat is thought to be nearer to Africa, Mauritius and the Seychelles rather than spread widely over the Indo-Pacific area. The Red Sea *C. paucifasciatus* has a faint spot in the dorsal fin and a slightly different shape to the orange area (which is, in fact, almost red). *C. mertensii* and *C. xanthurus* are also very similar in appearance to *C. chrysurus*.

Below: Chaetodon chrysurus
If any fish is truly aptly named, this beautiful butterflyfish must be it, for the scales, seen at the right angle, are of a wonderfully pearly hue.

Chaetodon collare

Pakistani Butterflyfish

☐ **Distribution:** Indian Ocean.

☐ **Length:** 150mm/6in (wild), 100mm/4in (aquarium).

☐ **Diet and feeding:** Most frozen marine foods and greenstuff.

☐ **Aquarium behaviour:** May be intolerant of other members of its own, or other, species.

☐ **Invertebrate compatibility:** No, not to be trusted.

The brown coloration of *C. collare* is unusual for a butterflyfish. It is reputed to be difficult to keep, although not all authorities agree on this. Species from different locations may have different feeding requirements, the species from rocky outcrops being easier to satisfy in captivity than those from coral reefs. Not a suitable fish for the beginner.

Below: Chaetodon collare
From the coast of East Africa, right across the Indian Ocean to Melanesia, this fish is a common sight around the coral reefs. Beginners to marine fishkeeping should avoid this species.

Chaetodon ephipippium
Saddleback Butterflyfish

- **Distribution:** Indo-Pacific.
- **Length:** 230mm/9in (wild).
- **Diet and feeding:** Crustaceans. Grazer.
- **Aquarium behaviour:** May be intolerant of other members of its own, or other, species.
- **Invertebrate compatibility:** No, not to be trusted.

Easily recognizable by the white-edged dark 'saddle' that covers the rear upper portion of the body and dorsal fin. The females become plumper at breeding time. It may be difficult to accustom these fish to a successful aquarium feeding pattern.

Above: Chaetodon ephipippium
This is one of the more sensitive butterflyfishes; make sure a specimen is feeding properly before you purchase it.

Below: Chaetodon falcula
In the wild, this fish is confined to the Indian Ocean. Like most species in this family, it is not for the beginner.

Chaetodon falcula
Double-saddled Butterflyfish; Pig-faced Butterflyfish

- **Distribution:** Indian Ocean.
- **Length:** 150mm/6in (wild), 100-125mm/4-5in (aquarium).
- **Diet and feeding:** Crustaceans, coral polyps, algae. Grazer.
- **Aquarium behaviour:** Aggressive towards similar species.
- **Invertebrate compatibility:** No, not to be trusted.

Two dark saddle markings cross the top of the body. The dorsal, anal and caudal fins are yellow, and there is a black spot or bar on the caudal peduncle. The body and head are white. A vertical black bar runs down the side of the head and there are many vertical thin lines on the body. This species is often confused with *C. ulietensis*, which is found across a wider area of the Pacific Ocean, and has slightly lower reaching 'saddles' and less yellow on top of the body and dorsal fin. Both species can be found available.

Chaetodon frembli
Blue-striped Butterflyfish

☐ **Distribution:** Indo-Pacific, Red Sea.

☐ **Length:** 200mm/8in (wild).

☐ **Diet and feeding:** Crustaceans, coral polyps, algae. Grazer.

☐ **Aquarium behaviour:** Calm community fish.

☐ **Invertebrate compatibility:** No, not to be trusted.

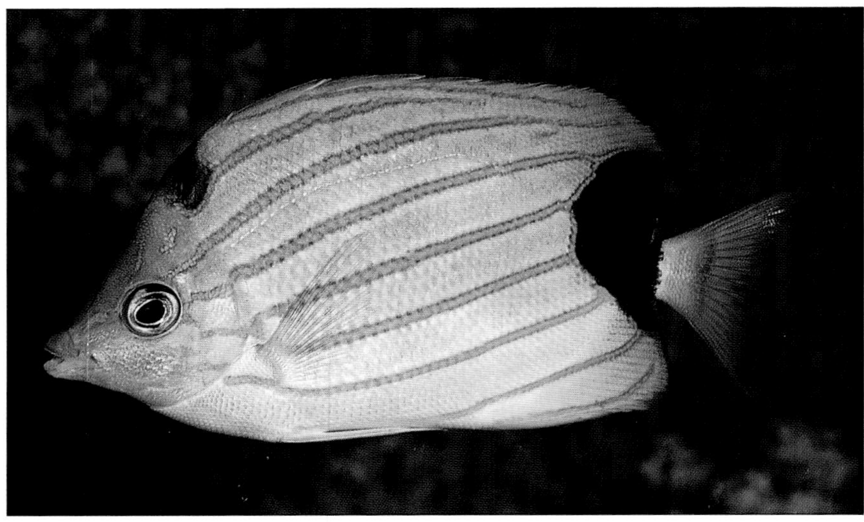

The yellow body is marked with upward slanting diagonal blue lines. A black mark appears immediately in front of the dorsal fin, and the black of the caudal peduncle extends into the rear of the dorsal and anal fins. The caudal fin has white, black and yellow vertical bars. This butterflyfish lacks the usual black bar through the eye. Not an easy species to keep.

Above: Chaetodon frembli
This species does not share the characteristic butterflyfish pattern, in which the real eye is hidden in a vertical dark band.

Chaetodon kleini

Klein's Butterflyfish; Sunburst Butterflyfish

☐ **Distribution:** Indo-Pacific.

☐ **Length:** 125mm/5in (wild), 100mm/4in (aquarium).

☐ **Diet and feeding:** Crustaceans, coral polyps, algae. Grazer.

☐ **Aquarium behaviour:** Peaceful.

☐ **Invertebrate compatibility:** No, not to be trusted.

Left: Chaetodon kleini
The obvious wide bands of the juvenile have faded by the time the fish reaches adulthood, as here. Only the black bar remains as a contrast to the sunburst colour of the body. Klein's Butterflyfish is thought to be the easiest member of the family to keep.

This is a more subtly coloured fish; its black eye bar is followed by a grey bar and the white forebody changes to a golden yellow. The dorsal and anal fins, plus the front part of the caudal fin, are a matching gold-yellow. The mouth is black. *C. kleini* is considered to be the easiest of all butterflyfishes to keep, being hardy once it has settled into the aquarium.

Chaetodon lunula

Racoon Butterflyfish

☐ **Distribution:** Indo-Pacific.

☐ **Length:** 200mm/8in (wild)

☐ **Diet and feeding:** Crustaceans, coral polyps, algae. Grazer.

☐ **Aquarium behaviour:** Usually peaceful with other fish, but will eat corals.

Above: Chaetodon lunula
Juvenile forms of the Racoon Butterflyfish have an 'eye-spot' in the rear part of the dorsal fin, but this fades with age. Another difference between young and adult fishes is that the adult fish has more yellow on the snout. This peaceful fish is relatively easy to keep and can have a fairly long lifespan in the aquarium.

☐ **Invertebrate compatibility:** No, not to be trusted.

A white-edged black bar runs down over the eye and immediately sweeps up again into the mid-dorsal area. A white bar crosses this bar immediately behind the eye. A black blotch appears on the caudal peduncle, a feature missing in the otherwise similar species, *C. fasciatus*, *C. lunula* is fairly long-lived in the aquarium and will readily accept most foods.

Chaetodon melannotus
Black-backed Butterflyfish

- **Distribution:** Indo-Pacific.
- **Length:** 150mm/6in (wild).
- **Diet and feeding:** Crustaceans, coral polyps, algae. Grazer.
- **Aquarium behaviour:** A peaceful, but difficult, fish.
- **Invertebrate compatibility:** No, not to be trusted.

The white body is crossed by diagonal thin black stripes and bordered by yellow dorsal, anal and caudal fins. A black eye bar divides the yellow head.

Chaetodon punctofasciatus
Spot-banded Butterflyfish

- **Distribution:** A wide distribution throughout the Pacific.
- **Length:** 100mm/4in (wild).
- **Diet and feeding:** Coral polyps. Frozen foods. Grazer.
- **Aquarium behaviour:** May be intolerant of other members of its own, or other, species.
- **Invertebrate compatibility:** No, not to be trusted.

The vertical black stripes end halfway down the body, and turn into many spots. A black spot appears immediately in front of the dorsal fin. The eye bar is yellow with a black edge.

Top right: Chaetodon melannotus
For hobbyists requiring absolute accuracy in fish descriptions, this species should perhaps be renamed the Black-sided Butterflyfish.

Right: Chaetodon punctofasciatus
This species has a wide distribution, ranging from the China Sea in the north, out to the Philippines, and south as far as Australia's Great Barrier Reef.

Chaetodon semilarvatus

Addis Butterflyfish; Lemonpeel Butterflyfish; Golden Butterflyfish

☐ **Distribution:** Indian Ocean, Red Sea.

☐ **Length:** 200mm/8in (wild).

☐ **Diet and feeding:** Crustaceans, coral polyps, algae. Grazer.

☐ **Aquarium behaviour:** May be intolerant of other members of its own, or other, species. Difficult.

☐ **Invertebrate compatibility:** No, not to be trusted.

The yellow body is crossed by thin orange vertical lines. A blue-black inverted teardrop patch covers the eye. Red Sea specimens are difficult to obtain and thus costly.

Below: Chaetodon semilarvatus
The bright coloration and distinctive markings of this species make it a perfect photographic subject. Specimens from the Red Sea are difficult to obtain and therefore very expensive.

Chaetodon striatus
Banded Butterflyfish

- ☐ **Distribution:** Tropical Atlantic Ocean.
- ☐ **Length:** 150mm/6in (wild).
- ☐ **Diet and feeding:** Crustaceans, coral polyps, algae. Grazer.
- ☐ **Aquarium behaviour:** May be intolerant of other members of its own, or other, species.
- ☐ **Invertebrate compatibility:** No, not to be trusted.

An easily recognizable species with four dark bands across its body. A continuous dark band passes through the outer edges of the dorsal, caudal and anal fins to connect with the ends of the third vertical band. The juvenile form has a white-ringed black spot on the soft dorsal fin. A good community fish.

Take care not to shock or otherwise stress this easily frightened fish during transportation and introduction into the aquarium.

Above: Chaetodon striatus
The black and white stripes of the Banded Butterflyfish make it easily recognizable and are reminiscent of the markings of the freshwater angelfish.

Below: Chaetodon vagabundus
The Vagabond Butterflyfish is a long-standing favourite; a peaceful fish that would make a good introduction to the marine aquarium.

Chaetodon vagabundus
Vagabond Butterflyfish; Criss-cross Butterflyfish

- ☐ **Distribution:** Indo-Pacific.
- ☐ **Length:** 200mm/8in (wild).
- ☐ **Diet and feeding:** Crustaceans, coral polyps, algae. Grazer.
- ☐ **Aquarium behaviour:** Peaceful.
- ☐ **Invertebrate compatibility:** No, not to be trusted.

Diagonal lines cross the white body in two directions. Black bars cross the eye and fringe the rear part of the body. The rear part of the dorsal and anal fins are gold-yellow edged with black; the yellow caudal fin has two black vertical bars. A similar species is *C. pictus*, often classified as a subspecies or a colour variant. *C. vagabundus*, like all marines, appreciates good water conditions.

Chelmon rostratus

Copper-band Butterflyfish

☐ **Distribution:** Indo-Pacific, Red Sea.

☐ **Length:** 170mm/6.7in (wild).

☐ **Diet and feeding:** Frozen foods, small animal foods, algae. Picks in between coral heads.

☐ **Aquarium behaviour:** Aggressive towards members of its own species. Difficult.

☐ **Invertebrate compatibility:** No, not to be trusted.

The yellow-orange vertical bands on the body have blue-black edging. These distinctive colours, coupled with the false 'eye-spot' at the rear of the upper body, make this fish difficult to confuse with any other. It may take time to acclimatize to aquarium foods. It is very sensitive to deteriorating water conditions.

Above: Chelmon rostratus
The outstanding colours and attractive (and unusual) shape of this fish should be all the inducement you need to keep it in the best aquarium conditions.

Above: Forcipiger flavissimus
Note how the black triangle on this species camouflages the eye.

Far right: Heniochus acuminatus
The Wimplefish is often confused with the Moorish Idol (Zanclus sp.).

Forcipiger flavissimus
Long-nosed Butterflyfish

☐ **Distribution:** Indo-Pacific, Red Sea.

☐ **Length:** 200mm/8in (wild), 100-150mm/4-6in (aquarium).

☐ **Diet and feeding:** Small animal foods, algae. Picks in between coral heads.

☐ **Aquarium behaviour:** Not as aggressive as *C. rostratus*.

☐ **Invertebrate compatibility:** No, not to be trusted.

The body, dorsal, anal, and pelvic fins are bright yellow, but a black triangle disrupts the contours of the head. The lower jaw is white, and the caudal fin is clear. A false 'eye spot' on the anal fin confuses predators. It is similar in its aquarium requirements and treatment to *C. rostratus*. The Big Long-nosed Butterflyfish *(F. longirostris)* is similar, but less common, with a longer snout.

Heniochus acuminatus
Wimplefish; Pennant Coralfish
Poor Man's Moorish Idol

☐ **Distribution:** Indo-Pacific, Red Sea.

☐ **Length:** 180mm/7in (wild).

☐ **Diet and feeding:** Most frozen marine foods and greenstuff. Grazer.

☐ **Aquarium behaviour:** Companionable.

☐ **Invertebrate compatibility:** No, not to be trusted.

Two wide, forward-sloping black bands cross the white body. The rear parts of the dorsal, pectoral and anal fins are yellow while the pelvic fins are black. The front few rays of the dorsal fin are much extended. These fish appreciate plenty of swimming room and young specimens act as cleanerfishes. Other species, such as the Horned Coralfish (*H. chrysostomus*) are rarely imported. *H. acuminatus* varies little in juvenile and adult coloration, but other species in the genus differ; some adults develop protuberances on the forehead.

This is an excellent substitute for the Moorish Idol (*Zanclus canescens*), which has a very poor survival rate in captivity.

Family: CIRRHITIDAE

Hawkfishes

Family chacteristics
Despite their attractive appearance and friendliness, Hawkfishes are predators – albeit of small prey. They rest or 'perch' on a piece of coral and wait for food to pass by, at which point they dash out and seize it. Reproduction in these fishes is by demersal eggs, i.e. the eggs are laid and fertilized on a firm surface, where they subsequently hatch. In the nine genera there are some 32 species, most of which are not commonly kept in the aquarium. The largest species described has a maximum length of 55cm (22in).

Diet and feeding
In the wild, these fishes will take small invertebrates – shrimps, etc. – and smaller fishes. In the aquarium, provide live foods and suitable meaty frozen foods.

Aquarium behaviour
Hawkfishes will appreciate plenty of 'perching places' in the aquarium. Despite their predatory nature, they appear not to harm sedentary invertebrates such as tubeworms, soft corals, etc.

Neocirrhites armatus
Scarlet Hawkfish

☐ **Distribution:** Central and Western Pacific.

☐ **Length:** 75mm/3in (wild)

☐ **Diet and feeding:** Accepts most marine frozen and live foods of a suitable size. Once settled in the aquarium, it will also accept marine flake.

☐ **Aquarium behaviour:** Peaceful.

☐ **Invertebrate compatibility:** Yes, generally well behaved.

This extremely attractive fish is much sought after by aquarists and usually commands quite a high price as a consequence. It is not a good swimmer and spends much of its time resting on rocks and Gorgonians waiting to ambush small crustaceans and plankton. Fortunately, it is not a threat in the home aquarium and makes an ideal community addition.

Below: Neocirrhites armatus
The aptly named Scarlet Hawkfish is regularly imported, but not in large numbers. It is a very popular fish in short supply and, although quite expensive, is not difficult to keep. N. armatus *seems to fare best in a mixed fish and invertebrate system, where it also tends to look more natural.*

Oxycirrhites typus
Longnosed Hawkfish

☐ **Distribution:** Indian Ocean mainly.

☐ **Length:** 100mm/4in (wild).

☐ **Diet and feeding:** Most frozen marine foods. Sits on coral or a rock, then dashes out to grab food.

☐ **Aquarium behaviour:** Peaceful. Can be kept in small groups.

☐ **Invertebrate compatibility:** Yes, generally well behaved.

The elongate body of this hardy fish is covered with a squared pattern of bright red lines. The snout is very long and suited to probing the coral crevices for food. There are small cirri, or crestlike growths, at the end of each dorsal fin spine and on the nostrils. The female is larger than the male and the male has darker red lower jaws. There are black edges to the pelvic and caudal fins.

In nature, spawnings occur from dusk onwards. Reports of aquarium spawnings suggest that the female lays patches of adhesive eggs after courtship activity.

Below: Oxycirrhites typus
The Long-nosed Hawkfish depends on its natural coloration and markings to provide camouflage as it perches on a suitable sea whip or sea fan waiting to ambush its next unsuspecting meal, which will usually consist of a shrimp or other unfortunate crustacean!

Family: DIODONTIDAE

Porcupinefishes

Family characteristics
Porcupinefishes are very similar to the other 'inflatable' fishes, the puffers (see pages 298-301). They can be distinguished from the pufferfishes, however, by the spines on their scales and by their front teeth, which are fused together. Hard crustacean foods present little problem to them. The pelvic fins are absent. Normally the spines are held flat, but in times of danger they stand out from the body as the fish inflates itself. The appearance and inflatability of the porcupinefishes make them interesting subjects for the aquarium.

Diet and feeding
Earthworms, shrimps, crab meat and other meaty foods can be given, but cut food into pieces for smaller specimens.

Aquarium behaviour
Although they grow very large in the wild, porcupinefishes rarely grow as big in captivity. Nevertheless, be sure to keep them alone in a large aquarium. You may find that specimens become hand tame. It may be a temptation to encourage these fish to inflate, but this should be resisted as it is very stressful for the individual.

Chilomycterus schoepfi
Spiny Boxfish; Striped Burrfish; Burrfish

☐ **Distribution:** Tropical Atlantic, Caribbean.

☐ **Length:** 300mm/12in (wild).

☐ **Diet and feeding:** Crustaceans, molluscs, meat foods. Bold.

☐ **Aquarium behaviour:** Aggressive among themselves. Do not keep them with small fishes.

☐ **Invertebrate compatibility:** Not suitable.

The undulating dark lines on its yellow body provide *C. schoepfi* with excellent camouflage, and a first line of defence; then the short spines – fixed and usually held erect – may be called upon to play their part. Not as liable to inflate itself as other related species.

Below: Chilomycterus schoepfi
The short spines of this species are kept erect – a constant defence against predation or capture. In addition, its coloration provides good camouflage in its natural environment.

Diodon holacanthus

Long-spined Porcupinefish; Balloonfish

☐ **Distribution:** All warm seas.

☐ **Length:** 500mm/20in (wild), 150mm/6in (aquarium).

☐ **Diet and feeding:** Crustaceans, molluscs, meat foods. Bold.

☐ **Aquarium behaviour:** Do not keep with small fishes.

☐ **Invertebrate compatibility:** Not suitable as invertebrates are its main food.

The colour patterning on this species is blotched rather than lined, but it serves the same excellent purpose – to disguise the fish as part of the surrounding underwater scenery.

Above: Diodon holacanthus
The Long-spined Porcupinefish is one of the most commonly found species, being native worldwide. It feeds on crustaceans, so do not include it in an aquarium containing invertebrates.

Diodon hystrix

Common Porcupinefish; Porcupine Puffer

☐ **Distribution:** All warm seas.

☐ **Length:** 900mm/36in (wild), considerably smaller in the aquarium.

☐ **Diet and feeding:** Crustaceans, molluscs, meat foods. Bold.

☐ **Aquarium behaviour:** Generally peaceful with other fishes.

☐ **Invertebrate compatibility:** Not suitable.

This species has longer spines held more flatly against the body. It is not constantly active, remaining at rest for long periods until hunger or some other action-provoking event stirs it. You will need to keep the tank efficiently filtered to cope with these fishes, which can sometimes prove 'messy eaters'.

Above: Diodon hystrix
Despite its formidable adult size, the Common Porcupinefish poses little threat to smaller fishes, though, again, it should not be kept in a mixed fish and invertebrate set-up and its aquarium will need good filtration.

Family: GOBIIDAE

Gobies

Family characteristics

Comparatively little is known about this very large family, which – paradoxically – contains one of the smallest known vertebrates (*Pandaka* sp). In the wild, gobies are found in several different locations: tidal shallow beaches; on the coral reef itself; and on the muddy seabed. Some species are found in fresh water. All rely on having a secure bolt hole in which to hide when danger threatens. Such 'bolt holes' may be located within sponges, caves, crevices or may simply be burrows in the seabed.

The gobies are endearing little characters for the aquarium. Unlike the blennies, the colours of the gobies can be quite brilliant. Their bodies are elongate, the head blunt with high-set eyes. Gobies can be further distinguished from blennies, with whom they share a similar habitat, by the presence of a 'suction-disc' formed by the fusion of the pelvic fins.

Sexing gobies can be difficult, although females may become distended with eggs at breeding time and there are the typical differences in the size and shape of the genital papillae – if you can see them! (The genital papillae are breeding tubes that extend from the vent of each fish; usually longer in females than in males.) In some species, the male may change colour or develop longer fins during the breeding period. Spawning occurs in burrows or in sheltered areas, with the eggs being guarded by the male. Several gobies have been spawned in captivity. *Gobiosoma oceanops* and *Lythrypnus dalli*, for example, will breed willingly in the aquarium, but rearing the young fry is not easy. The young of *G. oceanops* have been reared with more success than the smaller fry of *L. dalli*.

Diet and feeding

Gobies are carnivorous fishes that will eat brineshrimp, finely chopped meat foods, frozen foods and *Daphnia*.

Aquarium behaviour

Many reef-dwelling species provide cleaning services for larger fishes, the cleaning sequence following the pattern described for the Cleaner Wrasse (see pages 216-217).

Gobiodon citrinus
Lemon Goby

- ☐ **Distribution:** Indo-Pacific.
- ☐ **Length:** 30mm/1.2in (wild)
- ☐ **Diet and feeding:** Once settled, will accept most marine foods of a suitable size. Particularly fond of live foods.
- ☐ **Aquarium behaviour:** Very peaceful.
- ☐ **Invertebrate compatibility:** Good.

In common with many gobies, *G. citrinus* is not a good swimmer and spends much of its time perched in the branches of gorgonians or on rocks with a good vantage point. The mucus of this species is known to be poisonous and a protection against being eaten by other fish. However, it is not known to cause a toxic problem.

Below left: Gobiodon citrinus
Beginners and experienced aquarists alike will find this species an absolute delight. It is not a difficult species to keep but should ideally be kept in a mixed aquarium – it looks rather out of place in a fish-only tank.

Gobiodon okinawae
Yellow Goby

- ☐ **Distribution:** Pacific Ocean.
- ☐ **Length:** 30mm/1.2in (wild).
- ☐ **Diet and feeding:** Will readily accept small particles of most marine fare, including frozen, live and flake foods. Live foods are particularly relished, especially when the fish is first settling in.
- ☐ **Aquarium behaviour:** Very peaceful, except with the same species.
- ☐ **Invertebrate compatibility:** Excellent.

Although small, the Yellow Goby is highly territorial and, once settled into an aquarium, will very rarely tolerate other individuals of the same species, even in a fairly large tank. Sometimes a pair may be identified and introduced at the same time, in which case a spawning may be possible but, so far, none of these very desirable little fish have been raised to adulthood. Poor water quality is not tolerated, and the fish will refuse to eat and may turn a dirty brown colour as a result. If no improvement is made, death usually follows.

Below: Gobiodon okinawae
The Yellow Goby is, in common with many other gobies, a very poor swimmer and prefers to remain perched on favourite vantage points. Once settled, it shows little concern for other inhabitants that pose no threat.

Gobiosoma oceanops
Neon Goby

☐ **Distribution:** Western Atlantic, especially Florida, and the Gulf of Mexico.

☐ **Length:** 60mm/2.4in (wild), 25mm/1in (aquarium).

☐ **Diet and feeding:** Parasites, small crustaceans and plankton. Bold nibbler; bottom feeder.

☐ **Aquarium behaviour:** Peaceful and uninhibited.

☐ **Invertebrate compatibility:** Ideal.

Two characteristics distinguish this most familiar goby: the electric blue coloration of the longitudinal line on the body and the cleaning services it offers to other fishes. The species can be positively identified by the gap visible between the two blue lines on the snout when the fish is seen from above; other species have connected lines or other markings between the ends of the lines.

G. oceanops has been bred in the aquarium and is now regularly bred on a commercial basis. Pairing occurs spontaneously. Before spawning, the male's colour darkens and he courts the female with exaggerated swimming motions, assuming a position on the aquarium floor until the female takes notice of him. Spawning activity occurs in a cave or other similar sheltered area. The fertilized eggs hatch after 7-12 days. In the wild, the fry feed on planktonic foods for the first few weeks. In the aquarium, start the fry off with cultured rotifers followed by newly hatched brineshrimp.

Unfortunately, these eminently suitable (and practicable) aquarium subjects are relatively shortlived – perhaps only a year or two, but their breeding possibilities should enable you to propagate them for several generations if given the ideal conditions. Hopefully, one day, all Neon Gobies will be tank raised.

Above: Gobiosoma oceanops
This colourful goby is peaceful, doesn't need a large tank, and will spawn quite readily given the correct conditions.

Below: Lythrypnus dalli
A number of Blue-banded Gobies could share a reasonably sized tank without too much quarrelling.

Lythrypnus dalli
Blue-banded Goby; Catalina Goby

☐ **Distribution:** Californian Pacific coast.

☐ **Length:** 60mm/2.4in (wild), 25mm/1in (aquarium).

☐ **Diet and feeding:** Small crustaceans and other small marine organisms. Live foods preferred. Bottom feeder.

☐ **Aquarium behaviour:** Peaceful with small fishes but may be bullied by larger fishes.

☐ **Invertebrate compatibility:** Ideal.

The red body is crossed by brilliant blue vertical lines and the first dorsal fin has an elongated ray. The male has longer dorsal fin spines than the female. Despite territorial requirements several fish will share even a reasonably small aquarium quite happily, but they are not naturally a longlived species. This species does not require the same high water temperatures as other marine fish. This fish has been spawned successfully in the aquarium.

Valenciennea puellaris
Orange-spotted Goby

- ☐ **Distribution:** Indo-Pacific.
- ☐ **Length:** 150mm/6in (wild), 100mm/4in (aquarium).
- ☐ **Diet and feeding:** Once settled, will accept most marine fare of a suitable size, including frozen, live and flake foods.
- ☐ **Aquarium behaviour:** Very peaceful. An excellent fish for the community aquarium.
- ☐ **Invertebrate compatibility:** Generally good, but may upset sessile invertebrates with its digging activities.

The Orange-spotted Goby is a common fish throughout the Indo-Pacific. The patterning on the body may vary widely from region to region, sometimes making identification a little difficult. This species is an excellent aquarium subject and a very good choice for the beginner. It requires a sandy substrate in which to dig and burrow.

Valenciennea strigata
Blue-cheek Goby

- ☐ **Distribution:** Western Pacific and Indian Oceans.
- ☐ **Length:** 180mm/7in (wild).
- ☐ **Diet and feeding:** Thrives on nearly all marine frozen, live and flake foods.
- ☐ **Aquarium behaviour:** Very peaceful. A good community fish.
- ☐ **Invertebrate compatibility:** Generally good, but may upset sessile invertebrates with its digging activities.

V. strigata, which is closely related to the previous species, *V. puellaris,* constantly digs and sifts the sand for food particles. This can be a boon for aquarists with undergravel filtration as the activity helps to keep the substrate loose and less likely to compact. *V. strigata* also enjoys the company of its own species and may generally be considered safe to keep in pairs or small groups where space and filtration capacity allows. This easy-to-keep fish makes an ideal introduction to gobies.

Top: Valenciennea puellaris
The Orange-spotted Goby is a popular fish with many aquarists, who like to observe its interesting digging habits.

Above: Valenciennea strigata
The Blue-cheek Goby enjoys the company of its own species and a pair are often observed following each other.

Family: GRAMMIDAE

Fairy Basslets; Pygmy Basslets

Family characteristics
This small group of fish are confined to the Caribbean and only three species are known to date – the ever popular *Gramma loreto,* the Royal Gramma; *Gramma melacara,* the Black-Cap Gramma; and lastly, the very rare *Gramma linki* (not featured here).

In common with their closely related cousins, the Pseudochromids (see pages 280-283), these fish are shy and secretive. They spend most of their lives within the maze of reef crevices and are highly territorial in nature. They lead largely solitary lives, coming together only at breeding times. The Royal Gramma (*Gramma loreto),* although often aggressive with its own kind, has been regularly spawned in the aquarium.

Diet and feeding
The wild diet of these fish is largely made up of drifting planktonic animals and crustaceans. Most frozen and live marine foods are accepted within the aquarium. The Royal Gramma may also accept flake foods. *Gramma melacara* will need a little more care and may need to be tempted with live brineshrimp and *Mysis* initially.

Aquarium behaviour
Gramma melacara is highly territorial and may not be kept with its own or similar species. The Royal Gramma may be tempted, in a large enough aquarium, to form a breeding unit of one male to several females. Aprroach this with care, however, as two males will fight, usually to the death.

Above: Gramma loreto
As far as coloration goes, if big is beautiful then small can be simply stunning – as this Royal Gramma shows. A cave-dwelling fish, it is often very possessive, positively resenting any intrusion by other fishes into its chosen home. It is equally intolerant of others of its own kind (though you may be able to keep a pair in a large tank). An aquarium stocked with many soft corals and hideaways suits it perfectly.

Gramma loreto
Royal Gramma

☐ **Distribution:** Western Atlantic.

☐ **Length:** 130mm/5in (wild), 75mm/3in (aquarium).

☐ **Diet and feeding:** Eats a wide range of foods, including chopped shrimp and live brineshrimp.

☐ **Aquarium behaviour:** This cave-dwelling fish should be acclimatized gradually to bright light. It may resent other cave-dwelling species, particularly the Yellow-headed Jawfish, (see page 231). Aggressive towards its own kind, but pairings are possible in a large tank.

☐ **Invertebrate compatibility:** Yes, ideal.

The main feature of this species is its remarkable colouring. The front half of the body is magenta, the rear half bright golden-yellow. A thin black line slants backwards through the eye. These somewhat secretive cave dwellers should not be kept with boisterous species. An almost identical species, *Pseudochromis paccagnellae* (see page 282) has a narrow white line dividing the two main body colours.

Spawning activity has been observed – paradoxically, not in nature but in captivity. Four fish grouped themselves into two 'pairs', each comprising one small and one large fish. The larger fish lined a pit in the sand with strands of algae glued together with a glandular secretion and the pair spawned 'stickleback' fashion. The smaller fish was enticed into the pit several times, closely followed by the larger of the two, who then stood guard over the pit full of eggs. Unfortunately, the fry were not raised successfully, but this does shed light on the possible reproductive methods practised by this species. The dissimilar sizes of the fishes making up the 'pairs' seems to bear out other reports that the male fish is usually larger than the female where both fishes are of the same age.

Above: Gramma melacara
The Black-cap Gramma positively thrives in a mainly invertebrate aquarium. Although never on constant show, it will make regular appearances.

Gramma melacara
Black-Cap Gramma

☐ **Distribution:** Caribbean.

☐ **Length:** 100mm/4in.

☐ **Diet and feeding:** Prefers live foods but will usually accept frozen marine fare after an initial settling-in period.

☐ **Aquarium behaviour:** Shy and secretive by nature. Requires a comprehensive arrangement of rockwork in which to hide.

☐ **Invertebrate compatibility:** Ideal.

The common name Black-Cap is certainly apt in this case, for the purple body is only disturbed by a black patch over the crown of the head. This most attractive fish is extremely territorial and should be kept in the absence of its own, or similar, species. Overly aggressive specimens have been known to bite their keeper's hand! Having said that, these fish make ideal additions to the invertebrate aquarium.

Family: HAEMULIDAE

Grunts

Family characteristics
Grunts can be distinguished from the similar-looking snappers by differences in their dentition. Many grind their pharyngeal teeth, the resulting sound being amplified by the swimbladder. Juveniles often perform cleaning services for other fishes.

Diet and feeding
Members of this family of fishes eat well, enjoying a diet of small fishes, shrimps and dried foods.

Aquarium behaviour
Grunts may grow too quickly for the average aquarium.

Above: Anisotremus virginicus
Provided they are given a suitably large aquarium, these juvenile Porkfish will live quite happily together. They are not difficult to keep and will accept a wide variety of foods.

Anisotremus virginicus
Porkfish

☐ **Distribution:** Caribbean.

☐ **Length:** 300mm/12in (wild).

☐ **Diet and feeding:** In the wild, brittle starfish, crustaceans, etc. In the aquarium, chopped meaty foods etc. Nocturnal feeder.

☐ **Aquarium behaviour:** Keep juvenile specimens only. A large tank will suit them well.

☐ **Invertebrate compatibility:** Voracious predators on all forms of invertebrates and so should be kept in a fish-only aquarium.

The body is triangular, the highest part being just behind the head. The steep forehead is fairly long and the eyes are large. The yellow body is streaked with bright blue lines and two black bars cross the head region, one through the eye and one just behind the gill cover. The juvenile coloration is different; the cream body has black horizontal stripes and a black blotch on the caudal peduncle. The head is yellow and the larger fins have red marks on their edges.

The common collective name of grunts comes from the noise these fishes make when they are taken from the water. They are very similar in appearance to the Majestic Snapper, (see page 223).

Family: HOLOCENTRIDAE

Squirrelfishes

Family characteristics
Squirrelfishes are large-eyed nocturnal fishes that hide by day among crevices in the coral reefs of the Indo-Pacific and Atlantic Oceans. They usually have red patterning on their elongate bodies, spines on the gill covers and sharp rays on the fins. The dorsal fin looks as if it has two separate parts: a long-based spiny part at the front and a high triangular softer rayed section at the back. The scales and gill cover are extremely rough; take great care when netting or handling, as this can easily damage the fish.

Diet and feeding
In the aquarium, squirrelfishes rapidly adjust to a daytime eating routine and a diet consisting of chopped worm foods and small fish.

Aquarium behaviour
Squirrelfishes are very active and need a sufficiently large aquarium to accommodate their energetic way of life. Remember that other small fishes may not welcome such boisterous companions.

Holocentrus diadema
Common Squirrelfish

☐ **Distribution:** Indo-Pacific.

☐ **Length:** 300m/12in (wild).

☐ **Diet and feeding:** All foods. Bold.

☐ **Aquarium behaviour:** Do not keep with small fishes.

☐ **Invertebrate compatibility:** Yes, but may be unsafe with small crustaceans.

Horizontal red lines and a red dorsal fin make this common fish a very colourful addition to any sufficiently large aquarium. In nature, it is a nocturnal species and therefore needs some hiding places in which to rest during the day. It does adapt to aquarium life, however, and will swim around in daylight hours.

Below: Holocentrus diadema
In the wild, these strikingly attractive fishes swim in large shoals among the coral reefs. Their relatively large size and constant activity render them less suited to the average aquarium, but if you can provide adequate swimming space and plenty of companions, this fish will prove a good addition to the tank.

Holocentrus rufus
White-tip Squirrelfish

- ☐ **Distribution:** Western Atlantic.
- ☐ **Length:** 200mm/8in (wild).
- ☐ **Diet and feeding:** Crustaceans and meaty foods. Bold.
- ☐ **Aquarium behaviour:** Shoaling fish for a large aquarium.
- ☐ **Invertebrate compatibility:** Yes, except with small crustaceans.

Holocentrus rufus is a similar colour to other squirrelfishes, but it has a white triangular mark on each dorsal fin spine. Reasonably fearless, predatory squirrelfishes can hold their own with grunts and even moray eels; they will meet any threats to their safety with grunting noises and quivering actions.

Above: Holocentrus rufus
A feature of the White-tipped Squirrelfish is the long rear part of the dorsal fin; the upper part of the caudal fin is larger than the lower.

Myripristis murdjan
Big-eye Squirrelfish; Blotcheye

- ☐ **Distribution:** Indo-Pacific.
- ☐ **Length:** 300mm/12in (wild).
- ☐ **Diet and feeding:** Crustaceans and meaty foods. Bold.
- ☐ **Aquarium behaviour:** Peaceful.
- ☐ **Invertebrate compatibility:** Will eat small crustaceans.

The Big-eye Squirrelfish clearly lives up to its popular name! The organs in question are used to good advantage at night, when the fish is active. The red edge on each scale gives this fish a reticulated appearance. There is a dark red vertical area behind the gill cover.

It lacks the spine on the rear of the gill cover that is carried by members of the genus *Holocentrus*. Although the squirrelfishes are peaceful, do not be tempted to include smaller fishes in their tank.

Above: Myripristis murdjan
Although the aptly named Big-Eyed Squirrelfish is generally peaceful, it would be wise to avoid keeping it with smaller fishes, which might provide an easy and tasty meal. As its huge eyes suggest, this is a nocturnal species.

Family: LABRIDAE

Wrasses

Family characteristics
The Labridae is a very large family, encompassing about 400 species. It is not surprising, therefore, that the body shape varies; some wrasses are cylindrical, while others are much deeper bodied. Like many other marine fishes, wrasses swim without making much use of the caudal fin, which is mainly used for steering or held in reserve for emergencies. The main propulsion comes from the pectoral fins.

Sex reversal is quite common in wrasses, the necessary change occurring in single-sexed groups as required. (The female stage always precedes the male one.) Reproductive activity can occur between pairs or collectively in groups. In both cases, the fishes spiral upwards towards the surface to spawn. Occasionally, this activity is based around a preselected territory. Coastal species take advantage of the outgoing tide to sweep the fertilized eggs away from the reef to safety. Species from temperate zones in Europe and the Mediterranean build spawning nests of algae or sand.

Diet and feeding
Feeding habits vary from species to species, but most relish molluscs and crustaceans. They will take brineshrimps, shrimps, and most frozen marine fare.

Aquarium behaviour
Juvenile forms are quite suitable for the aquarium. Wrasses and rainbowfishes are interesting for several reasons: the juvenile coloration patterns are different from those of adult fishes. Many bury themselves in the sand for long periods during the day as well as at night time, so a sandy substrate is essential. Others spin mucus cocoons in which to rest; and a number of fishes perform 'cleaning services' on other species, removing parasites in the process. Fishes in this group are usually quite active and therefore may disturb more sedate fishes in the aquarium.

Bodianus pulchellus
Cuban Hogfish; Spotfin Hogfish

☐ **Distribution:** Western Atlantic.

☐ **Length:** 250mm/10in (wild), 150mm/6in (aquarium).

☐ **Diet and feeding:** Crustaceans, shellfish meat. Bold bottom feeder.

☐ **Aquarium behaviour:** Generally peaceful although small fishes in the aquarium may not be entirely safe.

☐ **Invertebrate compatibility:** Safe when young, but become destructive with age and size.

The front of the body is red, divided by a white horizontal band; the upper part of the back is bright yellow. There is a black spot at the end of the pectoral fins. Juveniles are yellow with a dark spot on the front of the dorsal fin, a colour scheme similar to that of the juvenile form of *Thalassoma bifasciatum* (see page 220). It is likely that both these species have evolved similar markings to signal their cleaning services. Usually it is quite easy to acclimatize these fishes to aquarium foods.

Above: Bodianus pulchellus
This smart Cuban Hogfish from the western Atlantic is easy to acclimatize to aquarium life. It is best kept with fishes of equal or larger size.

Bodianus rufus
Spanish Hogfish

☐ **Distribution:** Western Atlantic.

☐ **Length:** 600mm/24in (wild), 200mm/8in (aquarium).

☐ **Diet and feeding:** Crustaceans, shellfish meat. Bold bottom feeder.

☐ **Aquarium behaviour:** Peaceful.

☐ **Invertebrate compatibility:** Safe when young, but become destructive with age and size.

Juvenile specimens are yellow with an area of blue along the upper body. Adult fishes show the standard red and yellow coloration, although the proportions may vary according to the habitat and depth of water. Like other members of the genus, juveniles perform cleaning actions on other fishes.

Above: Bodianus rufus
A brightly coloured juvenile specimen of this wrasse from the Caribbean. This is a peaceful community fish.

Below: Cirrhilabrus rubriventralis
The male of a pair will show off his splendid markings to the female, dashing in front of her, flaring his fins.

Cirrhilabrus rubriventralis
Dwarf Parrot Wrasse; Sea Fighter

☐ **Distribution:** Indian Ocean.

☐ **Length:** 75mm/3in (wild)

☐ **Diet and feeding:** Will accept most marine fare, including frozen, live and flake foods.

☐ **Aquarium behaviour:** Peaceful community fish.

☐ **Invertebrate compatibility:** Good.

An extremely attractive species with distinct male and female coloration. The male is much more intensely coloured than the female and has an elongated leading edge to the dorsal fin. In suitably sized tanks it is possible to keep a pair, or one male and several females, together. In this arrangement, the male will intensify his colours and display to the females by dashing in front of them flaring his fins. Optimum water conditions are essential for this fish.

Above: Coris angulata
The adult Twin-spot Wrasse not only loses the spots seen in the juvenile, but also outgrows most home aquariums.

Coris angulata
Twin-spot Wrasse

☐ **Distribution:** Indo-Pacific, Red Sea.

☐ **Length:** 1200mm/48in (wild), 200-300mm/8-12in (aquarium).

☐ **Diet and feeding:** Small marine animals, live foods. Bottom feeder.

☐ **Aquarium behaviour:** Peaceful but grows very quickly.

☐ **Invertebrate compatibility:** Safe when young, but become destructive with age and size.

A spectacularly coloured species, both as a juvenile and as an adult. When young, this fish is white with two prominent orange spots on the dorsal surface. The front of the body, together with the fins, is covered with dark spots and there are two white-edged black blotches on the dorsal fin. The adult is green with yellow-edged purple fins and is referred to as the Napoleon Wrasse.

Coris formosa
African Clown Wrasse

☐ **Distribution:** Indian Ocean.

☐ **Length:** 300mm/12in (wild), 200mm/8in (aquarium).

☐ **Diet and feeding:** Small marine animals, live foods. Bottom feeder.

☐ **Aquarium behaviour:** Peaceful but grows large.

☐ **Invertebrate compatibility:** Safe when young, but become destructive with age and size.

The juvenile fish is dark brown with a thick vertical white band crossing the body and dorsal fin just behind the gill cover. Two shorter bands cross the head and two more appear on the rear of the dorsal fin and caudal peduncle. The caudal fin is white. In the adult, the head and body are green-brown and two green-blue stripes run in front of and behind the gill cover. The dorsal fin is red with an elongated first ray, the anal fin is green and purple, and the caudal fin is red, bordered with white.

Below: Coris formosa
Adults lack these white markings.

Coris gaimardi

Clown Wrasse; Red Labrid

☐ **Distribution:** Indo-Pacific.

☐ **Length:** 300mm/12in (wild), 150mm/6in (aquarium).

☐ **Diet and feeding:** Crustaceans, shellfish meat. Bold bottom feeder.

☐ **Aquarium behaviour:** May quarrel among themselves.

☐ **Invertebrate compatibility:** Safe when young, but become destructive with age and size.

Juveniles are similar to *C. formosa* but are orange rather than brown; the middle white band does not extend right down the body and the dorsal fin lacks a spot. Adults are brown-violet with many blue spots. The dorsal and anal fins are red, the caudal fin is yellow. There are blue markings on the face. These can be nervous fishes that dash about when first introduced into the aquarium, so try not to shock them.

Above: Coris gaimardi (adult)
Here, the final adult colours of the Clown Wrasse are established. The blue facial markings and spotted body bear little resemblance to the appearance of the young fish shown below.

Below: Coris gaimardi (juvenile)
The first colour stage of the Clown Wrasse is orange, with white markings on the body similar to, but less extensive than, those of C. formosa.

Gomphosus caeruleus

Birdmouth Wrasse

☐ **Distribution:** Indo-Pacific.

☐ **Length:** 250mm/10in (wild).

☐ **Diet and feeding:** Small animal life gathered from coral crevices.

In the aquarium, they will take brineshrimp, *Mysis* shrimp, krill and chopped fish meats, plus some green foods. Grazer.

☐ **Aquarium behaviour:** Peaceful.

☐ **Invertebrate compatibility:** Safe when young, but become destructive with age and size.

The body in adult males is blue-green; younger males, and females, are brown. The snout is elongated. A very active fish that is constantly on the move around the aquarium. This species looks and swims like a dolphin. Juveniles act as cleaners.

Below: Gomphosus caeruleus
The Birdmouth Wrasse is a very active species, always on the move around the aquarium. Generally, this species is very peaceful, and minds its own business, but its constant movement may annoy more leisurely or smaller species and specimens often become more destructive with age and size.

Halichoeres chrysus

Banana Wrasse; Golden Rainbowfish.

☐ **Distribution:** Western Pacific.

☐ **Length:** 100mm/4in (wild).

☐ **Diet and feeding:** Easily fed with most marine frozen, live and flake foods.

☐ **Aquarium behaviour:** Peaceful. A good community fish.

☐ **Invertebrate compatibility:** Very good.

Like most wrasses, *H. chrysus* needs a substrate of soft coral sand under which to retreat during the hours of darkness and when frightened. This very attractive species has a rich egg-yellow body and a clear caudal fin. In adulthood, the facial area develops green markings, making this an even more desirable fish.

Halichoeres trispilus

Four-spot Wrasse; Banana Wrasse

☐ **Distribution:** Indian Ocean.

☐ **Length:** 100mm/4in (wild).

☐ **Diet and feeding:** Accepts most marine frozen and live foods.

☐ **Aquarium behaviour:** A peaceful community fish.

☐ **Invertebrate compatibility:** Very good.

At first glance, *H. trispilus* and *H. chrysus* would appear to be one and the same fish. However, they are found in separate oceans and *H. trispilus* is white in the lower half of the body. Its common name of Four-Spot Wrasse derives from the small black spots, three of which are found on the dorsal fin and one on the caudal peduncle. This is an ideal fish for the beginner.

Labroides dimidiatus

Cleaner Wrasse

☐ **Distribution:** Indo-Pacific.

☐ **Length:** 100mm/4in (wild).

☐ **Diet and feeding:** Skin parasites of other fishes in the wild; in captivity, finely chopped meat foods make an excellent substitute. Bold.

☐ **Aquarium behaviour:** Peaceful.

☐ **Invertebrate compatibility:** Safe.

This is the most familiar of the wrasses because of its cleaning activities. This cleaning process, also practised by some gobies and Cleaner Shrimps, is almost ritualistic. When approached by a Cleaner Wrasse, the subject fish – or host – often remains stationary with fins spread, in a head-up or head-

Above left: Halichoeres chrysus
Many species possess the common name Banana Wrasse; perhaps this completely yellow fish deserves it more than most.

Above: Halichoeres trispilus
An ideal fish for beginners, the Four-spot Wrasse is colourful, readily available and disease resistant.

Right: Labroides dimidiatus
A true asset to the aquarium, the Cleaner Wrasse provides a service much appreciated by the other tank inmates.

down attitude. Sometimes the colours of the host fish fade, maybe so that the Cleaner Wrasse can see any parasites more clearly.

The elongate blue body of the Cleaner Wrasse has a horizontal dark stripe from snout to caudal fin. The mouth is terminal, and it is this feature that distinguishes *Labroides dimidiatus* from the predatory lookalike *Aspidontus taeniatus*, the so-called False Cleanerfish.

Lienardella fasciata
Harlequin Tuskfish

☐ **Distribution:** Western Pacific.

☐ **Length:** 600mm/24in (wild), 350mm/14in (aquarium).

☐ **Diet and feeding:** Generally quite easily fed on meaty marine foods, including shrimps, mussels and squid.

☐ **Aquarium behaviour:** A peaceful community subject if kept with fish of the same size or larger.

☐ **Invertebrate compatibility:** Definitely not.

The Harlequin Tuskfish is an extremely attractive species with a set of menacing teeth that belie its peaceful nature – at least with fish it is incapable of swallowing! Although small specimens are available, it should be noted that this fish, when fed correctly, is capable of reaching a fairly large size in the aquarium and adequate room will be required.

Left: Lienardella fasciata
Despite its large size, the Harlequin Tuskfish is very peaceful.

Below: Novaclichthys taeniourus
Keep this Wrasse in a species tank or with equal-sized tankmates.

Novaculichthys taeniorus
Dragon Wrasse

☐ **Distribution:** Indo-Pacific.

☐ **Length:** 200mm/8in (wild); 60mm/2.5in (aquarium).

☐ **Diet and feeding:** Crustaceans, meaty foods. Bottom feeder.

☐ **Aquarium behaviour:** Peaceful when young.

☐ **Invertebrate compatibility:** Safe.

The blotchy green coloration and elongated first rays of the dorsal fin are features of the juvenile; adult fishes are brown with marks radiating from the eye; these fade as the fish grows older. Keep it with similarly sized tankmates as this species is intimidated by larger, more aggressive, fish.

Left: Pseudocheilinus hexataenia
The Pyjama Wrasse is a constantly busy fish, always on the look out for small pieces of food missed by its tankmates. Once settled, it shows little regard for other fish, as long as they are not of the same species or with similar markings, otherwise fighting will occur.

Right: Thalassoma bifasciatum
Adult, fully coloured male Bluehead Wrasse make a colourful and peaceful addition to a suitable fish community aquarium. The juveniles, in common with several other species, are called Banana Wrasse but tend to be more sensitive than the adults and require water of the highest quality to do well.

Below right: Thalassoma lunare
A distinguishing feature of the adult Moon Wrasse is the bright yellow central section to the caudal fin and its green/ blue edging at the top and bottom. Note the radiating facial pattern around the eye; many species share this striking characteristic.

Pseudocheilinus hexataenia

Pyjama Wrasse; Six-line Wrasse

☐ **Distribution:** Indo-Pacific.

☐ **Length:** 50mm/2in (wild), 75mm/3in (aquarium).

☐ **Diet and feeding:** Will readily accept most marine frozen, live and flake foods.

☐ **Aquarium behaviour:** Peaceful, except with the same, or similar, species.

☐ **Invertebrate compatibility:** Ideal.

P. hexataenia has many of the attributes of an ideal aquarium fish: it rarely bothers invertebrates or other fish (as long as they are not of its own kind, or similar), it is colourful, easily fed, interesting in its activities and generally very inexpensive. This disease-resistant species can be heartily recommended to any newcomer to the hobby.

Thalassoma bifasciatum

Bluehead Wrasse

☐ **Distribution:** Caribbean.

☐ **Length:** 140mm/5.5in (wild).

☐ **Diet and feeding:** Crustaceans, meaty foods. Bottom feeder. Most specimens have a very healthy appetite but may need weaning off live brineshrimp on to other, more convenient, meaty foods.

☐ **Aquarium behaviour:** Peaceful.

☐ **Invertebrate compatibility:** Become destructive with age and size.

This fish undergoes remarkable colour changes: juveniles are yellow (the shallow water types are white) with a dark spot on the front of the dorsal fin and/or a dark horizontal stripe along the body. Dominant males develop the characteristic blue head and green body separated by contrasting black and white bands. This colour pattern acts as the focus for their harem formation.

Thalassoma lunare

Moon Wrasse; Lyretail Wrasse; Green Parrot Wrasse

☐ **Distribution:** Indo-Pacific, Red Sea.

☐ **Length:** 330mm/13in (wild).

☐ **Diet and feeding:** All meaty foods. Greedy bottom feeder.

☐ **Aquarium behaviour:** Active all day, then sleeps deeply at night. Its constant daytime movement may disturb smaller fishes and it may attack new additions to the tank, regardless of their size. Needs plenty of room.

☐ **Invertebrate compatibility:** Become destructive with age and size.

Adult specimens lose the dark blotches of the juvenile and are bright green with red and blue patterns on the head. The centre of the caudal fin is bright yellow, while the 'lyretail' effect is given by the green/blue edging.

Family: LUTJANIDAE

Snappers

Family characteristics
The snappers are a large and varied group of fishes, many of which are caught commercially for food purposes. Of those species that may be kept in the aquarium, most are only suitable as juveniles, as growth is quick and ultimate sizes can be quite unmanageable, even for the most enthusiastic aquarist. In many cases, the attractive coloration of the juveniles fades quite badly with age. Spawning is virtually unknown in captivity.

Diet and feeding
In the wild, these fishes feed on small fish and invertebrates. In the aquarium, a good, varied diet of meaty foods should be provided. This should include live river shrimp, frozen prawns, mussels, squid and lancefish.

Aquarium behaviour
Snappers are predatory fishes and should not be trusted with smaller species. They make fine specimen fish when young and can become very tame, although most will outgrow the average hobbyist's tank quite quickly. Snappers are best kept singly but are usually peaceful with other fish of the same, or larger, size. Plenty of room is needed if they are to achieve their full potential.

Lutjanus sebae
Emperor Snapper

☐ **Distribution:** Indo-Pacific.

☐ **Length:** 900mm/36in (wild).

☐ **Diet and feeding:** Animal and meaty foods. Bold.

☐ **Aquarium behaviour:** Although peaceful, do not keep this species with smaller fishes. Despite its attractive coloration, it will soon outgrow the tank, and is therefore not really suitable for anything but the largest public aquarium.

☐ **Invertebrate compatibility:** Unsuitable.

The white body has three red-brown transverse bands: the first runs from the snout up the forehead and the second is 'L-shaped' running vertically down from the dorsal fin to the pelvic fins and along the ventral surface into the front half of the anal fin. The third band is crescent shaped, beginning in the rear of the dorsal fin and crossing the caudal peduncle into the lower half of the caudal fin, which has a similarly coloured brown bar on the top edge.

Below: Lutjanus sebae
The Emperor Snapper is popular not only with marine aquarists – it also makes good eating! Sadly, the striking coloration fades with age.

Symphorichthys spilurus
Majestic Snapper

☐ **Distribution:** Pacific.

☐ **Length:** 320mm/12.6in (wild).

☐ **Diet and feeding:** Meaty foods. Bold feeder.

☐ **Aquarium behaviour:** Do not keep with smaller fishes.

☐ **Invertebrate compatibility:** Unsuitable.

The yellow body has horizontal blue lines and the fins are yellow. Two vertical black bars cross the head and there is a distinguishing white-ringed black blotch on the caudal peduncle. The dorsal fin develops extremely long filamentous extensions. The anal fin also has long extensions, which virtually mirror those of the dorsal.

Above: Symphorichthys spilurus
Being of a peaceful temperament, the Majestic Snapper makes a good community fish with other species that are as large as, or larger than, itself. Tankmates should, in any event, not be inclined to nip fins!

Family: MICRODESMIDAE

Wormfishes

Family characteristics
Firefishes were originally included in the family Blenniidae (blennies), subsequently placed in with the family Gobiidae (gobies) and have now found a home with the Microdesmids (Hoese, 1986, and Birdsong, 1988). This family consists of approximately 36 species of eel-like fishes, hence the common name of wormfishes (a not very flattering but, nonetheless, very apt description).

In the wild, firefishes may be seen hovering in groups close to the reef, head into the current, feeding on small planktonic animals that drift their way. All possess a favourite 'bolthole' in the reef into which they rapidly retreat at the first sign of danger.

Three species are represented in the genus: *Nemateleotris magnifica* (Firefish), *N. decora* (Purple Firefish) and the rarely seen, but superbly coloured, *N. helfrichi.* The first dorsal ray is greatly extended in all three species, particularly so in *N. magnifica.* The function of this ray is to act as a signalling device to other firefish and, additionally, to provide a 'locking' mechanism when the fish is positioned in its rocky retreat.

Aquarium spawnings are extremely rare and, to date, no larvae have been raised.

Diet and feeding
Small planktonic animals are taken in the wild. In the aquarium, firefishes will accept nearly all live, frozen and flake foods of a suitable size.

Aquarium behaviour
These are fairly nervous fishes, requiring plenty of rockwork crevices into which to retreat when disturbed and as a night-time shelter. In the absence of suitable rockwork; or in the company of boisterous companions, firefishes have a tendency to jump out of the water; therefore a tight-fitting cover glass is recommended.

Firefishes may be kept in small groups, but each fish will need a small territory of 10-20 square centimetres (1½-3 sq in) vertically. A hierarchy is usually established, the most dominant fish taking the most desirable position.

Nemateleotris decora
Purple Firefish

☐ **Distribution:** Indo-Pacific.

☐ **Length:** 75mm/3in (wild).

☐ **Diet and feeding:** Most marine frozen, live and flake foods.

☐ **Aquarium behaviour:** Peaceful.

☐ **Invertebrate compatibility:** Ideal.

This species is closely related to *N. magnifica,* but has a splendid purple coloration and a shorter first dorsal ray. Like its cousin, it is generally very peaceful, but squabbles may occur if the fish are kept in cramped conditions where required territory is at a premium. Provide plenty of rockwork so that this Firefish has somewhere to hide. Under active lighting the purple/ blue colour at the margins of the fins is shown to its best effect.

Left: Nemateleotris decora
The Purple Firefish is far less common than N. magnifica *and consequently commands a higher price. Many aquarists do not see this as a deterrent, however, as this colourful fish makes a very desirable addition to the mixed aquarium.*

Above: Nemateleotris magnifica
The beautifully coloured Firefish never ventures too far from its bolthole. If kept in a sufficiently large aquarium, several will live quite happily together.

Nemateleotris magnifica
Firefish

☐ **Distribution:** Indo-Pacific.

☐ **Length:** 60mm/2.4in (wild).

☐ **Diet and feeding:** Small crustaceans, plankton and other small live foods. Bottom feeder.

☐ **Aquarium behaviour:** Peaceful once established.

☐ **Invertebrate compatibility:** Yes, ideal.

This beautifully coloured fish settles into aquarium life much more successfully if plenty of boltholes in the rockwork are available to it. The blue, green and yellow on the body gradually give way to a magnificent fiery red on the rear of the body and on the dorsal, anal and caudal fins. The elongated first dorsal fin is used to signal to other firefish, as well as providing a 'locking' device.

Family: MONOCANTHIDAE

Filefishes

Family characteristics
Filefishes, like the triggerfishes (family Balistidae, see pages 174-179) to whom they are related (and with whom they are classified by some authorites), have two dorsal fins, the first being a rudimentary spine which can be locked into position. The ventral fins are reduced to a single spine. The skin is rough in texture, which has given rise to the fishes' alternative common name of Leatherjackets. The teeth are developed for nibbling. Most species occur around Australia.

Diet and feeding
In the wild, these fishes use their tiny mouths to feed mainly on polyps and algae. This may cause initial problems in the aquarium until they can be persuaded to accept alternative foods.

Aquarium behaviour
Despite their similarity to triggerfishes, filefishes are generally smaller, less active and – once acclimatized and feeding well – make good additions to a community tank.

Chaetodermis pencilligerus
Tassel Filefish

☐ **Distribution:** Indo-Pacific.

☐ **Length:** 180mm/7in (wild).

☐ **Diet and feeding:** May have to be tempted with live foods initially, but thereafter should accept most marine fare.

☐ **Aquarium behaviour:** Peaceful.

☐ **Invertebrate compatibility:** No.

The Tassel Filefish is quickly becoming a firm favourite with many marine aquarists owing to its interesting, not to say unusual, shape and its obliging nature. Once settled in the aquarium, rate of growth is rapid (the length given above does not take into account the odd specimen that has been documented at 250mm/10in), and a large aquarium will quickly become necessary.

Below: Chaetodermis pencilligerus
If you are looking for something a little different, the Tassel Filefish could well be the answer. Its unusual appearance provides camouflage in its natural habitat among floating seaweeds.

Family: MONOCENTRIDIDAE

Pine-cone Fishes

Family characteristics
This small family contains some interesting fishes known to have existed millions of years ago. Their bodies are enclosed in the rigid covering of a few large scales fused together. They are deepwater fishes and it is thought that they use their light-generating organs to attract prey and for recognition purposes. These fishes are only occasionally available through dealers and therefore command a high price. The dorsal fin spines alternate to right and left rather than in the normal straight row.

Diet and feeding
Because of their deepwater origins, little is known of their natural diet. It probably consists mainly of small marine animals attracted to them by their light-generating organs. In the aquarium, offer live foods and then try to wean them on to other suitable foods.

Aquarium behaviour
You may find it advisable to keep these fishes in a species tank so that you can study them more closely.

Monocentrus japonicus
Pine-cone Fish

☐ **Distribution:** Indo-Pacific.

☐ **Length:** 160mm/6.3in (wild), 100-150mm/4-6in (aquarium).

☐ **Diet and feeding:** Provide chopped white fish meat or shellfish meat, such as mussel. Also supply frozen meaty foods.

☐ **Aquarium behaviour:** Keep in a dimly lit species aquarium.

☐ **Invertebrate compatibility:** Not recommended.

The head forms about one third of the body size. The large brass-coloured scales have dark edges and spiny centres. Spiny dorsal rays alternate from left to right. The pelvic fins are restricted to strong spines. May not thrive if kept at temperatures above 23°C(74°F) for long periods.

Below: Monocentrus japonicus
The Pine-cone Fish, one of the more unusual fishes for the aquarium, can boast an ancestry going back some millions of years. Although not commonly encountered in retail outlets, it is worth considering if you are looking for something different.

Family: MONODACTYLIDAE

Fingerfishes

Family characteristics
These silver rhomboidal fishes are reminiscent of the freshwater angelfishes. They are found in coastal waters, particularly estuaries, often entering brackish or even fresh water. Although young specimens will thrive in slightly brackish water, they do even better in full strength salt water. Along with *Scatophagus* spp, they are scavengers, frequently found in dirty waters, where they appear to thrive in the conditions! Their scientific name '*Monodactylus*' means 'one finger' and refers to the shape and colour of the dorsal fin.

Diet and feeding
These fishes will eat any foods, including *Tubifex* worms.

Aquarium behaviour
Fast-moving shoaling fishes that may reach up to 150mm(6in) long in captivity.

Monodactylus argenteus

Fingerfish; Malayan Angel; Silver Batfish

☐ **Distribution:** Indo-Pacific.

☐ **Length:** 230mm/9in (wild).

☐ **Diet and feeding:** Will eat anything. Bold scavenger.

☐ **Aquarium behaviour:** Peaceful but constantly active. shoaling fishes.

☐ **Invertebrate compatibility:** Not recommended.

One or two black bars cross the front part of the silver body and the fins are yellow. The pelvic fins are rudimentary. These fishes are very fast swimmers when disturbed, and can be difficult to catch in the aquarium. They appear to thrive better when kept in shoals.

Above: Monodactylus argenteus
Although young specimens may be kept successfully in freshwater or brackish water tanks, adults really thrive in full-strength sea water. These active fishes need plenty of swimming space.

Monodactylus sebae
Striped Fingerfish

☐ **Distribution:** Eastern Atlantic, West African coast.

☐ **Length:** 200mm/8in (wild).

☐ **Diet and feeding:** Will eat anything. Bold scavenger.

☐ **Aquarium behaviour:** Peaceful, but restless.

☐ **Invertebrate compatibility:** Not recommended.

Monodactylus sebae is slightly darker than the previous species and the body is much taller. Two additional dark vertical stripes cross the body, one connecting the tips of the dorsal and anal fins, the other crossing the extreme end of the caudal peduncle. The pelvic fins are rudimentary. They appear to be less hardy than *M. argenteus*.

Below: Monodactylus sebae
The less common relative of M. argenteus *is also an active shoaling fish.*

Family: MURAENIDAE

Moray Eels

The tropical eels are often splendidly marked and all grow very long. Many are nocturnal and are hardly seen during the day, since they hide among caves and crevices. They detect their food by smell and are usually quite undemanding in captivity, providing that they have sufficient room, refuges and food. Keeping them in the company of small 'bite-sized' fishes is tempting providence a little too much. Needless to say, the aquarium should be tightly covered – and beware your fingers when feeding!

Breeding moray eels in captivity is unlikely because sexual maturity is reached only when the eels attain a large size. This stage is not normally reached in the confines of a domestic aquarium, and so successful breeding is doubtful even if a sufficient number of specimens are kept together to allow natural pairings to take place.

The Romans valued moray eels very highly; they were kept in captivity and favourite fish were bedecked with jewels! Wealthier Romans fed spare slaves to their morays!

Echnida nebulosa
Snowflake Moray

☐ **Distribution:** Indo-Pacific.

☐ **Length:** 1000mm/39in (wild), 600m/24in (aquarium).

☐ **Diet and feeding:** Requires meaty marine foods and relishes live river shrimp.

☐ **Aquarium behaviour:** Generally peaceful if kept with other fishes too large to swallow.

☐ **Invertebrate compatibility:** Possible, but not with crustaceans.

The Snowflake Moray is usually seen on sale as relatively small, juvenile specimens, but given the correct diet and aquarium conditions, it can grow very quickly. However, unlike many other moray species, it is unlikely to reach an unmanageable size in the aquarium. Although this species can become hand-tame, it is still capable of giving a nasty bite and should be treated with respect.

Above right: Echnida nebulosa
Although the Snowflake Moray is usually bought as a small specimen, it is fast growing and requires spacious quarters.

Right: Gymnothorax tesselatus
Concentrating on the 'business end' of this species is very wise. The bite can be painful, even leading to infection – and that's only for humans.

Gymnothorax tesselatus
Reticulated Moray; Leopard Moray

☐ **Distribution:** Indo-Pacific.

☐ **Length:** 1500mm/60in (wild).

☐ **Diet and feeding:** Will eat anything it can swallow. Predatory ambushers.

☐ **Aquarium behaviour:** Do not keep with anything small.

☐ **Invertebrate compatibility:** Not safe with crustaceans.

This species can inflict a very painful bite, even leading to infection (and that's only for humans); just imagine encountering this predator if you were a fish! Only for the 'big tank' hobbyist or public aquariums.

The dark body is covered with a reticulated pattern of pale markings, producing an effect very similar to that of a giraffe's markings. The nostrils are tubular.

Family: OPISTOGNATHIDAE

Jawfishes

Family characteristics
Behind the large mouth and eyes of these fish is a tapering cylindrical body. The main appeal of jawfishes is their habit of constructing tunnels or burrows in the substrate into which they retreat when threatened. At night they use a small pebble or shell to cover the entrance.

While the commonly kept Yellow-headed Jawfish (*Opistognathus aurifrons*) shows no sexual dimorphism, males of other less familiar species, such as the Atlantic Yellow Jawfish (*O. gilberti*) and the Pacific Blue-Spotted Jawfish do undergo colour changes at breeding times. Perhaps the best guide to distinguishing the sexes is the fact that males take on the oral incubation of the eggs.

Diet and feeding
Hovering close to their burrowed tunnels, Jawfishes wait for their prey of crustaceans, small fishes and plankton. Some species are not so adventurous, preferring to remain in their holes waiting for small live foods to pass by.

Aquarium behaviour
Providing sufficient 'accommodation' is available, a number of these fishes can be kept together. They are easily frightened, retreating into their holes like lightning. These tolerant fishes bother nobody, but may be harassed by other cave-dwelling species. Jawfishes are excellent jumpers, so ensure that the tank has a closely fitting cover.

Opistognathus aurifrons
Yellow-headed Jawfish

☐ **Distribution:** Western Atlantic.

☐ **Length:** 125mm/5in (wild).

☐ **Diet and feeding:** Finely chopped shellfish meat. Makes rapid lunges from a vertical hovering position near its burrow to grab any passing food.

☐ **Aquarium behaviour:** Peaceful and rarely disturbed by other fishes.

☐ **Invertebrate compatibility:** Yes, ideal.

The delicately coloured yellow head is normally all you see of this fish, but the rest of the body is an equally beautiful pale blue. The eyes are large. It needs a reasonably soft substrate in which to excavate a burrow, entering the hole tail first at any sign of trouble. Like other jawfishes, it is a good jumper.

Right: Opistognathus aurifrons
On the rare occasions when it is seen outside its hiding place, the Yellow-headed Jawfish reveals that its slim body has the most delicate coloration. How the fish manages to retreat into its bolthole tail-first at such speed almost defies belief.

Family: OSTRACIIDAE

Boxfishes and Trunkfishes

Family characteristics
These fishes have a rigid body made up of bony plates covered with a sensitive skin that may be damaged by cleanerfishes. The only flexible part is the caudal peduncle, where the most obvious growth occurs rearwards. The pelvic fins are missing, although bony stumps may appear at the corners of the body box in some species. They are slow moving – some have been designated 'hovercraft fishes' by imaginative authors – and they do indeed have a similar form of locomotion, making rapid movements of the dorsal, anal and pectoral fins to good effect. When buying these fishes, avoid any with concave looking sides, as these never recover from this probable semi-starved state. Regular feeding is strongly urged.

Most are poisonous, releasing a poison into the water when threatened. In the confines of the aquarium, or in the transportation container, this often proves fatal both to the Boxfish and to other fishes. Some authorities advocate introducing these fish into the aquarium in advance of other fishes to reduce the chances of fatal consequences should the boxfishes become frightened.

Diet and feeding
These fishes will try anything, but appear to particularly relish live foods.

Aquarium behaviour
Some reports suggest that these fish resent the attentions of Cleaner Gobies or any other inquisitive fishes perhaps attracted by their slow swimming action.

Lactoria cornuta
Cowfish

☐ **Distribution:** Indo-Pacific.

☐ **Length:** 500mm/20in (wild); 400mm/16in (aquarium).

☐ **Diet and feeding:** Algae and crustaceans. These are shy bottom feeders.

☐ **Aquarium behaviour:** Intolerant of each other.

☐ **Invertebrate compatibility:** Generally yes, but may peck at tubeworms.

The two 'horns' on the head and two more projections at the bottom rear of the body make for easy identification. The body is brilliant yellow with bright blue spots in the centre of each segment of body 'armour plating'. Specimens in domestic aquariums do not usually reach very large sizes.

Above: Lactoria cornuta
This fish's large horny projections make the fish hard to swallow by predators, although its poisonous flesh would, in any case, inflict retribution.

Ostracion meleagris

Spotted Boxfish; Pacific Boxfish

- ☐ **Distribution:** Indo-Pacific.
- ☐ **Length:** 200mm/8in (wild).
- ☐ **Diet and feeding:** Crustaceans and greenstuff. Bottom feeder.
- ☐ **Aquarium behaviour:** Peaceful.
- ☐ **Invertebrate compatibility:** Generally yes, but may peck at tubeworms.

It now seems certain that *O. meleagris* appears in a distinct male and female form. The male is the more colourful of the species. The top of the body is black with white spots and the lower flanks are violet with yellow spots. The two sections are separated by a yellow line. The eye is yellow-gold. By contrast, the female is almost entirely black with white spots.

In a large enough tank, it is possible to keep a pair, although breeding is rarely known in captivity. This is a difficult fish that is prone to bacterial infections of the skin and eyes. Initial feeding may be a problem and usually demands all the skill of an experienced hobbyist. Excellent water quality at all times is essential for this species.

Below: Ostracion meleagris
Although often confused with young specimens of pufferfish, especially Arothron meleagris, *boxfishes rely on poisonous secretions to ward off predators rather than inflating their bodies, as do the pufferfishes. This is a difficult species to keep.*

Ostracion tuberculatum
Blue-spotted Boxfish

☐ **Distribution:** Indo-Pacific.

☐ **Length:** 450mm/18in (wild).

☐ **Diet and feeding:** Crustaceans and greenstuff. Bottom feeder.

☐ **Aquarium behaviour:** Peaceful; best left undisturbed.

☐ **Invertebrate compatibility:** Generally yes, but may peck at tubeworms.

The almost cube-shaped body of juveniles is light cream or yellow with dark blue spots; it is easy to imagine that they are animated dice, slowly swimming around looking for food. Adult fishes develop a more elongate body and the colour changes to a yellowy green, while the armoured plates on the body become more clearly defined. The fins are tinted yellow.

Above: Ostracion tuberculatum
This species really lives up to its popular name, especially when viewed from the angle captured here. A side view would reveal yellow fins, a pointed snout and longish caudal peduncle.

Tetrosomus gibbosus
Hovercraft Boxfish

☐ **Distribution:** Indo-Pacific.

☐ **Length:** 400mm/16in (wild), 100mm/4in (aquarium).

☐ **Diet and feeding:** Can be tempted to eat most marine frozen, live and flake foods of a suitable size.

☐ **Aquarium behaviour:** Peaceful, except with its own, or similar, species.

☐ **Invertebrate compatibility:** No, except when very small.

T. gibbosus is usually seen on sale as a juvenile specimen some 25mm/1in in length and will rarely exceed 100mm/4in in the aquarium. Its curious swimming habit – it appears to hover in mid-air – has given rise to its common name of Hovercraft Boxfish. It should be kept with other non-boisterous fish, as it is a prime target for fin-nipping species.

Below: Tetrosomus gibbosus
If you are looking for something different – say a fish that doesn't look look a fish, doesn't swim like a fish, but is full of charm – the Hovercraft Boxfish would make an excellent choice!

Family: PLATACIDAE

Batfishes

Family characteristics
The oval-bodied, high-finned Batfish is unmistakable. It is found in coastal and brackish waters and in mangrove swamps. It often lies on its side 'playing dead', floating like a leaf to avoid capture or detection. It now appears fairly certain that there are four species of batfish; *Platax orbicularis, P. pinnatus*, the rarer *P. tiera* (Longfinned Batfish) and *P. batavianus* (Marbled Batfish). The latter two are rarely available to the hobbyist. Adult fishes are less colourful than juveniles. Some leading authorities clarify batfishes as belonging to the subfamily Platacinae of the family Ephippididae (the spadefishes).

Diet and feeding
These fishes may be difficult to accustom to the usual commercial marine foods and patience will be needed, especially with *P. pinnatus*. Try to purchase juvenile specimens that are already feeding.

Aquarium behaviour
The Batfish usually adapts to captivity well, not quarrelling with similarly sized tankmates. It does need a spacious tank, however, as it grows very quickly. The shape of the body dictates the need for a very deep tank to enable the fish to develop proportionately.

Platax orbicularis

Batfish; Orbiculate Batfish; Round Batfish

☐ **Distribution:** Indo-Pacific.

☐ **Length:** 500mm/20in (wild), 380mm/15in (aquarium).

☐ **Diet and feeding:** Will eat anything. Scavenger.

☐ **Aquarium behaviour:** Peaceful, but grows fast. Keep away from boisterous fin-nipping species.

☐ **Invertebrate compatibility:** Usually well behaved.

The body is round, with large rounded fins. There are one or two dark stripes on the head and front part of the body, but these fade with age. Young specimens have more elongated fins and also more red coloration.

Right: Platax orbicularis
This is a young specimen, showing the typical dark red-brown stripes; adults are less colourful. Allow a generous depth of water and plenty of swimming space for these tall-finned fishes.

Platax pinnatus
Red-faced Batfish

☐ **Distribution:** Indo-Pacific.

☐ **Length:** 500mm/20in (wild), 450mm/18in (aquarium).

☐ **Diet and feeding:** Can be difficult to start feeding. Live brine shrimp should be offered regularly.

☐ **Aquarium behaviour:** Peaceful, but grows fast. Keep away from boisterous fin-nipping species.

☐ **Invertebrate compatibility:** Usually well behaved.

This is a difficult fish to keep, demanding plenty of room and excellent water conditions. Do not choose this species unless you are prepared to invest the time and patience needed. Only juveniles from a reliable source (the best possible handling) will do well in the aquarium. This is definitely not a fish for the beginner. The body shape is much shorter and higher than in *P. orbicularis* and the fins are very elongate. The colour is much darker, with a red outline to the body and fins. It is a pity that it should lose such magnificent colours and gracefulness with advancing age.

Below: Platax pinnatus
The red edges of the fins outline this splendid fish to perfection.

Family: PLECTORHYNCHIDAE

Sweetlips

Family characteristics
Fishes in this family are often classified in the Haemulidae, alternatively known as the Pomadasydae. They resemble grunts or snappers, but differ from them in dentition details. The coloration of juveniles and adults differs quite dramatically. The sweetlips are confined to the Indo-Pacific Ocean areas.

Diet and feeding
Crustaceans, live animal and meaty foods. Shy slow eaters.

Aquarium behaviour
Juveniles are excellent subjects for a large quiet tank. They are gentle and independent natured and will usually totally ignore the other fish in their aquarium.

Plectorhynchus albovittatus

Yellow Sweetlips; Yellow-lined Sweetlips

☐ **Distribution:** Indo-Pacific, Red Sea.

☐ **Length:** 200mm/8in (wild).

☐ **Diet and feeding:** Crustaceans, animal and meaty foods. Bottom feeder.

☐ **Aquarium behaviour:** Hardy, but keep with non-boisterous fishes.

☐ **Invertebrate compatibility:** Yes, when small. Progressively more destructive with age.

In juveniles the body is yellow, with two white-bordered dark bands running the length of the body. The lower band is level with the terminal mouth and centre line of the fish. The patterning of the body extends into the rear of the yellow dorsal fin and into the caudal fin. Adult fishes lose this interesting coloration and become brown.

Below: Plectorhynchus albovittatus
Young fish, such as this, look very appealing, but they lose these colours with age; adults are brown. Juvenile Yellow Sweetlips are peaceful and make ideal subjects for a large, quiet aquarium.

Plectorhynchus chaetodonoides

Harlequin Sweetlips; Clown Sweetlips; Polka-dot Grunt

☐ **Distribution:** Pacific.

☐ **Length:** 450mm/18in (wild).

☐ **Diet and feeding:** Crustaceans, animal and meaty foods. (Small live or frozen shrimps will often get them feeding in the aquarium.) Bottom feeder.

☐ **Aquarium behaviour:** Shy; keep with non-boisterous fishes.

☐ **Invertebrate compatibility:** Yes, when small. Progressively more destructive with age.

Juveniles have a dark brown body covered with well-defined white blotches and this pattern is repeated on the fins. Adult fishes are a drab

brown with dark dots. Feeding requires special attention; be sure to offer only small portions.

Below and right: Plectorhynchus chaetodonoides
There is a striking difference between young and adult Harlequin Sweetlips.

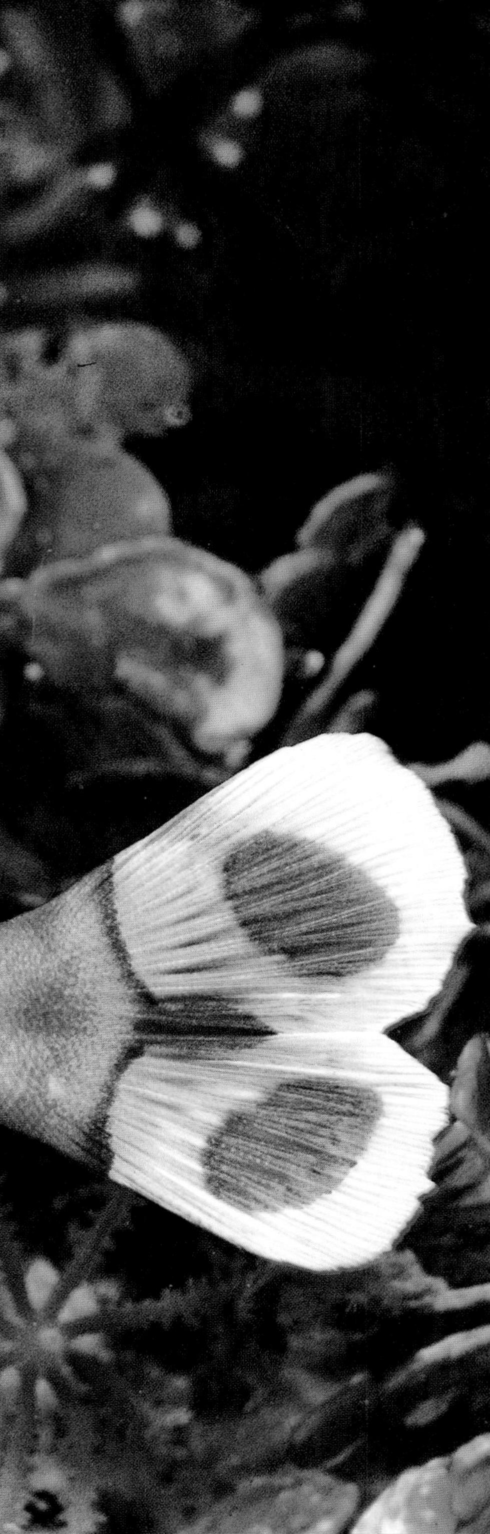

Plectorhynchus orientalis
Oriental Sweetlips

☐ **Distribution:** Indo-Pacific.

☐ **Length:** 400mm/16in (wild).

☐ **Diet and feeding:** Crustaceans, animal and meaty foods. Bottom feeder.

☐ **Aquarium behaviour:** Shy; keep with non-boisterous fishes.

☐ **Invertebrate compatibility:** Yes, when small. Progressively more destructive with age.

Juvenile fishes have large cream-yellow patches on a dark background. Adults may sometimes be confused with young *P. albovittatus*, although there are more stripes on *P. orientalis* and the coloration is not quite so yellow. In the aquarium, this species rarely exceeds 300mm (12in) in length.

Below: Pletorhynchus orientalis
Members of the sweetlips group are surprisingly shy; another even more unexpected feature is their habit of taking small morsels of food. This specimen is a juvenile; adults have stripes and are similar in coloration to the juvenile Yellow Sweetlips.

Family: PLOTOSIDAE

Catfishes

Family characteristics
Two features make it easy to identify the marine catfishes: the second dorsal and anal fins merge with the caudal fin, and there are barbels around the mouth. The spines preceding the dorsal and pectoral fins are venomous.

These fishes are very gregarious when young – species grouping together in a tight ball for safety – but this habit is lost (along with any colour pattern) when adult. In the wild, adult fishes may enter river systems. Aquarium spawnings have been reported, but so far the fry have not been reared successfully.

Diet and feeding
Chopped shellfish meats form an ideal food for these fishes in the aquarium.

Aquarium behaviour
Only juvenile specimens are suitable for the aquarium, as the adult fishes not only outgrow their juvenile coloration but also can become dangerous to inexperienced handlers. If a fairly large number are kept together in the aquarium, it is possible to witness the collective defence behaviour – 'balling' – as when threatened in the wild.

Plotosus lineatus

Saltwater Catfish

☐ **Distribution:** Indo-Pacific.

☐ **Length:** 300mm/12in (wild).

☐ **Diet and feeding:** Chopped shellfish meats. Bottom feeder.

☐ **Aquarium behaviour:** Peaceful. Prefers to be in a small shoal.

☐ **Invertebrate compatibility:** Yes.

Two parallel white lines run along the length of the dark body. The second dorsal and anal fins are very long-based and merge with the caudal fin. In the wild, young specimens shoal together, forming a tight, ball-like clump when threatened. In the aquarium, they are best kept in small shoals, since solitary specimens seem to pine away. The spines are venomous, so handle these fishes with care. (For action if stung, see page 287 – introduction to *Scorpaenidae*.)

This species presumably spawns in the same way as the freshwater Plotosid *Tandanus*, which constructs a nest of debris, sand or gravel. The male (usually identified simply because it does not lay the eggs) is said to guard the eggs after spawning has taken place.

Below: Plotosus lineatus
The habit of these smartly striped young specimens congregating together suggests that the catfish may be a good community subject. However, this fast-growing species soon loses its stripes and its sociable nature as it matures.

Poeciliidae

Black Mollies

☐ **Distribution:** 'Man-made' tank hybrids.

☐ **Length:** Male: 70mm/2.8in; female: 95mm/3.7in.

☐ **Diet and feeding:** Bold feeder. Appreciates most live foods, including *Daphnia* and midge larvae. Frozen foods, flake and some greenstuffs should also be fed.

☐ **Aquarium behaviour:** Peaceful.

☐ **Invertebrate compatibility:** Generally satisfactory, although some macro algae and delicate invertebrates may suffer.

Black Mollies are not normally associated with the marine aquarium; they are usually seen as freshwater community fishes. However, in the wild some species of molly live in brackish or fully marine conditions. Being hardy and nitrite tolerant, they can be used either as a non-aggressive fish to mature a new aquarium or as an unusual addition to graze on algae.

Black Mollies cannot, however, be taken straight from a freshwater environment and introduced into the marine aquarium; they must first be 'converted'. This is easily achieved by using an airline and valve to drip marine water at a rate of one drop per second into their container. As the container fills, the water should be discarded. The whole process will take 6-12 hours. (Converting back is the procedure in reverse.) Once 'converted' to a fully marine environment, it has been noted that colours intensify and general disease resistance improves. Breeding possibilities remain unaffected.

WARNING: Not all species of molly are suitable for convertion to marine conditions. Black hybrids and Hi-fins are generally fine but true species are not. If you are in any doubt, stick with the pure black hybrids.

Above: Black Mollies
Normally thought of as freshwater fish, many species of molly live in brackish or sea water in the wild. Freshwater specimens must be 'converted' to marine conditions; black hybrids, such as these, are the most suitable.

Family: POMACANTHIDAE

Angelfishes

Family characteristics

Despite the close similarities between angelfishes and butterflyfishes (see pages 186-197), the surest way of distinguishing between the two groups is to look for the spine found on a the gill cover of the former. As a general rule, angelfishes are also thicker set in the body and less ovoid in shape.

The Pomacanthids are an exceedingly attractive group of fish that vary widely in terms of size and colour. Some species may grow to exceed 600mm (24in) in the wild, whereas the dwarf species (see pages 244-249) may never grow any larger than 100mm (4in).

As juveniles, many of the larger angelfish have a different coloration pattern from the adults, and it is not always possible to identify these species with certainty; many are very similar at this stage – blue with white markings, or, sometimes, black with yellow markings. These juveniles commonly act as 'cleaner fish' to larger fish in the wild, and it is thought that the markings not only advertize this fact, but also distract the aggression that could be directed at them by older and fully coloured fish of the same species.

As with so many marine species, sexual differences are barely, if at all, distinguishable, although during the spawning season, females may be observed to be noticeably swollen with eggs. Spawning always occurs at dusk as a response to falling light levels and takes place between a single pair of fish only, although males of some species may mate with more than one female at different times. As with butterflyfishes, angelfishes ascend the water column and release eggs and sperm simultaneously. The fertilized eggs then float, hatch and develop in the planktonic layers for about one month, after which the juvenile fishes settle to the bottom. Although extremely difficult, several species of angelfishes have been spawned and reared successfully to adulthood in the aquarium.

Diet and feeding

Most angelfishes are omnivorous, feeding on a wide variety of smaller animals, algae, sponges and corals. Although members of the dwarf species (*Centropyge* sp.) rarely damage corals and sponges, the same cannot be said of large Pomacanthids and, indeed, their diet may consist entirely of sponges and corals. Adults of these species may be very reluctant to accept the normal foods available to the marine aquarist during the initial settling-in period.

Angelfishes should be offered a variety of foods, including live and frozen brineshrimp and *Mysis*, frozen squid, mussels, prawns, sponge-based foods, as well as some algae.

Aquarium behaviour

Only a few angelfishes can be recommended to the beginner, as most require some previous feeding and water management skills. Many species are particularly sensitive to deteriorating water conditions and quickly display their unhappiness by contracting various diseases, as well as losing interest in food.

The highly territorial nature of angelfishes means that mixing fish of the same, or similar, species within the confines of an average-sized aquarium is usually out of the question. Having said that, these are fish that can become very tame and accept food from the hand once their trust has been gained. The more difficult species should ideally be purchased as juveniles, as they seem to adapt much better to aquarium conditions.

Suitable rockwork should always be provided in which the fish can shelter at night and retreat into when disturbed. A comprehensive rockwork arrangement is essential for dwarf species, as this is where they spend much of their time. Make sure that larger species have plenty of swimming space in the aquarium.

Apolemichthys trimaculatus

Three-spot Angelfish; Flagfin Angelfish

☐ **Distribution:** Indo-Pacific.

☐ **Length:** 250mm/10in (wild).

☐ **Diet and feeding:** Mainly algae, but offer freeze-dried foods and greenstuff. Grazer.

Left: Apolemichthys trimaculatus
This fish's name refers to the three prominent spots on the body.

☐ **Aquarium behaviour:** Territorial, keep individual specimens only. This is not the easiest angelfish to maintain in captivity.

☐ **Invertebrate compatibility:** Yes, when small, but adults may do some damage.

The three 'spots' that give the fish its common name are around its head – one on top and one on each side of the body behind the gill covers. The lips are bright blue, and the anal fin is black with a broad white area immediately next to the body.

This species is fussy about water conditions and may also be difficult to acclimatize to aquarium life. Provide a variety of foods, particularly sponge-based.

Arusetta asfur
Purple Moon Angel

☐ **Distribution:** Indian Ocean, Persian Gulf and Red Sea.

☐ **Length:** 150mm/6in (wild).

☐ **Diet and feeding:** Meat foods and plenty of greenstuff. Grazer.

☐ **Aquarium behaviour:** Territorial, and should not be kept with the same, or similar, species.

☐ **Invertebrate compatibility:** Yes, when small. Progressively unsuitable with age and size.

This species has a yellow vertical bar across the blue body in front of the anal fin. In this respect it differs from a similar-looking species, *Pomacanthus maculosus*, whose yellow bar begins well into the anal fin. The dorsal and anal fins are elongated and the yellow colour is repeated on the caudal fin.

Arusetta asfur is regarded by some as a 'dwarf' angelfish, and this might be correct while the fish is still young, but as it grows into adulthood, the Purple Moon Angel behaves more like larger angelfish becoming progressively more destructive and quite aggressive in the mixed aquarium.

Above: Arusetta asfur
Compare the extended dorsal and anal fin outlines of this Indo-Pacific Angelfish with those of the smaller 'dwarf' species of the genus Centropyge.

Genus Centropyge
Dwarf Angelfishes

Species in the genus *Centropyge* deserve a special introduction, although we have maintained their position in the A-Z sequence of the angelfish section.

Most species are ideal aquarium fishes, principally because they are miniature versions of the larger angelfishes. Most specimens make ideal subjects for the invertebrate aquarium, being almost invariably well behaved, readily accepting aquarium conditions and eating all the usual commercial marine foods. In the wild, they are found more commonly at the base of the reef rather than among the coral polyps, although they are never far away from a safe retreat. Unlike some other angelfishes, *Centropyge* species more often than not associate in pairs, with several pairs sharing the same area. Their main diet appears to be algae, which they graze from the reef surfaces. Should treatment for White Spot, Oodinium or other protocoal diseases be required, these fishes will accept lower doses of a copper-based remedy for a longer time than normal, but may not tolerate the higher doses given to larger related species.

Centropyge acanthops
African Pygmy Angelfish; Fireball Angelfish

☐ **Distribution:** Indian Ocean, along the eastern seaboard of Africa.

☐ **Length:** 75mm/3in (wild).

☐ **Diet and feeding:** Meat foods and plenty of greenstuff. Grazer.

☐ **Aquarium behaviour:** Peaceful.

☐ **Invertebrate compatibility:** Generally well behaved in the invertebrate aquarium.

A blue fish with a yellow head and dorsal area, plus a pale yellow caudal fin. An ideal, peaceful aquarium subject. It is similar to *C. aurantonotus* (Flame-backed Angelfish) from the West Indies, which can be distinguished by its blue tail. The spine on the gill cover distinguishes this species as an angelfish, despite having a body more like a damselfish.

Below: Centropyge acanthops
Its diminutive size, attractive coloration, harmless disposition and interesting habits make the African Pygmy Angelfish an ideal choice for the mixed fish and invertebrate aquarium.

Centropyge argi

Pygmy Angelfish; Cherubfish; Purple Fireball

☐ **Distribution:** Western Atlantic.

☐ **Length:** 75mm/3in (wild).

☐ **Diet and feeding:** Meat foods and plenty of greenstuff. Grazer.

☐ **Aquarium behaviour:** Usually peaceful.

☐ **Invertebrate compatibility:** Generally well behaved in the invertebrate aquarium.

A deeper water fish, which lives around the base of the reef rather than at the top. The colour patterns around the head may vary in detail from one specimen to another and there is no difference in the juvenile colour form, as in other angelfishes. It is possible to keep compatible pairs in the aquarium, since natural territories are not particularly large.

Above: Centropyge argi
This attractive species is generally peaceful, and if two fishes appear to keep each other's company consistently, the result may be a spontaneous spawning in the aquarium.

Centropyge bicolor

Bicolor Cherub; Oriole Angel

☐ **Distribution:** Pacific.

☐ **Length:** 125mm/5in (wild).

☐ **Diet and feeding:** Meat foods and plenty of greenstuff. Grazer.

☐ **Aquarium behaviour:** Peaceful, providing plenty of hiding places are available.

☐ **Invertebrate compatibility:** Generally well behaved in the invertebrate aquarium.

The rear part of the body, from behind the head as far as the caudal fin, is bright purple-blue. The small bar across the head over the eye is the same bright shade, while the head and caudal fin are yellow. In groups, a solitary male will dominate a 'harem' of females. If the male is removed from the group or – as in nature – dies, then one of the females will change sex to replace him. This procedure occurs every time the group becomes 'male-less'. This fish is susceptible to disease. Use copper remedies with care.

Above: Centropyge bicolor
Literally, a two-colour angelfish. Juveniles are found in shallower waters than the adults. Despite its wide distrubtion in the Pacific, C. bicolor *is not found in Hawaii.*

Centropyge bispinosus
Coral Beauty

☐ **Distribution:** Indo-Pacific.

☐ **Length:** 120mm/4.7in (wild).

☐ **Diet and feeding:** Meat foods and plenty of greenstuff. Grazer.

☐ **Aquarium behaviour:** Will settle down if retreats are close at hand.

☐ **Invertebrate compatibility:** Generally well behaved in the invertebrate aquarium.

In young specimens, the head and body are outlined in deep purple; red flanks are vertically crossed by many thin purple lines. The adult fish has much larger areas of gold/ yellow on the flanks, again crossed by dark vertical stripes. The pattern is very variable, however; specimens from the Philippines, for example, have more purple and red coloration than those from Australasian waters.

Above: Centropyge bispinosus
The colour patterns of this species are very variable and depend on the native home of the individual specimen.

Centropyge eibli
Eibl's Angelfish

☐ **Distribution:** Indo-Pacific.

☐ **Length:** 150mm/6in (wild), 100mm/4in (aquarium).

☐ **Diet and feeding:** Most foods. Grazer.

☐ **Aquarium behaviour:** Peaceful.

☐ **Invertebrate compatibility:** Generally well behaved in the invertebrate aquarium.

The pale grey-gold body is crossed with gold and black lines, and some gold patterning appears in the anal fin. The rear part of the dorsal fin, the caudal peduncle and caudal fin are black, edged in pale blue. The eye is ringed with gold.

Above: Centropyge eibli
The combination of subtle colours of Eibl's Angelfish come as a pleasant surprise when compared to the more vivid – sometimes even gaudy – hues of other dwarf angelfishes.

Centropyge flavissimus

Lemonpeel Angelfish

☐ **Distribution:** Indo-Pacific.

☐ **Length:** 100mm/4in (wild).

☐ **Diet and feeding:** Predominantly greenstuff, but might be persuaded to take meaty foods. Grazer.

☐ **Aquarium behaviour:** Peaceful.

☐ **Invertebrate compatibility:** Generally well behaved in the invertebrate aquarium.

A plain yellow fish except for the blue outlines around the eye, bottom lip and gill cover edge.

Right: Centropyge flavissimus
The species may be easily distinguished from Centropyge heraldi *by the presence of blue rings around the eyes.*

Centropyge heraldi

Herald's Angelfish

☐ **Distribution:** Indo-Pacific.

☐ **Length:** 100mm/4in (wild).

☐ **Diet and feeding:** Mainly greenstuff, but also takes meaty foods. Grazer.

☐ **Aquarium behaviour:** Peaceful.

☐ **Invertebrate compatibility:** Generally well behaved in the invertebrate aquarium.

C. heraldi is also plain yellow, lacking even the blue details of *C. flavissimus*. Fijian specimens have a black edge to the dorsal fin.

Above: Centropyge heraldi
In the world of marine fishes, monocoloration is quite exceptional. This makes the totally yellow Herald's Angelfish an extremely easy fish to identify, and a popular choice.

Centropyge loriculus
Flame Angelfish

☐ **Distribution:** Pacific.

☐ **Length:** 100mm/4in (wild).

☐ **Diet and feeding:** Meat foods and plenty of greenstuff. Grazer.

☐ **Aquarium behaviour:** Peaceful.

☐ **Invertebrate compatibility:** Generally well behaved in the invertebrate aquarium.

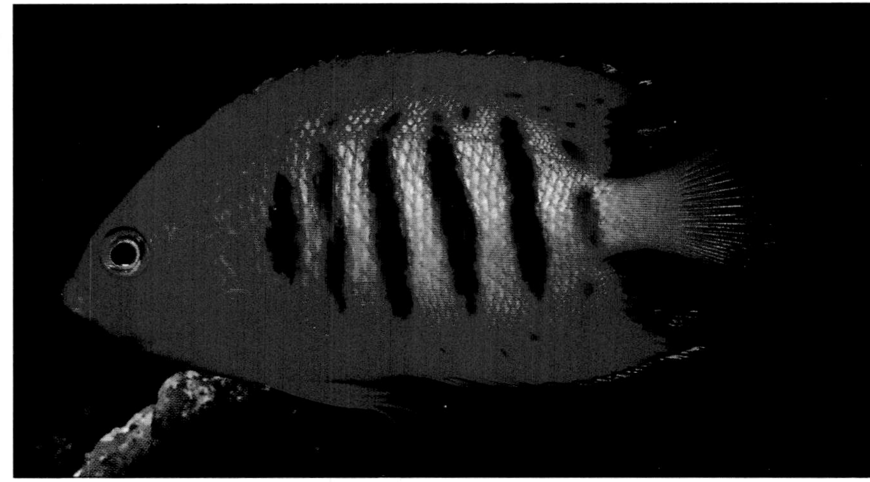

The fiery red-orange body has a central yellow area crossed by vertical dark bars. The dorsal and anal fins are similarly dark-tipped. The Flame Angelfish is not difficult to keep but does require excellent water conditions and a varied diet. Although generally expensive, this is a most rewarding fish to keep.

Above: Centropyge loriculus
The vivid coloration of this species clearly distinguishes it from any other dwarf angelfish.

Centropyge potteri
Potters Angel

☐ **Distribution:** Hawaiian Islands only.

☐ **Length:** 100mm/4in (wild).

☐ **Diet and feeding:** May initially be a difficult feeder, which should be tempted with live foods. When settled, it will usually accept the usual frozen marine food. Algae should be available to graze on as they make up an important part of this species' diet.

☐ **Aquarium behaviour:** Peaceful.

☐ **Invertebrate compatibility:** Very good.

C. potteri should not be regarded as an easy fish to keep; it demands excellent water quality and a varied diet with plenty of algae in it. However, this is a peaceful fish, which can often be kept with its own kind, much in the same way as *C. resplendens*. *C. potteri* is rather larger than most *Centropyge* species, in the middle size range between dwarf angels and the larger angels.

Above: Centropyge potteri
A peaceful, interesting species that can be kept in pairs as it is found in the wild around its native Hawaiian Islands.

Centropyge resplendens

Resplendent Angel

☐ **Distribution:** Eastern Atlantic, mainly Ascension Island and St. Helena Islands.

☐ **Length:** 40mm/1.5in (wild), 60mm/2.5in (aquarium).

☐ **Diet and feeding:** Easily fed on most marine frozen, live and vegetable flake foods. Appreciates a good growth of algae on which to browse.

☐ **Aquarium behaviour:** Peaceful.

☐ **Invertebrate compatibility:** Excellent.

The Resplendent Angel is one of the very few *Centropyge* species that not only tolerates its own species but even appreciates being kept in pairs or small groups in a larger aquarium. If maintained correctly, aquarium specimens usually attain a far larger size than those found in the wild, adapting very well to aquarium life. Altogether an excellent choice for the fish-only or living reef type tank.

Below: Centropyge resplendens
Unlike many other dwarf Angelfishes, this species can often be kept in pairs.

Centropyge vroliki

Pearl-scaled Angelfish

☐ **Distribution:** Pacific.

☐ **Length:** 120mm/4.7in (wild).

☐ **Diet and feeding:** Provide meat foods and plenty of greenstuff for this grazer.

☐ **Aquarium behaviour:** Territorial.

☐ **Invertebrate compatibility:** Ideal.

At first glance this species could be confused with *C. eibli*, but it lacks the vertical lines. The pale body is edged with dusky black dorsal, anal and caudal fins. The eye is ringed in gold, and the rear edge of the gill cover and the base of the pectoral fin are also gold.

Although widely available, this species may be less popular with fishkeepers simply because of its muted colours. It requires an elaborate rockwork structure in the aquarium to feel fully at home.

Above: Centropyge vroliki
Like its relative, C. eibli, *the Pearl-scaled Angelfish is not endowed with striking colours, but it deserves to be more popular due to an adaptable nature and ideal compatibility with all species of invertebrates. In addition, feeding usually presents no problem.*

Above: Chaetodontoplus conspicillatus
Sadly, the 'Jewel of the Angelfishes' is both rare and difficult to keep.

Right: Chaetodontoplus duboulayi
A rare, but generally peaceful, species.

Chaetodontoplus conspicillatus
Conspicuous Angelfish

- ☐ **Distribution:** Pacific.
- ☐ **Length:** 250mm/10in (wild).
- ☐ **Diet and feeding:** Crustaceans, coral polyps, algae. Grazer.
- ☐ **Aquarium behaviour:** Little is known about how well this species adapts to life in the aquarium.
- ☐ **Invertebrate compatibility:** Suitable when very young, but become destructive with age. Overall, not recommended.

The brown body is ringed by blue-edged dorsal and anal fins. The clearly defined eyes are a 'conspicuous' feature of the vivid yellow face; the mouth is a contrasting blue. Further areas of bright yellow appear at the base of the pectoral and caudal fins; the pelvic fins are blue.

This rare species – considered by many marine fishkeepers to be the 'Jewel of the Angelfishes' – is found mainly around Lord Howe Island, about 640km(400 miles) off the east coast of Australia.

Chaetodontoplus duboulayi
Scribbled Angelfish

- ☐ **Distribution:** Pacific.
- ☐ **Length:** 220mm/8.5in (wild).
- ☐ **Diet and feeding:** Crustaceans, coral polyps, algae. Grazer.
- ☐ **Aquarium behaviour:** Generally peaceful.
- ☐ **Invertebrate compatibility:** Suitable when very young, but become destructive with age.

The rear portion of the body from the gills, together with the anal and dorsal fins, is dark blue with scribbled markings. A vertical yellow bar behind the white gill cover is joined to the yellow caudal fin by a narrow yellow stripe along the top of the body. A dark bar covers the eye and the mouth is yellow. A nitrate-free, but algae-covered tank is ideal.

Chaetodontoplus septentrionalis
Blue Striped Angelfish

- **Distribution:** Western Pacific.
- **Length:** 210mm/8.25in (wild).
- **Diet and feeding:** Crustaceans, coral polyps, algae. Grazer.
- **Aquarium behaviour:** Not well documented.
- **Invertebrate compatibility:** Suitable when very young, but become destructive with age.

The brown body, dorsal and anal fins are covered with horizontal wavy blue lines. All the other fins are yellow. Juveniles are differently marked, being black with a yellow black-based caudal, and yellow margins to the dorsal and anal fins. The size at which the adult colour is assumed can be very variable.

Above: Chaetodontoplus septentrionalis
This species' brown body makes a contrasting background for the wavy blue stripes. It is rarely kept.

Below: Euxiphipops navarchus
When seen underwater, the dark blue areas, yellow saddle-back patch and yellow caudal fin help to disrupt the 'fish shape' outline of this species.

Euxiphipops navarchus
Blue-girdled Angelfish; Majestic Angelfish

- **Distribution:** Pacific.
- **Length:** 250mm/10in (wild).
- **Diet and feeding:** Meat foods and greenstuff. Grazer.
- **Aquarium behaviour:** Young specimens adapt better to aquarium life.
- **Invertebrate compatibility:** Suitable when very young, but become destructive with age. Overall, not recommended.

Blue-edged dark areas on the head and caudal peduncle of this fish are connected by a dark ventral surface. The rest of the body is rich orange flecked with fine blue iridescent spots. The plain orange anal and blue dorsal fins are both edged in pale blue, as are the dark pelvic fins. Like other large angelfishes, the juvenile form is dark blue with vertical white stripes.

Euxiphipops xanthometapon

Blue-faced Angelfish; Yellow-faced Angelfish; Blue-masked Angelfish

☐ **Distribution:** Indo-Pacific.

☐ **Length:** 380mm/15in (wild), 300mm/12in (aquarium).

☐ **Diet and feeding:** Meat foods and greenstuff. Grazer.

☐ **Aquarium behaviour:** Young specimens adapt better to aquarium life.

☐ **Invertebrate compatibility:** Suitable when very young, but become destructive with age. Overall, not recommended.

Despite the inclusion of 'xantho' (the Greek word for yellow) in the specific name, this fish is usually known as the Blue-faced Angelfish. Do not allow the attractive colouring and majestic appearance of this fish to tempt you unless you are an experienced fishkeeper; it needs special care. Juveniles are dark blue with white markings.

Below: Euxiphipops xanthometapon
This fish is difficult to keep, although juveniles are often found to be easier. Note the false eye on the dorsal fin.

Holacanthus bermudensis
Blue Angelfish

- ☐ **Distribution:** Western Atlantic.
- ☐ **Length:** 450mm/18in (wild).
- ☐ **Diet and feeding:** Meat foods and greenstuff. Grazer.
- ☐ **Aquarium behaviour:** Aggressive when young; grows large.
- ☐ **Invertebrate compatibility:** Suitable when very young, but become destructive with age. Overall, not recommended.

When adult, these fish are blue-grey in colour with yellow tips to the dorsal and anal fins. The juveniles of this striking species can be distinguished from those of the Queen Angelfish, *H. ciliaris*, by the straight blue vertical lines on their dark blue bodies. This species was formerly known as *H. Isabelita*.

Above: Holacanthus bermudensis
The beautiful blue body hues of this spectacular angelfish appear to change under varied lighting conditions.

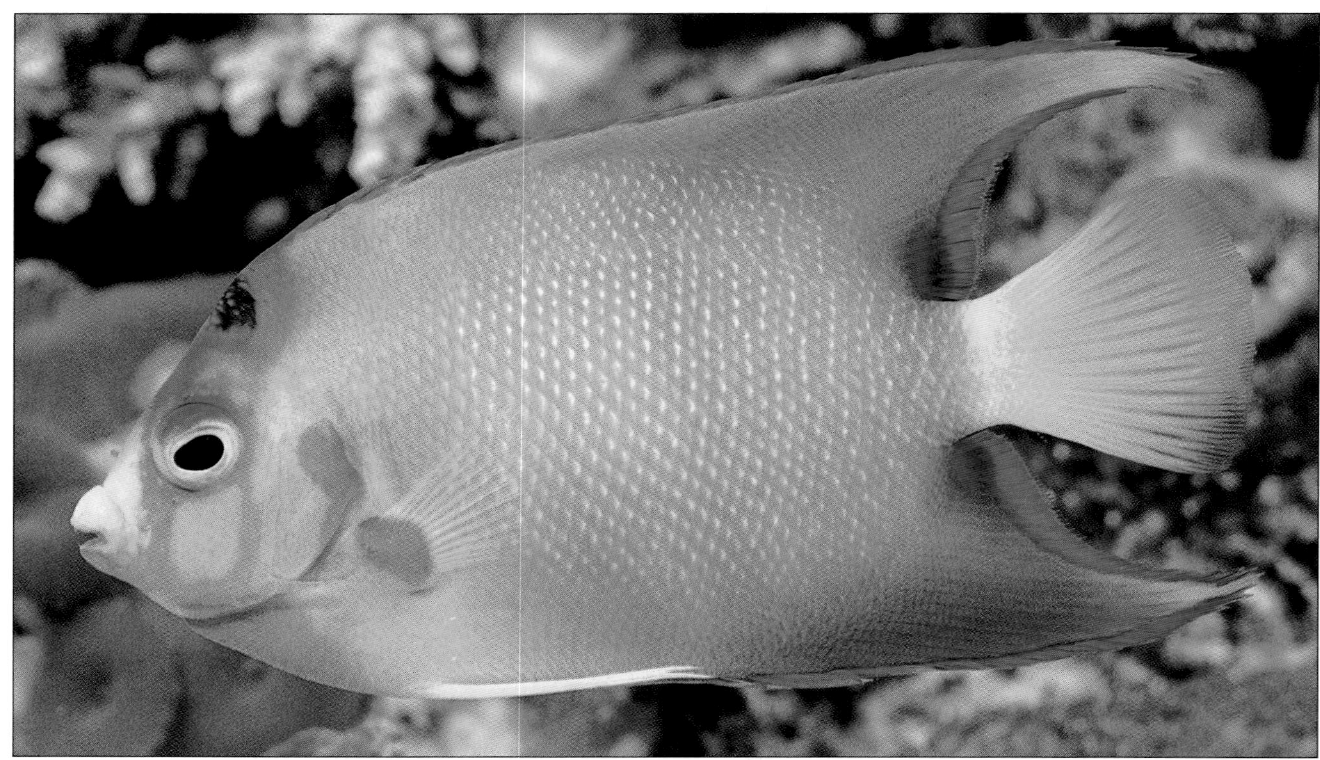

Holacanthus ciliaris
Queen Angelfish

- ☐ **Distribution:** Western Atlantic.
- ☐ **Length:** 450mm/18in (wild).
- ☐ **Diet and feeding:** Meat foods and greenstuff. Grazer.
- ☐ **Aquarium behaviour:** Aggressive when young; grows large. Intolerant of its own and similar species and can be very territorial.
- ☐ **Invertebrate compatibility:** Suitable when very young, but become destructive with age.

Above: Holocanthus ciliaris (adult)
When faced with this fish, who could deny its claim to be the 'Queen' of angelfish? Adult coloration may also be adopted at half the fish's maximum size, given the proper diet and spacious tank.

A very beautiful fish in the aquarium. Variations in colour pattern occur, but generally this species has more yellow than *H. bermudensis*. Hybrids between this species and *H. bermudensis* are classified as *'H. townsendi'* but this is a non-valid name. Young specimens of *H. ciliaris* have more curving blue vertical lines on the dark blue body than the young of *H. bermudensis*.

Queen Angelfish are reported to be prone to outbreaks of white spot disease, but can be successfully treated with copper-based remedies. They are quite resistant to such treatment, but proper management should reduce the likelihood of such outbreaks.

Below: Holocanthus ciliaris (juvenile)
This beautifully coloured and highly prized species just seems to go on improving with age. If you purchase it as a juvenile (shown here), and have a large enough tank, you will have the pleasure of witnessing its various colour progressions until it reaches the majestic adult form shown below left.

Holacanthus passer
King Angelfish

- ☐ **Distribution:** Pacific.
- ☐ **Length:** 450mm/18in (wild).
- ☐ **Diet and feeding:** Mainly greenstuff. Grazer.
- ☐ **Aquarium behaviour:** Aggressive; grows large.
- ☐ **Invertebrate compatibility:** Suitable when very young, but become destructive with age. Overall, not recommended.

The body is a dark brownish gold colour with a single vertical white stripe. The caudal fin is yellow. The dorsal and anal fins show gold patterning and edging. Young specimens have extra blue stripes on the rear of the body. These are extremely aggressive fish.

Above: Holocanthus passer
Only the yellow caudal fin and white stripe remain from the gold juvenile coloration. The blue stripes also merge.

Holacanthus tricolor

Rock Beauty

☐ **Distribution:** Western Atlantic.

☐ **Length:** 600mm/24in (wild), 300mm/12in (aquarium).

☐ **Diet and feeding:** In nature, sponges. Will eat meat foods and algae but may not thrive. Grazer.

☐ **Aquarium behaviour:** Progressively aggressive with age.

☐ **Invertebrate compatibility:** Suitable when very young, but become destructive with age. Overall, not recommended.

Juvenile forms of this fish are yellow with a blue-edged dark spot on the body, but this enlarges to cover two-thirds of the body as the fish matures into adult coloration.

This good-looking but aggressive species will offer a challenge to the experienced fishkeeper with a spacious aquarium. Feeding can be a problem, requiring patience and care; even when they appear to be feeding well, these fishes miss their normal diet of marine sponges. If the aquarium conditions are good, however, and you feed good-quality frozen foods, then you may well achieve success with this fish. Recently introduced sponge-based foods may prove helpful in the successful upkeep of this species. Again, juvenile specimens tend to adapt far better to aquarium life. Fish less than 25mm (1in) long are pure yellow with a neon-blue ocellus on the hind part of the body.

Above: Holacanthus tricolor
The Rock Beauty is an extremely attractive fish. However, it can be a hard species to acclimatize to aquarium diets and tends to be aggressive.

Below: Pomacanthus annularis
It is easy to see how the common name of 'Blue Ring Angelfish' was inspired. Unfortunately, this fish becomes territorial and destructive with age.

Pomacanthus annularis

Blue Ring Angelfish

☐ **Distribution:** Indo-Pacific.

☐ **Length:** 400mm/16in (wild), 250mm/10in (aquarium).

☐ **Diet and feeding:** Meat foods and greenstuff. Grazer.

☐ **Aquarium behaviour:** Territorial.

☐ **Invertebrate compatibility:** Suitable when very young, but become destructive with age.

Blue lines run from either side of the eye diagonally across the brown body. The lines rejoin at the top of the rear portion of the body. A dominant blue ring lies behind the gill cover. Juveniles are blue with a distinctive pattern of almost straight transverse white lines. Juveniles and adults were once considered to belong to different species.

Pomacanthus imperator
Emperor Angelfish

☐ **Distribution:** Indo-Pacific.

☐ **Length:** 400mm/16in (wild), 300mm/12in (aquarium).

☐ **Diet and feeding:** Animal foods and greenstuff. Grazer.

☐ **Aquarium behaviour:** Generally peaceful.

☐ **Invertebrate compatibility:** Suitable when very young, but become destructive with age. Overall, not recommended.

The yellow body is crossed with diagonal blue lines. The dark blue of the anal fin extends into a vertical wedge behind the gill cover. The eye is hidden in a blue-edged dark band. The caudal fin is yellow. Juveniles are dark blue with white semicircular or oval markings. Like all angels, this species requires the very best water conditions possible. Many fishkeepers have grown this species on from juvenile to adult.

Above: Pomacanthus imperator (adult)
Despite the colour changes apparent in this adult, the eye remains hidden beneath a dark bar, giving it protection against attack. Many juveniles have been successfully grown on to adulthood.

Below: Pomacanthus imperator (juvenile)
The beautiful pattern of distinctive white markings on a blue background provides excellent disruptive camouflage for the juvenile Emperor Angelfishes in the dappled light of the coral reef.

Pomacanthus paru
French Angelfish

☐ **Distribution:** Western Atlantic.

☐ **Length:** 300mm/12in (wild).

☐ **Diet and feeding:** Meat foods and greenstuff. Grazer.

☐ **Aquarium behaviour:** Young specimens may be 'nippy', since they act as cleaner fishes.

☐ **Invertebrate compatibility:** Suitable when very young, but become destructive with age. Overall, not recommended.

The young fish is black with bright yellow vertical bands. The adult fish is predominantly grey with bright speckles. Juvenile members of the Atlantic pomacanthids exhibit cleaning tendencies towards other fishes, and each angel's territory is recognized as a cleaning station.

Above and right: Pomacanthus paru
The impressive juvenile French Angelfish (above) has a pattern of yellow stripes on a black background. As the fish develops into a sub-adult (top right), the stripes begin to fade and the adult coloration appears (seen fully developed at below right).

Pomacanthus semicirculatus
Koran Angelfish

- **Distribution:** Indo-Pacific, Red Sea.
- **Length:** 400mm/16in (wild), 380mm/15in (aquarium).
- **Diet and feeding:** Meat foods and greenstuff. Grazer.
- **Aquarium behaviour:** Territorial.
- **Invertebrate compatibility:** Suitable when very young, but become destructive with age. Overall, not recommended.

The body is golden brown with blue speckles and the fins are outlined in blue. There are vertical blue lines on the head. The white markings on the juvenile are in the shape of semicircles rather than straight lines. During the colour change to adulthood, the markings on the caudal fin often resemble Arabic characters in the Koran – hence the common name.

Above: Pomacanthus semicirculatus (adult)
This near-adult form has almost lost the juvenile white markings.

Below: Pomacanthus semicirculatus (juvenile)
As in most angelfishes, the juvenile's coloration differs from the adult's.

Pygoplites diacanthus

Regal Angelfish; Royal Empress Angelfish

☐ **Distribution:** Indo-Pacific and Red Sea.

☐ **Length:** 250mm/10in (wild), 180mm/7in (aquarium).

☐ **Diet and feeding:** Sponges and algae in nature. In the tank, they will take frozen bloodworm, frozen *Mysis* shrimp, mussel meat, etc; even flake sometimes. Grazer.

☐ **Aquarium behaviour:** Shy, requires plenty of hiding places.

☐ **Invertebrate compatibility:** Suitable when very young, but become destructive with age. Overall, not recommended.

Dark-edged, bright orange slanting bands cross the body and extend into the dorsal and anal fins. The caudal fin is plain yellow. Feeding can be a problem, and may make it difficult to acclimatize this species to aquarium life. It requires a low nitrate level in the tank. Definitely a species for the experienced hobbyist only.

Specimens from the Philippines are relatively pale in colour, and consequently less desirable, and may be virtually impossible to feed. Those from Sri Lanka, the Maldives and the Red Sea will eat in good water conditions and are brighter in colour. The new sponge-based foods may prove helpful in facilitating the upkeep of this species. As some encouragement, one documented specimen of this species has grown 125mm (5in) during seven years in captivity.

Below: Pygoplites diacanthus
The Regal Angelfish is a species for the experienced aquarist; but if you can keep it in the very best of conditions and provide it with just the right diet, then over a period of years it will repay you by displaying amazing colours and, indeed, a truly regal manner.

Family: POMACENTRIDAE

Anemonefishes (Clownfishes) and Damselfishes

Family characteristics
Fishes within this family are usually divided into two distinct groups: the anemonefishes and the damselfishes.

Anemonefishes have come to represent the very essence of tropical marine fishkeeping; they are brilliantly coloured, full of character and relatively easy to keep. Many hobbyists would not consider an aquarium complete without one.

The curious 'waddling' swimming action of the anemonefishes, together with their appropriate markings, has given them their other collective common name of clownfishes. As their principal common name suggests, anemonefishes live in close association with sea anemones, especially *Heteractis* and *Stoichactis* species. The anemonefish was thought to be immune to the stinging cells of the sea anemone, but it now seems certain that the mucus on the fish prevents the stinging cells from being activated by masking the fish as potential prey.

The clownfish/anemone relationship is usually referred to as being symbiotic; in fact, it is commensal, which means that the fishes and anemones live in close proximity to one another, often to their mutual benefit. There may be some doubt about the benefit derived by the anemones in return for not stinging the fish. The favoured theory is that the anemonefishes, being highly territorial by nature, chase away fishes that might eat the host anemone.

Despite their close relationship in the wild, many anemonefishes will live quite happily in the aquarium without an anemone (and vice-versa), but then you will not see the fish behave as it does in nature. (It is worth noting that sea anemones are sensitive creatures and need special care and attention, see pages 317-322.) In the wild, large sea anemones can accommodate a whole group of anemonefish. Of these, only a dominant pair will breed, the rest remaining as male fish. If any disaster should remove the dominant female though, all is not lost; the dominant male will change sex and become a breeding female that will then pair off with the next dominant male.

Many anemones are only big enough to house a pair of fish, and all other prospective 'tenants' are seen off. This is more often than not the case in the aquarium and it is recommended that each anemone should host a pair of anemonefish only; any other fish may be remorselessly attacked and, if they are not killed, their lives will be made miserable. Very large tanks may accommodate several pairs of anemonefish without too much trouble, but smaller tanks should only house one pair, otherwise serious territorial disputes could ensue.

Anemonefish are fairly easy to pair, spawn and raise (see *Breeding fish*, pages 138-143); damselfish are slightly more difficult. In many countries, commercially bred anemonefish are now readily available and these should be purchased wherever possible to preserve wild stocks under pressure from pollution and habitat destruction.

Damselfishes are small busy fishes that bob constantly around the coral heads, using them as their territory and retreating into them when threatened. They are agile fishes – particularly when you are trying to catch them!

There are a number of similar-looking 'Electric-blue' or 'Blue Devil' fishes and also several blue-and-yellow coloured species. Because of these similarities, the nomenclature of this large group of fishes is, quite literally, a scientific minefield. Many authorities have endeavoured to reclassify the damsels, but this has only served thoroughly to confuse hobbyists, authors and scientists alike. Fortunately, for the purposes of the average hobbyist, all this matters little, as most damselfish share the same behaviour patterns.

Damselfishs' colours sometimes fade, which may be a response that helps the fish to blend in more effectively with the surroundings, or it may indicate undue stress in captivity. Because damselfishes are considered to be hardy, they are much abused, often suffering high ammonia and nitrite levels to mature a filter system. Apart from this being bad aquarium management, these species are no less likely to contract White Spot or Oodinium diseases than any other marine fish subject to adverse conditions, which could spell long-term disaster for a newly set-up aquarium.

Normally, there are no clear distinctions between the sexes. There is one method of determining sex by external observation – a technique similar to that used for determining sex in freshwater cichlids – and that is by looking at the genital papillae (often called the ovipositor). The male genital papilla is narrower and more pointed than the female's. Observations are best delayed until breeding activity is noticed, when the papillae are easier to see. Spawning in damselfishes entails the selection of a site and the laying and subsequent guarding of eggs.

Diet and feeding
In the aquarium, these fishes will take live foods, algae, frozen foods, flake etc. All species of damselfishes will take dried foods readily.

Aquarium behaviour
Anemonefishes are eminently suitable for keeping in the aquarium, where they will naturally associate with suitable anemones. In this way, you can keep a pair of Anemonefishes in a relatively small tank.

Damselfishes, despite their enormous popularity as a result of being colourful and hardy, do have a negative side: they are often aggressive and intolerant of their own, and other, species.

Abudefduf cyaneus
Blue Damsel

☐ **Distribution:** Indo-Pacific.

☐ **Length:** 60mm/2.4in (wild).

☐ **Diet and feeding:** Finely chopped meats and dried food. Bold feeder.

☐ **Aquarium behaviour:** May squabble with members of its own species. Keep singly or in shoals.

☐ **Invertebrate compatibility:** Yes, good choice.

Although some specimens may have yellow markings on the caudal fin and ventral area, the predominant colour of this fish is a stunning royal blue. There is some confusion about the positive classification of this species, since some authorities also refer to it as *Chrysiptera*.

Below: Abudefduf cyaneus
One of many blue damselfishes, this fish has more synonyms than most.

Abudefduf oxyodon
Blue-velvet Damselfish; Black Neon Damselfish; Blue-streak Devil

☐ **Distribution:** Pacific.

☐ **Length:** 110mm/4.3in (wild), 75mm/3in (aquarium).

☐ **Diet and feeding:** Finely chopped meats, algae and greenstuff. Bold.

☐ **Aquarium behaviour:** Aggressive.

☐ **Invertebrate compatibility:** Yes, good choice.

A vertical yellow stripe crosses the deep blue-black body just behind the head. The electric blue wavy lines on the head and upper part of the body fade with age.

Above: Abudefduf oxyodon
This handsome fish from the Pacific Ocean may not adapt well if it is in less than first-class condition.

Abudefduf saxatilis
Sergeant Major

- ☐ **Distribution:** Indo-Pacific, tropical Atlantic.
- ☐ **Length:** 150mm/6in (wild), 50mm/2in (aquarium).
- ☐ **Diet and feeding:** Finely chopped meats, algae and greenstuff. Bold grazer.
- ☐ **Aquarium behaviour:** Juveniles are very active; adults can become very aggressive.
- ☐ **Invertebrate compatibility:** Yes, good choice.

Five vertical dark bars cross the yellow/silvery body. Depending on the geographic location of the individuals, the caudal fin may be a dusky colour. Juvenile forms in the Atlantic have bright yellow upper parts on an otherwise silver body. However, it may lose its colours when disturbed. This is a hardy fish, and a good choice for the beginner. A shoal in a large tank is impressive.

Above: Abudefduf saxatilis
The Sergeant Major is widely distributed throughout the tropics. The male changes colour and an ovipositor appears from the vent during spawning. Eggs are laid on rocks, shells or coral.

Amphiprion akallopisos
Skunk Clown;

- ☐ **Distribution:** Indo-Pacific.
- ☐ **Length:** 75mm/3in (wild), 40-50mm/1.6-2in (aquarium).
- ☐ **Diet and feeding:** Small crustaceans, small live foods, algae, vegetable-based foods. Bold feeder.
- ☐ **Aquarium behaviour:** Peaceful but anemone-dependent.
- ☐ **Invertebrate compatibility:** Yes, ideal.

A white line runs along the very top of the brown-topped golden body, from a point level with the eye to the caudal peduncle. Some anemonefishes do not live up to the family's reputation as sea anemone dwellers, but the Skunk Clown seems to need the association more than other species.

Left: Amphiprion akallopisos
These yellow Skunk Clowns are doing what comes naturally, resting among the tentacles of their host sea anemone.

Amphiprion clarkii

Two-banded Anemonefish; Banded Clown; Clark's Anemonefish

☐ **Distribution:** Indo-Pacific.

☐ **Length:** 120mm/4.7in (wild), 75mm/3in (aquarium).

☐ **Diet and feeding:** Small crustaceans, small live foods, algae, vegetable-based foods. Bold feeder.

☐ **Aquarium behaviour:** Peaceful.

☐ **Invertebrate compatibility:** Yes, ideal.

This species is highly variable in coloration depending on its location, but generally the body is predominantly dark brown but for the ventral regions, which are yellow. All the fins, with the exception of the paler caudal fins, are bright yellow. Two tapering white vertical bars divide the body into thirds; in juvenile forms, there is a third white bar across the rear of the body.

Clark's Anemonefish is peaceful and makes an ideal choice for a mixed aquarium.

Below: Amphiprion clarkii
Clark's Anemonefish can be found in many colour variations and identification is therefore sometimes difficult. This bold fish is excellent for the community aquarium with little need for a host anemone in most cases.

Left: Amphiprion ephippium
This Tomato Clown is but one species so named, many others having the similar red body coloration with a dark patch.

Above: Amphiprion frenatus
Unlike the previous species, adult specimens of this Fire Clown retain the vertical white stripe into adulthood.

Amphiprion ephippium

Tomato Clown; Fire Clown; Red Saddleback Clown

- ☐ **Distribution:** Indo-Pacific.
- ☐ **Length:** 120mm/4.7in (wild), 75mm/3in (aquarium).
- ☐ **Diet and feeding:** Small crustaceans, small live foods, algae, vegetable-based foods. Bold feeder.
- ☐ **Aquarium behaviour:** Can be aggressive.
- ☐ **Invertebrate compatibility:** Yes, ideal.

This fish is often confused with *A. frenatus*, since both are a rich tomato-red with a black blurred blotch on the body rearwards of the gill cover. Juveniles have a white vertical bar just behind the head disappearing as the fish matures.

Amphiprion frenatus

Tomato Clown; Fire Clown; Bridled Clownfish

- ☐ **Distribution:** Pacific.
- ☐ **Length:** 75mm/3in (wild).
- ☐ **Diet and feeding:** Small crustaceans, small live foods, algae, vegetable-based foods. Bold feeder.
- ☐ **Aquarium behaviour:** May be quarrelsome in confined spaces.
- ☐ **Invertebrate compatibility:** Yes, ideal.

A. frenatus is very similar to *A. ephippium*, but it has the white stripe behind the head (sometimes two in juveniles) and the body blotch is often larger. The confusion is not helped by the fact that some authorities call this fish *A. ephippium* or *A. melanopus*.

Amphiprion nigripes
Black-footed Clownfish

☐ **Distribution:** Indian Ocean.

☐ **Length:** 80mm/3.2in (wild), 50mm/2in (aquarium).

☐ **Diet and feeding:** Eats plankton and crustaceans in the wild, but finely chopped foods are ideal in captivity. Bold feeder.

☐ **Aquarium behaviour:** Shy.

☐ **Invertebrate compatability:** Yes, ideal.

Although it is similar to the two previous species, *A. nigripes* is much more subtly coloured. It is a soft golden brown with a white stripe just behind the head. The pelvic fins are black, but the anal fin is not always so, hence the common name.

Above right: Amphiprion nigripes
A native of the Maldive Islands.

Amphiprion ocellaris
Common Clown; Percula Clown

☐ **Distribution:** Indo-Pacific.

☐ **Length:** 80mm/3.2in (wild), 50mm/2in (aquarium).

☐ **Diet and feeding:** Finely chopped foods. Bold feeder.

☐ **Aquarium behaviour:** Will exclude other anemonefishes from its territory.

☐ **Invertebrate compatibility:** Yes, ideal.

This is the clownfish that everyone recognizes, thanks to its bold and unforgettable coloration. There has been much debate on whether there is a similar, but distinct species called *A. percula*. In fact, this is a very colour-variable fish and the two fish are very probably one and the same species.

Right: Amphiprion ocellaris
'The essence of the coral reef.'

Amphiprion perideraion

Salmon Clownfish; Pink Skunk Clownfish

☐ **Distribution:** Pacific Ocean.

☐ **Length:** 80mm/3.2in (wild), 38mm/1.5in (aquarium).

☐ **Diet and feeding:** Finely chopped foods. Not quite as bold as other species.

☐ **Aquarium behaviour:** Shy.

☐ **Invertebrate compatibility:** Yes, ideal.

This species is very similar in colour to *A. akallopisos*, but can be easily distinguished from it by the vertical bar just behind the head. The body colour is perhaps a little more subdued and a white stripe reaches the snout. *A. perideraion* is rather more sensitive than other species and is best kept in a species tank with adequate space for sea anemones. Males have orange edging to the soft-rayed part of the dorsal fin and at the top and bottom of the caudal fin.

Below: Amphiprion perideraion
The Salmon Clownfish has a vertical bar and pink hue, which help distinguish it from similar white-backed species.

Amphiprion polymnus
Saddleback Clownfish

☐ **Distribution:** Pacific.

☐ **Length:** 120mm/4.7in (wild), 100mm/4in (aquarium).

☐ **Diet and feeding:** Small crustaceans, small live foods, algae, vegetable-based foods. Bold feeder.

☐ **Aquarium behaviour:** Can be territorial, and aggressive.

☐ **Invertebrate compatibility:** Yes, ideal.

The dark red-brown body is marked by two white bands; one broad band lies just behind the head, the other begins in the middle of the body and curves upwards into the rear part of the dorsal fin. There is also a dash of white along the top of the caudal fin.

Above: Amphiprion polymnus
The white markings on the dorsal area and the dark brown body make recognition of this species quite easy.

Chromis caerulea
Green Chromis

☐ **Distribution:** Indo-Pacific, Red Sea.

☐ **Length:** 100mm/4in (wild), 50mm/2in (aquarium).

☐ **Diet and feeding:** Chopped meats. Shy.

☐ **Aquarium behaviour:** Generally peaceful.

☐ **Invertebrate compatibility:** Yes, good choice.

This hardy colourful shoaling species has a brilliant green-blue sheen to the scales. The caudal fin is more deeply forked than in some damselfishes. Keep these fishes in shoals; individuals may go into decline. Ideally, a shoal should consist of at least six fishes.

Above: Chromis caerulea
Like many damselfishes, the peaceful Green Chromis has a gregarious nature and appreciates being kept in a small shoal. It is a lively and attractive species and can safely be kept in a mixed fish and invertebrate set-up.

Chromis cyanea

Blue Chromis; Blue Reef Fish

☐ **Distribution:** Tropical Atlantic.

☐ **Length:** 50mm/2in (wild).

☐ **Diet and feeding:** Chopped meats. Dried foods.

☐ **Aquarium behaviour:** A peaceable shoaling fish that prefers to be with some of its own kind to feel at home.

☐ **Invertebrate compatibility:** Yes, good choice.

This species thrives in vigorously aerated water. The body colour is brilliant blue with some black specks, topped with a black dorsal surface. There are black edges to the dorsal and caudal fins. The eye is also dark. In shape and size (but not colour) *C. cyanea* closely resembles *C. multilineata*, the Grey Chromis.

At breeding time, a brown ovipositor extends from just in front of the anal fin in a similar manner to that of freshwater cichlids.

Above: Chromis cyanea
This peaceful shoaling fish is best kept with others of its kind, possibly in a reef aquarium. The normally narrow black area on the top of the male Blue Chromis spreads during spawning time and a brown ovipositor appears. The male usually guards the eggs.

Chromis xanthurus

Yellow-tailed Damselfish

☐ **Distribution:** Indo-Pacific.

☐ **Length:** 100mm/4in (wild), 50mm/2in (aquarium).

☐ **Diet and feeding:** Chopped meats and dried foods. Bold feeder.

☐ **Aquarium behaviour:** Can be aggressive.

☐ **Invertebrate compatibility:** Yes, good choice.

The deep royal blue body contrasts sharply with the bright yellow caudal fin and caudal peduncle. Again, there is some confusion over the correct name of this species, both *Pomacentrus caeruleus* and *Abudefduf parasema* are given by other sources.

Above: Chromis xanthurus
Quite understandably, Yellow-tailed Damsels are among the most popular fish in the marine hobby; they are colourful, hardy, disease resistant and will eat almost all marine food. They are also, however, highly territorial.

Dascyllus aruanus

Humbug; White-tailed Damselfish

☐ **Distribution:** Indo-Pacific.

☐ **Length:** 80mm/3.2in (wild), 75mm/3in (aquarium).

☐ **Diet and feeding:** Chopped meats. Bold feeder.

☐ **Aquarium behaviour:** Aggressive towards its own kind and very territorial.

☐ **Invertebrate compatibility:** Yes, a good choice.

This white fish has three black bars across the body. The front bar covers the eye and follows the slope of the head up into the first rays of the dorsal fin. The rear two bars extend into the pelvic and anal fins and also into the dorsal fin, where they are linked by a horizontal bar along the top part of the fin. The caudal fin is unmarked. This is the hardiest of the damsels.

Left: Dascyllus aruanus
This fish shares its common name with the similarly coloured confection. It is relatively hardy, but very territorial.

Dascyllus carneus

Cloudy Damsel; Blue-spotted Dascyllus

☐ **Distribution:** Indo-Pacific.

☐ **Length:** 80mm/3.2in (wild).

☐ **Diet and feeding:** Chopped foods. Dried foods. Bold.

☐ **Aquarium behaviour:** Aggressive towards its own kind.

☐ **Invertebrate compatibility:** Yes, a good choice.

All the fins, except the white caudal, are black and the body is greyish brown with a pattern of blue dots. There is a white patch on the top of the body, towards the front part of the dorsal fin and immediately behind a black bar, which covers the pectoral fin. A similar fish, *D. reticulatus*, is an overall grey, lacks the white patch and has a vertical black bar running from the rear of the dorsal to the rear of the anal fin.

Below: Dascyllus carneus
Of a similar size, but less starkly coloured than the Humbug, the Cloudy Damsel has more grey-brown in its body.

Dascyllus marginatus

Marginate Damselfish; Marginate Puller

☐ **Distribution:** Red Sea.

☐ **Length:** 100mm/4in (wild).

☐ **Diet and feeding:** Chopped meats. Dried foods. Bold feeder.

☐ **Aquarium behaviour:** Aggressive and territorial.

☐ **Invertebrate compatibility:** Yes, a good choice.

A brown area slopes backwards from the front of the black-edged dorsal fin to the point of the anal fin. The rest of the body is cream in colour. This active fish will shelter among coral during the night.

Below: Dascyllus marginatus
Like all Dascyllus *species, this fish occasionally makes quite audible purring or clicking sounds*

Dascyllus melanurus

Black-tailed Humbug

☐ **Distribution:** West Pacific.

☐ **Length:** 75mm/3in (wild).

☐ **Diet and feeding:** Chopped foods. Dried foods. Bold feeder. Frozen mysis and brineshrimp.

☐ **Aquarium behaviour:** Aggressive and territorial.

☐ **Invertebrate compatibility:** Yes, good choice.

This fish is very similar to *D. aruanus*, except that the black bars are more vertical and a black bar crosses the caudal fin.

Above: Dascyllus melanurus
This black and white damsel is, like its almost lookalike relative, the Humbug, a shoaling fish. It is found over a more limited area, however, being confined to the western Pacific Ocean around the Philippines and Melanesia. It is an aggressively territorial species that is best housed with other fish that can take care of themselves.

Dascyllus trimaculatus
Domino Damsel; Three-spot Damselfish

☐ **Distribution:** Indo-Pacific, Red Sea.

☐ **Length:** 125mm/5in (wild), 75mm/3in (aquarium).

☐ **Diet and feeding:** Chopped meats and dried foods. Bold.

☐ **Aquarium behaviour:** Territorial.

☐ **Invertebrate compatibility:** Yes, good choice.

This fish is velvety black overall, including the fins. The only markings are the three spots from which one of the comon names is derived. There is one white spot on each upper flank, midway along the length of the dorsal fin; the third spot is situated on the centre of the head, just behind the eye. The spots fade with age.

Below: Dascyllus trimaculatus
This very common damselfish is instantly recognizable by the three white spots on its body, and it would be very hard to imagine a more appropriate popular name for it. Unfortunately, the spots usually fade with age.

Paraglyphidodon melanopus
Yellow-backed Damselfish

☐ **Distribution:** Indo-Pacific.

☐ **Length:** 75mm/3in (wild).

☐ **Diet and feeding:** Chopped meats. Bold feeder.

☐ **Aquarium behaviour:** May be aggressive towards its own, and smaller, species.

☐ **Invertebrate compatibility:** Yes, good choice.

An oblique bright yellow band runs from the snout to the tip of the dorsal fin above a pale violet body. The anal and pelvic fins are light blue, edged with black. The caudal fin is edged with yellow. A spacious tank with plenty of hiding places suits this brilliantly coloured fish very well.

Above: Paraglyphidodon melanopus
The combination of black-edged pelvic fins and brilliant colours of this damselfish has inspired several alternative common names, including Bow-tie Damsel, Bluefin Damsel and Royal Damsel. It is found over a wide area of the Indo-Pacific.

Above: Pomacentrus coeruleus
The brilliant electic blue colour of the Blue Devil makes it an instant eye-catcher in the dealer's tanks, and it will certainly add an extra splash of colour to the home aquarium.

Pomacentrus coeruleus
Blue Devil; Electric-blue Damsel

☐ **Distribution:** Indo-Pacific.

☐ **Length:** 100mm/4in (wild), 50mm/2in (aquarium).

☐ **Diet and feeding:** Chopped meats. Dried food. Bold feeder.

☐ **Aquarium behaviour:** Extremely pugnacious.

☐ **Invertebrate compatibility:** Yes, good choice.

The bright blue coloration of this fish really makes it stand out in the aquarium. There may be some black facial markings. It is a hardy species and lives peacefully in small groups when young but may turn aggressive when adult.

Pomacentrus melanochir
Blue-finned Damsel

☐ **Distribution:** Pacific.

☐ **Length:** 80mm/3.2in (wild).

☐ **Diet and feeding:** Chopped meats. Dried foods.

☐ **Aquarium behaviour:** Pugnacious.

☐ **Invertebrate compatibility:** Yes, good choice.

This rare blue damsel can be identified by the dark edge to each scale and defined blue patterning on the head. The dorsal, anal and caudal fins are more extended than on other species. Pectoral fins are yellowish.

Below: Pomacentrus melanochir
The extended finnage of this damselfish make it easy to identify.

Pomacentrus violascens

Yellow-tailed Demoiselle

- **Distribution:** Pacific.
- **Length:**80mm/3.2in (wild), 50mm/2in (aquarium).
- **Diet and feeding:** Chopped meats. Dried food. Bold feeder.
- **Aquarium behaviour:** Pugnacious.
- **Invertebrate compatability:** Yes, good choice.

The markings on *Pomacentrus violascens* resemble those of *P. melanochir*, but the tips of the dorsal and anal fins are yellow and the yellow of the caudal fin does not spread quite so far onto the body.

Left: Pomacentrus violascens
This beautiful damsel is slightly more sensitve than others in this family.

Left: Premnas biaculeatus
An attractive deep-red clownfish.

Above: Stegastes leucostictus
Common, and suitable for the beginner.

Premnas biaculeatus
Maroon Clownfish

☐ **Distribution:** Pacific Ocean.

☐ **Length:** 150mm/6in (wild), 100mm/4in (aquarium).

☐ **Diet and feeding:** Finely chopped foods. Bold.

☐ **Aquarium behaviour:** Aggressive towards other anemonefishes and its own species, if not a mated pair.

☐ **Invertebrate compatibility:** Yes, ideal.

This larger species differs from other clownfishes by having two spines beneath the eye, as well as the usual small spines on the back edge of the gill cover. The body is a deep rich red with three narrow white bands crossing it, behind the head, midway along the body and just behind the dorsal and anal fins.

Stegastes leucostictus
Beau Gregory

☐ **Distribution:** Caribbean.

☐ **Length:** 150mm/6in (wild), 50mm/2in (aquarium).

☐ **Diet and feeding:** Animal and vegetable matter. Dried foods. Bold feeder.

☐ **Aquarium behaviour:** Aggressive.

☐ **Invertebrate compatibility:** Yes, a good choice.

The yellow body is topped by a golden brown area covered in bright blue dots. There is a dark blotch at the rear of the dorsal fin. All the other fins are yellow. This common damsel is hardy enough for the beginner, but may bully fishes with similar feeding habits; kept alongside species with different feeding habits it is not so aggressive.

Family: PSEUDOCHROMIDAE

Pygmy Basslets/Dottybacks

Family characteristics

Many of the behavioural patterns of both pygmy basslets (Pseudochromidae) and fairy basslets (Grammidae) are essentially the same, the main difference being geographical location; the former group originates from the Red Sea and parts of the Indo-Pacific, while the latter are confined to the Caribbean. The pygmy basslets are a reasonably large group of fishes spread over a wide area. The vast majority are to be found within the Red Sea and adjacent areas and, as imports are restricted from these parts of the world, numbers are at a premium and specimens usually command high prices.

Pygmy basslets are generally very shy but highly territorial in nature, spending much of their time travelling the maze of crevices within the coral reef structure, occasionally dashing out to capture a morsel of food carried in the current.

Little is known of the reproduction process of this family and reports of aquarium spawning are extremely rare. To date, no larvae have been raised successfully.

Diet and feeding

Small crustaceans and drifting plankton make up much of the wild diet of these fishes. In the aquarium, much of the normal frozen and live marine fare is readily acceptable after an initial settling-in period. Flake foods are not appreciated by most species at any time.

Aquarium behaviour

These fishes are highly territorial by nature and will usually be very intolerant of the same, or similar, species. A good arrangement of rockwork is essential to satisfy their secretive habits, although most individuals acclimatize quite well, losing a good deal of their shyness once established.

Pseudochromis diadema
Flash-back Gramma

☐ **Distribution:** Western Pacific.

☐ **Length:** 55mm/2.2in (wild).

☐ **Diet and feeding:** Will readily accept most marine frozen and live foods; even flake.

☐ **Aquarium behaviour:** Peaceful, but requires plenty of hiding places.

☐ **Invertebrate compatibility:** Ideal.

Left: Pseudochromis diadema
The Flash-back Gramma is a beautiful fish often overlooked by aquarists. Given the right environment, it is easy to keep and will thrive for many years.

P. diadema is almost totally yellow with a wedge of purple beginning at the snout, running across the back and disappearing at the caudal peduncle. Although generally a peaceful fish, it will not tolerate its own, or similar, species, but may be regarded as a good beginner's fish if this is taken into account.

Pseudochromis dutoiti
Neon-back Gramma

☐ **Distribution:** Central Indian Ocean.

☐ **Length:** 88mm/3.5in (wild).

☐ **Diet and feeding:** Live foods are recommended, but frozen marine fare is usually acceptable once the fish has settled in. Flake foods are nearly always rejected.

Above: Pseudochromis dutoiti
The Neon-back Gramma is occasionally imported and is a popular, if expensive, choice. It is money well spent, however, as you will be rewarded with a naturally inquisitive fish, full of character.

☐ **Aquarium behaviour:** Shy but territorial. Aggressive towards fish of the same, or similar, species.

☐ **Invertebrate compatibility:** Ideal.

P. dutoiti is always popular when it appears on sale and makes an ideal addition to the living reef aquarium. However, it can become highly aggressive towards its own kind, or similar fish. Like *P. flavivertex,* it is not a beginner's fish and will usually need extra care where feeding is concerned.

Pseudochromis flavivertex
Sunrise Dottyback

☐ **Distribution:** Red Sea.

☐ **Length:** 70mm/2.75in (wild).

☐ **Diet and feeding:** Favours live foods but will eventually accept frozen marine fare. Flake is nearly always rejected.

☐ **Aquarium behaviour:** Has a shy, secretive nature and requires plenty of rockwork in which to hide.

☐ **Invertebrate compatibility:** Ideal.

The Sunrise Dottyback certainly lives up to its name – its cobalt blue body has a bright yellow band running from the tip of the nose, across the back and into the tail, giving the impression of a tropical sunrise. It should be kept on its own or in the company of dissimilar fish if fighting is to be avoided. Although not a beginner's fish, *P. flavivertex* makes a highly attractive addition to the invertebrate aquarium for those with more experience.

Above: Pseudochromis flavivertex
Like its cousin, P. dutoiti, *this fish is only an occasional, and expensive, import. But, such is its beauty, many cannot resist the temptation. It does best in a mixed fish/invertebrate tank.*

Below: Pseudochromis paccagnellae
The False Gramma requires similar aquarium conditions to its lookalike, the Royal Gramma. Make sure that you provide plenty of retreats in the aquarium to help it feel secure.

Pseudochromis paccagnellae
False Gramma; Dottyback; Royal Dottyback; Paccagnella's Dottyback

☐ **Distribution:** Pacific.

☐ **Length:** 50mm/2in (wild).

☐ **Diet and feeding:** Finely chopped meat foods, brineshrimp.

☐ **Aquarium behaviour:** Do not keep with similar fishes. May tend to nip at other fishes.

☐ **Invertebrate compatibility:** Ideal.

This species is almost identical to *Gramma loreto,* but a thin white line – often incomplete or hard to see – divides the two body colours.

Above: Pseudochromis porphyreus
The Strawberry Gramma is a fish full of character; it is bold and generally fearless, even with much larger fish. Colourful, disease resistant and fairly inexpensive, it is a popular choice.

Pseudochromis porphyreus
Strawberry Gramma

☐ **Distribution:** Central and Western Pacific.

☐ **Length:** 55mm/2.2in (wild), 75mm/2.75in (aquarium).

☐ **Diet and feeding:** Easily fed. Will accept most marine frozen, live and flake foods.

☐ **Aquarium behaviour:** Bold. Can be very aggressive towards its own kind and similar species.

☐ **Invertebrate compatibility:** Very good.

There is always an exception to every rule and, in many respects, *P. porphyreus* is it. Most pygmy basslets are shy and secretive but, once settled, the Strawberry Gramma can be bold and aggressive, intolerant of its own kind and even unrelated fish it takes a disliking to. However, it is still a desirable aquarium addition and its tough constitution makes it ideal for the beginner.

Family: SCATOPHAGIDAE

Butterfishes/Scats

Family characteristics
Like the Monodactylidae, the fishes in this family are also estuarine and can be kept with some success in brackish water or even freshwater aquariums. The family, which has only four species in two genera, is found around many of the islands of the Malay Archipelago to New Guinea and Northern Australia. In the latter region they are confined to tidal zones.

Diet and feeding
These fishes will eat anything, including greenfood, such as lettuce, spinach and green peas.

Aquarium behaviour
It is usual to keep scats in the company of fingerfishes (*Monodactylus* species, see pages 228-229). They need plenty of swimming space.

Above: Scatophagus argus
An active fish that will eat anything.

Scatophagus argus
Scat; Argus Fish

☐ **Distribution:** Indo-Pacific.

☐ **Length:** 300mm/12in (wild).

☐ **Diet and feeding:** Will eat anything, including greenstuff. Scavenger.

☐ **Aquarium behaviour:** Peaceful.

☐ **Invertebrate compatibility:** Generally not recommended.

Like *Monodactylus* sp., the Scat is almost equally at home in salt, brackish or even fresh water, but it thrives best in sea water. It frequents coastal and estuarine waters, where it is assured of a good supply of animal waste and other unsavoury material. (Its scientific name means 'excrement eater'.) The oblong body is laterally compressed, reminiscent of butterflyfishes and angelfishes. It is green-brown with a number of large dark spots, which become less prominent on adult fishes. A deep notch divides the spiny first part and the soft-rayed rear section of the dorsal fin. Juveniles have more red coloration, especially on the fins.

Family: SCIAENIDAE

Croakers and Drums

Family characteristics
Most of the species likely to be suitable for the aquarium come from the western Atlantic, although a species from the eastern Pacific, is another possible contender.

The fishes in this family are also capable of making sounds by resonating the swimbladder. Their strikingly marked bodies are usually elongated, often with a characteristic high first dorsal fin.

Diet and feeding
Most species may pose problems in their day to day care, being somewhat fussy eaters; success in the aquarium relies upon a constant supply of small live foods.

Aquarium behaviour
Fine with peaceable tankmates. Will spawn in the aquarium if provided with ideal conditions.

Equetus acuminatus
Cubbyu; High Hat

☐ **Distribution:** Caribbean.

☐ **Length:** 250mm/10in (wild), 150mm/6in (aquarium).

☐ **Diet and feeding:** Crustaceans, molluscs, soft-bodied invertebrates; live foods preferred in captivity. Slow bottom feeder.

☐ **Aquarium behaviour:** The long fins may be tempting to other fish, so be sure to keep this species with non-agressive tankmates.

☐ **Invertebrate compatibility:** No, destructive.

The main feature of this fish is the very tall first dorsal fin, which is carried erect. The pale body is covered with many horizontal black bands and the black fins have white leading rays. The chin barbels are used to detect food swimming below the fish, which then snaps downward to catch its prey. This species is probably the hardiest of the genus.

Above: Equetus acuminatus
This is a bottom-feeding fish – note the small barbels underneath the mouth.

Equetus lanceolatus

Jack-knife Fish; Ribbonfish

☐ **Distribution:** Caribbean.

☐ **Length:** 250mm/10in (wild).

☐ **Diet and feeding:** Crustaceans, molluscs, soft-bodied invertebrates. Slow bottom feeder.

☐ **Aquarium behaviour:** Its fins may be attacked by other fish. Can be aggressive towards its own kind when adult. A difficult species requiring care.

☐ **Invertebrate compatibility:** No, destructive.

The high first dorsal fin of this very beautiful fish has a white-edged black line through it, that continues like a crescent through the body to the tip of the caudal fin. This gives the fish a forward sloping appearance. Further vertical black bars cross the eye and the body just behind the head. A delicate fish in captivity. A similar-looking species, *E. punctatus*, can easily be confused with the Jack-knife Fish.

Above: Equetus lanceolatus
The strikingly attractive Jack-knife Fish is unfortunately rather delicate, and succumbs easily to shock and stress. It can also be aggressive towards its own kind when adult.

Family: SCORPAENIDAE

Dragonfishes, Lionfishes, Scorpionfishes and Turkeyfishes

Family characteristics
Here are the exotic 'villains' of the aquarium. They are predatory carnivores that glide up to their prey and engulf it with their large mouths. The highly ornamental fins are not just there for decoration either, since they have venomous stinging cells and will inflict a very painful wound. HANDLE THESE FISHES WITH CARE. If you are stung, bathing the affected area in very hot water will alleviate the pain and help to 'coagulate' the poison.

During spawning, the pair of fishes rises to the upper levels of the water and a gelatinous ball of eggs is released. When they are 10-12mm (about 0.5in) long, the fry sink to the bottom of the aquarium.

Diet and feeding
These fish will very often only take live foods in the initial stages of captivity – usually guppies or mollies – but, with a little patience, nearly every specimen can be weaned onto a diet of dead Lancefish and other meaty frozen foods. The ethics of feeding one live fish to another must, of course, be carefully considered by aquarists.

Aquarium behaviour
Members of the Scorpaenidae are usually peaceful in captivity, but do not put temptation their way by keeping them with small fishes. Lionfishes need plenty of room in which to manoeuvre.

Dendrochirus brachypterus
Turkeyfish; Short-finned Lionfish

☐ **Distribution:** Indo-Pacific, Red Sea.

☐ **Length:** 170mm/6.7in (wild), 100mm/4in (aquarium).

☐ **Diet and feeding:** Small fishes, meat foods. Sedentary, engulfs passing prey.

☐ **Aquarium behaviour:** Keep in a species aquarium or together with larger fish.

☐ **Invertebrate compatibility:** Generally yes, but will eat crustaceans.

A very ornate fish. The red-brown body has many white-edged vertical bars. The dorsal fin is multirayed and tissue spans the elongated rays. When spread, the fins have more obvious transverse patterning. The male has a longer pectoral fin and larger head than the female. At breeding time, the male darkens in colour; females become paler. This species does not grow as large as *Pterois* spp and hence it has attracted the alternative popular name of Dwarf Lionfish.

Above: Dendrochirus brachypterus
Camouflage and a venomous sting protect this species in the wild.

Pterois antennata

Scorpionfish; Spotfin Lionfish

- **Distribution:** Indo-Pacific, Red Sea.
- **Length:** 250mm/10in (wild), 100-150mm/4-6in (aquarium).
- **Diet and feeding:** Generally live foods such as small fishes, but all Lionfishes can be acclimatized to take frozen shrimps and similar items. A slow-swimming fish that takes sudden gulps of food.
- **Aquarium behaviour:** Predatory.
- **Invertebrate compatibility:** Generally yes, but will eat crustaceans.

The red bands on the body are wider and less numerous than on *P. volitans*. The white rays of the dorsal and pectoral fins are very elongated.

Above: Pterois antennata
The stationary lurking Scorpionfish is often dismissed by unsuspecting victims as a harmless piece of floating seaweed.

Below: Pterois radiata
The dark bars across the head and body of this graceful fish are accentuated by thin white borders on each side.

Pterois radiata

White-fin Lionfish; Tail-bar Lionfish

- **Distribution:** Indo-Pacific, Red Sea.
- **Length:** 250mm/10in (wild), 150mm/6in (aquarium).
- **Diet and feeding:** Smaller fishes and meaty foods as described for *P. antennata*. Slow-swimming sudden gulper.
- **Aquarium behaviour:** Predatory.
- **Invertebrate compatibility:** Generally yes, but will eat crustaceans.

Again, the red bands on the body are wider and less numerous than on *P. volitans*. The white rays of the dorsal and pectoral fins are very elongated and graceful. At breeding time, males of all *Pterois* species darken, while females become paler and have larger abdomens.

Pterois volitans

Lionfish; Scorpionfish

☐ **Distribution:** Indo-Pacific.

☐ **Length:** 350mm/14in (wild).

☐ **Diet and feeding:** Smaller fishes and suitable meaty foods. Slow-swimming sudden gulper.

☐ **Aquarium behaviour:** Keep with fish too large to be eaten.

☐ **Invertebrate compatibility:** Generally yes, but will eat crustaceans.

This is the most well-known fish in this group. The dorsal fin rays are quite separate and the pectoral fins are only partially filled with tissue. The pelvic fins are red, and the anal and caudal fins are fairly clear. Thick and thin red bands alternate across the body and there are tentacle-like growths above the eyes.

Below: Pterois volitans
This species can be very colour variable and even an extreme black form exists. Such highly prized variants appear on the market from time to time, but, as expected, command very high prices. Lionfish should be encouraged to accept 'dead' foods as soon as possible.

Family: SERRANIDAE

Sea Basses and Groupers

Family characteristics
Many juvenile forms of this large family of predatory fishes have become aquarium favourites. Most of the species within this group are hermaphrodite, and some therefore lack any clear sexual dimorphism. Even so, many species undergo colour changes during breeding, turning darker, paler, or taking on a bicolour pattern. Not surprisingly, 'females' become distended with eggs – another clue to their likely functional sex. This is a large and varied family with over 370 species represented in tropical and temperate seas worldwide.

Diet and feeding
You should include crustaceans and meaty foods in the diet of these fishes.

Aquarium behaviour
The majority of species need a large aquarium.

Anthias squamipinnis

Wreckfish; Orange Sea Perch; Lyre-tail Coralfish; Anthias

☐ **Distribution:** Indo-Pacific.

☐ **Length:** 125mm/5in (wild).

☐ **Diet and feeding:** Preferably live foods, or meat foods. Bold and prefers moving foods.

☐ **Aquarium behaviour:** Peaceful.

☐ **Invertebrate compatibility:** Yes, ideal.

This very beautiful orange-red fish has elongated rays in the dorsal fin, a deeply forked caudal fin and long pelvic fins. It is a shoaling species that needs companions of the same species. Males have an elongated third dorsal spine are usually larger and more conspicuously coloured than females. Dominant males are quite happy for a harem to follow them. Although these fish perform courtship behaviour in captivity, they have not yet been bred.

Left: Anthias squamipinnis
The Wreckfish is a shoaling species; dominant males often have a harem.

Calloplesiops altivelis

Marine Betta; Comet Grouper

☐ **Distribution:** Indo-Pacific.

☐ **Length:** 150mm/6in (wild).

☐ **Diet and feeding:** Small fishes, meaty foods. Predatory.

☐ **Aquarium behaviour:** Err on the side of caution, and do not keep with small fishes.

☐ **Invertebrate compatibility:** Yes, ideal.

Above: Calloplesiops altivelis
The fins of this fish are very similar to those of the freshwater Siamese Fighting Fish, Betta splendens, *hence the popular name. Avoid keeping smaller fishes in the same aquarium.*

A very beautiful and deceptive fish: the trick is to decide which way it is facing, since the dorsal fin has a 'false-eye' marking near its rear edge. The dark brown body is covered with light blue spots and all the fins are very elongated. This species spends much of its time in a 'head down' hunting position. Its tail allegedly resembles the head of the moray eel – a useful defence against predators.

Above: Cephalopholis miniatus
Ranging from the Red Sea to the mid-Pacific, the Coral Trout inhabits the coral reefs, looking for a meal of smaller fishes. In the aquarium, it often hides away in caves or under ledges, denying the fishkeeper a view of its spectacular colouring. An alternative, and very apt, common name for this species is Jewel Bass. The Coral Trout grows quite large in the aquarium and so is generally beyond the scope of the average hobbyist.

Cephalopholis miniatus

Coral Trout; Red Grouper; Coral Rock Cod

☐ **Distribution:** Indo-Pacific.

☐ **Length:** 450mm/18in (wild).

☐ **Diet and feeding:** Smaller fishes and meaty foods. Predatory.

☐ **Aquarium behaviour:** Do not keep with small fishes.

☐ **Invertebrate compatibility:** Yes, ideal.

The body and the dorsal, anal and caudal fins of *C. miniatus* are bright red and covered with bright blue spots. However, the pectoral and pelvic fins are plain red. Other fishes bear a resemblance to this species, but they do not have the distinguishing rounded caudal fin. A large, well-filtered aquarium is essential for this fast-growing fish.

Chromileptis altivelis

Panther Grouper; Polka-Dot Grouper

☐ **Distribution:** Indo-Pacific.

☐ **Length:** 500mm/20in (wild), 300mm/12in (aquarium).

☐ **Diet and feeding:** Live foods. Bold feeder.

☐ **Aquarium behaviour:** It is better not to keep this species with smaller fishes. However, its smallish mouth makes it the least harmful of all the grouper fishes.

☐ **Invertebrate compatibility:** Not recommended.

Juveniles have black blotches on a white body – effective disruptive camouflage. As the fish matures, these blotches increase in number but decrease in size. The result is a very graceful fish, and one that is constantly on the move in the tank.

Below: Chromileptis altivelis
These splendid juveniles in fine colour live up to their common name. As is often the case with beautiful fishes, however, they are very predatory.

Right: Grammistes sexlineatus
Introduce this grouper to a large aquarium ahead of suitably sized tankmates and it may become tame.

Grammistes sexlineatus

Golden-stripe Grouper; Sixline Grouper

☐ **Distribution:** Indo-Pacific.

☐ **Length:** 250mm/10in (wild).

☐ **Diet and feeding:** Animal and meaty foods. Bold.

☐ **Aquarium behaviour:** Do not keep with smaller fishes.

☐ **Invertebrate compatibility:** Not recommended.

Alternate black and white horizontal stripes cover the body. Although a good aquarium subject, it can give off toxic secretions when frightened, annoyed or even in the process of dying. It is unlikely to reach its full size when in captivity, unless kept in an extremely large aquarium.

Family: SIGANIDAE

Rabbitfishes

Family characteristics
The rabbitfishes have deep oblong bodies and are fairly laterally compressed. The mouth is small and equipped for browsing on algae and other vegetation. The spines on the dorsal and anal fins are venomous, so be sure to handle these fishes extremely carefully. Their alternative common name is 'Spinefoot', a reference to the fact that unsuspecting waders who disturb grazing fish risk a wound on the foot caused by the fishes' spines. Juveniles are often more brightly coloured than adults.

Only a dozen or so species belong to this family, but they have an economic significance in the tropics, where they are caught for food. The one species that is especially familiar to hobbyists, *Lo vulpinus*, has a tubular mouth, which contrasts with the normal rabbit-shaped mouth of species in this family.

Some reports of spawning in captivity – albeit of species not featured here – indicate that changing some of the water, or even decreasing its depth, may trigger spawning.

Diet and feeding
Rabbitfishes must have vegetable matter in their diet, although they will adapt to established dried foods and live foods in the aquarium.

Aquarium behaviour
Rabbitfishes are active, fast-growing fishes that need plenty of swimming space.

Lo vulpinus

Foxface; Fox-fish; Badgerfish

☐ **Distribution:** Pacific.

☐ **Length:** 250mm/10in (wild).

☐ **Diet and feeding:** Most foods, but must have vegetable matter. Bold grazer that adopts a typical 'head-down' feeding attitude.

☐ **Aquarium behaviour:** Lively but peaceable, although it may be aggressive towards its own kind.

☐ **Invertebrate compatibility:** Not recommended.

Below: Lo vulpinus
The Foxface, or Badgerfish, has a tubular mouth, which is rather at variance with the more rabbitlike shape characteristic of other members of this family. When first introduced into a new aquarium, it may lose its distinctive coloration in favour of a temporary blotched appearance.

The white head has two broad black bands: one runs obliquely back from the snout, through the eye and up the forehead; the second band is triangular, beginning below the throat and ending behind the gill cover. This coloration obviously gave rise to the common name of Badgerfish among European hobbyists, more familiar with the badger than other hobbyists, who, for some reason, feel the fish's face looks more like that of a fox. Although superficially similar to the surgeonfishes, it has no spine on the caudal peduncle, and the pelvic fins are not very well developed, having only a few rays.

Above: Siganus virgatus
Remember that the dorsal and anal spines of this species are venomous.

Siganus virgatus

Silver Badgerfish; Double-barred Spinefoot

☐ **Distribution:** Pacific.

☐ **Length:** 260mm/10.2in (wild).

☐ **Diet and feeding:** Live foods, meat foods and plenty of greenstuff. Bold grazer.

☐ **Aquarium behaviour:** Lively but peaceable, although it may be aggressive towards fellow members of its own species.

☐ **Invertebrate compatibility:** Not recommended.

The silvery yellow body is more oval and the head more rounded than in the previous species. Again, the head has two badger-like black bars, the second of which begins narrowly just below the pectoral fins and broadens as it runs up to the top of the body. The head and forepart of the body are covered with blue lines, producing an intricate pattern.

Family: SYNGNATHIDAE

Pipefishes and Seahorses

Family characteristics
Every fishkeeper loves the seahorse, and the equally appealing pipefish, which could be described as a 'straightened out' version of the seahorse. Pipefishes are found among crevices on coral reefs, whereas seahorses, being poor swimmers, anchor themselves to coral branches with their prehensile tails. Many pipefishes are estuarine species, and are therefore able to tolerate varying salinities, even entering fresh water.

When seahorses reproduce, the female uses her ovipositor tube to deposit the eggs into the male's abdominal pouch, where they are fertilized and subsequently incubated. Incubation periods range from two weeks to two months, depending on the species.

Diet and feeding
Seahorses and pipefishes have small mouths and require quantities of small live foods to thrive; brineshrimp and rotifers are suitable, even *Daphnia* would be satisfactory if other live foods are in short supply.

Aquarium behaviour
Pipefishes and seahorses do best in a quiet aquarium. Many hobbyists have great difficulty in keeping seahorses for any length of time, for two main reasons: firstly, these are sensitive fish requiring excellent water quality all of the time; secondly, they are constant feeders and three or four good feeds a day is highly recommended.

Collection from the wild usually occurs by accident, when the fish are caught up in shrimp nets. This is extremely traumatic for the fish and may give some clue as to their unwillingness to adapt well to aquarium conditions. Always make sure seahorses and pipefishes are feeding well before you buy them.

Above: Doryrhamphus excisus
Pipefish are close cousins of the seahorse and should be treated in much the same way: a quiet tank, plenty of small livefoods and good water quality.

Doryrhamphus excisus
Bluestripe Pipefish

☐ **Distribution:** Indian and Western Pacific Oceans.

☐ **Length:** 70mm/2.75in (wild).

☐ **Diet and feeding:** Prefers live brine shrimp but may accept small frozen shrimp once settled.

☐ **Aquarium behaviour:** Very peaceful; needs a quiet aquarium.

☐ **Invertebrate compatibility:** Ideal.

Given the optimum conditions, this is one of the few pipefish that do well in the aquarium environment. An ideal situation for this fish – a close relative of the seahorse – would be a quiet invertebrate or species tank. Take care that food portions are small enough for it to swallow. It is important to long-term success that newly purchased specimens are slowly acclimatized.

Hippocampus erectus

Florida Seahorse; Northern Seahorse

☐ **Distribution:** Western Atlantic.

☐ **Length:** 150mm/6in (wild).

☐ **Diet and feeding:** Small animal foods. Browser.

☐ **Aquarium behaviour:** Needs quiet, non-boisterous companions.

☐ **Invertebrate compatibility:** Ideal.

The pelvic and caudal fins are absent, and the anal fin is very small. The tail is prehensile. The coloration of this species is variable; individuals may be grey, brown, yellow or red. The male incubates the young in the abdominal pouch. This species is also frequently referred to as *H. hudsonius*.

Right: Hippocampus erectus
A pale individual of this elegant species. Seahorses adopt a vertical position when at rest. When swimming, they lean forward, propulsion being provided by the fanlike dorsal fin.

Below: Hippocampus kuda
Apart from the fascination of its unusal body shape, with its equine appearance, and amusing activity among the coral branches, the seahorse also displays a very different method of reproduction.

Hippocampus kuda

Yellow Seahorse; Pacific Seahorse

☐ **Distribution:** Indo-Pacific.

☐ **Length:** 250mm/10in (wild) – measured vertically.

☐ **Diet and feeding:** Plenty of live foods, very small crustaceans, brineshrimp. *Daphnia* etc. Browser.

☐ **Aquarium behaviour:** Best kept in a species tank.

☐ **Invertebrate compatibility:** Ideal.

Newly imported specimens may be grey, but once they have settled into the aquarium, the body may take on a yellow hue. The colour of specimens can vary widely, however. An irresistible fish with a fascinating method of reproduction. The male incubates the fertilized eggs in his pouch for four to five weeks before they hatch. This species needs anchorage points in the aquarium, such as marine algae and other suitably branched decorations. The male's brood pouch is the end of an evolutionary process that started with the seahorses' relatives glueing the eggs to the underside of the body for protection.

Family: TETRAODONTIDAE

Puffers

Family characteristics
Puffers are generally smaller than porcupinefishes and smooth scaled. Their jaws are fused, but a divided bone serves as front teeth. '*Tetraodon*' means four toothed (two teeth at the top and two at the bottom), whereas '*Diodon*' means two teeth (one at the top and one at the bottom). These fishes use their pectoral fins to achieve highly manoeuvrable propulsion, but the pelvic fins are absent. Their inflating capabilities vary from species to species; *Tetraodon* sp. – some of which are freshwater – are 'fully inflatable', but members of the genus *Canthigaster* can only partially inflate. The flesh of all species is poisonous.

Diet and feeding
Puffers will eat readily in the aquarium, taking finely chopped meat foods. They have a bold feeding manner.

Aquarium behaviour
Generally peaceful but occasionally may be aggressive towards other fishes. Do not keep with invertebrates.

Arothron hispidus

White-spotted Blowfish; Stars and Stripes Puffer

☐ **Distribution :** Indo-Pacific, Red Sea.

☐ **Length:** 500mm/20in (wild).

☐ **Diet and feeding:** Finely chopped meat foods. Cruncher.

☐ **Aquarium behaviour:** Peaceful. Do not keep with invertebrates.

☐ **Invertebrate compatibility:** No, will eat invertebrates.

The distinctive features of this species are the number of bluish white spots over the patchy grey body. These spots are not so pronounced in adult fishes. Just behind the gill cover, and at the base of the pectoral fins, there is a dark patch surrounded by a circular yellow pattern. Like most puffers, the flesh is poisonous. The caudal fin is often seen clamped shut and plays little part in propulsion. Pufferfish have their teeth fused together to form four powerful teeth at the front of the mouth, which they use to crunch up molluscs and crustaceans.

Left: Arothron hispidus
Like all puffers, this species will inflate its body when disturbed or frightened, but do not provoke it. Just in front of the white-rimmed eyes, two tentacle-like nostrils are visible.

Below: Arothron meleagris
Because this species is a rather large and messy eater, its tank will need good filtration and you should make sure that all traces of uneaten food are removed to avoid undue pollution.

Arothron meleagris

Spotted Puffer; Guinea Fowl Puffer; Golden Puffer

☐ **Distribution:** Indo-Pacific, Red Sea.

☐ **Length:** 300mm/12in (wild).

☐ **Diet and feeding:** Finely chopped meaty foods. Cruncher.

☐ **Aquarium behaviour:** Peaceful, but do not keep with invertebrates.

☐ **Invertebrate compatibility:** No, will eat invertebrates.

Although a plain yellow colour phase occurs, normally the brown-grey body is densely covered with white spots. When kept in a spacious aquarium, it will be less likely to release its poison under stress from other fishes. Scrupulous attention to water quality must be paid, as this fish is a very messy eater. Its unconsumed portions of food will rapidly pollute the water unless great care is taken to remove them.

Canthigaster solandri

Sharpnosed Puffer; False-eye Puffer/ Toby

☐ **Distribution:** Indo-Pacific, Red Sea.

☐ **Length:** 120mm/4.7in (wild), 50mm/2in (aquarium).

☐ **Diet and feeding:** Finely chopped meat foods. Bold cruncher.

☐ **Aquarium behaviour:** Peaceful, except towards members of its own kind.

☐ **Invertebrate compatibility:** No, will eat invertebrates.

This spectacularly patterned fish has a gold-brown body and a caudal fin covered with pale spots. A blue wavy line replaces the spots on the upper part of the body and a large white-edged black spot appears at the base of the dorsal fin. The fish swims with its caudal fin folded. The pelvic fins are absent.

Canthigaster valentini

Black-saddled Puffer; Valentine Puffer

☐ **Distribution:** Indo-Pacific.

☐ **Length:** 200mm/8in (wild), 75mm/3in (aquarium).

☐ **Diet and feeding:** Finely chopped meaty foods. Bold cruncher.

☐ **Aquarium behaviour:** Peaceful, although it has a reputation for nipping the fins of species with long fins, and may not tolerate its own kind.

☐ **Invertebrate compatibility:** No, will eat invertebrates.

The lower half of the body is cream in colour and covered with small brown dots. The upper part has four saddle-shaped dark areas; the one covering the forehead also has blue lines. These blue lines also occur on the two narrow vertical bars that reach three-quarters of the way down the sides of the fish between the head and dorsal fin. There is a final plain patch on the top of the caudal peduncle. A black spot at the base of the dorsal fin may merge with the other dark markings. The bases of the fins are red, but for the caudal fin, which is yellow. The pelvic fins are absent.

Right: Canthigaster valentini
The bold Black-saddled Puffer has strong jaws with which it can crunch coral.

Below: Canthigaster solandri
This species has an attractive spotted pattern, with bright radiating stripes around the eyes and top of the body.

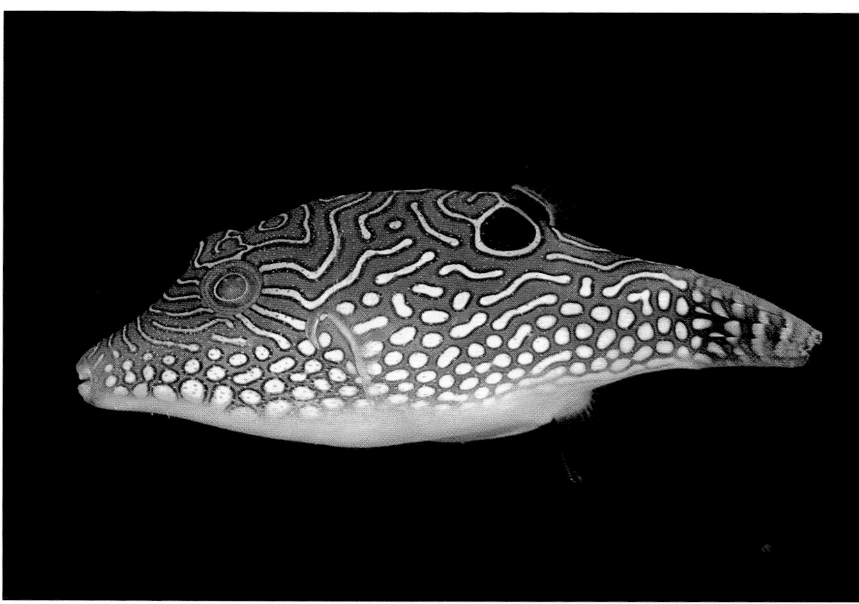

PART FIVE

TROPICAL MARINE INVERTEBRATES

There are many more species of invertebrates in the world than there are vertebrates, but within the aquarium hobby it is the fishes on which most emphasis is placed. The following section presents a selection of invertebrates suitable for the aquarium, arranged roughly in order of complexity (that is, the most biologically advanced are last). Certain species that are not recommended, either because they are dangerous to other species or to the hobbyist, or because they may not survive long in captivity are featured in Appendix Two on pages 382-383.

Fortunately, few tropical marine invertebrates are threatened with extinction, but there is concern that some may be declining in number. For example, the Queen Conch and the Spiny Lobster have traditionally been important food sources for coastal people but are increasingly becoming food for rich tourists, and some popular shells have been over collected for the ornamental shell trade. On a more positive note, it is worth remembering that, compared to the number of species caught for food or destined for the jewellery and curio market, the number of animals captured for the aquarium is very small, and with the sophisticated equipment available today, many have a good chance of surviving in the aquarium at least as long as they would have done in the wild. Finally, it is worth making the point that by observing their invertebrates, recording their findings and publishing their results, aquarists can contribute to the general fund of information about these fascinating creatures.

Left: *The Red Hermit Crab may reach the size of an adult human fist with an appetite to match, but for many marine aquarists, the strange beauty and interesting behaviour of such invertebrates make them irresistible.*

Phylum: PORIFERA

Sponges

Adocia sp.

Blue Tubular Sponge

This intensely blue species is imported fairly regularly from Indonesia, but is never available in large quantities. Damaged specimens will turn progressively whiter as the living cells die, leaving behind the supporting structure. Once it has recovered from the initial transition from one tank to another, the Blue Tubular Sponge is very hardy and grows surprisingly rapidly, particularly in an aquarium with fairly slow-moving water. Given suitable conditions it will also grow quickly from small pieces. Never remove any sponges from the water; if air pockets form within them they will decline and die.

In the wild, many small animals live within sponges and, on rare occasions, small crabs, shrimps and gobies are found in imported specimens. Other animals may live on the outer surface. Try to avoid introducing 'undesirable' subjects into the tank.

Below: Adocia sp.
Few other invertebrates are blue, so this easy-to-maintain animal provides a bold splash of colour in the aquarium. In slack or slow-moving water this species will develop a branching form.

Axinellid sp.

Orange Cup Sponge

Sri Lanka, Singapore and Indonesia are the main sources of supply for this yellow-orange species with its distinctive cup or bowl shape. They often prove to be one of the hardiest species but, unfortunately, are often shipped in insufficient water, leaving the edges exposed to the air so that they may turn pale and begin to crumble. It is important to check that all sponges are intact before you buy them. Ensure that the tank is not brightly illuminated when you introduce this sponge and that there is sufficient water movement to prevent debris accumulating in the cup. Growth is slow. Several other types of yellow or orange sponges are regularly imported and most do well in the right conditions.

Right: Axinellid sp.
The Indo-Pacific Orange Cup Sponge is readily available and easy to maintain if you prevent algae from smothering it.

Haliclona compressa

Red Tree Sponge

This bright orange-red species is very common in the Caribbean Sea and regularly imported. Most specimens are about 20cm (8in) tall, but larger examples are sometimes available and, with their interesting branched habit, they provide a dramatic splash of colour. It is important to select a specimen with the base attached to a piece of rock and with no white or pale patches on the arms. This species appreciates a reasonable water flow and, like all sponges, prefers somewhat dim lighting conditions. In too bright a situation, the branches often become covered with encrusting algae that choke the sponge and eventually kill it.

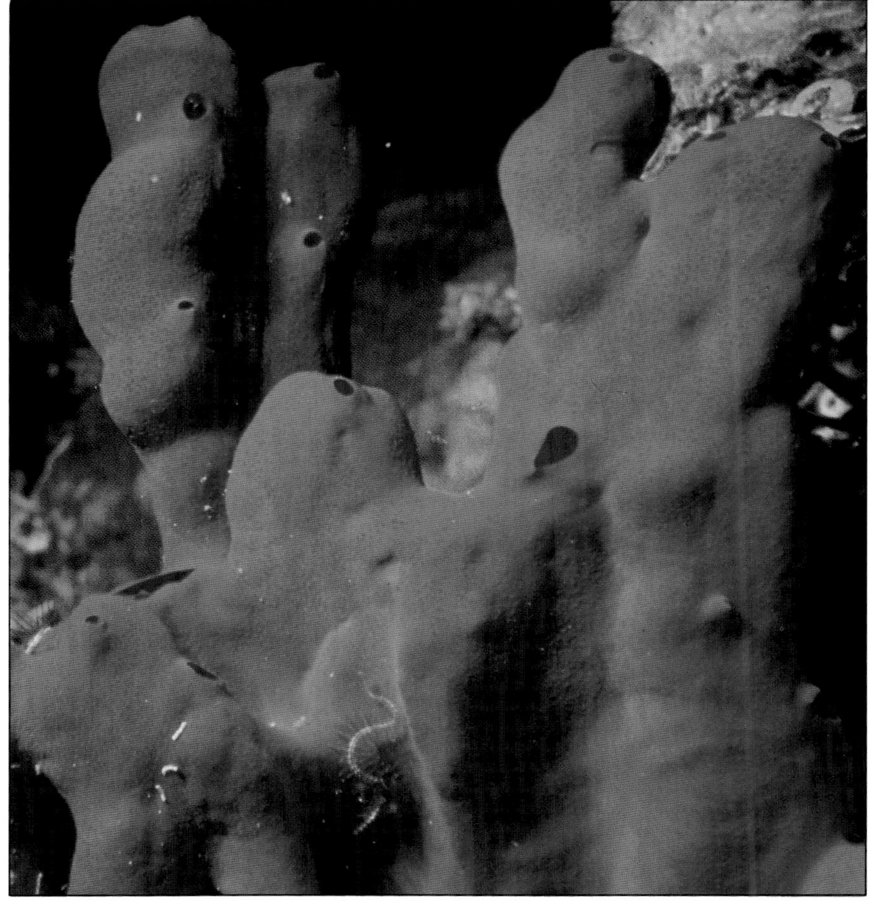

Right: Haliclona compressa
This striking Red Sea species is typically beige-pink but, as with many sponges, the colour is very variable. Avoid damaged specimens and do not allow them to touch corals or anemones.

Phylum: CNIDARIA

Hard Corals, Horny Corals, Jellyfish, Polyps, Sea Anemones, Sea Pens, Soft Corals

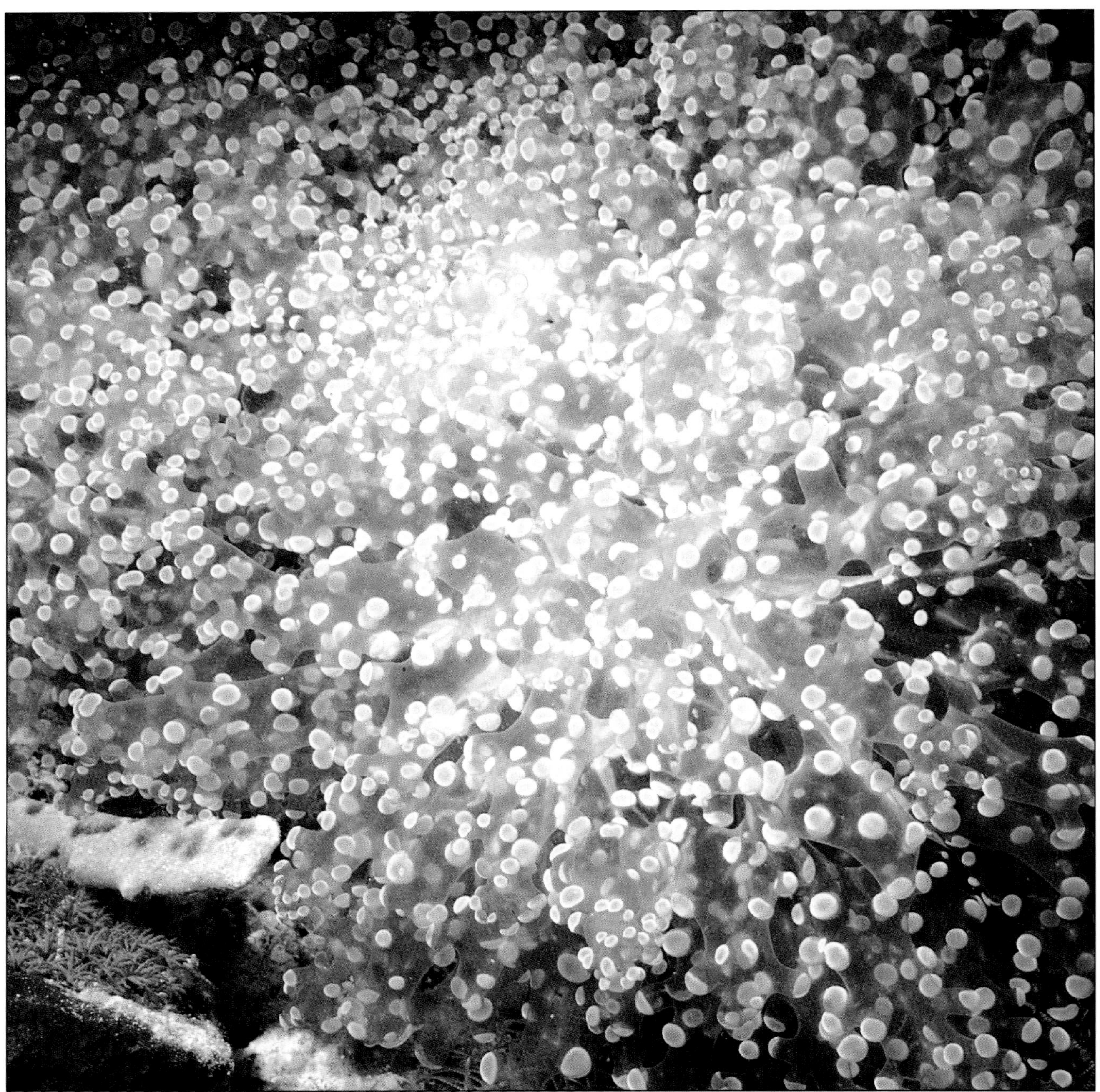

Above: Euphyllia divisa
A species known as Frogspawn Coral.

HARD, TRUE OR STONY CORALS

Euphyllia sp.
Vase Coral; Frogspawn Coral

Considerable confusion still surrounds the nomenclature of many corals and, until recently, much classification work was based solely on the dead coral skeletons, with no consideration of the living animal. Much of this confusion is found in the genus *Euphyllia,* which includes several well-known and popular corals.

The tentacles of all these specimens are very pronounced and comparable with those of sea anemones, although they vary in shape. Vase Coral may have round or crescent-tipped tentacles, while those of Frogspawn Coral are semi-transparent and irregularly bubblelike. An exception is Fox Coral, in which the polyps are like a row of flat toadstools. All species require optimum water and lighting conditions, otherwise lifespans will be unnaturally short.

Euphyllia picteti
Tooth Coral

Euphyllia picteti has only become widely available in the past few years, but is already firmly established as a favourite and specimens are quickly snapped up. When deflated they are fairly unprepossessing, but within a few hours of introduction to the tank they swell to four times the area of their supporting skeleton. The flesh is usually a fluorescent green, or occasionally blue, lined with anemonelike tentacles that frequently have vivid orange tips. The green colouring is due to the coral's symbiotic algae, so strong lighting is essential. This coral will take sizeable pieces of food and the tentacles pack a powerful sting; they are quite capable of raising a painful rash on a careless aquarist's arm, or killing any sessile invertebrates placed too close to them in the aquarium. Excellent water conditions are essential for long-term success.

Above: Euphyllia picteti
This beautiful species is popular, but often more costly than related species.

Above: Favites sp.
In this striking picture, a Red Sea species demonstrates the surprising ability of many corals to fluoresce under ultraviolet light. Providing that you choose a whole specimen that is not damaged, it should do well in the invertebrate aquarium. Unfortunately, many of the specimens seen for sale have been hacked from a larger coral head and invariably die in captivity.

Favites sp.
Moon Coral

These attractive dark green corals are closely related to the Brain Corals (see page 310), but here the meanders are subdivided into numerous single pockets, each housing a polyp. The polyps are interlinked, which causes a major problem with this type of coral. All too often the specimens received by importers are merely pieces hacked from large coral heads and in these cases, even with the best care, they almost invariably die. *Favites* are among the most light-sensitive corals, but can take supplementary food. If decorative algae are growing in the tank, ensure that leaf fronds do not rob the coral of light. Moon Corals fluoresce in ultraviolet light.

Galaxea fascicularis

Star Coral

This distinctive coral has a very attractive skeleton. Small stubs arise from the central core, with polyps sitting on each of the star-shaped ends. Singapore is the main source of this brown species, but as there are often considerable losses in transport it has not achieved any great popularity.

The Star Coral is by no means impossible to keep, but it requires similar conditions to *Goniopora* (see below) and cannot be recommended for the newcomer to the hobby.

Goniopora lobata

G. lobata is common throughout the Indo-Pacific and is one of the most frequently imported corals. Its attractive feathery appearance, combined with its usually low price, ensures that this is often the first stony coral that many aquarists keep. Unfortunately, it is not necessarily a good choice, since it demands perfect water conditions and very good lighting.

Without sufficient light, the zooxanthellae will not function properly, and with too much food in the water, the polyps will not expand. Furthermore, *Goniopora* species are easily damaged. The polyps are not individual animals, rather outgrowths from the skin covering the ball-like skeleton. When the animal inflates with water to expand the polyps, the skin is stretched taut, becomes thin and is easily punctured. Sea urchins, sharp-footed crustaceans and tumbles from rocks are major causes of such punctures, which usually lead to a persistent infection that quickly engulfs the coral.

There are several species of *Goniopora;* one of the most attractive has rather thin, creamy polyps with purple centres. Treat them with great care. The *Porites* corals of the Caribbean and Pacific are closely related, but rarely imported and just as difficult to maintain in captivity.

Above: Galaxea fascicularis
Star Coral is rarely seen in good condition, but here the colour is good and polys extended. This species is not for beginners; it requires perfect water conditions and excellent lighting.

Below: Goniopora lobata
Stony corals should be erect and well expanded. Bacterial infection may result if the flesh is damaged. Shrinking polyps indicate poor lighting and water; always provide the best of both.

Heliofungia actiniformis
Plate Coral

The various species of *Heliofungia* are easily confused with sea anemones, since their circular or oval bodies are covered with long tentacles that completely hide the ridged skeleton.

Most corals are a collection of polyps, but *Heliofungia* is a solitary polyp with one central mouth. Zooxanthellae can tint them green or pink. As well as deriving nourishment from the zooxanthellae, *Heliofungia* will take chopped fish and shrimp in small quantities in the aquarium.

Heliofungia fare best when placed directly onto a coral sand substrate where they can receive good light and a moderate flow of water. Do not position them on rocks, otherwise the delicate tissue around the edge of the coral may tear and open up a path for infection. When buying specimens, check that all the tentacles are erect and that there are no bald patches.

H. actiniformis is roughly circular, as are most of the related species, but *Herpolitha limax*, which sports many short, brown tentacles, forms a long oval.

Leptoria sp.
Brain Coral

Brain corals can reach massive proportions, but small specimens are strongly recommended for an aquarium with good lighting. The optimum size for aquarium specimens is about 10-15cm (4-6in); larger ones tend to be damaged in transport. Most species are various shades of brown, but some are a vivid green and others a pale purple-pink. Brain corals receive much of their food from the action of symbiotic algae, but they will supplement this with plankton.

Occasionally, you may see small tentacles around the edges of the sinuous channels of the Brain Coral. These can be extended to sting nearby corals and are particularly prominent in the closely related Caribbean species, *Meandrina meandrites.*

Right: Leptoria sp.
It's easy to see how this species gained the common name 'Brain Coral'. One of nature's most fascinating structures.

Below: Heliofungia actiniformis
Here, the tentacles are semi extended, revealing the green-tinged body.

Plerogyra sinuosa
Bubble Coral

This accommodating species can be highly recommended as a first stony coral. The common name is a very apt description, for during the day the polyp mouths and tentacles are covered in a mass of bubbles. These may be fawn coloured in the best specimens. At night, the bubbles deflate somewhat and the coral erects flowing, 6cm (2.4in)-long stinging tentacles to capture small shrimps in the wild. In the aquarium this coral will accept whole shrimps and pieces of fish gently tucked among the bubbles. If regularly fed, a Bubble Coral can increase its expanded diameter by some 50 percent within a few weeks. Weekly feeding is sufficient and even this can be suspended if the coral is given sufficient light.

The best specimens come from Sri Lanka and Indonesia, but somewhat similar species, often greenish or light brown, are found throughout the Indo-Pacific. Do not place any coral species too close to one another.

Below: Plerogyra sinuosa
Like many other corals, this species possesses zooxanthellae algae within its tissues. Intense lighting is essential if it is to reach full potential.

Above: Tubastrea aurea
When it expands – which it does mainly at night – T. aurea *is a most dramatic coral, resembling a bunch of golden chrysanthemums.*

Tubastrea aurea
Sun Coral

This vivid orange coral lives at the mouth of, or inside, caves and crevices in Indo-Pacific reefs. It is an extremely common species and large numbers are exported annually. Living as they do in a shady habitat, they have no need of symbiotic algae and rely on trapping food particles with their abundant yellowish tentacles.

Place the coral in a shady spot in the tank and consider each polyp as an individual small anemone. If it is reluctant to open, tempt the polyps to expand and 'flower' by squeezing a shrimp head into the water. A few minutes later the polyps will open and you can feed each one a small piece of shrimp.

Newly introduced Sun Corals may not open for a week or more. From then on, if properly fed, you can expect the colony to expand by producing new polyps at the base of the mature ones. In the wild, colonies grow up to 50cm (20in) across, but 10cm (4in) is a more normal size in the aquarium.

There are several similar species, of which the Indonesian *Balanophyllia gemmifera* is a good choice for the aquarium. It is larger and even easier to feed than *T. aurea.* The related species *Dendrophyllia gracilis* has an attractive branchlike form and is only infrequently offered for sale. *Tubastrea aurea* requires optimum water conditions.

Above: Tubipora musica
The structure of its red skeleton has given rise to the common name of this attractive coral. Aquarium specimens are usually broken from larger heads.

Tubipora musica
Organ Pipe Coral

This species is much more familiar to aquarists as a dead skeleton for tank decoration than as a living animal. It is one of the few corals with a naturally red skeleton, a very attractive feature when not overgrown with algae. When it is alive, the top of the interlinked red pipelike skeleton houses a mass of short but active brown polyps. These pulse with the flow of water in similar fashion to *Anthelia* (see page 324). The polyps are all interconnected and, as specimens are usually fragments of much larger pieces, their life in the aquarium is generally limited.

HORNY CORALS

Gorgonia flabellum
Sea Fan

Sea Fans are very closely related to Sea Whips, but in this species one main branch grows out in a very flat plane, the myriad small offshoots linking together to form a lace-fan appearance. Sea Fans are particularly common on Caribbean reefs, and at one time many were collected for the curio trade. Fortunately, this practice is now greatly reduced, but dried specimens of Sea Fans and Sea Whips are still occasionally offered as aquarium decoration.

When properly cured (i.e. made safe for aquarium use), Sea Fans should look like black lace. Before cleaning, they are often yellow or pink and should never be used in this state, as the dried tissue will rot in the tank and pose a major pollution problem. Although Sea Fans are more difficult to maintain than Sea Whips, they can survive in captivity, so let us hope that the dried Sea Fan trade will soon be a thing of the past.

Small, 15cm (6in) specimens are best for the aquarium, as larger animals are difficult to transport without damaging the tissue.

Muricea muricata
Sea Whip

This Caribbean species is one of many that produce a cluster of 'finger', or whiplike, extensions. Sea Whips are found throughout the tropics, usually in areas of strong water movement, and appear in all the colours of the rainbow. Most are fairly easy to maintain, the thicker fingered species having proved generally the most hardy.

Like Leather Corals, the best specimens are attached to a small portion of stone or coral. This ensures that the base is not broken and allows you to position the animal in a water current without risk of the soft flesh rubbing against the rockwork. When buying specimens, check that all the fingers are intact and that there are no exposed areas of dark chitinous skeleton. Bacterial infection can easily begin at such sites.

In nocturnal Sea Whips, the mat of small polyps only emerges at night. Under ideal conditions, they may grown 2.5cm (1in) a month.

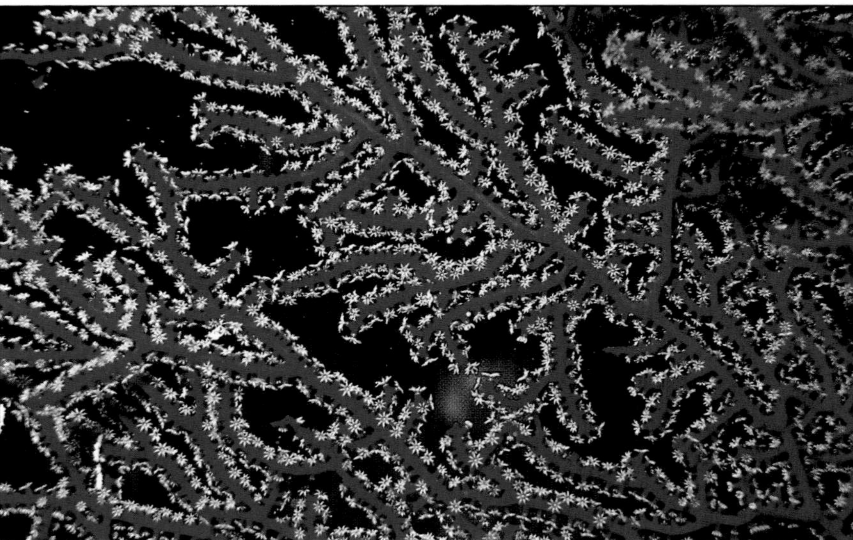

Top: Gorgonia flabellum
This close-up view clearly shows the structure of a typical Sea Fan.

Above: Muricea muricata
Feed sparingly when polyps are extended. Good water circulation in the tank is essential.

JELLYFISH

Cassiopeia andromeda
Upside-down Jellyfish

Jellyfish are familiar to beachcombers throughout the world, but virtually unknown within the hobby. *C. andromeda* is the only species ever offered for sale and the only one suitable for the aquarium. It is found throughout the Red Sea and the Indo-Pacific region and can reach up to 30cm (12in) in diameter. Only small specimens, up to 8cm (3.2in), are generally available.

Most jellyfish trail their arms behind them as they swim, but *Cassiopeia* spends much of its time lying on the substrate, with its tentacles upwards, wafting in the current. Among the tentacles are small bladderlike growths, filled with zooxanthellae that provide much of the animal's food. It therefore needs intense lighting, and you can supplement the diet with newly hatched brineshrimp. However, even with the best care, it rarely lives long in an aquarium and should therefore be left to experienced aquarists.

Below: Cassiopeia andromeda
This species needs a specialized aquarium, with intense lighting, optimum water quality, a soft sandy substrate and plenty of room.

POLYPS

Rhodactis spp.
Mushroom Polyps

Mushroom Polyps – or Mushroom Anemones, as they are sometimes known – are available as colonies clustered on small pieces of rock. They have been one of the staple additions to the invertebrate tank for many years, but are still justifiably popular with hobbyists.

There are many species; most of them measure 2-5cm (0.8-2in) in diameter, although a few giants can reach 15-20cm (6-8in), and these are very dramatic. Most species are green or brown, and often the two colours are combined in radiating stripes. Reddish brown and blue specimens are available from Indonesia but are somewhat expensive. It has been found that these red and blue pigments act as a light filter, which prevents the animal being 'sunburnt'. If the aquarium is not brightly illuminated, these attractive colours disappear, allowing more light through to the zooxanthellae, but resulting in a drab, brownish animal.

A particularly attractive species, with a rather tufted appearance to its pale bluish green polyps, is often found on living rock imported from the Caribbean.

Zoanthus sociatus
Green Polyps

There is a huge range of *Zoanthus* species and their relatives, all of which are generally sold under the title 'polyp colony'. The zoanthids mark something of a halfway house between the corals and the sea anemones. The polyps are usually found in clusters and are often interconnected at the base. However, they have many more tentacles than the true corals and no calcareous skeleton. All the 'polyp colonies' are among the easiest species in the phylum Cnidaria to keep. Most require good water quality and good lighting, but very little else. In good conditions, mature polyps often multiply by budding new, small polyps at the base so allow room for new growth.

Most species are coloured in various shades of green, brown and beige, or combinations of the three, but several bright yellow types are also regularly available.

Top: Rhodactis spp.
The many forms of Rhodactis *all have the typical mushroom shape seen here.*

Above: Zoanthus sociatus
Coral polyps are one of the mainstays of the reef tank and usually easy to keep.

SEA ANEMONES

Anthopsis koseirensis
Pink Malu Anemone

This attractive pinkish purple species is structurally very similar to *Heteractis malu* (see page 320) and is widely considered to be a colour form of the latter species – hence the common name. *A. koseirensis* is rather less common in the wild than *H. malu* and commands a higher price, but its appealing coloration, ease of maintenance and the willingness of all species of clownfishes to form a commensal relationship with it justifies its cost. It is particularly attractive if the illumination is supplemented with a red-enhancing light.

In the past, many anemones were artificially coloured by immersing them in a solution of food colouring to produce blue, green, orange and scarlet specimens. While the food dye itself appeared to cause no obvious problems, few specimens survived long after this treatment – possibly because of the effect it had on the colour of light reaching the vital zooxanthellae. Fortunately, this practice seems to have died out, but you should treat with suspicion any malu anemones in colours other than purple-pink, pale yellow and pale brown.

Below: Anthopsis koseirensis
This beautiful pink species is popular with hobbyists and clownfishes. This one houses a pair of Common Clowns.

Condylactis gigantea
Caribbean Anemone

This long-tentacled anemone is the most popular and commonly exported species from the Caribbean sea. The body can be white, brown or pink, and the tentacles are usually pink or white with a more intense pink tip.

Condylactis are very easy to keep, requiring only moderate lighting and a steady, but not vigorous, water flow. They are easily fed by dropping small pieces of fish or shrimp among the tentacles once or twice a week. As a general rule, do not feed anemones with a liquid invertebrate diet.

Despite their pleasant colouring and ease of maintenance, however, *Condylactis* are not as popular as the Pacific anemones, because the various *Amphiprion* clownfishes will only very rarely set up home within their tentacles.

Above: Condylactis gigantea
The common Caribbean Anemone is found in a variety of colours.

Heteractis aurora
Sand Anemone

The Sand Anemone's scientific name has undergone a change (Dunn 1981), from *Radianthus simplex*. This greyish white species is easily distinguished by its tentacles, which are thickened to give a ringed appearance and have a tendency to lie flat against the surface disc. These are among the commonest anemones in their Indo-Pacific home range.

As their common name suggests, they are happiest placed on the substrate, rather than on rockwork, and will often anchor their foot through the sand and onto the undergravel filter plate or base glass of the tank. When disturbed, they can rapidly deflate and disappear beneath the substrate, thus escaping the attention of predators.

H. aurora is a small species, rarely more than 15cm (6in) in diameter, and is easy to feed with small pieces of fish or shrimp once or twice a week. Although easy to maintain for long periods, it is often thought to have only limited attraction for clownfishes. However, several *Amphiprion* species have been recorded with this anemone and *Amphiprion clarkii* have been observed with *H. aurora* in reef areas off Borneo. It is a very suitable species for the beginner or the hobbyist on a limited budget.

Below: Heteractis aurora
The Sand Anemone is common on coral gravel beds in lagoons and at reef edges.

Heteractis magnifica

Purple Base Anemone

Heteractis magnifica is one of the large anemones that regularly plays host to clownfishes. Previously known as *Radianthus ritteri,* it was one of the few whose scientific name seemed to cause no confusion! Unfortunately, the new name *Heteractis magnifica* (Dunn 1981) has been very slow to achieve the same familiarity.

This anemone is found throughout the Indian Ocean and the Indo-Pacific region. Specimens from Sri Lanka typically have a purple body with buff or light brown tentacles. A more attractive form with a scarlet body and pure white tentacles is exported from Kenya. Both are easy to keep, but in good conditions they may reach 70cm (27.5in) in diameter and quickly grow too large for all but the biggest aquarium.

At first sight, *H. magnifica,* like all anemones, appears rooted in one position, but this particular species has an annoying habit of climbing slowly up the tank glass, thus presenting a rather unattractive view to the aquarist. By gently teasing the foot loose with the ball of the thumb, you can easily move them, but take great care to avoid tearing the very delicate flesh.

Below: Heteractis magnifica
The large Heteractis magnifica *is often included in shipments from Sri Lanka. This beautiful anemone is a popular aquarium species, which, under good lighting and water conditions thrives, making an ideal host to clownfishes.*

Heteractis malu

Malu Anemone

Until recently, this species was widely known as *Radianthus malu* and will be much more familiar to experienced aquarists under this name. Malu Anemones are imported in large numbers from Singapore, Indonesia and the Philippines, and are one of the staples of the hobby. *H. malu* is very attractive to clownfishes and an ideal species for most invertebrate aquariums.

Specimens are available in sizes ranging from 10 to 40cm (4 to 16in) in diameter, but they are capable of growing even larger. All the colour forms of the Malu Anemone display the distinctive purple-red tips to the tentacles, which are regularly tapered, up to 5cm (2in) long and evenly spaced across the disc.

Given intense illumination, the lighter forms will turn brown with the development of the zooxanthellae algae that supply much of the anemone's nutritional requirements. In most situations, you can offer *H. malu* a similar diet to *H. aurora* and, like all anemones, it will benefit from regular additions of a vitamin supplement.

This species is more likely to stay where you put it than some others, but it is quite capable of moving if your choice of site is not suitable. When introducing this species, and other anemones, to the tank, ensure that they do not rest 'face-down' on the sand. Anemones 'breathe' through the tentacles and quickly die if water movement around the tentacles is restricted.

Remember that all anemones accumulate waste products within their body cavities. To void these, they periodically collapse, pumping out the stale and polluted water within their body and often producing a stream of brown mucus at the same time. Occasionally, a sizeable anemone may shrink to the size of a golf ball. This is not a matter for concern, provided it does not happen more than once a day and the anemone does not stay closed for more than 24 hours. In this event, it may be taken as a sign that a major change of the aquarium water is overdue. Many anemones will contract when lacking in sufficient illumination or as a result of poor water conditions.

Below: Heteractis malu
Clownfishes rarely venture far from their host anemone and even lay their eggs under its protective mantle.

Heteractis sp.
Gelam Anemone

In this species we have another example of the confusion that exists in the specific names for anemones. Although it is considered here as a *Heteractis* species, Gelam Anemones are structurally different from the Malu Anemones with which they share their genus name. Gelam Anemones have shorter tentacles – which often have swollen tips – hence the alternative common name of Bubble Anemones.

Their small size – up to 20cm (8in) – and good colouring make them justifiably popular. The most attractive Gelam Anemones have rusty red tentacles and the very best have purple bodies. They are easy to keep, feeding on small pieces of shrimp or shellfish, and most clownfishes will use them.

Gelam Anemones have a tendency to roam around the aquarium, but can be encouraged to settle if they are placed in an opened clam shell or between two scallop shells wedged into the substrate. They usually confine themselves to the lower half of the tank, unlike *H. magnifica,* which often seeks out the highest point. This species is particularly soft bodied; check that there are no tears in the body, as these usually prove fatal. Avoid buying very pale specimens, which have lost their symbiotic algae.

Left: Heteractis sp.
A typical feature of the Gelam Anemones are the swollen tips to the tentacles. The body may be red-purple or brown and is normally hidden among the rocks.

Pachycerianthus mana
Fireworks Anemone; Tube Anemone

The ceriantbid anemones are an interesting group found in all the world's warmer waters. Their chief characteristic is that they live within a tube formed of mucus and detritus gleaned from the soft substrates they inhabit. They also have many very long, thin tentacles and a very powerful sting.

P. mana is an Indo-Pacific species that often has banded tentacles, while other close relatives show colours ranging from pure white, through yellow to maroon and near-black. Here again, the strength of their sting precludes them from acting as hosts for clownfish. Their 20cm (8in)-long tentacles make them a threat to neighbouring invertebrates and fishes.

Cerianthids are night feeders, usually remaining in their tubes during daylight hours. They are easy to feed on finely chopped fish and shrimp every other day, but in view of the risk they pose to other animals, think carefully before introducing them to a well-populated aquarium.

Left: Pachycerianthus mana
The Fireworks Anemone lives up to its common name in appearance. Its tentacles are lined with very powerful poisonous stinging cells.

Above: Stoichactis gigas
This giant anemone has a powerful sting; avoid keeping it with other anemones or close to corals. It is popular with clownfishes and green and brown specimens are often available.

Stoichactis gigas
Carpet Anemone; Blanket Anemone

As the scientific name would suggest, this is one of the largest species of sea anemone, with wild specimens approaching 1m (39in) in diameter. Smaller specimens are popular with aquarists, but are no longer as readily available as in previous years, when large numbers were exported from Sri Lanka. Most were white or pale brown, but there was a steady supply of blue, purple and fluorescent green specimens. These are now rare in the hobby and command high prices. Nonetheless, this is a very hardy and long-lived species and worth seeking out.

All anemones have stinging cells with which they catch plankton, small fish and crustaceans, but this is one of the few in the hobby that can sting man. The short (1cm/0.4in), densely packed tentacles feel very sticky when touched; their effect is one of multitudes of barbed stinging cells being fired into the flesh. Stings on particularly sensitive areas, such as the wrist and inside of the forearms, can produce an annoying rash that may last several days or, on rare occasions, considerably longer.

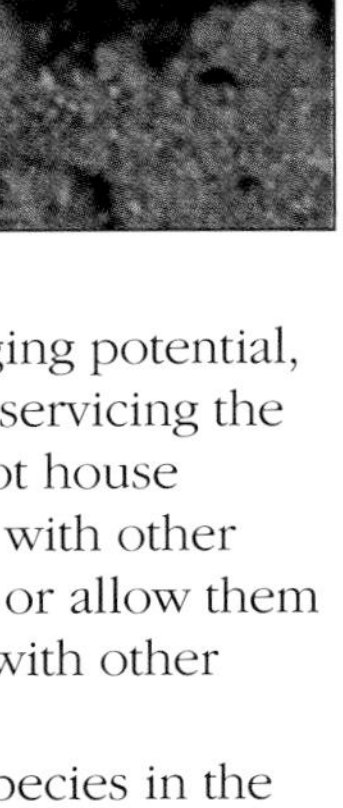

In view of this stinging potential, be very careful when servicing the aquarium – and do not house *Stoichactis* anemones with other families of anemones or allow them to come into contact with other invertebrates.

You can feed this species in the same way as the Gelam Anemones, but you may find it necessary to wriggle the food into the tentacles to elicit a stinging response before the food is passed to the central mouth and engulfed.

SEA PEN

Cavernularia obesa
Sea Pen

Sea Pens are an attractive and interesting group of animals, only rarely seen within the hobby. Their central tubular body is supported by a calcium 'spine' that resembles the quill of a feather, hence their common name. A distinct foot burrows into the substrate and anchors the animal in position in the fairly turbulent waters that they often inhabit.

During the day, the body, which may be orange, yellow buff or white, is contracted. Throughout the night, and occasionally during daylight hours, the body expands and previously hidden feathery polyps appear all over the animal as it starts to feed on plankton and organic detritus. Sea Pens can give off an eerie greenish blue light when disturbed. They move slowly through the sand and, in view of their habits, are not suitable for the total system aquarium with a shallow substrate.

Below: Cavernularia obesa
At night-time, the delicately branched polyps expand in the water current to capture minute food particles.

SOFT CORALS

Anthelia glauca
Pulse Coral

The Pulse Corals are a comparatively recent introduction to the hobby, but as Indonesian imports become more common they are justifiably increasing in popularity. *Anthelia* and the closely related *Xenia elongata* are two of the easiest corals to keep and both can be expected to spread and multiply in the aquarium.

Anthelia consists of a cluster of very feathery polyps that join at the base to form a foot anchoring the coral to a rocky substrate. *X. elongata* is similar but more treelike, the body splitting into branches that bear the polyps. The common name for both these corals comes from the continual rhythmic opening and closing of the polyps as they appear to feed. Both species require adequate lighting and appreciate a good current of water.

Above: Xenia elongata
Although very similar to Anthelia glauca, *this species of soft coral has a more branched appearance. Both need good lighting and water circulation.*

Below: Anthelia glauca
The attractive Pulse Coral is highly recommended for the invertebrate aquarium. It spreads quickly, colonizing neighbouring rocks.

Dendronephthya rubeola

Red Cauliflower Coral

This delicately branched species is one of the most attractive of the soft corals and the easiest of several lookalike species to maintain. *D. rubeola* lives on sand and mud sediments in the Indo-Pacific, where it anchors itself into position with a number of thick, fleshy, rootlike growths from its base. This method of attachment makes it much easier to collect this species than *Dendronephthya klunzingeri,* for example, which anchors itself to rocks and is easily damaged during collection.

During the day, these species contract into a red-and-white ball. The loose calcareous spicules, which support the flesh like a disjointed skeleton, project through the skin and make an uncomfortable handful. At night, or under subdued lighting, the animal takes in water to feed. Very large specimens reach over 1m (39in) in height, but more typical aquarium specimens are 15-20cm (6-8in) high. All the Cauliflower Corals feed on the very smallest particles.

Sarcophyton trocheliophorum

Leather Coral; Elephant Ear Coral

The Leather Corals are very widespread throughout the Indo-Pacific tropical seas and *S. trocheliophorum* is the most frequently imported. The common name comes from both the texture and colour of the animal when it retracts its polyps.

In the wild, they can form soft, undulated plates over 1m (39in) in diameter, the top surface clothed with a carpet of 1cm (0.4in)-high, delicate polyps. One of the best forms for the aquarium grows as a convoluted mushroom. Given good lighting, they fare very well and can be expected to increase in size.

When disturbed, the polyps retract and it is not unusual for them to take several days to re-open when, for example, they are transferred from one aquarium to another. This species can be strongly recommended as a first coral for the beginner. The best specimens are attached to a small piece of rock. Make sure that the base is undamaged, with no decomposing white areas. Use a small-bore siphon to remove any sediment that accumulates within the 'mushroom'.

Top: Dendronephthya rubeola
The coloured Cauliflower Corals require a constant supply of fine food and good water movement to survive. Specimens grow rapidly under good conditions.

Above: Sarcophyton trocheliophorum
The mushroom-shaped Leather Coral expands its polyps to feed. With the right conditions, it will grow steadily.

Phylum: PLATYHELMINTHES

Flatworms

Pseudoceros splendidus
Red-rim Flatworm

This vivid red, black and white species is one of the few occasionally offered for sale. Although somewhat nocturnal in its habits, it usually does well if not subject to predation. The bright colours of this group of animals are believed to serve a protective function, and few fish will eat them because of their foul-tasting mucus. However, many crabs and shrimps will quickly devour, or badly damage, flatworms. There are many small and insignificant species, one of these – reddish brown and 3-4mm (0.12-0.16in) long – can reach plague proportions (see page 384). Always remove it from a living reef aquarium, as there is no predator that will eliminate it naturally without damaging other desirable invertebrates.

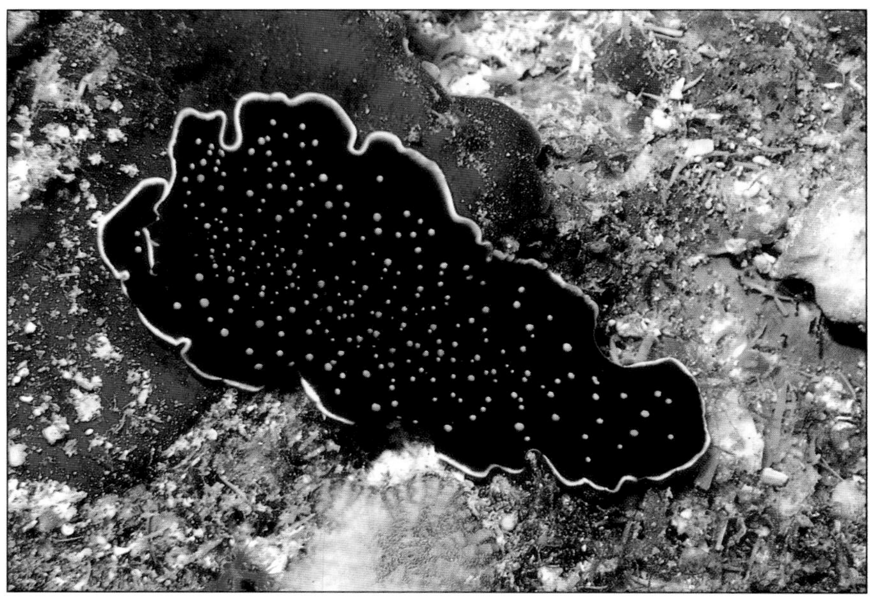

Above: Thysanozoon flavomaculatum
In the past, this attractive species was occasionally imported by accident among shipments of living rock.

Below: Pseudoceros splendidus
Most flatworm species are nocturnal, but Pseudoceros splendidus *appears during the day, when its coloration, warning of a foul taste, deters predators.*

Phylum: ANNELIDA

Segmented Worms

SABELLID SPECIES (FANWORMS)

Sabellastarte magnifica; S. sanctijosephi

Fanworm; Featherduster Worm; Tubeworm

Among the huge numbers of featherduster worms and tubeworms imported each year from Singapore, Sri Lanka and Indonesia, these particular species are justifiably popular. The body of the worm is encased in a parchment tube buried in the substrate, with the feathery head extended for feeding. At the approach of danger, the feathery tentacles are very rapidly withdrawn into the tube. They are not fussy about their lighting requirements and are easily satisfied with brineshrimp *nauplii* and rotifers.

It is by no means unusual for these species to reproduce in the home aquarium. When this is about to happen, the first signs are usually evident early in the morning, when the animals emit smoky plumes of either eggs or sperm. The adult worms then often shed their feathery heads, which prevents them eating the larvae that develop very shortly after the fertilization process is complete.

Tubeworms also shed their 'feathers' if attacked by predators, as well as in response to poor water conditions or the shock of being moved. If this happens, remove the head but leave the tube in position, and after two or three weeks a short, stubby feathered head will normally reappear and eventually grow back to its former glory.

Below: Sabellastarte magnifica
Featherduster worms are imported in huge numbers, and in a wide variety of colours, from Sri Lanka, Singapore and Indonesia, and are ideal for newcomers to the marine aquarium hobby. The cilia, or 'feathers', clearly visible here, are used to trap fine particles of food, which are then channelled to the creature's central mouth.

SERPULID COLONIES (TUBEWORMS)

Serpulid worms differ from Sabellids in that they produce a stony tube and are usually considerably smaller. The most commonly available species lives in colonies, with its tubes embedded in *Porites* coral. The 1cm (0.4in) diameter worms are often very brightly coloured, with heads of red, blue, black, white and yellow – in contrast to the beige through brown to maroon heads of *Sabellastarte*. *Spirobranchus giganteus,* the Christmas Tree Worm, is common in the Caribbean and the Indo-Pacific. It is so-named on account of the two branches of spiralling tentacles that emerge from the tube. Featherduster clusters from the Caribbean are small intertwined clumps of rocky tubed Serpulid Worms, usually with red- or rust-coloured heads. Take care that these species do not become overgrown with algae.

Above: Serpulid sp.
This large Serpulid species is a fairly demanding variety and easily damaged.

Below: Serpulid sp.
This small but attractive Caribbean species lives in small aggregations.

Phylum: CHELICERATA

Horseshoe Crabs

Limulus polyphemus

Horseshoe Crab; King Crab

The Horseshoe Crab is not in fact a crab, but is more closely related to spiders, scorpions and mites than to crabs. The few living species are the only representatives of a very ancient lineage. *Limulus polyphemus* is the largest species and can reach 50cm (20in) in size. It is found on mud and sand flats on the east coast of America. Small specimens are available on the American market, but in Europe one of the three western Pacific species is more likely to be on offer. These do not grow as large and make entertaining, if somewhat clumsy, aquarium specimens. They spend a large part of their time burrowing under the substrate and can play a valuable role in keeping the sand loose in undergravel filter systems.

Worms, algae and small shellfish form the natural diet of Horseshoe Crabs. They are unlikely to find sufficient food if left to scavenge, so provide small particles of squid, cockles and shrimps.

Above: Limulus polyphemus
The Horseshoe Crab is rather a clumsy aquarium occupant and will topple delicate corals quite easily. It may be better to keep it in a species tank, where it can be given an adequate diet, and provided with room to burrow in a deep, sandy substrate, which is essential to its well-being.

Phylum: CRUSTACEA

Barnacles, Crabs, Lobsters and Shrimps

BARNACLES

Lepas anserifera
Gooseneck Barnacles

Lepas species are occasionally available, but require large quantities of fine food, which can put a strain on the filtration systems of most marine aquariums. Small conical barnacles sometimes grow up spontaneously, or may be introduced on living corals.

Left: Lepas anserifera
A small colony of Gooseneck Barnacles clustered on a piece of submerged driftwood. Although common in the tropics, they are rarely seen for sale.

Above: Lepas anserifera
Barnacles are fascinating creatures to observe, using their delicate feet to capture small, drifting particles of food and wafting them into their mouths.

Above: Calappa flammea
The Shame-faced Crab is not a retiring creature, but a powerful omnivore, capable of devouring many sessile invertebrates in its quest for food.

CRABS

Calappa flammea
Shame-faced Crab

The Shame-faced Crab is one of the few typical crab-shaped crustaceans that you might consider for the home aquarium. A number of similar species are characterized by their over-developed but weak claws. These are normally held in front of the mouthparts with just the eyes peeping over – hence their common name.

Calappa are very efficient scavengers and will also break open and eat various types of molluscs. They are well camouflaged with algal growth on the carapace, or they may spend much of their time buried beneath the substrate – a habit that makes them interesting aquarium inhabitants.

Dardanus megistos

Red Hermit Crab

Hermit crabs vary quite considerably in size and colour, from the blue-legged hermits from Singapore and the tiny thumbnail-sized species commonly shipped from the Caribbean to the giant *Aniculus maximus,* which has attractive golden yellow legs but is a fearsome predator that will devour anything that comes within reach of its powerful claws. *D. megistos* is one of the largest species, and fist-sized specimens are by no means uncommon.

Unlike most crabs, the hermit crab's abdomen extends out from the body, with no hard protective shell on the rear. It protects itself by taking over the shells of various univalve molluscs – often by eating the previous and rightful owner. Despite the weight of some of these shells, hermit crabs are very active climbers and their inquisitive nature endears them to many hobbyists. However, they have very catholic tastes and a large specimen is capable of causing considerable damage within a well-stocked living-reef aquarium. They are useful scavengers, particularly in tanks with sizeable fishes, but will rarely fit into the average aquarium set-up.

Above: Dardanus megistos
Given its size and large appetite, this crab is better suited to a species tank.

Below: Lybia tessellata
An attractive crab for a smaller tank with suitable benign companions.

Lybia tessellata

Boxing Crab

The small Boxing Crabs rarely grow more than 3cm (1.2in) long and make ideal aquarium occupants, particularly for small tanks, where they will not get 'lost in the crowd'.

Boxing Crabs are the only examples of invertebrates known to use tools. While the Anemone Hermit Crab, *Pagurus prideauxi,* merely shelters beneath anemones, these small crabs collect a tiny anemone in each claw and actively wave them at encroaching predators as a warning. Furthermore, even though these crabs use their first pair of walking legs to search the substrate detritus for food, they will happily collect food from the anemones. Only when they change their exoskeleton will *Lybia* deliberately release the anemones and carefully set them aside until the new shell hardens. Then they pick them up and press them into service once more.

There are several species of *Lybia,* but the nomenclature is in some confusion. All are attractive and very interesting, well worth a place in the tank. Small pieces of meaty marine fare are readily accepted.

Neopetrolisthes ohshimai

Anemone Crab

N. ohshimai is one of a small group of porcelain crabs that have evolved an immunity to anemone stings and, like *Amphiprion* clownfishes, can live among the tentacles of their venomous hosts for protection from predators. Measuring barely 2.5cm (1in) across the carapace, they are among the smallest crabs and make ideal aquarium specimens.

The crabs live in the same types of anemones as clownfishes and will use their well-developed claws on any clownfish that tries to evict them from their chosen home. For feeding purposes, however, the crab uses feathery projections on its jaw processes to trap particulate matter. As they are so small, Anemone Crabs are particularly vulnerable when changing their shells, so provide plenty of hiding places and do not house them with larger, more aggressive crustaceans.

The Indo-Pacific *N. ohshimai* has an irregularly spotted pattern that can vary depending on where it was found. *Neopetrolisthes maculatus* is densely covered with small chocolate spots on a white background, which give it an overall pinkish appearance. The very rare *N. alobatus* from East Africa has widely spaced, almost circular, dark brown spots of varying sizes, producing a polka-dot effect.

Above: Neopetrolisthes ohshimai
An Anemone Crab in a Heteractis *anemone. This species will feel more secure housed in a fairly small tank.*

Pagurus prideauxi
Anemone Hermit Crab

Several species of *Pagurus* hermit crabs have gone one step better in their search for protection by actively encouraging certain species of stinging sea anemones to colonize their shells and ward off predators. Like all crustaceans, they periodically shed their hard outer skeleton, so be sure to include a few spare shells among the tank's decorations to provide new homes for the growing crabs.

Pagurus not only find new and suitably sized shells into which they can rapidly slip their delicate abdomens, but they also tease their anemones off the old shell and deliberately replace them on the new one. The anemones appear to accept this willingly, because as the crabs rip up their food, many small pieces drift away and into the anemones' tentacles. *Pagurus* are large, destructive crabs and will only suit the aquarist looking for a 'one-off' speciality animal.

Below: Pagurus prideauxi
This crab protects itself by encouraging anemones to colonize its shell.

Stenorhynchus seticornis
Arrow Crab

The Arrow Crab gets its common name from the distinctly triangular, arrowhead-shaped body. This feature, together with its very long thin legs, results in a creature too closely reminiscent of a spider to appeal to many tastes. This is regrettable, as Arrow Crabs are attractive, easily maintained aquarium subjects.

S. seticornis has a leg span of about 15cm (6in) and is generally well behaved, although it may pull at featherduster worms, as small, burrowing worms form a major part of its natural diet. In captivity, it will eat any meaty food and has the added advantage of being one of the few creatures that will happily consume the carnivorous, scavenging Bristleworms *(Hermodice carunculata)*, which are sometimes accidentally introduced into the aquarium.

Unless you have a very large aquarium, it is not a good idea to keep two Arrow Crabs together, as they almost invariably fight – the loser having all its legs removed before being eaten.

Below: Stenorhynchus seticornis
Within this limited family of spiderlike crabs, the Caribbean species shown here is the most readily available. Do not worry if a specimen loses a limb during transportation; it will quickly regrow. The Arrow Crab is not a swift mover, so you will have the opportunity to study it at leisure.

LOBSTERS

Enoplometopus occidentalis

Red Dwarf Lobster

This vivid red species is the most attractive of the various lobster species and, with its relatively large claws, looks like the typical fishmonger's lobster. The Red Dwarf Lobster grows to a length of about 12cm (4.7in) and looks very dramatic, but its largely nocturnal habits mean that you will generally catch only the occasional fleeting glimpse of your specimen.

Enoplometopus is highly territorial and quickly despatches any similar species and many of the more commonly available shrimps. It is also quite capable of catching and killing small fishes, particularly when these are 'dozing' at night. Think carefully before introducing *Enoplometopus* into your aquarium, since removing a particularly aggressive specimen at a later date may involve you in a complete strip down of the tank.

The similar, but rarer, pacific *E. holthuisi* is slimmer and can be easily distinguished by a white bullseye-like mark on either side of the thorax. Two rather purplish pink species are imported from the Indo-Pacific region and both are smaller than *E. occidentalis*. *E. debelius* has a pale pink body, liberally covered with almost round, purplish red spots. *E. daumi* has a pale purple-brown body, becoming more richly purple towards the head and claws. These two species are even more shy and retiring than their red relative shown left.

Left: Enoplometopus occidentalis
Naturally nocturnal, but usually learns to scavenge in daylight hours.

Below: Panulirus versicolor
A very popular species – but it has a healthy appetite and rapid growth rate.

Panulirus versicolor

Purple Spiny Lobster

This attractive purple and white banded species is the most attractive member of a large and commercially valuable family of animals and a worthy addition to the aquarium. There are major fisheries of its relatives in both the Caribbean and Mediterranean.

Very young specimens of *P. versicolor* are commonly imported from Singapore and Indonesia. They have a body length of 5-7cm (2-3in), the long, rasplike antennae adding a further 10-15cm (4-6in). An adult body length of 20cm (8in) is by no means unusual. These efficient scavengers thrive in captivity on a diet of frozen fish and shrimp. Although not deliberately destructive, they can cause damage with their sharp feet, or by jerking backwards to evade a threat, either real or imagined.

Several other species of *Panulirus* are occasionally available, usually in shades of reddish brown, but these grow even larger and are suitable only for a very large aquarium. Like the purple species, their long antennae are easily broken in confined spaces and, although they will grow with successive shell changes, the animal loses much of its appeal to the aquarist if these appendages are broken.

The Slipper Lobster, *Scyllarides nodifer,* is a close relative, but instead of antennae this species has well-developed plates around the head to dig through the substrate seeking food. It is dull-coloured and of more interest to the specialist.

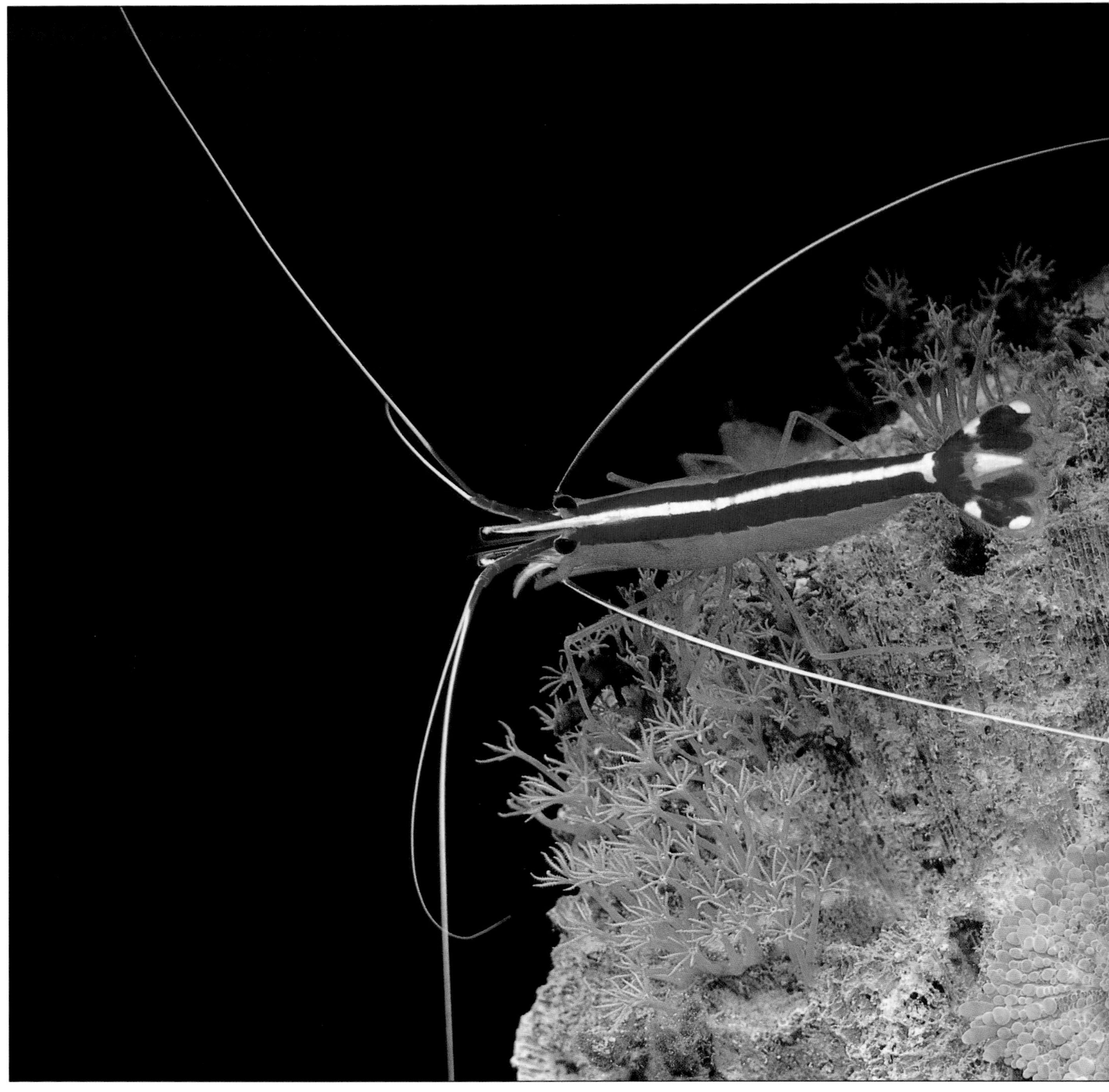

SHRIMPS

Lysmata amboinensis
Cleaner Shrimp

The common name for these very attractive and sociable shrimps derives from their natural cleaning behaviour. In the wild, on Indo-Pacific reefs, they will pick parasites, damaged skin, etc., from many species of fishes, particularly moray eels and large groupers. The fish clearly appreciate these attentions and only rarely eat what would otherwise seem an attractive morsel.

Lysmata lack the dramatic claws of *Stenopus,* but many are attractively coloured. The common Indo-Pacific *L. amboinensis* has a scarlet back with a white stripe running from between the eyes to the base of the tail. The tail is marked with three white patches. The very similar but, in Europe, much rarer Caribbean *L. grabhami* has a white stripe running to the tip of the tail, which is edged, rather than blotched, in white.

Above: Lysmata amboinensis
It is easy to see why the Cleaner Shrimp is a favourite with aquarists.

Both species reach about 8cm (3.2in) in body length, and make very desirable aquarium inhabitants, being long-lived and easy to care for. They are particularly attractive when kept together in groups of

four or five, when they may perform group cleaning activities on fishes.

Both species regularly breed in the aquarium, the females developing large quantities of green eggs under the abdomen. Unfortunately, the newly hatched shrimps usually provide a welcome addition to the menu of the tank's other inhabitants, or are quickly swept into the filter system. Raising these shrimps to adulthood in captivity is rare and difficult.

Lysmata debelius
Blood Shrimp

This intensely red and white spotted species caused a considerable stir within the hobby when it was first introduced in the early 1980s. Early specimens were all imported from Sri Lanka, but they have also been found in Indonesia and now, although this is still one of the more expensive shrimps, it is easily obtainable.

L. debelius is somewhat shyer than *L. amboinensis,* but after a few days adjusting to the aquarium conditions – and with the reassurance that there are plenty of convenient boltholes available – it will soon settle down and do very well.

Several other *Lysmata* species occasionally appear for sale. Most are either banded or striped in combinations of white, pink, beige and red. *L. rathbunae* comes from the Caribbean, while *Lysmata californica* is found on the west coast of the USA. *L. vittata* is an almost transparent Pacific species, while the blotched pink and white *L. kukenthali* comes from the Pacific Ocean. A Mediterranean species, *L. seticaudata,* and *L. wurdemanni* from the western Atlantic share similar red and white longitudinal markings.

Below: Lysmata debelius
The aptly named Blood Shrimp is easy to maintain and long lived.

Periclimenes brevicarpalis
Anemone Shrimp

P. brevicarpalis is the commonest species in a family of very interesting and easily maintained shrimps. They have acquired their common name from their habit of living among the stinging tentacles of sea anemones for protection against predators, rather like clownfishes and Anemone Crabs.

These species are rarely more than 2.5cm (1in) long and are often almost totally transparent, which makes them very difficult to see if you are unaware of their presence. *P. brevicarpalis* is transparent with white blotches. It occurs throughout the Indo-Pacific region, where it often shares anemones with clownfishes.

The very delicately formed *P. holthuisi* from the Indo-Pacific, and the Caribbean *P. pedersoni,* are glasslike with fine purple markings. *P. imperator* is found in the Red Sea and Indian Ocean and is very variable in colour. Bright red specimens have been found living among the gill tufts of large, similarly coloured sea slugs, such as *Hexabranchus imperialis*, the

Spanish Dancer (see page 347). All Anemone Shrimps will accept almost any small food items and will thrive in captivity. Do take care not to put these creatures at risk from larger predatory species, however; most crabs and shrimps can stalk unharmed through anemone tentacles and an Anemone Shrimp would make a welcome addition to their diet.

Left: Periclimenes brevicarpalis
This glasslike Anemone Shrimp and its relative P. pedersoni *are delicate species that do not appreciate boisterous neighbours, though they are fairly easy to maintain in captivity.*

Above: Rhynchocinetes uritai
Candy Shrimps are commom in the wild, frequently imported and inexpensive. They make interesting aquarium subjects and, as they are quite hardy, are ideal for newcomers to the hobby.

Rhynchocinetes uritai
Candy Shrimp; Dancing Shrimp

This group of shrimps is distinguished by having a movable rostrum (head spine) and very protuberant eyes. There are many attractive species, but *R. uritai* is the only species regularly available. It is found throughout the Indian Ocean and Indo-Pacific regions and exported in large numbers, making them among the cheapest shrimps to buy. They do best in small groups, when they will lose much of the shyness they display if kept singly. Males have large but ineffective claws, so in view of their lack of defensive armament, do not house them with larger, potentially more aggressive crustaceans. On occasion, they will pester corals and anemones, but are generally harmless. Candy Shrimps grow to about 3cm (1.2in) and are ideal specimens for beginners to keep.

Saron rectirostris

Monkey Shrimp

This interesting species and its relatives are comparatively recent introductions to the hobby, with specimens being shipped from Indonesia and Hawaii. They can be distinguished by the strong spines or hooks along the thorax and between the eyes.

S. rectirostris has purple legs and a pale body spotted with brown. *S. inermis* has greyish spots on the pale front portion, while the rear half of the body is more brown in colour. *S. marmoratus* is brownish green, with the body heavily coated with hairlike extensions. In all species, the males have a greatly elongated first pair of walking legs. In *S. marmoratus* these are attractively banded in reddish brown and buff.

They are good scavengers, taking any meaty food, but are essentially nocturnal and thus rarely seen during daylight hours.

Above: Saron marmoratus
All the Saron *species tend to be rather shy and difficult to see; here,* S. marmoratus *is camouflaged among the fronds of a cactus algae,* Halimeda *sp.*

Below: Stenopus hispidus
The brightly coloured and impressive Boxing Shrimp is the most commonly imported, and one of the most popular, shrimp species available to aquarists.

Stenopus hispidus
Boxing Shrimp; Coral-banded Shrimp

The attractive Boxing Shrimp is one of the most commonly imported and justifiably popular species available to hobbyists. *Stenopus* are bold animals and, once settled into a new environment, will rarely hide for long. A large specimen with its 6cm (2.4in)-body looks very impressive as its long claws and delicate white antennae wave in the current. Unless you can be sure of buying a compatible pair, house only one specimen in the tank. However, *S. hispidus* generally mixes quite safely and happily with other species of shrimp.

There are several species of *Stenopus* and as the hobby expands, so more appear on the market, albeit in very limited numbers. *Stenopus spinosus* is found in the Mediterranean and is essentially gold-yellow overall. The Caribbean is home to *S. scutellatus*, which has red-and-white claws and tail, but a yellow thorax. It can be distinguished from the smaller *S. zanzibaricus* by the two scarlet dots near the mouth. *S. tenuirostris* from the Indo-Pacific is another small, and lightly built, species with a purplish blue thorax.

The giant of the family is the rare and very expensive *Stenopus pyrsonotus* from Hawaii, which grows at least 50 percent longer than *S. hispidus*. *S. pyrsonotus* is white throughout, except for a striking, broad, red band down the length of the body. The only similar species is the very small (2-3cm/0.8-1.2in) *S. earlei,* which has a pale body with a red stripe along each side, forming a 'V' shape at the tail. The base of the claws is reddish.

Stenopus are particularly vulnerable when they shed their exoskeletons and thus need plenty of hiding places to enable them to evade predators while the new shell hardens. Legs, claws or antennae are often lost or damaged, but these quickly regrow. All *Stenopus* are omnivorous, taking almost any commercial foods.

Above: Synalpheus sp.
The greatly enlarged snapping claw of this Pistol Shrimp is clearly visible here as it rests on a Tridacna *clam. The reason for the attraction of this species – and for its common name – lies in the loud pistol crack sound that it is able to produce by snapping this huge claw (its victims are stunned by the shock waves when they come within range). Unfortunately, it is normally an extremely secretive species.*

Synalpheus sp.
Pistol Shrimp; Snapping Shrimp

Small specimens of Pistol Shrimps are frequently introduced to the marine aquarium by accident, along with pieces of living rock. They often occur in the water canals of sponges. Most are pale brown or green, but there are a few very attractive orange and red species. However, they are all confirmed recluses and of limited interest to most hobbyists.

Their common name comes from the pistol crack sound they are able to produce, a sound so similar to cracking glass that many a hobbyist has had a nasty shock! All Pistol Shrimps have one greatly enlarged claw, usually the right. By snapping this shut they produce a shock wave through the surrounding water, stunning the small shrimps that make up a major part of their natural diet. With a maximum body length of about 5cm (2in), they pose little, if any, threat to the other inhabitants of the tank and should not be confused with Mantis Shrimps (see page 383).

Phylum: MOLLUSCA

Bivalves, Cephalopods, Sea Slugs and Univalves

Above: Lima scabra
The vivid colouring of the Flame Scallop explains its popularity. This Caribbean species has lookalike relatives throughout the tropics. Feed regularly with a good-quality liquid preparation.

BIVALVES

Lima scabra
Flame Scallop

This very attractive Caribbean species grows to about 6cm (2.4in) in diameter. The shell is unremarkable, but the body flesh is an intense scarlet. In the most popular of the two forms of *L. scabra,* the fringe of tentacles around the lip of the shell is also red, while in the other, the tentacles are off-white.

Position these scallops in a hollow or crevice towards the front of the tank where, hopefully, they will settle and attach themselves with wiry threads. Without an anchoring point, they may gravitate towards the back of the tank and be lost.

Flame Scallops are filter-feeders and have fairly heavy appetites. The commonest cause of death, other than predation, is long-term starvation due to insufficient supplementary feeding or an over-efficient filter system.

Flame Scallops are a very popular food item for many animals, but are able to escape predators by clapping their shells together and using the resultant force to jet through the water. The Indo-Pacific lookalike *Promantellum vigens* has another useful defence system. The scallop's usual tactic is to flee the scene of battle, but if this fails, *P. vigens* defends itself with its tentacles. These are very sticky and easily detached from the body, and thus prove an irritating deterrent to many potentially predatory fish.

Occasionally, Flame Scallops reproduce in the aquarium and small clusters of spats – miniature, almost transparent 0.5cm (0.2in) diameter scallops – are found in caves and under rocks.

An interesting Philippine species has recently appeared on the market. It is similar in size and coloration to the red form of *Lima scabra* and has rippling luminous lines just inside the shell that flick on and off. We do not yet know what benefit these lines confer on the so-called Flashing Scallop.

Spondylus americanus

Thorny Oyster

As its scientific name would suggest, this is a Caribbean species. Both valves of the shell have long, thornlike extensions and, when cleaned, the shell is very attractive and a favourite with collectors. When the animal is alive, the thorns are often heavily covered with growths of sponge, hydroids and algae, which camouflage the animal.

Spondylus aurantius is a very similar Indo-Pacific species with shorter thorns. This species is often coated with a vivid red sponge and, at 20cm (8in) in diameter, it is twice the size of *S. americanus*.

Both species are found in caves and under overhangs and thus do not appreciate bright lighting. Unfortunately, they appear short-lived in the aquarium and, because of the pressure from shell collectors, who pay high prices for good specimens, they are usually too expensive to appeal to hobbyists.

Very few other bivalves are deliberately added to the aquarium, but they are quite often introduced accidentally. Small specimens are often found growing on sea whips and sea fans, and many burrowing species are introduced with 'living-rock'. Some of the best Caribbean rock is heavily populated with burrowers and mussel species. Take great care to remove any air pockets from this type of rock, as tunnelling bivalves may otherwise die and cause very serious ammonia and nitrite pollution problems.

Above: Spondylus americanus
This species, one of the more expensive marine invertebrates, demands excellent water quality and an adequate supply of particulate food in the home aquarium.

Below: Tridacna crocea
Brightly coloured species such as this are justifiably popular. Usually seen at about 10cm(4in), they can reach twice this length, but are slow growing.

Tridacna spp.

Giant Clams

The various *Tridacna* species are probably the most popular bivalves, and justifiably so. The shell, particularly that of *T. crocea*, often shows deep flutes along the ridges, while the fleshy mantle of most species can be the most intense, almost fluorescent, blue and green. The largest species is *T. gigas*, the Giant Clam of Hollywood fame, which can reach a weight of over 100kg (220lbs), and is particularly common on the Great Barrier Reef of Australia. Its shell is often covered with algae and coralline growths and the mantle is generally greenish brown. It has been heavily over-fished and is largely protected.

Tridacna maxima and *T. crocea* are of more interest to the hobbyist and are regularly imported from Indonesia and Singapore. *T. maxima* can reach 30cm (12in) in length, and some of the most attractive specimens have green and brown striped mantles, while others may show a chocolate and cream blotched pattern. The most dramatically coloured blue specimens of *T. crocea* grow to around 15cm (6in).

All clams are filter feeders, drawing water through one siphon, filtering out planktonic organisms, and exhaling the cleaned water through the other. They are all heavily dependent on intense lighting. In fact, much of the colouring in the mantle is due to the zooxanthellae algae living in the tissue. These algae utilize sunlight for photosynthesis and produce the majority of the clam's food.

CEPHALOPODS

Nautilus macromphalus
Nautilus

For many years, Nautilus were thought to be extremely rare and to occur only in very deep waters. Recently, however, large numbers have been found and caught by research teams off Indo-Pacific reefs. It appears that they retreat to the depths, often hundreds of feet down during the day, but float up into shallower water at night and use their many tentacles to catch small fish and shrimps.

Very occasionally, the better wholesalers may obtain specimens of Nautilus, but the supply is so limited and the demand so great that their price is likely to remain beyond the reach of most hobbyists for the foreseeable future. Nonetheless, those specimens that have appeared have proved viable in the aquarium and, despite their essentially nocturnal habits, have many admirers.

Right: Nautilus macromphalus
Nautilus shells are readily available, but the live animal is rarely for sale.

Octopus cyaneus
Common Tropical Octopus

Octopi are the most advanced cephalopods and have lost all trace of their ancestral shells. Most species are less than 60cm (24in) in diameter – and none approach the horror-story dimensions prized by the early Hollywood film makers. *Octopus cyaneus* rarely reaches more than 30cm (12in) across and is typical of the small tropical species shipped in considerable numbers from the Far East. It is common on many reefs and easily captured by overturning stones under which it lurks at the water's edge at low tide. This and other species are able to control not only the colour of their skin, but also its texture. When at rest and relaxed, most octopi are fairly smooth skinned and their colour matches their background. When angered or frightened, they rapidly become much darker or lighter and their skin folds into eruptions resembling algal growth.

Like many octopus species, *O. cyaneus* is an ideal aquarium inhabitant for those prepared to make some effort on its behalf. Although not particularly light sensitive, all octopi demand perfect water conditions and will not tolerate any form of pollution. The aquarium must contain a number of suitable caves as hiding places and a tight-fitting lid, as octopi are notorious explorers, squeezing their boneless bodies through the smallest of openings. Many an octopus has met a dry and dusty end on the carpet, thanks to its owner's carelessness. Suitable tankmates include corals, sponges, featherduster worms, and some echinoderms. Crustaceans and fish, unless intended as food, have no place in the octopus tank.

The octopus should be the last introduction to the tank, as it resents further disturbance. Allow it to become used to the dark, leaving the tank unlit for a day after the animal's release. Take the greatest care during this period; octopi are sensitive creatures and if badly upset will eject sepia ink into the water. This natural defence mechanism can cause major problems in the tank, and if the animal 'inks' in its shipping container it is likely to die.

A happy octopus is a greedy feeder, and laboratory tests have shown that it is quick to learn how to obtain food – even unscrewing bottle tops to get at the food within. Do not overfeed these ever-hungry creatures; they can generate more wastes than the average filter system is capable of dealing with in an acceptably short period. A regular feed of one or two shrimps or small frozen fish per day will comfortably satisfy all but the largest species.

It is not a good idea to house two octopi in any but very large aquariums, as they will usually fight. The female octopus is fertilized internally and occasionally a gravid specimen will produce fertile eggs in the aquarium. She may hang these from the roof of a cave or carry them about with her. The female does not normally feed during the incubation period and generally dies shortly after the eggs hatch, producing miniatures of their parents. The small hatchlings can be kept together and commercial producers in America are now supplying their country's growing number of public and educational aquariums. Breeding and rearing is still a great challenge for the specialist hobbyist and results should be more common as techniques are refined.

Above: Octopus cyaneus
The powerful sucker-lined arms are clearly visible on this Common Octopus.

Below: Sepia plangon
Cuttlefish are efficient hunters, not to be trusted with fish or crustaceans.

Sepia plangon
Cuttlefish

The brittle supporting blade inside cuttlefish of the *Sepia* genus is very familiar to birdkeepers. Unfortunately, cuttlefishbone is the closest most of us will ever come to having a cuttlefish, although *S. plangon* is a common species in the tropical Indo-Pacific, while *S. officinalis* occurs throughout the northeastern Atlantic and the Mediterranean Sea. The latter is a very common and popular animal in European public aquariums, where it can enjoy the large tanks that these very active animals require.

Unlike their relative, the octopus, squids and cuttlefish are fast-swimming and very active hunters. Like an octopus, they have eight arms around the mouth, but they also have two longer and rapidly extendable arms to catch prey.

Very little is known about the behaviour of the vast majority of squid and cuttlefish species because they are difficult to catch undamaged and many live in very deep water. Those few species that have been studied display a variety of interesting behaviour patterns. Many are capable of very rapid colour changes and, in the case of *Sepia,* waves of colour wash over the body when they are excited or agitated. Many squid species show luminescent patches and it is believed that some species communicate with each other with a system of colour codes.

Very occasionally, small species, such as *Loliguncula brevis,* are imported from the Gulf of Mexico. This has very large pigment cells (chromatophores) that produce a kaleidoscope of reds and black. Given plenty of swimming room, it might prove viable in the home aquarium. All squid and cuttlefish require optimum water conditions and are particularly sensitive to low oxygen levels. Most will not tolerate salinities lower than those of their native waters. Being extremely predatory, cuttlefish can be trusted only in a species aquarium, or with sessile invertebrates.

SEA SLUGS

The sea slugs are univalve molluscs that have lost the valve (shell) and have become more mobile. Some of the more primitive sea slugs still have a very tiny, residual shell, but they cannot withdraw into it.

Below: Aplysia dactylomela
The Sea Hare is one of the easiest nudibranchs to maintain, given large quantities of vegetable matter.

Bottom: Chromidoris quadricolor
The bright colours of these common nudibranchs probably serve to warn off predators. Note the retractable tentacles, characteristic of dorids.

Aplysia sp.
Sea Hare

The Sea Hares are an entertaining, if not particularly attractive, group of sea slugs. Typically, they resemble a greenish brown lemon, with continually waving flaps along each side. They have earlike projections on the head, and it is these and their habit of grazing on seaweed that gives them their common name.

Most specimens offered for sale are shipped from the Caribbean, but very similar species are found throughout the world. They are by far the easiest type of sea slug to maintain for any length of time, although the first few days in a new aquarium can be a testing period. They require good water conditions and a continual supply of vegetable matter, preferably in the form of algae. If these few necessities are met, they can survive in captivity for two years or more. Since the invertebrate aquarium occasionally suffers from a plague of green algae, Sea Hares can provide one of the most useful and harmless answers to this problem.

The common Caribbean Sea Hare, *A. dactylomela,* can grow to over 30cm (12in), although smaller specimens of 6-8cm (2.4-3.2in) are most commonly seen. It is a strong swimmer, making good use of the parapodial flaps around its body.

Chromodoris quadricolor
Striped Nudibranch

The dorids are the largest group of nudibranchs and include some of the most vividly coloured animals found in the sea. *C. quadricolor* though striking in its black, white and orange livery, is by no means exceptional. Members of this group typically have two retractable tentacles on the head and a ring of gills, again retractable, towards the rear. Specimens rarely grow more than 6cm (2.4in) long.

Although commonly available and among the cheapest of sea slugs, their life expectancy in captivity is short. Again, the problem is to provide the correct diet. All are predatory, feeding on a wide range of sessile invertebrates, from sponges to barnacles, sea squirts to soft corals, and most seem limited to just one prey species. In the Red Sea, *C. quadricolor* feeds on the red sponge, *Latruncnlia.* Until more is known of the requirements of *Chromodoris* species and a suitable alternative diet is available, they are best left in the wild.

Other available dorid species include *Gymnodoris ceylonica,* which lays strings of yellow eggs; *Polycera capensis,* a sea squirt feeder; the green, yellow and black *Tambja affinis,* and the sponge-feeding, white *Casella atromarginata.*

Hexabranchus imperialis
Spanish Dancer

The Spanish Dancer is one of the largest and most dramatically coloured nudibranchs available. It is imported in small but regular quantities from all parts of the Indo-Pacific, in sizes ranging from 6-15cm (2.4-6in). When at rest, or browsing over rocks, the mantle of the Spanish Dancer is folded and marbled red, pink and white in colour. It is not until it swims that its full glory is revealed. The mantle unfolds to reveal an expanse of vivid crimson with a white border and then, with an action like a butterfly-stroke swimmer, it 'flies' through the water, earning its name.

The similar, and even more dramatically scarlet *Hexabranchus sanguineus* can be found on reefs in the Red Sea, but it is some years since this species was available commercially. Both species seem almost immune to fish attack and one small shrimp, *Periclimenes imperator,* takes advantage of this to hide among the gill tufts of *H. sanguineus.*

Spanish Dancers will often lay eggs in captivity, producing a 3-4cm (1.2-1.6in) diameter rosette of pink gelatinous ribbon containing thousands of eggs. Unfortunately, neither these, nor the adult animal, generally succeed in the aquarium. The adults are reputed to be omnivorous scavengers, but from their limited survival rate it seems likely that a significant ingredient is missing from their diet. *H. sanguineus* is said to feed on sponges and sea squirts and has been observed feeding on the Elephant Ear Coral, *Sarcophyton trocheliophorum.* These species are not really suited to aquarium life.

Spurilla sp.
Spiny Nudibranch

Spurilla is one of a large group of nudibranchs known as aeolids, most commonly found in cooler waters, although there are some tropical species. Most are fairly small, measuring up to 3cm (1.2in) and, although common as accidental introductions, are rarely available commercially. Small grey species similar to *Spurilla* are common on *Goniopora* coral, but generally go unnoticed. As accidentals they usually fare better than the dorids, as they are usually introduced on their food animals.

This group characteristically has two long tentacles on the head and numerous spikelike protuberances on the back. They are often brightly coloured, but without the striping common in dorids. They generally feed on anemones and corals, but some eat molluscs and fish eggs.

One particularly interesting species is *Glaucus atlanticus.* This blue-grey species is oceanic, living at the surface where it hunts various floating coelenterates,including the notorious Man-of-War Jellyfish. Not only is it immune to the jellyfish's stings, but it can store them within its own body to deter predators, which might eat the otherwise defenceless *Glaucus.*

There are many thousands of species of sea slugs and many occasionally appear on the market. Among the most common are the 'warty slugs', which are often covered in pimples, but show no external gills or tentacles. The duller green-brown species are generally longer lived than the more brightly coloured types.

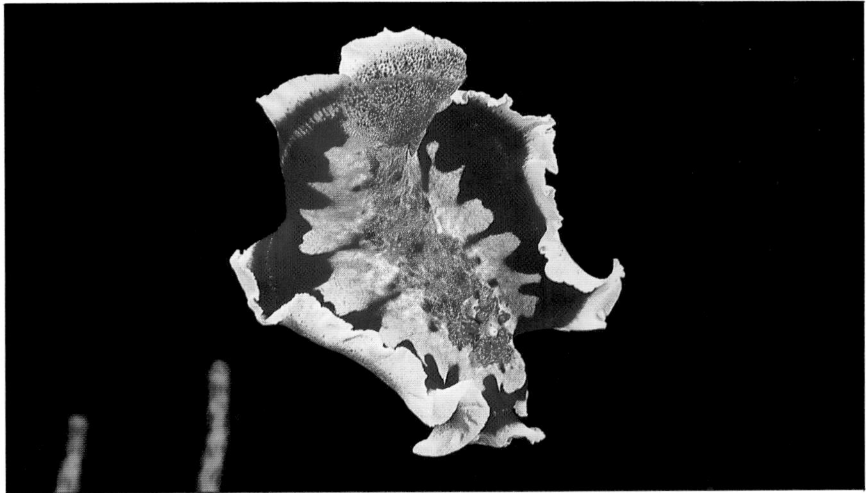

Above: Hexabranchus imperialis
The spectacular Spanish Dancer is, sadly, not long-lived in the aquarium.

Below: Pteraeolidia ianthina
This attractive blue species is one of the many aeolid nudibranchs.

Above: Cypraea tigris
The spotted shell of the Tiger Cowrie is largely covered by the fleshy mantle, an extension of its foot.

UNIVALVES

Cypraea tigris
Tiger Cowrie

The Tiger Cowrie is one of a large group of sea snails of interest not only to aquarists, but also to shell collectors. Some cowries are extremely rare and command very high prices among collectors, but the Tiger Cowrie is not one of these. All the cowries have characteristic highly polished oval and domed shells, many of which sport very decorative patterns. This colouring is normally well concealed by the fleshy mantle – an extension of the body that folds up and over the shell. The mantle is usually decorated with tufts and tassles and is inconspicuously coloured, providing good camouflage.

Tiger Cowries are commonly imported from Singapore at about 7.5cm (3in) long and are among the easiest invertebrates to keep. They feed avidly on *Caulerpa* species of seaweed and graze the less decorative hairy algae, but must have some animal matter; small pieces of fish and shellfish meat are suitable. A mature environment and good aeration are essential.

Cowries have two major drawbacks; firstly, many are primarily nocturnal and hide under rocks during the day, and secondly, they are somewhat clumsy. They have a powerful foot that is not easily dislodged and often tumble corals and other sessile invertebrates from their allocated position in the aquarium. Additionally, some species and specimens develop a taste for both hard and soft corals.

Among the other regularly available species are *C. arabica* from the Indo-Pacific, a slightly smaller species with a netlike shell pattern; *C. pantherina,* which is somewhat similar to *C. tigris,* and *C. nucleus,* characterized by the furry appearance of its mantle.

Above: Lambis lambis
The attractive underside of this Spider Shell (several species are sold under this common name). The top surface is normally camouflaged with algal growth – effective protection in the wild.

Below: Strombus gigas
When disturbed, S. gigas *retracts into its shell, as shown here. The heavy armour is proof against most would-be predators. This large mollusc is likely to appeal most to the specialist.*

Lambis lambis
Spider Shell

A number of Indo-Pacific species are sold under the name Spider, or Millipede, Shell. All are characterized by the five or more long, thin and often sharp extensions to the shell, and all species have a very long and horny foot with which they are able to right themselves if they are inadvertently upturned.

Various other species and families of univalves appear on the market from time to time, but few are of interest to aquarists. Moon shells, olives, murex, tulips and whelks are all predators and have no place in a 'living-reef' set-up. Top shells, limpets and chitons are largely vegetarian and can be treated like cowries and conchs.

Strombus gigas
Queen Conch

The Queen Conch is a very important commercial food animal in its native habitats and huge numbers of dead shells are exported for decoration and the curio market. It is one of the largest molluscs available to the hobbyist, reaching 25cm (10in) or more, and is thus likely to be of greater interest to the specialist. At one time, strictly enforced regulations put a limitation on the size at which *S. gigas* could be taken from the sea and no small specimens were available to the hobbyist. In recent years, however, there has been a huge increase in breeding and farming this species, and small specimens, up to 5cm (2in), are now obtainable on the American market and it cannot be long before they are more widely available to hobbyists.

This species is found on sand and sea-grass fields throughout the Caribbean, where it eats algae and detritus. Its attractive brown and pink shell should prove popular with aquarists, but make due allowance for the size of the fully grown animal; it will require an aquarium of some considerable size in which to roam about unrestricted.

Phylum: ECHINODERMATA

Basket and Brittle Stars, Sea Cucumbers, Sea Lilies, Sea Urchins and Starfishes

Above: Astrophyton muricatum
The delicate tracery of the Basket Star's arms is well illustrated here.

Below: Ophiomastix venosa
The small central disc and five slender arms are typical of this group.

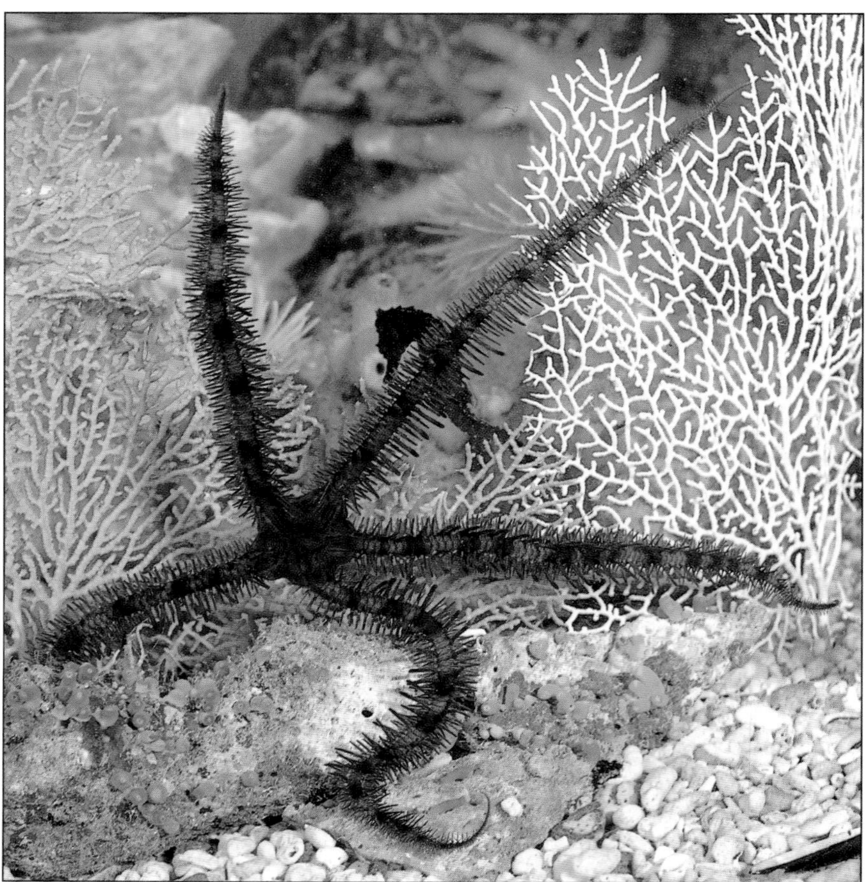

BASKET AND BRITTLE STARS

Astrophyton muricatum
Basket Starfish

Most imports of the fascinating Basket Star come from the Caribbean, but similar species are found in other oceans. They are very efficient feeders and require a good supply of food to thrive. They also need plenty of room to spread their 50cm (20in)-long arms, so they are clearly not animals for small tanks.

Given suitable conditions, these are long-lived creatures in the aquarium, but their strictly nocturnal habits limit their popularity to all but the most dedicated hobbyists. Their colours are generally restricted to greys, beige, browns and combinations of these. Provide a suitable liquid feed only when the arms are fully extended; nearly always at night.

Ophiomastix venosa
Brittle Star

Brittle Stars are regularly imported from the tropics and are not expensive, but because they spend most of their time hidden from view, they are not particularly popular. However, they are valuable scavengers, particularly in living reef tanks, which often have many crevices that trap excess food. Furthermore, they will not harm sessile invertebrates, such as corals and featherduster worms.

Brittle Stars have an efficient sense of smell to detect food and a surprising turn of speed. If a promise of food awaits them, they will sprint from one end of the aquarium to the other in seconds.

Ophiomyxa flaccida is a typical smooth-armed Caribbean species that reaches approximately 15cm (6in) in diameter. This species is often seen entangled among the spines of *Diadema* sea urchins, where it is comparatively safe.

Above: Cucumaria miniata
Yellow specimens of this small Sea Cucumber are less often seen than the pink form, which is regularly imported. Both species do much better in an 'established' living reef aquarium. That is to say, one that is at least six months old, if not more.

SEA CUCUMBERS

Cucumaria miniata
Feather Cucumber

Feather Cucumbers may be among the smallest members of their family, but they are some of the most attractive. There are several similar species, but the most common one, from Singapore, has a bright pink body and five longitudinal rows of bright yellow tube feet. In this species, the mouth tentacles are developed into feathery growths that the animal uses to trap planktonic organisms and other food items drifting in the water. Feed sea cucumbers with live brineshrimp and rotifers.

This and the following species are among the few that may successfully reproduce in a domestic aquarium. Where two or more of the 6cm (2.4in)-long adults are present you may find small clusters of miniatures adhering to the sides of the tank.

Pseudocolochirus axiologus
Sea Apple

This very attractive species of sea cucumber has been given the somewhat confusing common name of 'Sea Apple' to differentiate it from all other cucumbers. It is by far the most strikingly coloured and popular species in the family.

The Indonesian form of *P. axiologus* typically has an ovate, greyish pink body up to 10cm (4in) long, with rows of tube feet defined in pink, orange or yellow. The head of the animal is crowned with a ring of feathery tentacles, which it uses for filter feeding. As the animal feeds, it pushes each tentacle in turn lugubriously into its mouth in the centre of the ring, rather like a child sucking toffee from its fingers. These tentacles vary in colour from pale yellow through to crimson. Do not keep Sea Apples with any fish species that might peck at the feathery tentacles.

P. axiologus is an easy species to maintain in the aquarium, provided it is given plenty of fine food. All too often, however, they slowly starve, becoming progressively smaller until, at about 3cm (1.2in) long, they give up the fight. Feed live brineshrimp and rotifers several times daily.

There is an even more striking giant form of *P. axiologus* from the Great Barrier Reef of Australia. Its body may be 15cm (6in) or more long, and is usually a rich purple colour with tube feet outlined in scarlet. The tentacles are purple and pure white. This desirable form is too expensive for many aquarists.

Stichopus chloronotus
Black Cucumber

Sea cucumbers are a large, varied and largely unprepossessing family within the echinoderms. Looking like a dark, shrivelled and discarded cucumber, *S. chloronotus* is a fairly typical example of the group. It is found on coral rubble throughout the Indo-Pacific region where, like many of its relations, it swallows mouthfuls of gravel and detritus, digesting any organic material and ejecting the residue from its rear.

This species is commonly available from Sri Lanka and, although very hardy, is not sufficiently attractive to appeal to most hobbyists. Nonetheless, it is a useful scavenger, particularly in an aquarium where organic material may begin to accumulate in a thin layer of unfiltered substrate.

Top: Pseudocolochirus axiologus
The Sea Apple has been a mainstay of the aquarium hobby for many years. The red tentacles are efficient traps for particles of food.

Above: Stichopus chloronotus
The Black Cucumber is one of the commonest Indo-Pacific species, though not one of the most popular. It is sometimes host to small fishes, which seek refuge in the cloacal chamber.

SEA LILIES

Himerometra robustipinna

Red Crinoid; Feather Starfish

H. robustipinna, from Singapore and Indonesia, reaches about 18cm (7in) in diameter and is one of the most attractive species. *Lamprometra palmata* is one of several common brownish species that achieves a similar size, while others are occasionally available in shades from yellow through orange to black. All these species require very careful acclimatization to the aquarium, as they react badly to rapid changes in salinity and pH. Do not house them with large, boisterous or 'pecky' fishes.

Crinoids feed mainly at night, climbing to a high point on the reef and then extending their arms to trap small particles of food falling from the surface of the sea. Nevertheless, in captivity they are also very decorative during daylight hours when they are unable to retreat to the cavities they would normally seek out in the wild.

Remember that these animals are very brittle. If they are caught by a strong water current or attacked by other animals, one or more arms is easily broken. In the wild, these will regenerate very quickly, but in the aquarium they require perfect water conditions and a great deal of suitable food, in the form of pulverized shrimp or fish, algal fragments and newly hatched brineshrimp, if they are to recover.

In the wild, many small starfishes, shrimps and gobies live a well-camouflaged existence among the arms of crinoids; these 'extra' species are infrequent, but welcome, bonuses in the tank.

Below: Himerometra robustipinna
This vivid red species, one of the most attractive sea lilies, is shown here with its arms extended for feeding.

SEA URCHINS

Diadema savignyi

Long-spined Sea Urchin

D. savignyi is just one member of a large genus found throughout tropical and subtropical seas. It may be uncomfortably familiar to holiday makers who have received painful wounds from treading on these animals. The spines are long, extremely sharp and, in some species, venomous. Despite this, they make good aquarium inhabitants, grazing over algae-covered rocks and surviving for a number of years. Unfortunately, their sharp spines can puncture and damage corals and sea anemones.

D. savignyi is rather unusual in its genus in that the dark spines become lighter and banded at night. Most *Diadema* species have banded spines as juveniles, but black or dark brown spines when mature.

Above: Diadema savignyi
The long needle-sharp spines typical of this family of urchins are clearly visible on this Indo-Pacific species. They can cause painful injuries; handle this species with care.

Below: Echinometra mathaei
This common species uses its spines and tube feet to amble over the coral rubble of the lagoon as it seeks out algae and detritus. A valuable scavenger in the aquarium and easy to feed.

Echinometra mathaei

Common Urchin

As its common name suggests, this Indo-Pacific species is not only widespread in the wild, but frequently available to hobbyists. Although its spines are shorter and considerably blunter than those of *Diadema savignyi,* take care when handling it. If you are unlucky enough to be stung by *E. mathaei* or *D. savignyi*, bathe the affected area with very hot water to help neutralize the poison. The pain usually subsides in an hour or two.

E. mathaei is easy to maintain in captivity and will accept a wide variety of food. Unfortunately, it seems to spend a great deal of time hidden behind, or under, rocks and is most active at night. Bear in mind that the tube feet provide the urchin with a very strong grip on the substrate, allowing it to go almost anywhere it pleases, and in doing so it can easily tumble rockwork.

The shell of the Common Urchin can reach a diameter of about 10cm (4in), but most animals are about half this size and these make the better aquarium specimens.

Eucidaris tribuloides
Mine Urchin

This small species only reaches about 5cm (2in) in diameter and, although not particularly attractive, it is a hardy species. It spends most of the day hidden in crevices in rocks, only emerging to feed at night, and is included here to avoid confusion with the *Heterocentrotus* Pencil Urchins, below.

Left: Eucidaris tribuloides
The Mine Urchin is a common export from Florida. Unfortunately, its nocturnal habits have restricted its popularity within the hobby, though it is a relatively hardy species.

Left: Heterocentrotus mammilatus
The distinctive heavy, thick spines would seem to be rather an encumbrance to the Pencil Urchin as it roams across a Hawaiian reef. This species is expensive but fairly easy to maintain.

Heterocentrotus mammillatus
Pencil Urchin

The Pencil Urchins of the genus *Heterocentrotus* are generally considered the most attractive and desirable sea urchins but, sadly, they are neither as common in the wild nor as regularly imported as other species. This ensures that they command a price roughly twice that of most others. In *Heterocentrotus mammillatus* – and the closely related *H. trigonarius* – the spines are reduced in number, but those that remain are greatly thickened and resemble a 5-7.5cm (2-3in) pencil stub. Indeed, you can use these spines instead of chalk to write on a slate or stone tablet as did the Ancient Egyptians. Unfortunately, Pencil Urchins are often commercially fished to provide component parts for the wind chimes for sale in gift shops.

Pencil Urchins make admirable aquarium inhabitants, but be sure to keep the pH level of the water at the high end of the range. They eat algae, lettuce and small particles of meaty foods.

STARFISHES

Choriaster granulatus
Giant Kenya Starfish

This species is probably the largest starfish available to the hobbyist on a regular basis. It can reach up to 30cm (12in) in diameter and is heavily built, with five thick fleshy arms. Unfortunately, this very attractive red and buff species is generally only imported when it has attained a size too great to appeal to the average hobbyist. This, and the proportionately high air freight costs, ensure that *C. granulatus* remains a species for the specialist.

The animal gets it scientific name from the small gill processes that protrude through the skin to give the arms a granular appearance. Most specimens are imported from Kenya, but it also occurs throughout the Indo-Pacific region, where it feeds on coral polyps and other immobile invertebrates.

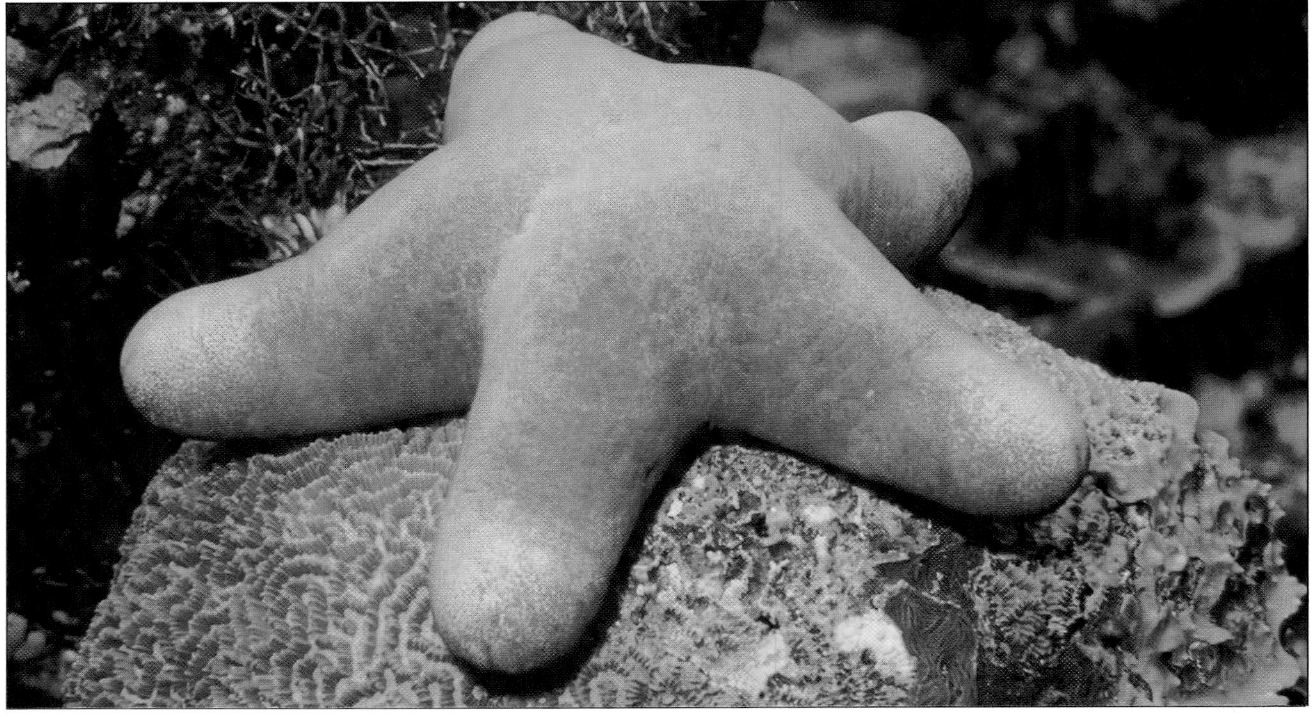

Culcita novaeguinea
Bun Starfish

The adult of this large 20cm (8in), Indo-Pacific species has a completely different body form from that of the typical starfish. As a youngster, it shows the typical five-pointed star shape familiar to us all, but as it matures the arms broaden and thicken to produce an almost regular pentagon. The comparatively thick body makes this one of the heaviest starfish in the world.

At their smaller sizes, this and the related *C. schmideliana* make very attractive aquarium inhabitants but, unfortunately, they are not common and only rarely appear in retailers' shops. The dorsal surface is often attractively marked with a pattern of dark raised tubercles.

Bun Stars do best in lightly decorated tanks, as they will often wedge themselves among rocks and risk puncturing their skin, thus opening a route for bacterial infections. They are also somewhat clumsy animals and may dislodge and damage loosely positioned corals as they move around the tank.

Above: Choriaster granulatus
A giant starfish for the specialist.

Below: Culcita novaeguinea
Most Bun Stars have a beige-brown dorsal surface, but colourful undersides.

Fromia elegans
Red Starfish

This bright red species is another common import in shipments from Indonesia and the surrounding region. In view of the sensitivity of the water vascular system, it is important to avoid rapid changes in salinity when acclimatizing starfishes to the aquarium.

F. elegans is one of the smallest starfish species, reaching only 8cm (3.2in) in diameter. Juveniles have black tips to the arms, but these disappear as the animal matures. *F. elegans* requires a similar diet to *F. monilis* but is often eaten by more aggressive tankmates, such as Hermit Crabs and large starfishes.

Right: Fromia elegans
The Red Starfish is commonly imported and easy to keep provided you buy undamaged specimens and avoid more aggressive tankmates.

Below right: Fromia monilis
The Orange Starfish provides a welcome splash of colour among the greens and browns of a well-stocked 'living reef' aquarium. It is inexpensive, easy to maintain and justifiably popular.

Fromia monilis
Orange Starfish

This vivid orange and red species is one of the most popular and commonly imported starfish. Regular supplies from Sri Lanka and Indonesia ensure that they are within the financial reach of all marine hobbyists. They rarely grow more than 6cm (2.4in) in diameter, but can reach up to 10cm (4in).

Bear in mind that starfish's water vascular system is easily damaged, so examine all starfishes before you buy them to ensure that they are in good condition, particularly the tips of the arms, and that the body is not limp and flaccid. A starfish with any such defects is unlikely to survive.

This species will not harm other invertebrates and feeds happily on small pieces of shrimp or shellfish. Highly recommended for the marine invertebrate tank.

Linckia laevigata

Blue Starfish

The Blue Starfish is undoubtedly one of the most dramatically coloured of all marine invertebrates. While blue is a common colour among marine fishes, it is very unusual in invertebrates, and the pure, intense, occasionally almost purple, blue of *Linckia laevigata* makes it look almost artificial.

This species has been regularly imported from Singapore, Sri Lanka and the Philippines almost since the beginning of the marine hobby, and is now often considered a little 'old hat' by experienced hobbyists. Nonetheless, the species has many factors in its favour. It is quite inexpensive, feeds well and, unlike some species, spends a considerable part of the day on view. But there is one particular caution; this species seems particularly prone to parasitization by a small species of bivalve mollusc that burrows into the animal, usually from the underside of one of the arms. If left in place, it will ultimately penetrate the critically sensitive vascular system. These parasites are easily removed with a gentle thumbnail, but it is always wise to examine Blue Starfishes carefully before buying them and to reject any that show evidence of damaged skin.

Below: Linckia laevigata
Three bright Blue Starfishes cross a patch of the Great Barrier Reef in search of edible detritus.

Pentaceraster mammillatus

Common Knobbed Starfish

This species is extremely variable in colour. The background is mostly brown or green, and the knobs – which are substantially smaller than those of *P. lincki* – may be white, yellow, orange, brown or black. Most commonly around 8cm (3.2in), they can reach twice this size.

As its name suggests, this is a common species, regularly included in imports from Singapore, the source of many of the cheapest invertebrates available to many hobbyists. Like its relative *P. lincki,* it is a greedy feeder, capable of everting the stomach in order to digest food. A suitable diet can include shredded prawn and brineshrimp; do not allow uneaten food to pollute the tank.

Above: Pentaceraster mammilatus
This is a common colour form of this most variable species.

Below: Protoreaster lincki
The intense, cherry-red patterning of this species has ensured its popularity.

Protoreaster lincki

Red-knobbed Starfish

The Red-knobbed Starfish is a widely distributed Indo-Pacific species that can reach up to 30cm (12in) in diameter. It is mostly offered for sale at about half this size, and its long, vivid red dorsal spikes ensure that it makes an impact in the aquarium. The most attractive specimens have a red, netlike, pattern on an off-white background, and are quickly snapped up by hobbyists. Unfortunately, most collectors are not aware of a general rule that applies to starfishes, namely that knobbly backed starfish are omnivorous, if slow, predators, while most of the tropical, smooth-armed species are less harmful scavengers. This ignorance often results in Red-knobbed Starfish being introduced to an aquarium well stocked with corals, molluscs and other sessile animals, all of which seem to provide grist to this insatiable animal's mill.

In the right circumstances, Red-knobbed Starfish are rewarding and long-lived aqaurium animals. Feed them by placing them directly onto 1.25cm (0.5in) pieces of fish, squid or shellfish.

Phylum: CHORDATA

Sea Squirts

The phylum Chordata is mainly composed of animals with backbones, but members of two subgroups are generally considered as invertebrates, since they lack a true backbone. The sea squirts *Distomus* spp. (class Ascidiacea) are the only ones of interest to most hobbyists and even these usually arrive by accident. Small specimens are common introductions on pieces of living rock – most often white, beige or reddish species. They thrive with no additional care other than that given to the other inhabitants of the aquarium.

There are more than a thousand species of sea squirts. Some form mats of small specimens, others are large 50cm (20in) individuals. They have a leathery baglike body, with large inlet and outlet siphons. As water is drawn through these tubes, small particles of food are filtered out. Sea squirts are found in every colour and combination of colours, but their general inactivity means that they have never become very popular. Very small, but regular, liquid feeds are generally beneficial.

Above: Cyclosalpa polae
In this large red species the inhalant and exhalant siphons are clearly visible.

Below: Didemnum molle
One of many sea squirts found in large aggregations, typically in deep water.

Right: Pycnoclavella detorta
Several of the smaller sea squirts, such as this semi-transparent species, live in tight colonies in the wild.

Below: Rhopalaea crassa
This attractive blue species is one of the most appealing sea squirts, but is only rarely available.

PART SIX

THE COLDWATER AQUARIUM

Since sea water extends outside the tropical zones to all regions of the world, you should not overlook the possibility of keeping fishes from cooler waters. Because the sun shines less brightly at higher latitudes, less light penetrates the water in temperate regions. In addition, the water is often less clear, due to pollution and the heavy concentration of silt and mud constantly stirred up by coastal traffic. Fishes from these waters are not as brilliantly coloured as their tropical relatives, but they do offer one very real advantage for the hobbyist in temperate parts of the world – they are less expensive to obtain. In fact, if you live fairly near to the seashore, you can collect your own specimens absolutely free! (Coldwater marine species are not generally available from the usual aquatic stores.)

There are also many invertebrates to collect – many sea anemones are very colourful, bearing in mind their murky habitat – and there is also the advantage that should any species outgrow the tank, or outstay its welcome by antisocial adult behaviour, you can return it to the wild to continue its natural lifespan.

Despite the apparent convenience of keeping the local species, you may find problems arising during the summer months; as you enjoy the warm sun, the water temperature in the aquarium may rise uncomfortably high for its occupants and you may need to take steps to cool it down. Blennies, butterfishes, gobies and the marine species of stickleback are all small enough to be suitable for the aquarium in the long term. Juvenile forms of larger species, such as bass, grey mullet and wrasses, outgrow their aquarium before long and must be returned to the wild.

Left: *The Black Scorpionfish* (Scorpaena porcus) *should be handled with extreme care, owing to its venomous spines. However, it does make an unusual and interesting addition to the coldwater marine aquarium.*

Collecting and General Care

Coldwater species require the same aquarium conditions as those described for tropical species, with the obvious omission of heating equipment. Although substrate biological filtration is adequate, you should provide some extra water movement to create surface turbulence and to ensure well-oxygenated water.

As most of the species collected from the wild are likely to be rockpool inhabitants, furnish the aquarium with numerous retreats to recreate their natural habitat.

The biggest problem will be temperature regulation; in summer the average water temperature in the aquarium will be higher than you might expect to find in nature. Provide extra aeration at these times and improvize some kind of cooling system. The serious hobbyist may even consider fitting a cooling plant, or using a refrigerator to cool water in an outside filter system. There are a few 'aquarium' cooling units available, so check this out as well.

Feeding is not usually difficult, as most fishes are more than willing to accept fish and shellfish meats. Only the fishes with the smallest mouths, such as pipefishes and sea sticklebacks, will require copious amounts of tiny live food.

Regular water changes will stabilize the water conditions. If you check the specific gravity, remember that it will give a higher reading at the lower water temperatures, probably about 1.025 at 15°C (59°F).

If you prepare the aquarium before you collect your fish, try to make sure that the water is the same specific gravity as the natural sea water in the rockpools.

You must be well prepared to transport the livestock that you capture. Large plactic buckets with clip-on lids are ideal, although a double thickness of plastic film may be an adequate substitute for a lid. You will find that a battery-operated air pump, supplying air to an airstone in the water, will give the fish a better chance of surviving a long journey home. This is especially important during the summer months, when the journey may take longer.

Collect specimens with care; rocks surrounding the rockpools are usually covered in very slippery seaweeds, so wear suitable footwear. Consult tide timetables in advance to ensure that you get the maximum collecting time. Do not forget the incoming tide. Remember also to leave the rockpool in a fit state for the animals left behind: if you collect invertebrates, such as sea anemones or starfishes, collect site and animal together, replacing any rocks that you remove with others to restore the number of hiding places in the pool. Transport anemones and other invertebrates separately from the fish; anemones will sting the fish in the close confines of a bucket, and fish may eat small invertebrates, such as shrimps, during transit.

Never over-collect. Not only is this bad practice from the conservation point of view, but it is also false insurance; it is better for the majority of specimens in a small collection to survive than to arrive home with none at all.

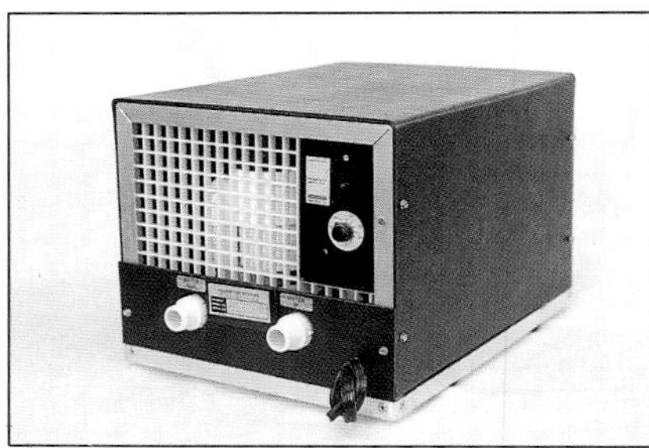

Left: *Nearly all coldwater aquariums will need some form of cooling equipment. This one is specially made for the purpose and fully adjustable.*

Below: *Keeping marines from cooler native shores can be very informative, and they can be fascinating to observe. Choose suitable companions with care.*

Coldwater Marine Fishes

Family: BLENNIIDAE
Blennies

These are most common in rockpools, where they are found hiding under overhanging rocks. They are often confused with gobies, but they lack the 'suction cup' formed by the fusion of the pelvic fins. Most blennies have 'tentacles' or a crest, described as 'cirri', positioned over the eye.

Aidablennius sphynx
Sphinx Blenny

☐ **Distribution:** Adriatic and Mediterranean.

☐ **Length:** 80mm (3.2in).

☐ **Diet:** All meaty worm foods.

☐ **Feeding manner:** Bottom feeder.

☐ **Aquarium compatibility:** May be territorial.

Once this fish leaves the security of its favourite bolt-hole, you can see that it is a most attractively coloured fish with dark bands crossing the body. It usually swims with the dorsal fin lowered, but raises it when alarmed. It spawns in caves, males physically cornering any passing female inside.

Lipophrys nigriceps
Black-headed Blenny

☐ **Distribution:** Mediterranean.

☐ **Length:** 40mm (1.6in).

☐ **Feeding manner:** Bottom feeder.

☐ **Aquarium compatibility:** May be territorial.

Whoever gave this fish its common name seems to have disregarded the predominant red of the body, concentrating instead on the darker reticulated pattern of the head region. *B. nigriceps* shares its habitat with the almost identical *Trypterygion minor*, from which it may be distinguished by the absence of a small extra dorsal fin in front of the main dorsal fins.

Lipophrys pavo
Peacock Blenny

☐ **Distribution:** Mediterranean.

☐ **Length:** 100mm (4in).

☐ **Diet:** Worm foods.

☐ **Feeding manner:** Bottom feeder.

☐ **Aquarium compatibility:** Territorial; needs plenty of retreats in which to hide.

Two obvious characteristics identify this species: the helmet-shaped hump above the eye in mature males and the blue-edged black spot just behind the eye. Blue-edged dark bands cross the green-yellow body.

Below left: Aidablennius sphynx
The Sphinx Blenny can be territorial.

Below: Lipophrys pavo
The Peacock Blenny is quite hardy.

Lipophrys pholis
Shanny

- **Distribution:** Mediterranean, Eastern Atlantic form West Africa to Scotland.
- **Length:** 160mm (6.3in).
- **Diet:** Live foods, meat and worm foods.
- **Feeding manner:** Bottom feeder.
- **Aquarium compatibility:** Gregarious, but can be hard to please when it comes to a choice of hiding places; whelk shells are often acceptable.

Like all blennies, these fish prefer a tank with plenty of hideaways. However, they also like to bask in the light, sometimes emerging from the water to do so. There are no cirri on the head.

Above: Lipophrys pholis
The Shanny is a widely distributed species and is quite easy to collect.

Parablennius gattorugine
Tompot Blenny

- **Distribution:** Mediterranean, Eastern Atlantic from West Africa to Scotland.
- **Length:** 200mm (8in).
- **Diet:** Live foods, meat and worm foods.
- **Feeding manner:** Bottom feeder.
- **Aquarium compatibility:** Can be territorial and may worry smaller fishes – and themselves be worried by larger ones.

These fishes prefer a tank decorated with medium-sized stones, under which they can hide. They can become tame, quite happy to make friends with you.

Parablennius rouxi
Striped Blenny

- **Distribution:** Mediterranean.
- **Length:** 70mm (2.75in).
- **Diet:** All meaty, worm foods.
- **Feeding manner:** Bottom feeder.
- **Aquarium compatibility:** Most blennies will live quite happily with sessile invertebrates, but crustaceans will be unsafe.

A distinctive fish with a horizontal dark stripe from head to tail. The fins are colourless.

Above left: Parablennius gattorugine
The Tompot Blenny has some six attractive dark bars crossing its body vertically. Once established in the aquarium, it can become quite tame.

Above: Parablennius rouxi
The Striped Blenny is distributed mainly throughout the Mediterranean and is easily identified by a dark stripe running horizontally from head to tail.

Spinachia spinachia
Fifteen-spined Stickleback

☐ **Distribution:** Northeastern Atlantic.

☐ **Length:** 200mm (8in).

☐ **Diet:** Very small animal life.

☐ **Feeding manner:** Midwater feeder.

☐ **Aquarium compatibility:** Fin nipper; keep separately.

This species must have frequent meals of tiny live foods; brineshrimp are probably the most useful food for this purpose. The Stickleback lives for only about two years in the wild, and its life expectancy will be even shorter unless the feeding problem is solved.

Above right: Spinachia spinachia
An unusual and fascinating subject.

Family: GASTEROSTEIDAE
Sticklebacks

Although freshwater sticklebacks (*Gasterosteus* spp.) are able to tolerate some degree of salinity, there is one species within the family – *Spinachia spinachia* – that spends its entire life in marine conditions. Like its freshwater relatives, it also builds a nest in which to spawn, fabricating the structure from plant fragments stuck together with a secreted fluid.

Lepadogaster candollei
Connemara Clingfish

☐ **Distribution:** Eastern Atlantic, Mediterranean, Black Sea.

☐ **Length:** 75mm (3in).

☐ **Diet:** Worm foods.

☐ **Feeding manner:** Bottom feeder.

☐ **Aquarium compatibility:** Not known.

The common name refers to the ability of the fish to cling to rocks and other surfaces by means of a suction disc formed by the pelvic fins. Colours may vary but generally include reds, browns and greens; males have red dots on the head and on the lower part of the long-based dorsal fin.

Family: GOBIESOCIDAE
Clingfishes

Clingfishes are small, shore or shallow water dwelling species. The Gobiesocidae family has a wide range of body shapes, but in all species the front part of the head is flattened. All members of the family lack scales and have only one dorsal and one anal fin. Their eyes are large and often dorsal, the better for them to see their prey. The papillae on their sucking disc are often used in identifying the species. Clingfishes are sedentary fishes, using their ventral fins, which are specially modified into suckers, to enable them to remain attached to rocks, algae or any other substrate (hence their common name). Despite their apparent immobility, however, they are active carnivores.

Family: GOBIIDAE
Gobies

Gobies have no lateral line system along the flanks of the body, instead, sensory pores connected to the nervous system appear on the head and over the body. Gobies can live quite a long time, records show they have survived for up to ten years. A very large family, gobies inhabit many types of water – tropical and temperate, freshwater, brackish and full salt water.

Gobius cruentatus
Red mouthed Goby

☐ **Distribution:** Eastern Atlantic, North Africa to southern Ireland.

☐ **Length:** 180mm (7in).

☐ **Diet:** Small crustaceans, worm foods, shellfish meats, small fishes.

☐ **Feeding manner:** Bottom feeder.

☐ **Aquarium compatibility:** Territorial at times.

Gobies are found on both sandy and rocky shores. Sand-dwelling species are naturally camouflaged, whereas rock-dwellers can be much more colourful.

Gobius niger
Black Goby

- **Distribution:** Mediterranean, Black Sea and eastern Atlantic.
- **Length:** 150mm (6in).
- **Diet:** Worm foods, small crustaceans.
- **Feeding manner:** Bottom feeder.
- **Aquarium compatibility:** Territorial at times.

A generally dark blotched fish, but how it 'colours up' in captivity depends a great deal on the colour of its surroundings. It is very rarely black! Another scientific name for this fish is *Gobius jozo*.

Pomatoschistus minutus
Sand Goby

- **Distribution:** Eastern Atlantic, Mediterranean and Black Sea.
- **Length:** 95mm (3.7in).
- **Diet:** Worm foods.

Above: Pomatoschistus minutus
The Sand Goby is a shy species. Choose its aquarium companions with care (it is best kept with its own kind).

- **Feeding manner:** Bottom feeder.
- **Aquarium compatibility:** Probably shy and likely to be predated upon by other fish. This species is best kept in a tank with its own kind.

Its natural camouflage colouring makes this fish difficult to see when you are collecting it. Being a sand colour, it will 'feel at home' with a similarly coloured covering on the aquarium floor.

Family: LABRIDAE
Wrasses

Like their tropical relatives, wrasses from temperate waters can also be brightly coloured. In fact, their colour can lead to identification and sexing problems; colour varies not only between the sexes (that of the male also changing at breeding time) but also depending on the mood of the fish and on the colour of the substrate! Sex reversals are also not uncommon. Juveniles act as cleaner fishes to other fishes, and many species hide away in crevices or bury themselves in the sand at night.

Coris julis
Rainbow Wrasse

- **Distribution:** Mediterranean eastern Atlantic.
- **Length:** 250mm (10in).
- **Diet:** Small marine animals, live foods.
- **Feeding manner:** Bottom feeder, although it will take surface plankton.
- **Aquarium compatibility:** Peaceful.

The long, slender, green-brown body has a horizontal white-red stripe. The eyes are red. These fishes are hermaphrodites, the females turning into fully functional males. Aquarium specimens are active during the day, but bury themselves in the substrate at night. This behaviour has not been observed in this species in the wild. Like their tropical relatives, juveniles act as cleaner fishes.

Below: Coris julis
Coloration of the Rainbow Wrasse varies depending on location and sex. Deeper water fish are red-brown; females have a pale spot on the gill cover base.

Anthias anthias

- ☐ **Distribution:** Mediterranean, eastern Atlantic as far north as Biscay.
- ☐ **Length:** 240mm (9.5in).
- ☐ **Diet:** A varied selection of animal and meaty foods.
- ☐ **Feeding manner:** Bold.
- ☐ **Aquarium compatibility:** Peaceful.

The body is golden brown with blue speckling and the facial markings are blue. The long pelvic fins are yellow and blue. In the wild, coloration may appear different because part of the colour spectrum of light is lost in deep waters due to absorption.

Right: Anthias anthias
It is surprising that collectors have not yet given this beautifully coloured fish a popular name.

Pholis gunnellus

Butterfish; Gunnell

- **Distribution:** Eastern and western Atlantic.
- **Length:** 250mm (10in).
- **Diet:** Crustaceans, worms, molluscs, shellfish meats.
- **Feeding manner:** Bottom feeder.
- **Aquarium compatibility:** Do not keep with small invertebrates.

The eel-like body has a long-based dorsal fin that is twice as long as the anal fin. It may have transverse dark bands on the body and white-edged markings along the base of the dorsal fin. This species is found under stones.

Family: PHOLIDIDAE
Gunnells

Often seen in the same areas as blennies, gunnells are slender cylindrical fishes with a dorsal fin running the entire length of the back. The anal fin is also long based, occupying almost the rear half of the body. Both the dorsal and anal fins are limited to just one ray. Species found on both sides of the North Atlantic Ocean and also on the northern Pacific coast of America.

Above: Pholis gunnellus
This fish usually hides under rocks.

Below: Scorpaena porcus
Handle the Scorpionfish with care!

Serranus hepatus

Brown Comber

- **Distribution:** Mediterranean, eastern Atlantic (Senegal to Portugal).
- **Length:** 130mm (5in).
- **Diet:** Animal and meaty foods.
- **Feeding manner:** Bold.
- **Aquarium compatibility:** Although no reliable information is available, you should not keep this species with smaller fishes.

The reddish brown body has four or five vertical dark bars across it. The undersides are pale. There is a black blotch on the dorsal fin at the junction of the hard and soft rays.

Scorpaena porcus

Black Scorpionfish

- **Distribution:** Mediterranean and eastern Atlantic (Biscay and further south).
- **Length:** 250mm (10in).
- **Diet:** Small fishes.
- **Feeding manner:** Lies in wait for passing prey.
- **Aquarium compatibility:** Nocturnal and distinctly unsociable. This is definitely a fish that should be kept in a separate tank.

The reddish brown mottled coloration makes this fish hard to see as it lies on the seabed. Not only is it a danger to other fishes, but also to swimmers who may inadvertently step on it. Use very hot water to bathe any wound, which may turn septic.

Family: SCORPAENIDAE
Scorpionfishes

Although they lack the ornate finnage of the tropical scorpionfishes, species from temperate waters are just as dangerous; the spines on the head are very venomous. When disturbed during the day, these sedentary nocturnal fishes swim only a short distance before settling again to await any passing prey.

Coldwater Marine Invertebrates

Above: Cleona celata
Sponges require excellent conditions.

Below: Actinia equina
A beautiful Beadlet Anemone.

Left: Urticina falina
It is a common fallacy that coldwater invertebrates are dull; this Dahlia Anemone would grace any tank.

Sponges
Sponges are usually difficult to keep in the aquarium as they are very sensitive to adverse water conditions. They must have well-oxygenated, crystal-clear water and are not all compatible with sea anemones. They attach themselves to shells, even those that contain crabs. If this happens, they will devour the shell and in turn become the home of the crab. *Suberites domuncula* is a common Mediterranean and Atlantic species.

Sea anemones
Beadlet anemones (*Actinia equina*) can be found in a variety of colours. The columns can be red, green or brown and the tentacles are usually the same colour, but not always. They move around the aquarium, providing splashes of colour in an ever-changing pattern.

Actinia equina has two sub-species *A. equina var. mesembryanthemum*, the Beadlet Anemone from the North and South Atlantic and the Mediterranean, is a very common sight in coldwater rockpools. The body and tentacles are bright red, but the body contracts to a dull red sphere just as you reach for it. *A. equina var. fragacea*, the strawberry variant, is usually red with green spots – just like a strawberry. Its tentacles are usually red, but can be a paler pink. It is larger than the Beadlet and is found in the slightly deeper waters of the northeastern Atlantic and the Mediterranean.

The long tentacles of *Anemonia viridis (sulcata)*, the Snakelocks Anemone, are not fully retractable. Because it prefers strong light, it is found very close to the water surface in the northeastern Atlantic and Mediterranean. In the same waters you will find *Bunodactis verrucosa*, the Wartlet or Gem Anemone. It has tentacles with ringed markings and vertical rows of wartlike growths on its body, hence the common name.

Cerianthus membranaceus, the Cylinder Rose, is almost a cross between a sea anemone and a tubeworm, with a longer cylindrical body and less stocky in shape. The tube is often partially buried in the sand. It is a delicate animal that needs careful handling, although it may be able to regenerate a damaged tube fairly easily. Its tentacles vary in colour from species to species and are toxic to most fishes; for this reason, too, you should place other sea anemones beyond its reach. Unlike some sea anemones, *Cerianthus* does not move about the aquarium.

Although a fairly large anemone, *Condylactis aurantiaca* from the Mediterranean, has relatively short brown, white-ringed tentacles tipped with violet. Some *Epizoanthus* species are also native to the Mediterranean. They only grow to around 10mm (0.4in), but colonies can be found on rocks just below the waterline, where the constant water movement ensures a regular delivery of food.

Urticina (Tealia) felina var. *coriacea*, the Dahlia Anemone from the North Atlantic and northeastern Pacific, has a body covered with warts, sand and fragments of shell. Tentacles surround the patterned mouth disc. A similar species, *U. crassicornis*, occurs on the east coast of North America. *U. lofotensis* has white and pink tentacles on a red body and, with the larger *U. columbiana*, occurs in the northeastern Pacific. There is also a deepwater species *U. eques*.

Crabs

Although crabs seem to be endearing little creatures, the majority of 'free-swimming' species grow too large and become a disruptive influence in the aquarium. A better choice would be the smaller Hermit Crabs (*Pagarus* spp.), which interestingly shed their adopted shell for larger premises as they increase in size (see page 333 for the tropical species).

Below: Homanus gammanus
The juvenile Common Lobster makes an ideal subject for the coldwater single-species aquarium, but will need quite a large tank as it grows.

Top: Eupagurus bernherdus
A Hermit Crab is ideal for an aquarium.

Above: Leander serratus
Common Prawns are quick-moving.

Prawns and shrimps

It is easy to capture species of *Palaemon*, *Crangon* and *Hippolyte* – small shrimps and prawns – from rockpools in the northeastern and northwestern Atlantic and the Mediterranean. *Lysmata* is an interesting Mediterranean species, *L. seticaudata* being very similarly marked to the Indo-Pacific species *Rhynchonectes uritae*. Prawns and shrimps are excellent scavengers and often act as cleaners to other fishes. Egg-carrying females may

Above: Chlamys operculans
Don't keep Queen Scallops with starfish!

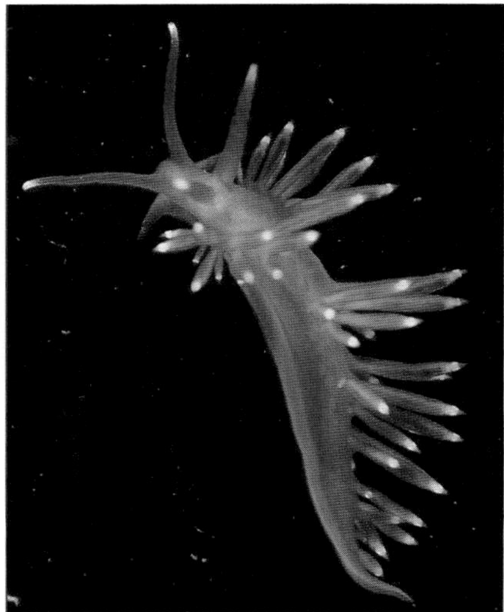

Right: Copyphella pedata
Nudibranchs need special dietary care.

Above: Echinus esculientes
Edible Sea Urchins are easy to collect.

Below: Luidia ciliaris
A predatory starfish.

provide extra numbers for the coldwater marine aquarium.

Shellfish

When you are collecting from rockpools, do not forget that there are some surprisingly active shellfish that will add extra interest to the aquarium. Species of limpet (*Patella*) and winkle (*Littorina*) are quite suitable. Do not ignore empty shells; a collection of shells of various sizes make ideal homes for a growing hermit crab.

Nudibranchs

Relatively colourful species occur in the Mediterranean and northeastern Atlantic. *Chromodoris* and *Hypselodoris* are typical genera of these molluscs.

Sea urchins

Like their tropical relatives, sea urchins from temperate waters can also make interesting aquarium species. The Black Urchin, *Arbacia lixula*, from the Mediterranean is a purple-black in colour and looks like a short-spined version of the tropical *Diadema antillarum*.

Starfishes

The following species are among the wide range of starfishes found in temperate waters.

Asteria rubens is commonly found in the northeastern Atlantic, where it feeds on mussels and scallops, prising them apart with its feet and introducing its stomach into the shell. The skin of this species is covered with many tubercles.

Astropecten aranciacus, the Red Comb Star from the Mediterranean and northeastern Atlantic, is a large predatory starfish (up to 500mm/20in) with comblike teeth along the edges of its arms.

Echinaster sepositus, a Mediterranean species, grows to 300mm (12in). Fertilized eggs develop directly into small starfishes.

Ophidiaster ophidianus, another red starfish from the Mediterranean, grows to 200mm (8in). The long arms issuing from an almost non-existent central 'body' of this starfish are cylindrical in section rather than flat, with sharply tapering ends.

Sea squirts

Sea squirts are vase-shaped bivalves that draw in water through one valve, trapping suspended minute food on a mucus-covered pharyngeal basket, and then exhale the water through the second siphon. *Halocynthia papillosa,* about 100mm (4in) tall, is red-orange in colour with many bristles around the siphons. It is common in the Mediterranean.

APPENDIX ONE: MARINE ALGAE

To freshwater hobbyists coming to marines for the first time, the mention of 'algae' is likely to conjure up a picture of greenish brown slime growing over plants and masses of hairlike tendrils choking the aquarium. By contrast, marine aquarists consider the different forms of algae as allies.

The species of alga that live within the tissues of corals and anemones – the zooxanthellae – provide food and help with the elimination of the animals' waste products. Small encrusting, and generally insignificant, algae coat the rockwork, producing a more natural-looking scene and providing a continually available food source for many browsing invertebrates and fishes. The larger species include many decorative forms, and these are the marine equivalent of plants in a freshwater tank.

The encrusting species and those that form furry 'lawns' on rocks generally arrive as accidental introductions with living rock, or as small particles included in the water when you buy invertebrate specimens. The larger, decorative species of algae are usually bought separately, but some are so prolific that you may be able to obtain 'cuttings' from neighbouring aquarists. They may be green, brown or red in colour.

Like most terrestrial plants, all algae species use chlorophyll to synthesize food, so require moderate to strong lighting. Commercial algae fertilizers are available, but these are only rarely necessary. Indeed, if other conditions are less than ideal, they can do more harm than good, by promoting undesirable species and increasing nitrate levels within the tank. Generally speaking, sufficient trace elements are dissolved within the water, and enough phosphates and nitrates are available from the animals' wastes to ensure good algal growth. In fact, by absorbing nitrates and phosphates as plant fertilizers, all forms of algae play an important role in maintaining good water quality in the aquarium.

Above: *Careful harvesting of algae growing in the aquarium is essential to prevent an impressive invertebrate display from being overrun and to ensure that species are not deprived of beneficial light.*

In the early days of the newly established invertebrate aquarium, you may encounter a problem with excessive growth of unwanted or undesirable forms of algae. This is most common where high-intensity lighting is provided and mats of green, hairlike algae form as a result. Generally speaking, the sequence of events is as follows. The aquarist provides sufficient light for zooxanthellae to function but, when the tank is new, large expanses of rock are exposed to this light. As there are few corals and anemones to utilize the light, algae are able to prosper. However, as soon as more corals and similar invertebrates are added to the tank, they begin to shade the algae and use the light themselves, eventually causing the algae to decline. Sea urchins and cowries will graze on green algae, but these animals are somewhat indiscriminating about the routes they follow and may damage sessile animals.

Although most marine algae can be safely encouraged to grow, there is a purple-brown alga that rapidly forms a spreading film over everything in the tank (see pages 91-93). Be sure to siphon any spots of this type of alga out of the tank as soon as you notice them. This problem is normally associated with overstocking, incorrect lighting, overfeeding, insufficient water movement within the tank, insufficient frequency (or quantity) of water changes, and excessive levels of nitrates. A series of partial water changes and an improvement in general conditions will usually solve the problem. On no account should you use the algae-killing preparations designed for ponds and freshwater aquariums in a marine system.

Above: Acetabularia spp.
Very attractive, but rarely available.

Acetabularia spp.
Mermaid's cup

This small and very delicate plant is one of the most attractive of the marine algae, but it is only rarely available to the hobbyist. The thin stipes, only 5cm (2in) long, are topped by pale blue-green caps like inverted toadstool heads. Unfortunately, the plant is easily damaged, both in transit and by other aquarium inhabitants, and is easily swamped by hairlike algae. It requires good light and less water movement than suits most invertebrates and algae.

Avrainvillea nigricans

This species is related to *Halimeda* spp. and *Pencillus capitatus*, but here the stipe ('stalk' or 'stem') is topped by a single, large, flattened blade, roughly circular and up to 10cm (4in) in diameter. Although hardy, the blades are often coated with brown encrusting algae, which detract from the plant's appeal. *Udotea* species are very similar in appearance and, from the aquarist's point of view, can be considered roughly the same.

Below: Avrainvillea sp.
A tropical Western Atlantic species.

Caulerpa spp.

The most commonly cultivated algae are the many *Caulerpa* species. Various types are found throughout the Caribbean, Mediterranean and Indo-Pacific regions and all are prolific. *Caulerpa* species may vary in colour from an intense lime green to a bluish brown, and they may grow 50cm (20in) tall or form low mats. Despite this variation, the basic structure is very similar. Growth develops from a main runner (stolan), with leaf stalks being produced from the top of the runner and a rootlike growth from the bottom. This 'holdfast' serves to anchor the plant body in position. It does not absorb water and food in the same manner as a terrestrial plant's roots; in marine algae, nutritional substances are absorbed through the leaves (blades).

The fronds of *Caulerpa* species are very thin-walled and filled with fluid. Because of this, it is important to acclimatize these plant-like blades very slowly to a new environment, especially in terms of specific gravity. If the transition is too sharp, changes in osmotic pressure can rupture the cell walls, causing an attractive green plant to change rapidly into a decomposing translucent slime.

Since some 'body fluid' will leak when pieces are removed for transplanting to other aquariums, it is safer to buy larger, rather than smaller, segments to reduce the proportion lost. This is particularly important if the tank houses fishes or invertebrates that may peck at the plant. A large sample has a much better chance than a small piece of surviving – and outgrowing – this minor pruning process.

In some circumstances, *Caulerpa* species grow so rampantly that they threaten to swamp, or at least severely shade, the various corals and polyps in the tank. Regular thinning of the growth is much more desirable than infrequent but heavy pruning, which may, on occasion, cause the collapse of the whole growth through excess fluid loss from the cut surfaces.

Most *Caulerpa* species are easy to grow, although the fleshier species require greater care than the more leathery types. The species can be distinguished by the form of the 'leaves'. The easiest to identify is probably *C. prolifera*. It has a thin, wiry runner, or stolon, typically up to 30cm (12in) tall and straplike blades up to 3cm (1.2in) wide. Occasionally, the blades develop as chains of heart-shaped sections, usually as a result of persistent damage to the growing tips. It is a good idea to obtain specimens still attached to rock; this will give them a good start in your tank. Marine algae is very brittle and cannot always support its own weight out of water, so handle it carefully.

Caulerpa mexicana and *C. sertularioides* have very attractive featherlike blades and both grow very rapidly. *C. racemosa* has short bunches (stipes) of spherical or ovate, berrylike growths on the vertical stalks and has earned the species the common name Grape Caulerpa. Although very attractive, it is rather slow growing and somewhat more demanding than most species.

Below: Caulerpa prolifera
As the name suggests, this species can be rampant, even in fairly poor conditions. Harvest it regularly to promote fresh, young growth.

Bottom: Caulerpa racemosa
The berry-like leaves of this Caulerpa *species make it easy to identify.*

Above: Caulerpa sertularioides
Another easily recognized species, with alternate blades arranged herringbone fashion from the main stem.

Below: Codiacea spp.
This slow-growing alga is fairly easy to maintain in the reef tank, where it will not be swamped by nuisance algae.

Above: Caulerpa taxifolia
An easy and very fast-growing species, identified by a profusion of divided blades attached to long runners.

Codiacea spp.

Several attractive members of this algae group are imported, primarily from the Caribbean. These species are known as calcareous algae because their 'leaves' are reinforced with calcium, absorbed from the sea water. This makes them much more rigid than *Caulerpa* species and less prone to predation. Given good lighting, a high pH level and regular use of a pH buffer solution, most species are easy to maintain, though often slow to reproduce.

Halimeda spp.

Typical specimens of these algae consist of a stipe, anchored into a soft substrate, from which grow numerous roughly circular or heart-shaped flat plates. New plates grow from the tips of the old ones. *H. discoidea* is one of the commonest species, its numerous 1.5cm (0.6in)-diameter plates giving the impression of a prickly pear-cactus – hence the common name Cactus Alga. *H. goreaui* and *H. opuntia* form very dense mats of tiny plates and look particularly attractive in a small aquarium. *H. copiosa* produces long chains of small plates and is very delicate and elegant.

Right: Halimeda discoidea
Unfortunately, this commonly available alga is easily overcome by filamentous problem algae in the aquarium.

Above: Pencillus captitatus
The appropriately named Shaving Brush!

Pencillus capitatus

Shaving brush

This is probably the most commonly imported of the Caribbean *Codiacea* and grows on a wide variety of substrates, its fleshy stipe often buried 7cm (2.75in) deep in the sand or mud. Its common name is very apt, as it perfectly resembles a green shaving brush. Although easily damaged in transit, intact specimens usually flourish, with small new growths appearing like rose suckers.

Rhipocephalus phoenix is similar in appearance, but has a crown made up of concentric rings of thin, flattened plates.

Above: Rhodophyceae
Red algae make a welcome change to the more common green species. On the whole, red algae grow very slowly.

Below: Valonia ventricosa
One of the more strange species of marine algae. It can quickly multiply to occupy favoured spots in the tank.

Rhodophyceae
Red algae

Several decorative species of maroon-red algae are occasionally available. Typically, these are anchored to a base rock by a thick stipe that rapidly branches to form a bushlike structure. Some species are quite stiff and erect, while others collapse if removed from water. The success rate with these types of algae is very variable. The best specimens are those that remain attached to a small rock and have few or no pale or faded tips to the branches.

Valonia ventricosa
Sailor's Eyeballs

This species produces a cluster of roughly spherical balls up to 5cm (2in) in diameter. Each ball is a single cell and it is this plant's claim to fame as the largest single-celled growth in the world that earns it a place here. *V. ventricosa* usually occurs as an accidental introduction into the aquarium and, given time, can make an attractive feature. The cells are easily punctured, however, so it is important that you handle them with great care.

APPENDIX TWO: SPECIES TO AVOID

TROPICAL MARINE FISHES

1

2

3

4

5

6

7

8

9

1 Aeoliscus strigatus
(Razorfish; Shrimpfish)
Generally possesses an unnaturally short life expectancy in captivity.

2 Apolemichthys arcuatus
(Bandit Angelfish; Banded Angelfish)
An extremely difficult fish to keep for long periods of time.

3 Centropyge multifasciatus
(Multibarred Angelfish)
An extremely difficult fish to keep for long periods of time.

4 Chaetodon capistratus
(Four-eyed Butterflyfish)
An extremely difficult fish to keep for long periods of time.

5 Chaetodon larvatus
(Red-headed Butterflyfish)
An extremely difficult fish to keep for long periods of time.

6 Chaetodon meyeri
(Meyer's Butterflyfish)
An extremely difficult fish to keep for long periods of time.

7 Chaetodon octofasciatus
(Eight-banded Butterflyfish)
An extremely difficult fish to keep for long periods of time.

8 Chaetodon ornatissimus
(Ornate Butterflyfish)
An extremely difficult fish to keep for long periods of time.

9 Chaetodon trifascialis
(Chevron Butterflyfish)
An extremely difficult fish to keep for long periods of time.

10 Chaetodon trifasciatus
(Rainbow or Redfin Butterflyfish)
An extremely difficult fish to keep for long periods of time.

11 Chaetodon xanthocephalus
(Yellowhead or Goldrim Butterflyfish)
An extremely difficult fish to keep for long periods of time.

12 Dunkerocampus dactyliophorus
(Banded Pipefish)
Generally does not survive for long in captivity.

13 Mirolabrichthys evansi
(Evan's Butterfly perch)
An extremely difficult fish to keep for long periods of time.

14 Mirolabrichthys tuke
(Purple Queen; Butterfly Perch)
An extremely difficult fish to keep for long periods of time.

15 Oxymonocanthus longirostris
(Long-nosed Filefish; Orange-green Filefish; Beaked Leatherjacket)
Rarely survives long in captivity.

16 Rhinomuraenia amboinensis
(Blue Ribbon Eel)
Does not usually survive for long periods in captivity.

17 Synanecja horrida
(Stonefish)
Potentially lethal if mishandled because of its very venomous spines.

18 Zanclus canescens
(Moorish Idol)
Does not generally survive for long periods in captivity.

TROPICAL MARINE INVERTEBRATES

1 Acanthaster planci
(Crown-of-thorns Starfish)
An unsuitable subject for the aquarium.

2 Acropora palmata
(Elkhorn Coral)
Collection of this large reef-building coral is ecologically unsound.

3 Aiptasia sp.
(Rock Anemone)
A very invasive pest in the aquarium.

4 Conus spp.
(Cone shells)
Capable of inflicting lethal injury.

5 Cyphoma gibbosum
(Flamingo Tongue)
Short-lived in captivity.

6 Hapalochlaena maculosa
(Blue Ring Octopus)
A dangerous species, capable of inflicting a lethal bite.

7 Hermodice carunculata
(Bristleworms; Fireworm)
These accidental introductions into the aquarium are carnivorous scavengers, and, in addition, their bristles will cause a painful rash if touched.

8 Hymenocera sp.
(Harlequin Shrimp; Orchid Shrimp)
Unsuitable for the aquarium as starfish (and possibly the tube feet of sea urchins) are their sole source of food!

9 Macropipus sp.
(Swimming Crab)
A predatory pest.

10 Millepora spp.
(Stinging Coral)
Can inflict very painful wounds.

11 Odontodactylus spp.
(Mantis Shrimp)
An extremely efficient predator, taking shrimps, crabs and fishes and damaging starfishes and featherduster worms. Can also inflict a serious wound.

12 Ovulum ovum
(Egg Cowrie)
Most specimens demand supplies of soft leather coral if they are to prosper.

13 Pseudoceros sp.
(Brown Flatworm)
A serious pest, capable of multiplying into an overwhelming aquarium plague.

14 Synapta maculata
(Worm Cucumber)
An unsuitable aquarium subject.

15 Toxopneustes pileolus
(Poison Urchin)
The spines are armed with a poison that can produce a very painful reaction.

16 Uca sp.
(Fiddler Crab)
Not a suitable aquarium subject.

GLOSSARY

Absorption The process of taking in and holding physically as a dry sponge takes in water. Liquid vitamins added to flake act in this manner.

Activated carbon Material used in mechanical/chemical filtration systems (external 'power filter' canister types) to remove, by adsorption, dissolved matter.

Adsorption The process by which organic molecules are chemically bonded onto a surface of a medium, such as activated carbon.

Algae Primitive plants, which may be either unicellular or large (e.g. kelp). They have plant characteristics, are almost exclusively aquatic and do not flower.

Ammonia (NH_3) First byproduct of decaying organic material; also excreted by the fishes' gills. Highly toxic to fishes and invertebrates.

Anal fin Single fin mounted vertically below the fish.

Artemia salina Scientific name of brine shrimp.

Barbel Whisker-like growth around the mouth; used for detecting food by taste.

Biological filtration Means of water filtration using bacteria, *Nitrosomonas* and *Nitrobacter*, to reduce otherwise toxic ammonium-based compounds to safer substances such as nitrates.

Bivalve A mollusc or shell-dwelling animal with two respiratory valves.

Brackish water Water containing approximately 10 percent sea water; found in estuaries where freshwater rivers enter the sea.

Brine shrimp Saltwater crustacean, *Artemia salina*, whose dry-stored eggs can be hatched to provide live food for fish or invertebrates.

Buffering action Ability of a liquid to maintain its pH value. Calcareous substrates may assist in this respect.

Cable tidy Commercial 'junction box' for neat and safe connection of electrical supply circuits.

Calcareous Formed of, or containing, calcium carbonate, a substance which may help to maintain a high pH of the aquarium water.

Caudal fin Single fin mounted vertically at the rear of the fish, the tail.

Caudal peduncle Part of fish's body joining the caudal fin to the main body.

Cirri Crestlike growths found above the eyes in some species, such as blennies.

Commensalism Living practical partnership, where one party derives more benefit than the other.

Copper Metal used in copper sulphate form as the basis for many marine aquarium remedies. Poisonous to fishes in excess, and even more so, at trace levels, to invertebrates.

Counter-current More efficient design of protein skimmer where the water flows against the main current of air, thereby giving a longer exposure time for collection of waste or sterilization if ozone is used.

Cover glass Panel of glass to form an anti-condensation, anti-evaporation protection placed on top of the aquarium immediately below the hood.

Cryptocaryon Parasitic infection, often referred to as the marine equivalent of the freshwater White Spot Disease, *Ichthyophthirius*.

Daphnia Freshwater crustacean, the water flea, occasionally used as food in the marine aquarium.

Demersal Term usually applied to eggs or to spawning action of fishes. Demersal eggs are heavier than water and are laid in prepared spawning sites on the sea bed. The fertilized eggs are then guarded by one or both adult fishes until hatching occurs.

Denitrification The removal of nitrate by anaerobic bacteria into nitrous oxide and then into free nitrogen gas. Used as a reliable method of keeping nitrates at a low level in the aquarium.

Diffuser An alternative name for wooden airstones.

Dorsal fin Single fin mounted vertically on top of the fish; some species have two dorsal fins, one behind the other. Many marine species have venomous rays in the dorsal fin, so handle them with care.

Dropsy Disease, where body fluids build up and produce a swollen body.

Filter feeder Animal (fish or invertebrate) that sifts water for microscopic food, e.g. pipefishes, tubeworms.

Filter medium Material used in filtration systems to remove suspended or dissolved organic substances from the water either mechanically, biologically or chemically.

Fin rot Bacterial ailment; the tissue between the rays of the fin rots away.

Foam fractionation Method of separating out proteinous substances from water by foaming action. Also known as protein skimming.

Fry Very young fish (see *Larvae*).

Fungus Parasitic infection, causing cotton-wool-like growths on the body.

Gallon (Imp) Measure of liquid volume (= 1.2 US gallons = 4.55 litres.)

Gallon (U.S.) Measure of liquid volume (= 0.83 Imp gallons = 3.8 litres.)

Gill flukes Trematode parasites, such as *Dactylogyrus*, that in severe infestation cause rapid breathing and gaping gills.

Gills Membranes through which fish absorb dissolved oxygen from the water during respiration.

Gravel tidy Plastic mesh fitted between layers of gravel to protect biological filtration systems from being exposed (and thus rendered ineffective) by digging fishes.

Hood Aquarium cover containing light fittings.

Hydrometer Device for measuring the specific gravity (S.G.) of the salt water, especially useful when making up synthetic mixes. May be either a free-floating or swing-needle type.

Impeller Electrically driven propeller that produces water flow through filters.

Irradiation Method of exposing food to gamma rays to sterilize it.

Larvae Often the first stage of very young marine fish; under-developed fish fry; also first reproductive stage of many invertebrates.

Lateral line Line of perforated scales along the flanks which lead to a pressure-sensitive nervous system. Enables fish to detect vibrations in surrounding water caused by other fishes, or reflected vibrations of their own movement from obstacles.

Length (standard) Length of fish (SL) measured from snout to end of main body; excludes caudal fin.

Litre measure of liquid volume (1 litre = 0.22 Imp gallons = 0.26 US gallons.)

Lymphocystis Viral ailment that causes cauliflower-like growths on skin and fins.

Mercury vapour Type of high-intensity lamp.

Mimicry The close resemblance of one creature to another. Specifically, the resemblance of predatory fishes to 'safe' fishes allowing them to gain unfair advantage over other animals.

Mouthbrooder Fishes than incubate fertilized eggs in the mouth.

Mysis Commercially available marine shrimp used as live and frozen food.

Nauplii Term used generally for the newly hatched form of brine shrimp.

Nitrate (NO_3) Less toxic ammonium compound produced by *Nitrobacter* bacteria from nitrite. Nitrate levels can be kept to a minimum by regular partial water changes; anaerobic filters convert nitrate back to free nitrogen.
Nitrification The process by which toxic nitrogenous compounds are converted by aerobic bacteria into less harmful substances, e.g. ammonia to nitrite to nitrate.
Nitrite (NO_2) Toxic ammonium compound produced by *Nitrosomonas* bacteria from ammonia. Toxic to fishes, and even more so to invertebrates.
Nitrobacter A species of aerobic bacterium essential in the biological filter to convert nitrite into far less harmful nitrate.
Nitrosomonas A species of aerobic bacterium utilized in the biological filter to convert ammonia into less toxic substances, e.g. nitrite.

Oodinium Single-celled parasite causing coral fish disease. Highly infectious, but curable with proprietary remedies.
Osmosis Passage of liquid through a semi-permeable membrane to dilute a more concentrated solution. Accounts for water losses through the skin of marine fishes, i.e. to the relatively stronger sea water, which they have to constantly drink to replenish these losses.
Ozone (O_3) Three-atom, unstable form of oxygen used as a disinfectant. Only to be used in conjunction with a protein skimmer, which prevents ozone coming into direct contact with fishes or invertebrates.
Ozonizer Device that produces ozone by high-voltage electrical discharge. Air from an air pump is passed through the ozonizer on its way to the protein skimmer.

Pectoral fins Paired fins, one on each side of the body immediately behind the gill cover.
Pelagic Strictly meaning 'of the open sea', this term is also applied to eggs and spawning methods. Pelagic eggs are lighter than water and are scattered after an ascending spawning action between a pair of fishes in open water. The fertilized eggs are then carried away by water currents.
Pelvic fins Paired fins on the ventral (lower) surface, usually immediately below the gill covers. Not all marine fishes have pelvic fins.
pH Measure of water acidity or alkalinity; the scale ranges from 1 (extremely acid) through 7 (neutral) to 14 (extremely alkaline). Sea water is normally around pH 8.3 and aquarium water should be kept in the range of pH 7.9 to 8.3. A falling pH indicates a partial water change is necessary or that there is a failure in the filtration sytstem.
Phytoplankton Extremely small plants (e.g. unicellular algae) that drift around in the water.
Power filters External canister-type filtration devices, usually fitted with an electric impeller to drive aquarium water through the enclosed filter media. Often used to prefilter water in 'reverse-flow' biological filtration systems.
Power head Electric impeller system fitted to biological filter return tubes to increase water flow.
Protein skimmer Device that removes proteinous substances from the water by fractionation: may be air-operated or electrically powered. Also used in conjunction with ozonized air for further water sterilization purposes.

Quarantine Mandatory period of separation for new fishes, to screen them from any latent diseases. Quarantine tanks must be maintained to the same high standard as the main aquarium to reduce stress when fishes are moved from one to the other. Can double as a treatment tank.

Rays Bony supports in fins.
Reverse-flow Alternative design of biological filtration system in which water flows up through the base covering instead of the more usual downward direction. Best powered by external power filters.

Salinity Measure of saltiness of the water. Quoted in terms of gm/litre. Natural sea water has a salinity of about 33.7 gm/litre.
Silicone sealant Adhesive used to bond glass or stop leaks. Use it to create rocks and coral formations, caves, etc. Use in well-ventilated conditions; it gives off heavy vapour smelling of vinegar. Allow at least 24 hours for it to cure. Be sure to use proper aquarium sealant, not the type sold for domestic use.
Siphon A length of tube with which to remove water from the aquarium; may also refer to inhalant organ of molluscs.
Spawning Act of reproduction involving the fertilization of the eggs. Many marine species have been observed spawning in captivity, but very few young fishes have been raised. Best chances so far are with clownfishes and Neon Gobies.
Specific gravity Ratio of density of measured liquid to that of pure water. Natural sea water has an S.G. of around 1.025, but marine aquarium fishes are normally kept in slightly lower density water (1.020-1.023) to avoid osmotic stress.
Starter Circuit necessary to initialize ('start') the discharge in fluorescent lighting.
Substrate Term for aquarium base covering.
Swimbladder Hydrostatic organ enabling fish to maintain chosen depth and position in water.
Symbiosis Relationship between two parties, each deriving mutual and indispensable benefit. Advanced form of commensalism.

Total system Term given to aquariums with built-in sophisticated filtration and other management systems providing full water treatment.
Trickle filter Slow filter, often involving inert granules, sand or algal system. Anaerobic types convert nitrates back to free nitrogen.
Tungsten Incandescent filament wire type of lighting. Not recommended for aquarium use: inefficient, 'unbalanced' spectral output and produces too much heat.
Turnover Water flow rate through a filter. For marine aquariums a high turnover is recommended.

Ultraviolet (UV) Type of light used as disinfectant, produced by a special tube usually enclosed in a surrounding water jacket through which aquarium water is passed. DO NOT LOOK AT AN OPERATING UV LAMP WITHOUT PROTECTIVE GOGGLES.
Undergravel filter Alternative name for biological filter acting as the substrate in an aquarium.

Ventral Undersurface of a fish. May be especially flattened in bottom-dwelling species.
Ventral fins Alternative name for pelvic fins.

Water change Regular replacement of a proportion (usually 20-25%) of aquarium water with new synthetic sea water. Helps to maintain low nitrate levels, correct pH levels and replaces trace elements. Aerate any stored synthetic sea water before use.
Wattage Unit of electrical consumption used to classify power of aquarium heater or brightness of lamps.

Zooplankton Extremely small animals that drift around in the water.

GENERAL INDEX

Page numbers in **bold** indicate major references, including accompanying photographs or illustrations. Page numbers in *italics* indicate captions and annotations to photographs and other illustrations. Text entries and references in panels are shown in normal type.

Right: Enoplometopus occidentalis
Red Dwarf Lobster.

SPECIES INDEX

Page numbers in **bold** indicate major references, including accompanying photographs or illustrations. Page numbers in *italics* indicate captions and annotations to photographs and other illustrations. Text entries and references in panels are shown in normal type.

A

B

D

E

F

T

U

V

W

Y

Z

PICTURE CREDITS

ARTISTS

Copyright of the artwork illustrations on the pages following the artists' names is the property of Interpet Publishing.

Rod Ferring: 27, 153
David Holmes (Garden Studio): 30, 31, 33, 37, 39, 41, 45, 47, 48, 49, 51, 52, 53
Phil Holmes/Stuart Watkinson: 24, 26, 68, 77, 81, 82, 83, 84, 85, 86, 88-89, 90, 93, 97, 99, 100, 101, 112, 141, 147, 150, 152

PHOTOGRAPHS

The publishers wish to thank the following photographers and agencies who have supplied photographs. These have been credited by page number and position on the page: (B)Bottom, (T)Top, (C)Centre, (BL)Bottom left, etc.

David Allison: 182-183(B), 207, 222, 227, 254(T), 259(B), 266-267, 281, 285, 332, 355(T), 360(T), 362-363, 376(T), 379(B)
Dr. Chris Andrews: 153(TL,C), 154(L,BC,R)
M P & C Piednoir/Aqua Press: 103(B)
Peter Biller: 234(T)
Biofotos: 259(T, Ian Took)
Bioquatic Photo - Alf J Nilsen (ajnilsen@online.no): 59, 61, 67, 75, 76, 80, 85, 92, 95(B), 104-105(B), 109(B), 110-111(B)
Bruce Coleman: 230(B, Alain Compost), 239(T)
Nick Dakin: 42(T), 91, 140, 147, 159, 225, 268(B), 282(B), 324(T), 325(B), 339
Andy Dalton: 260(T)
Max Gibbs: Endpapers, Half-title page, Copyright page, 22, 24, 28, 43, 46, 47, 49, 52, 66, 72(B), 124-125, 126, 127(T), 131, 132, 139(B), 155(C), 160-161, 163, 164, 165, 166, 168, 169, 170-171, 171, 172, 173, 175(T), 177(T), 178-179, 180, 181, 183(T), 184, 185, 186, 187, 188, 189, 190(B), 191, 192, 193, 194(T), 195, 196(L), 196-197, 198, 199, 200, 202, 203, 204, 205, 208, 210(B), 211, 212, 213(B), 214(T), 214-215, 217, 218-219, 220, 221, 223, 224, 226, 228, 229, 230(T), 231, 232, 233, 234(B), 235, 236, 237, 238-239(B), 240, 241, 242, 243, 244, 245, 246, 247, 248, 249(B), 250-251, 252(B), 253, 254(B), 255(B), 256, 257, 258, 260(B), 261, 263, 265, 267, 268(T), 269, 270(B), 271, 272-273, 274(B), 275, 277(T), 280, 283, 284, 286, 287, 288, 289, 290, 291, 292, 293(T), 300-301, 302-303, 313, 316(B), 327, 328(T), 331, 335, 336-337, 338-339, 345(T), 346(B), 347(T), 348, 350(B), 351, 352(T), 353, 357(T), 380(TR, CL, BL, BC), 381(TL, TC, CR), 383(CR)
Max Gibbs © Interpet Publishing: 156
Robert Harding Picture Library: 60
Martyn Haywood: 321(B), 359(T), 382(TR)
Les Holliday: 12, 13, 14, 15, 17, 19(B), 20, 21(B), 23(B), 35(B), 51(L), 53, 54, 55, 56, 57, 58, 61 (courtesy Operation Raleigh), 62, 136, 297(TR), 304(T), 314(B), 318(B), 357(B), 374
Andy Horton: 73, 364(B)
IKAN: 216 (Kleiter), 277 (Debelius)
Alex Kerstitch: 23(T), 35(T), 36, 42(B), 44, 63, 248(T), 279, 312(B), 325(T), 326(B), 328(B), 330(B), 343(T), 382(TL, CL, CR, BL, BR), 383(TL,C)
Lahaina Systems Ltd: 70, 364(T)
Frank Lane Picture Agency: 59 (T. Silvestris)
Jan-Eric Larsson: 201(B), 330(TL), 334, 391
Dick Mills: 250(TL)
Natural Science Photos: I. Bennett: 45, 309(B), 310, 330(TL), 352(B), 356(B), 358, 383(CL, BL); I Bennett & D.G. Myers:38(B); Mark Caney: 138; D. Hill: 16, 18, 34, 50, 314(T), 382(TC), 383(TR); Nat Fain: 21(T), 315, 318(T), 330(TR), 342, 383(BR); Paul Kay: 27, 40, 131, 132, 298-299, 366(T, BL), 367, 368, 370, 371, 372, 373; Alan Smith: 10-11, 37, 38(T), 51(R), 182(T), 264(T), 311, 333(B), 340(B), 350(T), 382(C)
Arend van den Nieuwenhuizen: 176, 177(B), 194(B), 206, 209, 213(T), 249(T), 213(T), 249(T), 264(B), 270(B), 270(T), 274(T), 276, 293(B), 294, 295, 296, 297(BL), 299, 307, 344, 346(T), 354(B), 355(B), 380(TC, C, CR, BR), 381(TR, CL, C, BL), 383(BC)
Oxford Scientific Films: 190(T), 214(B), 252(T, Steffen Hauser), 282(T, Max Gibbs), 329, 378(B)
Planet Earth Pictures: John Lithgow: 349(B); J. MackKinnon: 349(T); Christian Pétron: 366(BR), 369
Geoffrey Rogers © Interpet Publishing: Contents pages, 68, 71, 72(T), 74, 77, 78, 79, 81, 83, 84, 87(B), 88, 89, 90, 95(T), 96, 98, 99, 100, 101, 102, 104(T), 106-107, 108, 109(T), 110(T,L), 113, 114-123, 127(B), 128, 129, 130, 133, 134, 135, 137, 139(T), 142-145, 148-149, 151, 153(BL)
Royal Botanic Gardens, Kew: 375(B), 377(TR, © Andrew McRobb)
Mike Sandford: 175(B), 201(T), 210(T)
Gunther Spies: 32, 167, 255(T), 304, 305(B), 316(T), 321(T), 324(B), 356(T), 359(B)
Peter Stiles: 9, 69, 378(T)
Linda Stokoe: 377(B)
R. & V. Taylor: 381(BR)
William A. Tomey: Title page, 64-65, 157, 278(T), 278-279(B), 312(T), 317, 320, 322-323, 333(T), 240(T), 341, 345(B), 365(T), 375(T), 376(B), 377(TL), 379(T)
Tropical Marine Centre: 103(T)
Brent Whitaker: 154(TC), 155(T,B)

Acknowledgments

The publishers wish to thank the following individuals and organizations for their help in the preparation of this book:

Arcadia, Croydon, Surrey; Aquaworld, Warrington, Cheshire; Max Gibbs of The Goldfish Bowl; Heaver Tropics, Ash, Sevenoaks, Kent; NT Laboratories Ltd., Wateringbury, Kent; Swallow Aquatics, Southfleet, Kent and Colchester, Essex; Richard Sankey of The Tropical Marine Centre, Chorleywood, Herts; Terry Evans of Wetpets.